complete
landscaping

LOWE'S SERIES

Senior Editor Sally W. Smith

STAFF FOR LOWE'S COMPLETE LANDSCAPING

Editor Michael MacCaskey

Photo Editor Lynn Ocone

Art Director Bill Harvey

Design and Page Makeup Sylvie Vidrine, Michele Newkirk

Art Assistant Brianna de Mol

Copy Editor John Edmonds

Proofreader Mary Roybal

Indexer Kathy Barber

Prepress Coordinator Danielle Johnson

Production Specialist Linda M. Bouchard

Principal Illustrator Rik Olson

Additional Illustrators Anthony Davis, Debra Lambert, Lois Lovejoy, Jane McCreary, Mimi Osborne, Erin O'Toole, Lucy Sargeant, Lynn Severance, Wendy Smith-Griswold, Catherine M. Watters

For photography and design credits, see page 432.

A special thanks to the writers and editors who contributed to the development of the previous edition of *Lowe's Complete Landscaping*, especially Margaret McKinnon, A. Cort Sinnes, and Lance Walheim. Also thanks to Steven Cory, Carrie Davis, Scott Gibson, Doug and Karen Jimerson, Marty McNamara, Diane Slavik, and Ann Whitman.

On the Cover

Cover design by Vasken Guiragossian. Cover image, top: Photography by Mark Rutherford; styling by JoAnn Masaoka Van Atta. Cover image, bottom: Photography by Jack Coyier; design by Richard Krumweide, Architerra Design Group.

10 9 8 7 6 5 4 3 2 1 First printing February 2008

Copyright © 2008 Sunset Publishing Corporation, Menlo Park, CA 94025.

Second Edition. All rights reserved, including the right of reproduction in whole or in part in any form.

ISBN-13: 978-0-376-00927-2

ISBN-10: 0-376-00927-6

Library of Congress Control Number 2007940184

Printed in the United States.

Readers' note: Almost any do-it-yourself project involves a risk of some sort. Your tools, materials, and skills will vary, as will the conditions at your project site. Lowe's Companies, Inc., and its subsidiaries ("Lowe's") have made every effort to be complete and accurate in the instructions and other content contained in this publication. However, neither Lowe's nor the publisher will assume any responsibility or liability for damages or losses sustained or incurred in the course of your home improvement or repair project or in the course of your use of the item you create or repair. Always follow manufacturer's operating instructions in the use of tools, check and follow your local building codes, and observe all standard safety precautions.

welcome

"LET'S GROW SOMETHING TOGETHER." YES, THAT'S A LITTLE DIFFERENT FROM "LET'S BUILD SOMETHING Together," but at Lowe's we provide for landscapers as well as builders. We know that "home improvement" includes the yard as well as the home itself, and that's why each of our over 1,400 North American stores offers expert landscaping help along with all the products you'll need to build, or rebuild, your landscape.

This book, the second edition of *Lowe's Complete Landscaping*, is an extension of those services. It is a complete resource of both ideas and how-to information for people looking to get more use and beauty from the outdoor spaces around their homes. You'll find here a plain-language guide to making or remaking your garden and patio, including how to think about landscaping the way professionals do, how to collect and apply the ideas that are right for you, and then how to make those ideas real.

Browsing these pages is a little like taking a continent-wide garden tour. There are plenty of ideas for you to borrow or adapt in the pictures. Take a patio design from one garden, a pond idea from another, and a pergola plan from a third. Beyond these outdoor structures, the gardens in this book display every sort of plant—annuals, perennials, bulbs, shrubs, vines, trees, grasses, ground covers, vegetables, herbs, and wildflowers—and each image is a success story. There's probably no more efficient way to learn about plant combinations that really work than to study such beautiful home landscapes.

This and the other Lowe's books are part of our commitment to providing all the know-how you need for projects around your home. You'll find help with a range of projects in *Complete Home Improvement and Repair*, *Complete Home Decorating*, *Decorating with Paint & Color*, *Complete Patio & Deck*, and *Complete Tile & Flooring*, along with the Lowe's Creative Ideas series that includes *Organizing Your Home*, *Kids' Spaces*, *Makeovers*, and *Color*.

Remember that Lowe's also offers extensive assistance via Lowes.com and the in-store clinics conducted throughout the year, plus a range of installation services. And for those times when doing it yourself doesn't make sense, you can rely on our trained installers for that new deck, fence, or play set while you focus on the finishing details of the landscape.

Founded 62 years ago, Lowe's has been actively improving homes and landscapes from day one. If you want to make your landscape more beautiful, more practical, more *you*, let's grow something together.

LOWE'S COMPANIES, INC.

Robert Niblock
CEO and Chairman of the Board

Larry D. Stone
President and Chief Operating Officer

Nick Canter
Executive VP, Marketing and Merchandising

Bob Gfeller
Senior VP, Marketing

Theresa Anderson
Senior VP, General Merchandise Manager

Melissa S. Birdsong
VP, Trend and Design

Karena Bailey
VP, Merchandising

Sarah Wagner
Merchandising Director

contents

getting started

WHEN YOU FIRST CONTEMPLATE A NEW LANDSCAPE, THE

project is likely to seem overwhelming. Perhaps you can

see in your mind what you want, but how do you get there?

What do you do first? What should you tackle yourself, and

when should you plan to get help?

For many homeowners, landscaping is a very creative,

deeply satisfying experience. But depending upon your

ambitions, it's a project that may take many months to

complete. So it's important to match your goals to your

limits of time, resources, and energy. This is why, for some

people, landscaping is a work in progress, evolving over

several years.

The projects in this book are well within the reach of a

motivated do-it-yourselfer. None require specialized skills,

but some will be challenging, physically at

least. So take it

slowly and

enlist help

when necessary.

what you need and want
ASK YOURSELF THESE BASIC QUESTIONS

JUST AS YOU DON'T NEED TO BE AN INTERIOR DESIGNER TO DECORATE YOUR HOME, YOU DON'T need to be a landscape architect to design a garden. The first step is to evaluate your property and assess your own needs, then identify regional conditions that may influence your garden plans. If you don't feel confident tackling the job of garden design, you can save time and avoid mistakes by using professionals, especially if your property presents challenges like steep slopes or poor drainage.

Even in a tiny bed of 36 square feet, you can have a wealth of vegetables. Basil, bell peppers, eggplants, green beans, and a tomato plant grow in adjoining beds, and all is set off by a wall of color.

When you want to create a beautiful and functional place for relaxing outdoors, the reality of your bare or overgrown yard may seem daunting. Before getting down to work, close your eyes and picture your dream garden. Well-designed landscapes begin with decisions made before the first spadeful of earth is turned. Do you want an elegant entry and a formal front yard, or an outdoor room for casual living and entertaining? Do you want a plant-filled garden, or a durable one that can withstand tricycle wheels and a game of tag? Do you like to read and sunbathe or play badminton or croquet? Answering questions like these will help determine what you want in your outdoor space. Make a

checklist of features that are essential to you and your family and include them in your plan, but be prepared to compromise on the less important elements or create a timetable for including them later.

Like most homeowners, you probably have both aesthetic and practical aims in mind. You may want colorful flower borders as well as a productive vegetable garden. With careful landscape design, you can have both.

Your family's needs will also dictate other aspects of your design. If children or people who are elderly or disabled use the landscape, you may value safety and ease of movement. Secure fences are a safeguard against the potential dangers of swimming pools, driveways, and roads. Similarly, graded paths and ramps, night lighting, and stable railings on decks and stairs make a garden accessible to all who use it.

To make your landscape more comfortable, you can slightly modify the climate. Trees or shade structures offer respite from the heat, walls or dense plantings buffer strong winds, sun pockets collect warmth, and overheads provide cover on rainy days.

Also consider how much upkeep you're willing to take on. To reduce the amount of time and effort required, avoid high-maintenance features such as lawns, sheared hedges, or trees that litter. And installing an automatic irrigation system not only saves time but also delivers water most efficiently.

where do you begin?

The precise route that you'll navigate on the way from bare ground or old, worn-out yard to a pleasing landscape is as variable as you might imagine. But no matter how many twists and turns your own path takes, there are several steps that are shared by everyone, and those are collected here. Becoming familiar with them now will give you a sense of what to expect, whether you're doing it alone over a couple of years or whether you choose to work with designers and contractors.

collect ideas As you begin to think seriously about landscaping your garden, it will help greatly to collect pictures and ideas from gardening books like this one, as well as from magazines. Also visit gardens in your area, taking photographs as you go and noting which plants look best in which season. And stop by Lowe's to see new plants and the range of outdoor options available.

determine your climate zone You'll save time, money, and frustration by choosing plants that are proven performers in your area. You'll find what you need to know about plant hardiness on page 298.

get to know your soil To find out whether it is predominantly sand, clay, or loam, do this simple test. Thoroughly wet a small

ABOVE LEFT: If you'll be sharing your landscape with a pet, like Ozzie the Airedale, account for its needs as you plan.

ABOVE RIGHT: No space? Make a garden in a pot. This one combines *Stipa arundinacea* with 'Rustic Orange' coleus, blue-green *Euphorbia polychroma*, and trailing *Lysimachia nummularia*.

patch of soil. Wait for a day, then squeeze a handful firmly in your fist. If it forms a tight ball with a slippery feel, you have clay. If it feels gritty and crumbles when you open your hand, it's sandy. A moist yet slightly crumbly ball is closer to loam. To test your soil's pH (acidity or alkalinity), use one of the test kits sold at nurseries. If you'd like a more precise picture of your soil, have it tested by a commercial soil laboratory. Contact your local cooperative extension office for advice. For more about soil, see page 300.

study light patterns Is your site open to the sun all day, or is it largely in the shade? Which areas are sunny in the morning but shady in the afternoon, and vice versa? Will the house, trees, or other large structures cast shade in winter, when the sun is lower in the southern sky, but not in summer, when it arcs more directly overhead?

note special conditions If you're planting where deer frequently browse, you'll need to include a deer fence in your plan or to assemble lists of plants that deer are less likely to eat. If your garden is on a steep slope, mowing a lawn would be difficult and could be unsafe, so you might plant shrubs and ground covers or plan for terraces to mitigate the abrupt grade.

find a style Are you more comfortable in a casual or a formal setting? Do you prefer a tropical feel? Consider the architecture of your home and surroundings, and make sure the style you want will be a good fit. The style that's right for you is probably as unique as you are.

list uses How do you want to use your space? Do you dream of an entertainment area, a private sanctuary, or both? Do you want to grow vegetables and herbs or to compose a pretty picture of colorful flowers and foliage? Will children and pets play in the garden? Ask and listen to everyone who will use the space about what they want.

check local zoning laws Especially if you plan to do any major construction, check with your area's planning or permits office. Contact your water and utility companies so

you know the exact locations of underground cables or pipes before you put shovel to soil.

recycle Consider materials already on site or easy to obtain and think about how to incorporate them into your landscape. Examples are old flagstones or even broken concrete. If you uncover large stones when digging a flower bed, consider using them to border a path. If you're tearing down an old fence, use the boards to build a compost bin.

make a plan Draw a site plan (see page 176). Start by measuring the property's outer boundaries and then sketch in permanent features. Include all the features of the garden and indicate the location of your home's doors and windows. Draw a base plan to scale so you can play around with different possibilities. Lay a piece of tracing paper over your base plan and see where, for example, you'd like to locate a pool or rose beds or a bench for enjoying the view.

use design principles Include focal points like a special tree or a piece of art at the end of a sight line. Strive for some degree of symmetry and balance, even with something as simple as a matching pair of plants at the head of a path. For tips from landscape design professionals, see pages 188–193.

choose landscape floors If you want a lawn, check at Lowe's for advice on the grasses that do well in your area, and see pages 338–353, and pages 406–413. If you're putting in paths, decide whether to lay them out with stepping-stones, bricks, gravel, or mulch. Would a flagstone or brick patio meet your needs, or do you prefer a wooden deck? There's more about patios and decks beginning on page 76.

choose landscape walls and ceiling A fence may be the quickest and most obvious way to gain privacy, but a hedge or even a small tree can do the job in a softer, more organic way. To shade a dining area, a simple umbrella might suffice, but perhaps you'd prefer an arbor draped with flowering vines. For ideas, see pages 120–141.

LOWE'S QUICK TIP

It's smart for do-it-yourselfers to live on their property for at least a year before landscaping. It takes about that long to learn its idiosyncrasies and how you relate to it. For instance, after a year it will be clear where you need stepping-stones, or how big and what shape to make the deck.

clear the site Remove dead or unwanted plants. Protect the plants you're saving by either marking their location or protecting them from damage during construction.

rough-grade If you're starting from scratch, it's at this point that you'll want to shape the land as the plan requires. Make the rough grade lower than the final grade to allow for the depth of the sod or the paving that will come later. For more, see pages 204–205.

install utilities With the rough grade complete, install main irrigation lines. Wait until finish grading to set valve boxes and irrigation heads. Install electrical lines or conduits for them under areas that will be paved later or otherwise inaccessible.

complete construction At this point you can finish all construction, in particular any work that requires heavy equipment, such as walls, steps, patios, and decks.

finish grading Once construction is finished, establish the finish grade and complete the irrigation system. Install outdoor lighting at this stage and amend soil if necessary.

plant Once construction and grading are complete, and once there's no more need to work in areas that will become beds, it's time to plant. If you can, plan to plant in fall or early spring because these seasons are most favorable. If that's not doable, you might need to wait until the next fall or spring.

BELOW LEFT: Test your soil's pH. If it's extreme in either direction, adjust it with lime or sulfur.

BELOW RIGHT: Landscaping usually includes some demolition.

BOTTOM LEFT: Make a watering basin around a new plant to ensure the root ball receives water.

BOTTOM RIGHT: Amended planting soil is crumbly and rich in organic matter.

great landscapes

A GREAT LANDSCAPE CAN TAKE MANY FORMS: GRAND OR modest, formal or casual. In the final analysis, it is whatever works for you and your family. In all cases, it's a place where you can relax, entertain friends, perhaps play, and reconnect with nature.

But how do you get there? The photos in this chapter show some key design principles that go into making an outstanding landscape. An understanding of these principles will help you shape in your own yard a landscape that meets your needs and brings you delight. Easy to describe in the abstract, each principle is a subtle quality to experience. All begin with privacy, comfort, and style. Great landscapes interact with the surrounding environment and provide a connection with nature, season by season. They are both practical and beautiful. By following these principles, you can create your own personal paradise.

keep it private but open
PLAN FOR SECLUSION, BUT NOT TOO MUCH

IN WHOLE OR IN PART, WELL-PLANNED LANDSCAPES EXHIBIT THE RIGHT BALANCE OF PRIVATE AND open space. Visually and literally, a fence, wall, hedge, or planting of shrubs and trees transforms an area into a quiet, restful retreat. Fences and walls also do the practical task of keeping young children and wandering pets inside, and unwanted visitors outside.

A cozy spot for two is sheltered but not overpowered by the rich mixture of foliage textures and shapes. Chartreuse euphorbias are combined with lavender, red kangaroo paw, and silvery artemisia.

Depending on an enclosure's height, location, and screening properties, it can also provide privacy—an increasingly valuable commodity. The right amount of privacy allows you to live and work in the garden just as you wish, from singing to yourself as you sow seeds to stretching out on a chaise longue in the sun.

Does enclosing a garden always mean you're keeping the rest of the world away? Yes and no. Even if your landscape includes the most gloriously unlimited natural vista— whether a forest, mountain range, canyon, coastline, or desert—you'll probably want to enclose at least a portion of it, to create a sense of security. Conversely, if it's on a Manhattan rooftop, you'll have a safety barrier—but you'll want to leave a view.

Walk around your property identifying areas where you'll want covers or screens. Also try to evaluate how plantings and additional structures will affect your neighbors, the patterns of sun and shade in your garden, and any views you want to preserve.

BELOW LEFT: A redwood boardwalk, fringed with pink-flowered coral bells, connects a private deck to the main patio and the outdoor dining area.

BELOW RIGHT: Hydrangeas beckon visitors through the keyhole-shaped garden gate.

BOTTOM LEFT: Red poppies reach for sunlight as trees lightly screen afternoon heat.

BOTTOM RIGHT: Freestanding walls define areas without closing them off.

LOWE'S QUICK TIP

If you live where lawns merge into one another, a screen at the property line might seem antisocial. In that case, screen an area closer to the house, perhaps just around the patio.

be comfortable
FURNISHING YOUR OUTDOOR ROOM

LANDSCAPE DESIGNERS THINK ABOUT OUTDOOR SPACE MUCH AS ARCHITECTS AND INTERIOR designers think about indoor space—the needs, desires, and comfort of their clients come first. In an outdoor setting, this means providing just enough shade in summer and sun in winter, plus convenient places for sitting and lounging.

A rattan swing dangles from a steel frame that arches over a cozy sitting area. Reclaimed from a hillside overgrown with blackberries and ivy, the space is now a cool retreat.

Because walls, ceilings, and floors are such essential parts of any home, architects and interior designers don't need to discuss their importance with clients. But people may have difficulty thinking about elements they associate with indoor spaces as essential to an outdoor

space. Yet every well-designed landscape, large or small, has its own kind of walls, ceilings, and floors that must be considered from the very beginning of the design.

Beyond structural elements, landscape designers have concerns that are typical for

indoor spaces—furniture, lighting, traffic patterns, and cooking equipment, in addition to the kind of style the homeowner desires.

When you think of landscaping, don't think only of plants. Instead, think first about how you and your family and friends want to live outdoors. Put your own needs ahead of the plants you want to grow. Once you've taken care of those needs, go ahead and plant.

BELOW LEFT: Rainproof overhead shelter means an outdoor meal needn't be interrupted by rain. Shade cast by trees, including a stunning crape myrtle, adds to the enclosure.

BELOW RIGHT: An outdoor fireplace, grand enough for an Adirondack lodge, adds warmth with panache.

BOTTOM LEFT: Adjacent to a pool are hooks for towels and a low bench for drying off or stretching out.

BOTTOM RIGHT: A metal fire bowl is the center of a back-yard campfire circle that's surrounded by lush plantings.

express yourself

AFTER ALL, IT'S YOUR LANDSCAPE

KEEP IN MIND THAT YOUR LANDSCAPE BELONGS TO YOU AND THAT THE BEST OUTDOOR LANDSCAPES reflect the personalities, tastes, and interests of their owners. Wouldn't it be boring if people used only one standard to judge a successful landscape? Luckily, many people feel freer to express themselves in their outdoor surroundings than they do in their interior spaces, perhaps because the outdoor canvas is larger and has looser boundaries. And even if you're a little timid about showing off your own taste in the front yard, in the relative privacy of your backyard, your only rule may be that anything goes.

Take risks and have fun as you plan and plant. Here, a terra-cotta pot brimming with dusty miller hovers over a pink sea of sedum 'Autumn Joy'. The sculptural bowl supports water lilies, and waving above are the broad leaves of Japanese banana.

You're allowed to say, "It's my garden, and you don't have to like it." A tree house with a rope ladder? Brightly painted garden walls? Patio trees festooned year-round with little twinkling lights? A Victorian fretwork design on the deck railing? A pathway enlivened with a mosaic of bits of broken crockery? Why not?

BELOW LEFT: Accessorize your outdoor space with antique signs or other objects that have meaning to you.

BELOW RIGHT: This mini labyrinth is only 10 feet in diameter but is impossible to ignore. A double spiral of sod and decomposed granite, it's lined with moss-covered fieldstone and ornamental alliums.

BOTTOM LEFT: Folk art, such as this Mississippi Delta bottle tree, connects your landscape to cultural and regional traditions.

BOTTOM RIGHT: The simple design of this pavilion is adapted from pavilion designs in Bali. It's a 6-by-10-foot deck with 8-foot posts and a marine fabric roof.

embrace nature

INVITE IT IN, BUT STRIVE FOR BALANCE

GREAT LANDSCAPES EMBRACE NATURE. THEY BORROW CERTAIN PRACTICALITIES FROM THEIR INDOOR counterparts while effortlessly making the most of all that nature offers. Do what you can to bring in the natural world—the sky, clouds, birds, butterflies, breezes, shadows, stars, and views of the surrounding hills and landscapes.

If landscaping in your region presents obstacles, use those obstacles as starting points. For example, this tapestry of tough plants in a Southern California garden shrugs off drought and water shortages.

The trick is finding the right balance. Practically speaking, this may mean reducing the size of a patio and screening it, or making an overhead structure more open, to bring creature comforts into balance with the natural setting. This might mean that you'll still experience times of the day when it's too hot to sit outside or too windy for an outdoor meal. But you may feel that's a small price to pay for all the other joys of outdoor living.

Finding the right balance goes for wildlife too. Provide food, shelter, and water to encourage birds and butterflies to visit, or better, grow the kinds of plants they prefer. But also provide the right kind of barriers or deterrents to mosquitoes and deer.

TOP LEFT: Evaluate the existing virtues of your yard and use what you find. Here, a plain folding chair in a beautiful spot is available to take advantage of free moments. The surrounding planting beds are all free-form. The easy-care plants include vibrant yellow *Asteriscus maritimus* 'Gold Coin', white Santa Barbara daisy, and lavender. *Rosa banksiae* covers the arbor with sunny yellow blooms.

TOP RIGHT: Wild things, like this hummingbird, shortly find and adopt favorable places, such as a farm plow disk recycled and plumbed as a recirculating fountain.

ABOVE: Fiery autumn foliage of a Japanese maple tree shimmers with color behind the bent-stick love seat. Beside it, golden grasses and red penstemon cascade over the flagstone patio.

celebrate the seasons

REMEMBER, IT'S A GARDEN

ONE THING IS CERTAIN: A LANDSCAPE SHOWS OFF THE SEASONS IN WAYS INTERIOR ROOMS CANNOT. To get the most enjoyment, design for year-round interest. Trumpet spring with a display of flowering bulbs and annuals if you like, but don't neglect the beauty of a crab apple in fall. Place a dogwood prominently for its spring flowers but also to highlight its bare branches in winter.

Fiery fall colors aren't only for New England. The graceful branches and delicate leaves of a laceleaf Japanese maple burn bright red in a Northwest garden.

Changing the look of your interior rooms to match the seasons is doable and even fun, but it's sensible for only a few of us. Outdoor spaces are another matter. Nature is in charge, and the landscape will change whether you're ready or not. So make the most of it, from the profound seasonal changes of the Northeast and Midwest to the subtler but equally commanding variations of the South and West.

Imagine how your use of the landscape will vary from season to season. In spring, you'll probably want to be outdoors as much as possible. Summer is for entertaining and perhaps quiet times in the shade. During winter, more often than not you'll be inside looking out.

BELOW LEFT: Fall gardens in the Southeast can be a cacophonous medley of colors and textures, as demonstrated here. Tall goldenrod *(Solidago altissima)* arches high over flower stalks of silver grass and fountain grass. Coleus, dahlia, sedum 'Autumn Joy', and blue-flowered Tatarian aster are some of the other flowers here.

BELOW RIGHT: In the North, colorful berries in winter are visual relief for people, and food for wildlife. This cedar waxwing is making off with a berry of *Ilex verticillata* 'Red Sprite'.

BOTTOM: In late spring and early summer, "high season" in the Northwest, most plants are at their peak. Here, white and pink cosmos, roses, clematis, and salvia are highlights.

be practical
ACCOMMODATE YOUR FAMILY'S NEEDS

THE BEST LANDSCAPES ADDRESS THE PRACTICAL NEEDS OF THEIR OWNERS. JUST AS INDOORS, PEOPLE need room for their clutter, tools, equipment, and supplies. Every homeowner has to deal with trash cans and yard-waste bins and find a place to store them. And then there are the nuts-and-bolts aspects of accessories like pool equipment, irrigation timers, and air-conditioning units.

Side yards offer one of the most logical spots to place these practical necessities, especially if they can be grouped in one area. Bear in mind that pool and air-conditioning equipment can be annoying when running, so try not to install it under a bedroom window or where it could ruin an outdoor dinner party. Plan for safety and ease of movement. Gates, fences, and railings safeguard people against

dangers posed by swimming pools, driveways, busy streets, and elevated decks. Ramps and graded paths with smooth, firm surfaces will ease passage for the disabled and elderly and for young children. Night lighting permits safe movement and discourages intruders.

Also consider how much time you're willing to invest in maintenance. Lawns, swimming pools, hedges, and rose and

In small yards where usable space is limited, think about what you can do with the side yard. Formerly plain dirt, this yard now features a strip of lawn and a vegetable garden.

vegetable gardens all take time. If you have it, great. If you don't, steer clear. On the other hand, an automatic irrigation system can cut many hours of hand watering from your schedule.

While practical concerns may seem relatively minor in the overall scheme of things, you'll be glad you addressed them early in the planning stage instead of trying to figure out how to deal with them after the landscaping is completely installed.

TOP LEFT: Smooth paving is easier for unsteady legs to walk on, and it makes a handy surface for projects and crafts.

TOP RIGHT: This utility shed is integrated into the landscape, and slate pavers set into the lawn where sunlight filters through create enough surface for a small patio.

ABOVE LEFT: To make the most use of space, plan for necessities such as trash cans. These are shielded behind a fence.

ABOVE RIGHT: Boards lining the bottom of a wire fence keep Welsh springer spaniels from tunneling into the nicely landscaped front yard.

let beauty reign

FIND WAYS TO ADD THAT EXTRA SOMETHING

BEAUTY IN THE GARDEN TAKES MANY FORMS. MOST OFTEN, IT IS CONCEIVED OF AS FLOWERS, AND rightly so. The diversity of flowers guarantees the possibility of endless fascination. Leaves are also a rich source of garden color, and it is color that lasts much longer than flowers. Besides a host of remarkably diverse greens, you can find plants with leaves in shades of yellow, red, purple, blue, or gray.

Perhaps you assume that beauty is derived mostly from artfully chosen and combined plants. Often it is, but there is more to it than that. Sometimes it's a matter of presentation. A single plant displayed in a special container and sitting on a pedestal can be stunning. Beauty isn't a matter of complexity.

Similarly, to be beautiful plants don't need to be exotic or rare. Often it is the most ordinary plants that become extraordinary. It happens when such a plant is grown particularly well, matched with companion plants creatively, or presented well. A common but vigorous ivy is more beautiful than a rare plant that struggles to live.

Some landscapes are beautiful by virtue of their details, such as an artfully finished deck railing, a carefully laid pathway, or a

Moving water brings life and beauty into a garden. The urn in the center of this aboveground pool is filled nearly to its brim with stones, leaving half an inch of water for birds.

well-placed sculpture. Brightly painted walls and fences can elevate a simple landscape to a memorable one.

Great landscapes can take many forms and styles, but in the end, all are an unabashed celebration of beauty. Wherever it occurs, beauty is the reason you want to relax on the deck in the morning and linger outdoors as long as possible in the evening.

BELOW LEFT: The repeating shape of echeverias spreading around a water bowl echoes the bowl's circular shape.

BELOW RIGHT: Few trees exceed flowering cherries for their exquisite spring beauty.

BOTTOM LEFT: Tulips 'Pink Impression', 'Holland Glory', and 'Orange Emperor' complement the colors of this brick-walled garden.

BOTTOM RIGHT: The pink-and-silver flower heads of ruby grass 'Pink Crystals' glow in the evening light.

LOWE'S QUICK TIP

Beauty can be simple and is not necessarily showy, though it often is both. In gardens, beauty may be a graceful line, a passing butterfly, or an ordinary but charming plant.

themes and ideas

LANDSCAPES TAKE AS MANY FORMS AS THERE ARE DIFFERENT kinds of houses times the number of different homeowners. There is no one right way to do them, and there's certainly no simple recipe for success. The previous chapter presented seven guiding principles. In this chapter you'll find many examples of ways those principles have been personalized and adapted to various situations. For instance, are you more inclined to relax and entertain in your yard, or do you mostly want to garden? Do you live in the West where drought is common and wildfire is a threat, or in the Northeast in a shaded, cool woodland? Chances are that most readers will find their circumstances to be a combination of the themes presented here. Some of these ideas address practical issues, such as limited space or drought, and many are strictly for fun. The payoff comes when you incorporate a mix of these features into your landscape. Then you'll find it has become a place that you can use and enjoy.

creating curb appeal
IF IT LOOKS GOOD, IT IS GOOD

LANDSCAPING THAT ENHANCES YOUR HOUSE'S CURB APPEAL IS ONE OF THE BEST INVESTMENTS YOU can make. Yet for most homeowners, the front yard is far from ideal. It may be a virtual blank slate, with neither personality nor character, or be outdated, with a narrow walkway, a ring of shrubs around the foundation, and perhaps a concrete slab at the door.

Conifers look good year-round, so they're a good choice for prominent positions in northern regions. Conifers here, from left, are dwarf Colorado blue spruce, mugho pine, limber pine, and dwarf blue Scotch pine.

Conversely, your front yard may be so overgrown with foliage that the house is hidden. To transform your front yard, focus first on the entry walkway. Make it so clear, obvious, and easy to navigate that guests are never confused about the best route to the front door. Also make the path wide enough for two adults to comfortably walk side by side (see the diagrams on page 99). In addition, use materials for the path and driveway that complement and enhance your house's facade.

If you don't have the time to redo your landscape but need to spruce up the yard, here's how.

REMOVE BRUSH Rent a chipper-shredder to convert leaves and brush to usable mulch or compost.

PRUNE Remove dead or diseased limbs from trees and shrubs. Deadhead or remove spent annuals.

CLEAN UP Groom any edging that has started to look ragged from contact with mower blades or encroaching turfgrass. A power edger can create clean lines quickly.

MULCH New mulch improves your home's curb appeal.

ADD FLOWERING PLANTS These will help draw the eye away from spots you'd rather not have people looking at.

CLEAN THE DECK The cost and time investment are low, and the results are often impressive.

All landscapes should be a mixture of permanent and short-lived plants, but in the front yard, this mix is doubly important. Permanent plants, such as conifers, look lush and green from season to season, even in the North. They create structure and provide a stage for showier annuals and perennials. Select low-growing or dwarf conifers and broadleaf evergreens that are in scale with your home and won't soon block paths or windows.

Define the front entryway with accents of bold, colorful annuals, in containers or in a small planting bed, to be replanted seasonally. Containers also make the most of tight quarters, such as on the steps of a front porch.

ABOVE: A gracious path of brick pavers is the same width as the house's entry. Small containers anchor the path at the base of the steps, and large ones accent the front door.

BELOW: A planting of favorite perennials forms a mosaic of flowers and foliage in this sunny walkway border.

a passion for plants

THEY ARE THE FOCUS, AND THE RESULTS ARE COLORFUL

IF YOU'RE A PLANT LOVER, IF YOU BUY PLANTS AT NURSERIES, GARDEN CENTERS, PLANT SALES, GARAGE sales, and grocery stores without having the faintest idea of where you intend to plant them, you are a plant lover. And you need a special kind of landscape.

Orange lion's tail, pink kangaroo paw, and *Salvia* 'Indigo Spires' add bright accents to a gently curving border.

You might assume this approach would result in a disorganized landscape in which chaos is the rule. But usually the opposite is true. Plant lovers constantly pinch, tweak, rearrange, and reorder their gardens. It's that constant fussing that, over time, creates a beautiful garden.

The examples here show that you can be a plant lover and still leave some room in the garden for human inhabitants.

TOP: Oversized stepping-stone pads of brick pavers ease visitors past American boxwood, crape myrtle, oak, hydrangea, Lenten rose, hosta, astilbe, and geranium.

ABOVE: Combining white phlox with 'Casablanca' lilies makes this courtyard as compelling to the nose as to the eye.

smitten with roses?

BEAUTY, VARIETY, AND LUSCIOUS SCENTS ABOUND

RECENTLY INTRODUCED LANDSCAPE ROSES ARE FREE OF DISEASES AND PESTS. COMPARED TO THE roses or the last generation, these are essentially maintenance free. Like flower factories, they bloom more or less continuously throughout the growing season and demand little pruning.

The hardy floribunda rose 'Hot Cocoa' bears deep-rust-colored buds, which open to smoky, chocolate-orange blooms.

If you are fond of the familiar long-stemmed hybrid tea or other types such as grandifloras, floribundas, and English roses, you'll pay a price for all that beauty and fragrance. To do what they do so well—namely, produce quantities of beautiful, often fragrant flowers—these roses need special attention. Although hybrid teas can be planted among other plants, it's far easier to lavish them with what they require if

they grow in a small bed of their own. Ten to twelve hybrid teas make a magnificent display, provide plenty of flowers for cutting, and require a bed only 8 by 12 feet or so. Any shape of bed will do, but generations of gardeners have favored the formal look: square, round, or rectangular beds edged with stone, brick, or clipped boxwood. Often a fountain or sundial is placed in the center for added interest.

Nearly all roses demand a location that receives at least 6 hours of sun each day. Ideally, the bed will provide good air circulation and receive morning sun to help dry the plants' leaves early in the day (damp leaves invite disease).

Before planting, pay special attention to improving the soil with organic matter. The extra effort you put into improving the soil now will pay off in superior growth for years to come.

TOP LEFT: Clusters of light pink, wavy-petaled flowers cover 'Sparrieshoop' roses from spring through fall.

TOP RIGHT: 'Fourth of July' is a climbing rose that produces big sprays of semidouble red-and-white blooms.

ABOVE LEFT: Pink 'Carefree Wonder' is matched here with royal blue delphinium.

ABOVE RIGHT: In a formal rose garden, structures and ornaments are aligned along well-defined sight lines. Then roses are planted in distinct beds.

formal is serene

IT'S UNDERSTATED, ELEGANT, AND CALMING

FORMAL GARDENS MAY BE LARGE OR SMALL AND RURAL, SUBURBAN, OR URBAN. WHAT DEFINES A formal garden is a predominance of straight lines, geometric shapes, and classical symmetry. Symmetry means that what appears on one side of the garden is mirrored on the other side. The outermost dimensions are frequently rectangular, and this shape is repeated elsewhere in pools, patios, flower beds, and borders. Usually there is a limited number of kinds of plants, and they are sheared to reinforce the garden's lines. Often a single object, such as a statue, sundial, or large urn, serves as the center of interest. It's placed for optimum effect, usually toward the rear of the garden, and is directly visible from a favored viewing spot, either outside or indoors.

The symmetry of a formal garden relaxes the mind as much as the balmy air of a summer evening does the body. Soft lighting, comfortable furnishings, and water enhance the effect. The architecture, furniture, and use of concrete in this garden form a contemporary version of a formal garden.

If formal landscapes seem to be governed by rules, they are. The precedents of today's formal gardens stretch back to ancient Greece and Rome. Interestingly, while other garden styles come and go, formal gardens have remained steadily popular.

Formal gardens are well suited to certain kinds of architecture, including Georgian, Mediterranean, French, and Victorian, as well as to some modern houses. They also require a level site, or perhaps a series of terraces connected by steps.

TOP LEFT: A fountain with walls thick enough to provide seating, essential for close views of koi and water lilies, is the key feature of this Mediterranean-style courtyard. Sheared into spherical shapes adjacent to the fountain, boxwood grows in square concrete planters. Around the perimeter are 'Tiny Tower' Italian cypresses in pots and billowy sweet lavender *(Lavandula × heterophylla)* and, on the shady side, 'Goodwin Creek Grey' lavender.

TOP RIGHT: Symmetry is created with a flagstone pathway centered on the planter at the rear and a pair of large containers of verbena marking each side of the entrance.

ABOVE: Designed to be viewed from above, formally clipped evergreens offer year-round appeal, while the flowering borders at left and right change with each season. A sundial marks the garden's center.

asian style
CENTURIES OF GARDEN-MAKING KNOW-HOW

INHABITANTS OF ASIAN COUNTRIES HAVE ONE OF THE WORLD'S MOST ANCIENT GARDENING traditions. Naturally, what has taken thousands of years to refine and perfect is impossible to express in just a few words.

The Asian landscape tradition begins with an abiding reverence for nature. Therefore, it's not surprising that Asian cultures revered gardens.

Today's most successful and authentic Asian gardens embody the same spirit that led early Chinese garden makers to study and contemplate the beauty and mystery of wild landscapes. Returning to civilization, these early landscape designers attempted to re-create that beauty and mystery, essentially by

miniaturizing it. Along the way, design ideas developed that included a system of symbols. A rock of a certain shape depicts male energy, a pool represents female attributes, a crooked path prevents evil from passing, and a turtle-shaped rock represents nothing less than ten thousand eons.

Another important part of any Asian-style garden, grand or small, is a place for visitors to sit and contemplate and appreciate its beauty. If you intend to create a garden in

A Japanese-style overhead gracefully shelters a conversation area. On the other side of the low wall is a walkway that invites you to enjoy the view.

this style, be sure to emphasize this important component. At the same time, remember to keep the design simple. As with any formal landscape, much of the allure and beauty of Asian-style gardens is derived from the simplicity and purity of the designer's vision. Avoid the temptation to overdo it. Instead, ask yourself at each turn, "Will this enhance or diminish the scene I'm trying to create?"

BELOW LEFT: The attention to detail in this bamboo fence shows reverence for natural materials.

BELOW RIGHT: Water is important to all kinds of gardens, including Asian. Red azaleas and a thread-leaf Japanese maple accent this overflowing stone basin.

BOTTOM LEFT: Stone pavers crossing a stream are offset so that water can move around them.

BOTTOM RIGHT: A pagoda-style lantern emits a warm glow beside a pathway.

easy-care landscapes
FOCUS ON MINIMIZING UPKEEP

AN UNKEMPT LANDSCAPE CAN MAKE BOTH GARDENERS AND GUESTS UNCOMFORTABLE. THE PATIO furniture may look romantic when littered with a few fallen leaves. But when plants are struggling or uncared for, the atmosphere becomes subtly depressing. And where plants thrive, the mood is uplifting to the same degree.

Minimize yard maintenance by choosing plants that require minimal upkeep yet look good year-round. Flanking steps here are feathery, blue-green 'Hughes' juniper, silver-leafed snow-in-summer, and orange sedum 'Autumn Joy'.

One way to keep up with maintenance is to install a garden that essentially takes care of itself, with automated irrigation, large areas of paving, and tough evergreen shrubs. However, if you love to use a hose and to see the garden change with the seasons, such a solution won't appeal to you. One alternative is to develop a garden that reduces the tasks you dislike—pruning vigorous vines, perhaps—and includes tasks you enjoy, such as raking oak leaves off a gravel path or deadheading roses.

Excellent soil combined with plants that are well suited to your climate and conditions will get any garden off to a good start. Mulching will reduce the need for weeding, and an automated irrigation system will reduce the need for hand watering. If you dislike sweeping and raking, avoid planting trees and shrubs that drop messy fruits, flowers, and leaves. Unless you enjoy pruning, choose plants that won't outgrow their space. Group plants that have similar needs so they are easier to maintain.

BELOW: Bold but simple plantings—like this combination of river birches, grass-like liriope, and sedums—make for easy upkeep.

BOTTOM LEFT: In place of a lawn, a tranquil "streambed" of gravel meanders around the garden, punctuated by a few low-maintenance, flowering annuals and perennials, including pink cosmos and purple Russian sage.

BOTTOM RIGHT: Significant labor savers aren't necessarily complicated. For anyone who mows a lawn regularly, a mowing strip like this one will reduce both edging and weeding time.

spaces for kids
ROOM FOR PLAYING, GROWING, AND HANGING OUT

LANDSCAPES DESIGNED WITH THE NEEDS OF A BUSY FAMILY IN MIND PUT THE ACCENT ON FUN.
Consider anything and everything for active outdoor living, including swimming pools,
built-in kitchens, tree houses, sport courts, gazebos, children's play areas, dining areas,
saunas, swings, and spas.

Most kids take to garden-ing naturally; for them, it's educational play. With the garden adjacent to a playhouse, kids can move easily from one to the other.

One of the first decisions to make when you are planning a play yard is where to place it. Preschoolers feel safer and can be more easily watched if the play area is close to the house. You may prefer to corral older, noisier children farther away yet still within view.

Take into account sun, wind, and shade. Hot sun increases the risk of sunburn and can make metal slides, monkey bars, and concrete walks burning hot. To avoid both problems, install play sites on the cooler, north side of the yard. Areas of dappled shade are ideal.

If you have no spreading foliage and if the north side is not available, construct a simple canopy of lath or canvas, or somehow plan to shade a portion of the structure. Similar-ly, if your property is in the path of strong winds, build a play yard inside a windbreak of fencing or dense trees.

Allow at least a 6-foot fall zone around all sides of swings, slides, and climbing structures, and then cushion it well. A 3-inch layer of wood chips is one choice (increase the depth to 6 inches under a swing). Shredded bark ($^1/_4$-

to 1-inch particles of Douglas or white fir bark) holds up well, even in windy areas or on slopes. Sand provides another safe landing for falls—a depth of 12 inches is not too much. Building a low wall around a play yard helps contain loose materials, keeping the cushion thick and reducing the cost of replenishing. Turfgrass also makes a functional play surface, but avoid mixtures that contain clover, as its flowers attract bees. For maximum cushioning, keep grass about 2 inches high.

If your child will be pedaling a riding toy or tricycle, plan a smooth concrete path at least 24 inches wide. Gravel paths are frustrating for kids on wheels.

ABOVE LEFT: This family used their favorite pastime—hiking and camping—as a theme for their backyard landscape. The result is a space that both kids and parents use.

TOP RIGHT: Kids like to help, and engaging them in ways that are truly useful, such as in making compost, is easy.

ABOVE RIGHT: The sandbox and raised bed are surrounded by a fence and a soft surface—shredded recycled tires.

The need for property-line fencing is probably obvious. Securely fence the play area from the driveway, as well as from the pool, spa, or other body of water, such as a water garden. You may also need to fence off sharp or heavy tools, garden supplies, and garbage cans.

LOWE'S QUICK TIP

Offer kids a small garden plot of their own—even just a container or two—to grow plants of their choosing. Point them toward quick-growing vegetables, such as radishes and cherry tomatoes. Tall, fast-growing flowers like cosmos, zinnias, and sunflowers entice kids as well.

the magic of water features

THEY WILL TRANSFORM YOUR GARDEN

WATER GARDENING IS BOOMING BECAUSE HOMEOWNERS HAVE DISCOVERED THE BIG IMPACT THAT even a small pond or fountain can make—and how easy it is to include one. Because of this popularity, options are increasing. Fountains and ponds are the most common choices, but even something as simple as a birdbath adds a little of water's reflective charm to the garden while also doing something nice for the birds.

Placed among colorful flowers and foliage, a mossy stone basin invites birds to drink and bathe.

If you decide on a fountain or pool, you'll have plenty of choices. Select among them based on your preferences and the layout of your garden. Many terra-cotta and cast-concrete wall fountains come with recirculating pumps. Vinyl pond liners and fiberglass shells are available in many shapes, sizes, and depths, and they make installing a pool as basic as digging a hole (see pages 256–257). And you always have the option of adding a custom-designed pool, which is formed from reinforced concrete. Keep in mind that geometrically shaped pools look best in formal gardens, while free-form pools and waterfalls are best in informal landscapes.

Goldfish and koi add an exotic shimmer of life to the water, and both live for decades. Goldfish are more cold hardy. They over-winter in any pond that doesn't freeze solid and has some surface area free of ice.

BELOW LEFT: A fountain and a tranquil pool with horsetails and iris make a dramatic focal point. The fountain's copper back and water trough define the smooth stucco wall.

BELOW RIGHT: Splashing water from a reproduction antique fountain enlivens this garden retreat and masks noises from a nearby road.

BOTTOM LEFT: A cobble-and-concrete pool offers a tranquil place for reflection. Small rocks, flagstone, and boulders add texture and blend with the muted tones of surrounding plants.

BOTTOM RIGHT: A submerged pump in a 5½-foot-tall Southeast Asian urn creates a low spurt of burbling water.

making outdoor rooms
DIVIDE BIG, OPEN SPACES INTO INTIMATE ONES

WHEN A FENCE, HEDGE, OR MASONRY WALL ENCLOSES AN OUTDOOR SPACE, THE SETTING ESSENTIALLY becomes an outdoor room. The question, then, for homeowners and landscape designers is whether they want one big multipurpose room or a series of rooms designed for specific purposes. For example, you may want separate areas for a vegetable garden and outdoor cooking and eating. Or you may want a divider between a patio area and a utilitarian cutting garden or dog run. Making more boundaries and dividing up space is how you create that hidden retreat or sanctuary.

Brightly colored furnishings and accessories accent this patio's comfortable living area. A green-limbed palo verde tree and an ancient saguaro cactus rise behind the walls.

You can separate one area from another in a variety of ways. Fences, hedges, low walls, rows of shrubs, and lattice screens serve well. Being able to catch a glimpse of the adjoining room through an opening in a hedge or fence adds to the mystery and appeal, and it beckons visitors from one room to the next.

Although you might not think of your garden areas as outdoor rooms, many land-scapes already employ the concept to conceal a utility area for trash cans and garden equipment. How far you take the idea is up to you, but it can add both usefulness and livability to any size garden.

BELOW LEFT: Dividing this cramped, steep yard into a series of stacked outdoor rooms made creative use of a difficult site. A sunny dining terrace offers low walls for comfortable seating and overlooks the colorful, shaded, cozy flower garden below.

BELOW RIGHT: A hard-packed gravel path with contrasting stone steps leads into an intimate side yard garden room that is framed by symmetrical planting beds. A lily pool in the 7-foot-diameter steel livestock tank is the focal point, enjoyed from both the path and a living room window.

BOTTOM RIGHT: Give each garden room a well-defined entrance and an exit, and connect them with paths, as in this garden. The arbor over this entry is covered with a hop vine, and the view through it frames the checkerboard patio.

courtyard sanctuaries
THESE ARE COOL AND COZY PLACES

FROM THEIR ORIGINS IN ARID CLIMATES, COURTYARD GARDENS HOLD THE TRADITION OF BLOCKING out harsh surroundings while enclosing a cool, welcoming paradise. These oases are wonderful gardens to live with and in, functioning much like outdoor rooms.

This narrow, L-shaped side yard has all the charm of a more traditional, square, centrally located courtyard. Note the space-saving wall fountain and the comfortable seating.

Because they are enclosed, courtyard gardens are like distilled versions of larger landscapes. All of the elements are there—the floors, ceilings, and walls; the flowers, trees, and shrubs. But because the space is confined, each element is brought out in high relief, creating an impact out of proportion to its size.

The peace and calm afforded by these courtyard landscapes will invite your guests to linger. But without plenty of comfortable seating as a part of the plan, that invitation is no better than a tease. Use outdoor furniture, but also include in your plan low seat walls and built-in benches.

If you're considering a courtyard garden, don't fall prey to the "bigger is better" notion. For courtyards, small is beautiful—and comforting. You won't need to go overboard with plantings. A couple of well-chosen small trees (possibly even in containers), a few vines for the wall, perhaps a small boxwood hedge surrounding a fountain, and a pot or two of flowering annuals are all you need.

BELOW LEFT: Complete with a koi pond and ample seating, this courtyard was created in a small space. It includes a narrow water channel, or *rill*, set into the middle of the stairs.

BELOW RIGHT: Here, a Mediterranean-style courtyard blends terra-cotta tile squares with blue-glazed accents. The blue tiles echo the colors of the chairs and fence.

BOTTOM: Surrounded by a 12-foot-high stucco wall, this diminutive courtyard is private and feels secluded even though it adjoins a busy retail area.

when space is limited
SMALL MEANS CLOSE FOCUS AND BIG IMPACT

THE AVERAGE SIZE OF RESIDENTIAL BACKYARDS IS SHRINKING. INSTEAD OF EXPANSIVE, OPEN OUTDOOR spaces, more homeowners today have yards that are pocket-sized—perhaps just a balcony or rooftop on which to create a private paradise.

The homeowners reclaimed space in this Southern California backyard by pruning overgrown ficus trees into a tall hedge. That made room for a gravel-paved dining patio, fireplace, and lawn.

But size is relative. What matters most is not the physical dimensions of the space but the commitment to create a good design and to invest ingenuity in the effort.

Small gardens have certain advantages. Condensed spaces are naturally cozy and inviting. They bring each plant into sharper focus, making even a common red geranium in a terra-cotta pot seem special. Although weeds, dead leaves, and other garden debris stand out in a confined space, the effort to keep a small garden tidy is minimal compared to a large yard, leaving you more time to enjoy it. And because there is less to buy, you can create a very satisfying small landscape on a much more modest budget.

Scale is perhaps the most important design element to work with. Select plants or varieties of plants that are naturally compact and that have small leaves. Likewise, choose features, such as a fountain or pool, that are small in scale without sacrificing their function. With careful attention to the size of every element, you can fit many features of a larger landscape into the smallest of spaces.

BELOW LEFT: In many regions, a small, well-cared-for lawn makes more sense than a sprawling one. Give a small lawn an attractive shape and let its emerald green do the rest.

BELOW RIGHT: Clean lines and artful illusion transformed this compact backyard. A "floating" bench and a fire bowl created from a colored concrete planter are key features. Mondo grass grows between poured-concrete pavers.

BOTTOM LEFT: The angled patio and curving path make this small garden look larger than it is.

BOTTOM RIGHT: It feels roomy, but this patio is quite small. Old brick pavers, mature vines, and plenty of comfortable seating do the trick.

cottage garden charm
THE STYLE IS LIGHT AND LOOSE

A LANDSCAPE WITH THE PERSONALITY OF AN ENGLISH COTTAGE GARDEN HAS CHARM TO SPARE, usually in the form of plants climbing out of and spilling over their appointed spaces. Plants are grown and added at the whim of the gardener, and the only guiding principle is to include the gardener's favorite plants.

The effect is usually kaleidoscopic in character, with an old climbing rose, a clump of daylilies, a mat of nasturtiums, and a towering stand of hollyhocks surrounded by spots of color from cottage pinks, basket-of-gold, veronica, poppies, and other flowering and edible plants. The true cottage garden has an unplanned look, but it is as engaging as any landscape.

While this loose design approach may appeal to you, the more random and chaotic the plantings, the more important it becomes to have a strong skeleton that underlies everything, contributing a gentle but discernible sense of order.

As with any other landscape, start the design by defining utilitarian areas—pathways, patios, decks, and so on. Bear in mind that because cottage gardens are naturally unruly, paths need to be extra-wide to accommodate plants' exuberant growth. Leave enough room for outdoor activities like cooking, dining, and lounging, and then decide the shapes and sizes of the flowerbeds and borders.

There are no strict rules for planting a cottage garden. All kinds of plants—fruits, perennials, annuals, shrubs, and vines—are candidates.

The profuse, bountiful look associated with cottage gardens depends on plants that are not merely growing but thriving, and in order to thrive, they need the best possible soil. Improve yours before planting. You'll probably never get a second chance to do it right, so be sure to add generous amounts of organic matter to the soil, till it in deeply, and add whatever amendments may be necessary.

TOP LEFT: Pink sweet William and poppies play off yellow daylilies and silvery lamb's ears in this border.

TOP RIGHT: The charm of this cottage garden starts with the white picket fence and rose-clad arbor over the gate.

ABOVE LEFT: Pink flowers of 'Ballerina' rose and yellow 'Sun Goddess' rose complement the playfully painted blue door.

ABOVE RIGHT: A Mediterranean version of a cottage garden features roses, lavender, and rosemary, along with pink-flowering *Geranium incanum*.

a cook's garden

HERBS ARE KEPT CLOSE, AND THERE'S ROOM FOR EDIBLES

NOTHING IS QUITE SO SATISFYING TO COOKS AS BEING ABLE TO WALK OUT THE BACK DOOR TO pluck a sun-ripened tomato for a salad, or snip a sprig of parsley or basil for a pot of simmering soup. While a sprawling vegetable garden may work for some people, homeowners with smaller spaces can also enjoy the convenience of homegrown vegetables and herbs.

To make a kitchen garden with a contemporary look, a family installed a grid of nine concrete squares, each measuring 30 inches square and 14 inches tall. All have drainage holes except the center one, which is a recirculating fountain.

This is true even if you're a beginning gardener. Creating a garden that's both edible and attractive is well within your reach. Your garden doesn't have to be either all edible or all flowers. You can mix edibles with flowering perennials and annuals, essentially using vegetables as ornamentals. This allows you to enjoy small amounts of homegrown produce without a big commitment of time and space.

You can use herbs, with their distinctive fragrances and interesting colors, to line pathways, and put long-lived vegetables, cabbage for instance, in decorative containers. The colors and textures of leafy greens, such as Swiss chard, brighten late-season borders, while the shapes of dramatic plants, perhaps artichoke or rhubarb, lend a sculptural touch to a border.

LEFT: Both kids and vegetables thrive in a kitchen garden that's supervised by a scarecrow.

BELOW: Redwood-framed beds hold corn, tomatoes, and other summer crops.

BOTTOM LEFT: Raised wooden planters are finished with a mitered 2-by-6 seat rail, which eases herb harvest.

BOTTOM RIGHT: Gold-flowered signet marigolds weave among blue-green, red, and curly-leafed cabbages.

outdoor dining areas

MAKE THE MOST OF EATING ALFRESCO

AN OUTDOOR DINING AREA IS OFTEN THE CENTERPIECE OF AN ATTRACTIVE PATIO OR DECK. IT CAN also double as a craft center, sewing spot, or as a perfect place to play board games or enjoy other leisurely activities.

A brightly colored tablecloth accents a cozy dining nook hidden in a brick-paved rose garden. Potted plants add soft accents.

A functional and inviting outdoor dining area incorporates a careful balance of many of the site considerations and structural and design elements described in this book. For example, ensuring privacy, sufficient shade, and shelter from the elements—via trees, overhead structures, screening, and fences—will add

significantly to your enjoyment of the space. Defining the area with colorful plantings also adds appeal. In general, cool colors are relaxing and meditative, while warm colors tend to create a more energetic, active space.

Furniture is also important and today is available in a wide variety of materials. From

wrought iron to wicker, your choices are many and should fit the space and blend well with the surroundings, as well as be suitable for the climate. For sunny spots, a large umbrella is likely a necessity.

Outdoor dining rooms are most useful within easy access of the house. If you have a large property, however, you may decide to create yours in a more remote location for secluded and private gatherings.

PLANNING YOUR DINING SPACE

Whatever your choice of furniture, you need to figure out how best to use available space. Be sure to leave enough room for people to maneuver around the dining table and other furniture to serve and remove food. The illustration here shows one example of how to calculate clearances around furniture.

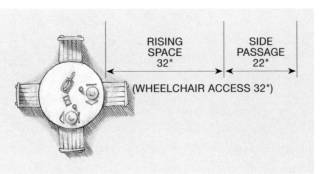

RISING SPACE 32"

SIDE PASSAGE 22"

(WHEELCHAIR ACCESS 32")

TOP LEFT: A traditional Southwest fireplace with seat wall is a gathering spot on chilly nights.

TOP RIGHT: The fence and mature shrubs enclose this dining area.

ABOVE LEFT: A fireplace with a stone hearth is the focal point of this combined outdoor kitchen and dining room.

ABOVE RIGHT: In mild climates, a tiled outdoor kitchen is a colorful alternative to wood or stone.

artistic landscapes

THE RESULTS ARE QUIRKY, PERSONAL, AND FUN

WHETHER THEIR OWNERS ARE ACTUALLY ARTISTS OR NOT, THE LANDSCAPES PICTURED ON THESE pages are certainly works of self-expression. Their creators let loose in their own backyards. Strong forms and bold colors alternate with soft textures and quiet corners. No surface is sacred. The door of a garden shed might be Day-Glo green, a patio may be made from an intricate mosaic of broken bits of crockery, or an old wheelbarrow might recall a Currier & Ives painting. Whimsy abounds, and simply delighting in the results is reason enough to enjoy these gardens.

Persicaria virginiana 'Painter's Palette' spreads around a sculpted rock and makes a frame for it.

It's interesting to note that artists' gardens are usually the expression of a single personality. Rare is the couple who can agree on whether fluorescent purple is an appealing color to paint a lawn chair. Garden—and relationship—harmony may by maintained by each partner having his or her own space.

BELOW LEFT: Eleven varieties of thyme grow in this circular bed, which is surrounded by a pebble mosaic representing Ouroboros—a snake or dragon that expresses the cyclical nature of life.

BELOW RIGHT: Bold use of color, such as the yellow door with chartreuse trim, is the sign of an artist's hand. It makes this garden visually delightful even when there are no flowers.

BOTTOM LEFT: Bright, artist-made floral ceramic tiles transform a concrete-block retaining wall. Gaillardia and nasturtiums growing in the bed behind the tiles were chosen to match their colors and motif.

BOTTOM RIGHT: A trompe l'oeil gate, painted on an otherwise blank stuccoed wall, invites visitors into an imaginary garden. Plants near the painting aid in the illusion.

- Be willing to experiment—and fail.
- Trust your own eye and experience.
- Look at familiar materials in new ways.

wildflowers are wild

SOW AND THEN LET NATURE DO ITS THING

WHEN MANY PEOPLE THINK OF WILDFLOWERS, THEY SEE THEM AS SUITABLE ONLY FOR LARGE plantings—spaces measured in acres instead of square feet. Wildflower mixes, however, are delightful, low-maintenance additions to landscapes of any size, whether planted in traditional borders, in a rough area out back, or as a replacement for a lawn.

In a Phoenix garden, desert bluebells and owl's clover fill the foreground, while a wall of pink-spired desert beard tongue rises in the rear. Yellow blooms of desert marigold and orange Arizona poppies add contrast.

Wildflowers are all about the spring show: Don't expect all-season good looks from them.

For the greatest success with wildflowers, pay attention to regional recommendations. Wildflowers that grow well in some regions are utter failures in others. For example,

California poppies return year after year in the desert Southwest but are overwhelmed by weeds and tall grasses in the rainy Southeast.

Take time to prepare the soil properly before sowing, and remove all weeds from the planting bed by hand, by repeated tilling, or, if you must, with an herbicide.

TOP LEFT: In New England the woodland native white wood aster *(Aster divaricatus)* is well suited to tree-shaded gardens. Like most other asters, it blooms in the fall.

TOP RIGHT: Penstemons thrive in the high-elevation West. Here, orange-red scarlet bugler penstemon *(Penstemon barbatus)* blooms with pink sunset penstemon *(P. clutei)*, purple Rocky Mountain penstemon *(P. strictus)*, and yellow columbine.

ABOVE LEFT: In New Mexico, an orderly row of blue mist *(Caryopteris)* lines an entry path, while yellow daisies of Mexican hat *(Ratibida columnifera)* and lavender-blue Russian sage *(Perovskia)* transition into the wilder, natural landscape.

ABOVE RIGHT: Native throughout most of eastern North America, perennial lupine *(Lupinus perennis)* starts from seed, dies with frost, then returns from its roots in spring.

shaded landscapes
LEAFY COVER OFFERS MANY OPPORTUNITIES

AS FORESTS AGE, A WHOLE NEW MICROCLIMATE IS CREATED. PLANTS THAT WERE AT ONE TIME dominant disappear, and new kinds of plants appear, ones that can flourish in the low light under a canopy of trees and can find the water and nutrients they need. An amazing variety of ferns, the nodding bluebells of early spring, the lyrical beauty of a dogwood tree in bloom, and azaleas are examples of these shade-loving woodland plants. Rhododendrons and camellias that add their resplendent blossoms to the spring green are other notable and extraordinary plants associated with woodlands.

Many woodland plants, including rhododendrons and azaleas, thrive in the shade cast by tall spruce and maple trees. What better place to cool off and rest on a warm spring afternoon?

If you're interested in creating a woodland garden and have the natural conditions to foster one, your best bet is to mimic nature's designs. If possible and at different times of year, explore on foot the naturally wooded areas in your community, and take along a notebook and a camera to record what you see. If plants catch your eye but are unknown to you, take photographs of them to a nursery, where staff members should be able to help you identify them. Don't be tempted to dig up plants from the wild. For one thing, it doesn't work very well: Wild plants rarely transplant successfully into gardens. But not only is it bad form, it's illegal in many areas.

Add a patio or deck where the view is particularly pleasant so that you can spend time enjoying your plants at close range.

BELOW: Under stately old pines and an enormous oak tree in Denver, shade-loving plants of varying textures include yellow-edged 'Frances Williams' hosta, white-edged 'Patriot' hosta, and the large leaves of 'Blue Giant' hosta.

BOTTOM LEFT: Lavender fronds of Japanese painted fern echo the bloom hues of a hellebore. *Polemonium reptans* 'Stairway to Heaven' adds cream-splashed foliage.

BOTTOM RIGHT: Sunlight trickling through the branches of mature trees creates the perfect environment for shade-loving bigleaf hydrangea *(Hydrangea macrophylla)*.

birds and butterflies
THEY'LL ENLIVEN YOUR LANDSCAPE

WHILE SOME PEOPLE DREAM OF PLANTING A ROSE GARDEN OR A VEGETABLE PATCH, WILDLIFE gardeners have visions of butterfly gardens and bird sanctuaries. Often this type of landscape has no lawn, or it's only a small one. Gone too are neatly trimmed shrub borders. In their place are informal plantings of annuals and perennials and meandering walks covered with pine needles or bark. Most contain at least one birdbath, fountain, or small pool for the fresh water that's essential to all forms of life.

All landscapes require regular upkeep, but informal plantings that attract wildlife are far less demanding than more traditional ones. Allow plants to find their natural forms instead of trimming them into tidy shapes. A weed here or there isn't such an eyesore when it's growing amid a profusion of billowing plants. And birds and butterflies won't notice whether it's a weed or a rare and exotic plant.

Though wildlife landscapes are informal, you'll want to define places to sit, relax, and take in the sights and sounds of your private sanctuary. A wooden bench under a spreading tree, a couple of chaise longues on a patio overlooking a small pond, or a clearing in a grove of trees for a picnic table and benches will provide human comfort and an enchanting vantage point.

Any water-holding depression, as in this natural outcrop of boulders, will draw birds after rainfall.

TOP LEFT: This corner of a garden was designed specifically to rejuvenate the busy owners. Quiet and comfortable, it also features a fountain with recirculating water and a bird feeder, because watching visiting birds and insects is itself relaxing.

TOP RIGHT: A monarch butterfly pauses for a drink at the blossom of a New England aster *(Aster novae-angliae).*

LEFT: A female Anna's hummingbird hovers over the bloom of a bottlebrush *(Callistemon).*

ABOVE: Trumpet honeysuckle *(Lonicera sempervirens),* a favorite of hummingbirds, clambers over a birdhouse intended for other feathered friends.

rock gardens
IF LIFE GIVES YOU STONES, MAKE A GARDEN

ROCK GARDENS ARE LANDSCAPES IN MINIATURE, simulations of boulder-strewn mountain slopes, rocky outcrops of coastal bluffs, or windswept high plains—all created with diminutive flowering and evergreen plants. Your property is a potential rock garden if it contains natural outcroppings or slopes with thin, gravelly soil that makes typical landscaping difficult.

Even in yards that are mostly stone, you can find space to grow attractive plants. Colorful conifers and flowering perennials, such as lady's mantle with chartreuse blooms, offer a charming contrast to the muted brown and gray boulders.

Traditional rock gardens rely on plants from high altitudes. Called alpine plants, they are low-growing plants that survive winter under a blanket of snow, and send roots deep into rocky crevices. In spring, they put forth brilliantly colored—and often very large—flowers.

Although strict practitioners of rock gardening insist upon using only plants and rocks that are native to alpine regions, most gardeners ask only that a plant look right in its rocky surroundings, caring little for the origin of the plant and even less about where the rocks might have come from. Modern rock gardens use any type of plant, as long as it is relatively delicate in scale.

Most plants adapted to rocky sites are naturally dwarf and low-growing. Some of the most useful plants are low-growing junipers, dwarf conifers, compact ground covers, and various mosses.

TOP LEFT: Several kinds of dianthus combined with stone-cress *(Aethionema × warleyense)* thrive and flower in the gaps between stones, with roots under a gravel mulch.

TOP RIGHT: Fringed with ferns and sweet woodruff, moss-mottled boulders in various shapes were placed by an expert but look as if they were revealed by nature.

ABOVE LEFT: Just a tiny crevice in a lichen-covered rock is more than enough space to make a comfortable home for hen and chickens.

ABOVE RIGHT: Cascading sedums, shore junipers, and woolly thyme soften the edges of this aged stone wall as they drape over it.

tropical flair

IT'S NOT ONLY FOR THE TROPICS

MORE THAN ANY OTHER STYLE, TROPICAL LANDSCAPES ARE ABOUT PLANTS. SWAYING PALMS, NEON-flowered bougainvillea spilling over the top of a roof, cannas rising rocket like beside a garden pool, and aptly named elephant's ears putting forth leaves the size of tablecloths are just a few of the treasures.

You can enjoy the look, if not the climate, of the tropics almost anywhere. Spiky New Zealand flax, red and yellow cannas, and giant bird of paradise are the tallest here. Chartreuse sweet potato vine grows in front of ruffled taro.

Mainstays of gardens in the lower and subtropical South, as well as the mild-winter West, tropical plants are hot items for gardeners just about everywhere. Tropical and semitropical plants revel in hot summers, and many will bloom nonstop through summer with spectacular flowers.

Creatively combining the different shapes and sizes of leaves of these exuberant plants is as rewarding as mixing different colors of flowers. Try juxtaposing plants with wide leaves with ones that have narrow or lance-shaped leaves. Or match small leaved plants with ones that have large leaves.

Don't let the prospect of cold winters keep you from trying tropicals in your garden. In marginal climates, gardeners can often preserve tropicals just by mulching them heavily in fall. Where this isn't enough, grow them in containers, bring them indoors before the first fall frost, then take them back outdoors the following spring.

BELOW LEFT: This slice of tropical paradise features palms and a ground cover of bromeliads.

BELOW RIGHT: With landscaping and Buddha statues, a simple redwood sleeping platform evokes southern Asia.

BOTTOM LEFT: A slate-tiled patio separates a grove of sculptural palms and a planting of tall horsetails.

BOTTOM RIGHT: The feel of Bali is conjured by this stylized pavilion surrounded by lush vegetation.

LOWE'S QUICK TIP

In spring, once night temperatures are above 55 degrees F, move outdoors tropical houseplants including croton, split-leaf philodendron, ti plant, fiddleleaf fig, and bromeliads.

container gardens

ADORN BALCONIES, ROOFTOPS, STAIRWAYS, AND FENCES

PLANTS IN CONTAINERS, LONG A STAPLE IN CITY GARDENS, LEND VERSATILITY TO ANY GARDEN. Containers can go almost anywhere—into sun or shade—to provide a bright splash of color or fill out a bare spot. They can become a focal point in their own right if the container has sufficient presence. Moreover, during a long winter, you can move plants in containers to a protected spot and perhaps prolong bloom.

Container gardening allows you to display plants where the soil is poor or even nonexistent. Place them along paths, on stairs, in sitting areas, and even on the tops and sides of walls and fences.

Among shade plants that are suitable for containers, some of the most striking effects come from those with unusual leaf markings and colorful foliage. Purple, red, and yellow foliage—found on coleus, caladium, and

Persian shield (*Strobilanthes dyerianus*)—makes a stunning foil for bright flowers and lush leaves.

Bold leaf shapes, of hostas for instance, can contrast handsomely with the fine-textured foliage of fringed bleeding heart (*Dicentra eximia*). Strap-leaved plants, such as agapanthus, can add drama and soften the harsher lines of other plants.

Choices for sunny locations are practically unlimited. Try flowering annuals beginning

Re-create a piece of North America's prairie by combining a clump of native grass with gloriosa daisy and purple cone flower.

with rosy pink petunias, erect blue mealycup sage (*Salvia farinacea* 'Victoria'), and white African daisies. Or match the pink floribunda rose 'Nearly Wild' with red-and-pink maiden pink (*Dianthus deltoides*). For large mixed plantings, select the central plant first, then choose plants with flowers that complement its growth habit and color. Annuals are perfect for containers, thanks to their shallow roots and vigorous growth, but most plants perform well as long as the container is large enough to accommodate the plant's roots.

BELOW LEFT: Bottomless culvert pipes lend an architectural element to this deck, and they give the billowing annual flowers a place to sink deep roots.

BELOW RIGHT: Thriving in steel livestock tanks are yellow santolina, blue fescue, silvery lamb's ears, and 'Otto Quast' Spanish lavender.

BOTTOM LEFT: Annuals and sculptural desert plants fill pots on both sides of this courtyard fountain, softening the expanse of paving.

BOTTOM RIGHT: Spikes of red salvia and mounds of flowering daisies complement the brick walls and pavers in this courtyard. Also in containers are other vines and shrubs that, combined, create a lush look.

LOWE'S QUICK TIPS

- Make sure containers allow for good water drainage.
- In containers, use a lightweight soil mix, not soil from the garden.
- Water and fertilize container plants regularly.

water-wise landscaping
DRY GARDENS ARE EXCITING IN MANY WAYS

WHERE RAIN IS SCARCE OR RESERVOIRS ARE EASILY OVERTAXED—WHETHER FROM A TEMPORARY weather condition or the prevailing climate—more and more gardeners are becoming conscious of their water use.

Spiky yucca and purple Dutch irises rise over blooming perennials in a Colorado garden, where plants need to be both drought and cold tolerant.

Many homeowners are forgoing large lawns and the sprawling beds of annuals that demand more in water than they return in pleasure. Instead, these gardeners group water-conserving plants together, and similarly arrange plants that need regular watering so that they can be efficiently watered at once, perhaps by a separate irrigation system schedule. Water-conserving plants are ones that are well adapted to the region's natural weather conditions.

Lowe's Garden Center stocks many plants that are well adapted to your particular region—plants more or less content to survive on the area's natural rainfall (or occasional lack of it). To make the most of what water you have, choose less thirsty plants.

Make sure your sprinklers deliver water as efficiently as possible, and don't waste water to overspray and runoff (see pages 208–215). Routinely incorporate organic mulch to improve your soil's ability to resist evaporation and retain moisture. A 1- to 2-inch layer of shredded bark or pine needles over soil and around plants reduces moisture loss, controls weeds, and slows erosion.

BELOW LEFT: A lush but lean garden includes yellow yarrow, blue Russian sage, chaste tree, and Chinese wisteria.

BELOW RIGHT: It's in early spring, when the intense blue pride of Madeira and golden California poppies bloom, that this Mediterranean garden is showiest.

BOTTOM LEFT: Ribbons of native buffalo grass between pavers look thirsty, but only monthly irrigation is required.

BOTTOM RIGHT: Weeks of drought won't faze yellow fernleaf yarrow or the red-and-yellow blanket flower.

preparing for wildfire

HOW LANDSCAPING CAN SAVE YOUR HOUSE

WILDFIRES HAVE LONG BEEN A FACT OF LIFE IN THE WEST AND ARE BECOMING SO IN OTHER REGIONS of the country. If you live where wildfires are a threat, one of the most important steps you can take to prevent losing your home is to manage the property around your house properly. Fire officials believe that clearing the brush at least 30 feet from the house can halve the odds of losing your house to fire. The exact distance to clear for your house is determined by slope, wind, neighborhood density, and your house's architecture and materials.

Poised above a fire-prone canyon, landscaping for this garden is as much about security as good looks. The lawn is a green buffer, and it's surrounded by low-growing plants that don't burn easily.

For years, common wisdom was to plant only fire-retardant plants. But experts now say such plants provide only false comfort. In California, fire-retardant plants did little to slow a rapidly advancing fire, especially where those plants were affected by drought, poorly maintained, or placed adjacent to a house with a wooden roof. In a high-intensity fire, everything burns. But some landscapes are safer than others. The guidelines listed on the facing page offer the best information to date. For more information, visit Lowes.com or Firewise Communities at firewise.org.

FIRESCAPING BASICS

- Eliminate fire ladders—plants of different heights that form a continuous fuel supply from the ground up to the tree canopy.
- Create a transition zone, if your lot size allows, 30 to 50 feet out from the house. In this area, leave only enough shrubs and low-growing plants to stabilize a slope.
- Regularly clean up leaves and other plant litter and remove overgrown brush.
- Clear all vegetation and debris from your roof and gutters several times a year.
- Keep plants well watered (assuming water supplies permit), especially those within 30 feet of the house. Keep grasses watered and green year-round.
- Thin crowns of clustered trees, trim limbs to 20 feet or more off the ground, and cut back any branches to 15 to 20 feet from the house. Prune out all dead branches.
- Clear out overhanging tree branches along the driveway and prune back bushy shrubs to ensure that fire trucks have easy access.

TOP LEFT: The home in the background was saved by the cleared space around it.

ABOVE LEFT: An underground sprinkler system helps keep the landscape from drying and becoming a fire hazard.

ABOVE: A professional arborist clears highly flammable deadwood from a mature oak tree.

patios, decks, and paths

FIRST THINGS FIRST. INSTEAD OF THINKING ABOUT A NEW PATIO or deck, think of a new outdoor room. The difference is more than semantic. When you think of your yard as a room, you consider not only how you'll use it but what ambience it should have, not only how it will take advantage of the sun or a view but also what its color scheme should be. Think in terms of its furnishings—seating and lighting, of course, but perhaps also a heater, a pizza oven, or a spa.

With these factors in mind, you can review this chapter and begin to zero in on whether you want a patio or a deck—or both. One good reason for decks is their versatility. And when it comes to patios, few projects can enlarge your home more quickly. Add to them paths and stairs, arbors and gazebos, and you have the basic decor of your outdoor room.

patios and decks
WHICH WILL WORK BETTER FOR YOU?

SOMETIMES THIS DECISION IS SIMPLY A MATTER OF STYLE, BUT MORE OFTEN IT IS DETERMINED BY your site. Decks have a number of advantages. The lumber is durable and resilient underfoot, and it doesn't store heat the way stone, brick, or concrete does. Hardwoods add a furniture-like elegance, and the choices of man-made and recycled products are becoming more attractive and rightly popular. Decks can also tame sloping, bumpy, or poorly draining sites.

Big pots planted with flowering maples (left) and orange-flowered canna (right) dress up a cozy deck that overhangs a pond.

Patios, on the other hand, lend an incomparable sense of permanence and tradition to a formal garden or house design. Among the choices are traditional brick or tile or elegant stone. Concrete pavers are rising stars, and they're easy to install yourself. And don't rule out concrete—you may be amazed at the jazzy techniques for coloring,

retexturing, and softening a concrete slab. Loose materials, such as pea gravel, bark, or wood chips, are still other options.

Or why not combine both patio and deck in one design? A blend of masonry and wood allows great flexibility in space, texture, and finished height.

TOP LEFT: Built above a mist-filled valley, this deck provides a scenic overlook and a front-row seat to a stunning view.

TOP RIGHT: A patio just steps from the kitchen door makes good use of a side yard.

ABOVE: This contemporary-style elevated deck contrasts the rich look of ipé wood decking with concrete columns.

LOWE'S QUICK TIP

For a complete reference on selecting the right patio or deck plus instructions for building one, see *Lowe's Complete Patio & Deck Book*.

matching house to patio

USE YOUR HOME FOR DESIGN INSPIRATION

EITHER A PATIO OR A DECK CAN BE MUCH MORE THAN A SIMPLE RECTANGLE OUTSIDE THE BACK DOOR. You might also consider a succession of patios and level changes, connected by steps, or design a secluded deck in an attractive corner of your property. Perhaps you could even reclaim a forsaken side yard. Here are some of the possibilities.

L- or U-shaped house A house with this shape cries out for a patio or deck. The surrounding house walls already form an enclosure, so a privacy screen and a decorative overhead structure, such as an arbor, a pergola, or even a simple roof, complete the room. Often such a site can be reached from several parts of the house.

detached site Perfect for serving as a quiet retreat, a detached patio or deck can be built on a flat or sloping lot and looks very much at home in a cottage garden. Reach it with a direct walkway or a meandering path. A roof, privacy screen, or small fountain can make such a detached patio or deck even more enjoyable.

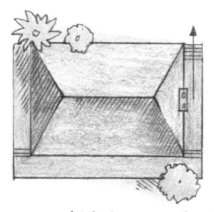

wraparound A flat lot is a natural candidate for a wraparound patio, which enlarges the apparent size of the house while allowing access from any room along its course. If your lot has a gentle grade, rise above it with a slightly elevated wraparound deck, which the Japanese call an engawa.

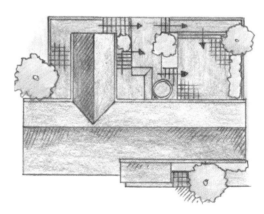

multilevel deck and patio A large lot, especially one with changes in elevation, can often accommodate decks and patios on different levels, linked by steps or pathways. Such a scheme works well when outdoor space must serve several purposes.

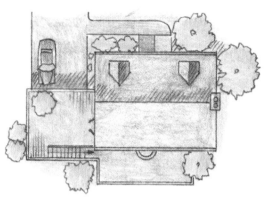

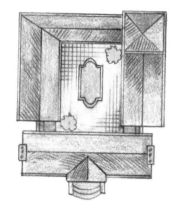

rooftop or balcony site No open space in the yard? Look up! A garage rooftop adjacent to a second-story living area may be ideal for a sunny outdoor lounging space. Or consider a small balcony patio with a built-in bench and planter box.

interior courtyard If you're designing a new home, consider incorporating an interior courtyard into your design. If you're remodeling, perhaps your new living space can enclose an existing patio area.

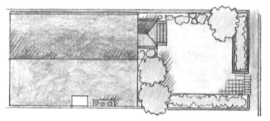

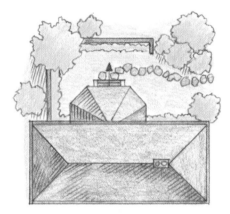

entry patio Pavers, plants, and a trickling fountain enclosed by a privacy wall transform an ordinary entry path into a private oasis. If a solid wall won't work, use a hedge, arbor, or trellis for screening.

porch Where summers swelter, the classic porch evokes traditional indoor-outdoor living. In bug country, screened porches or sunrooms make sense. Some porches can be shuttered when strong winds blow.

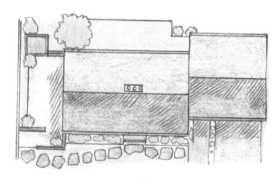

side-yard space A neglected side yard may be just the spot for a sheltered outdoor sitting area to brighten and expand a small bedroom or master bath. Or consider a container herb garden or sunny breakfast deck off the kitchen.

double-duty driveway A driveway can double as a masonry patio. Concrete turf blocks can support car traffic but yield a softer appearance than plain asphalt or concrete.

patio planning

CHOOSING SURFACES, STYLES, AND ACCESSORIES

TYPICALLY, DESIGNING A PATIO, AS OPPOSED TO A DECK, INVOLVES THE DESIGN OF THE ENTIRE yard, or at least a substantial part of it. Because a patio surface is only slightly above grade, it needs to be integrated with the landscaping. Often a patio serves as a transition between the house and the lawn, in the area that receives the most foot traffic. The lawn then becomes an extension of the patio. Neighboring foliage, such as trees, shrubs, vines, flower beds, and crevice plants, integrates the patio with the yard and contributes to its functionality.

An elegant brick fireplace provides a dramatic backdrop to a seating area and can be used for cooking.

If your patio will abut a tree, consult a nursery to determine whether the patio will damage the tree's root system. Take into account the rate of growth for the tree. In many cases, it is best to keep the patio at least 4 feet from the trunk. If the tree has shallow roots, it is likely preferable to install loose gravel or a raised deck rather than a concrete pad around the tree.

The first step in planning a patio is to focus on your family's needs and habits. Think about the way you spend your leisure time. Consider your lifestyle. Do you frequently entertain outdoors? If so, do you prefer casual or formal

entertaining? An important question is how much time you want to spend gardening and maintaining your yard. Do you have pets that may damage fragile patio plants and furniture? Your answers to these questions will determine some basic design elements for your patio.

Next, evaluate your garden's assets and liabilities. Even if you plan to hire a landscape architect or other professional, you need to have a good understanding of your existing landscape. Can the patio capitalize on a beautiful view? Is your property bounded by woods? Perhaps the design can take advantage of a sunny southern exposure, mature plantings, or one worthwhile element, such as an attractive tree.

Also consider potential design obstacles or handicaps. Is your lot on a steep slope? How much of the lot is exposed to street traffic and noise? Does your current patio open off the wrong room, get too much sun or shade, or lack sufficient space? You'll want to plan a patio that minimizes your yard's special problems.

The patio's exact location will depend largely on the size and contour of your lot, the way your house is sited, your preferred uses for the patio, and your climate.

For details on how to build a basic concrete patio, see pages 220–221.

successful patio design

Regardless of the size of your lot and the landscaping problems your property may present, successful patio design depends largely upon the following five key elements.

flexibility Your design needs to accommodate activities important to your family.

privacy As an extension of your indoor space, the patio should offer a similar feeling of privacy (see pages 122–123).

comfort You'll be most comfortable on a patio that's designed with your area's climate in mind.

safety Materials for paving have differing properties. Some, for example, become slippery when wet, while others are too sharp or uneven for children or for playing games. Consider the safety of traffic patterns from house to patio and from garden to patio. Provide adequate lighting at steps and along garden paths.

beauty Successful patios create a balance in an overall garden scheme. Materials should blend with those in the house, and colors and textures should harmonize with the landscaping and other decorative accents.

ABOVE LEFT: Diagonally placed brick pavers detail a path that leads to a color-matched garden seating area paved with flagstone.

ABOVE RIGHT: A small, private patio offers informal seating and quiet views. Planting space is maximized by use of containers and raised planters.

LOWE'S QUICK TIP

Check to see whether you need to obtain a permit and to have your patio inspected by your local building department. In many communities, a modest-size patio with pavers laid in soil or sand does not need to be inspected, whereas a concrete slab or a large patio does.

patio styles

When choosing a patio environment, decide whether you want a formal or informal effect. Formal landscapes are typically symmetrical, with straight lines, geometric patterns, and near-perfect balance. They often include neatly sheared hedges or topiaries and a fountain, pool, or sculpture. In addition, formal patios are best kept well maintained. Small rectangular plots are suited to the medieval knot-garden style, with brick or stone pathways and formal plantings radiating from a central foundation or sculpture. If you

Colorful squashes and potted plants add an autumnal touch to this patio, tiled in earthy tones to match the house.

replace the brick or stone with adobe and tile, the style becomes Spanish. Concrete lends a slightly industrial look to a formal patio garden. Seeded aggregates, as well as smooth-troweled and textured concrete, are modern in feel.

Informal styles, on the other hand, tend toward curves, asymmetry, and apparent randomness. These patios are often easier to maintain. Adjacent plantings are usually more informal as well. Contemporary designs may feature multilevel surfaces, planters, overheads, a swimming pool, or low-maintenance plantings. Irregular flagstone or mossy bricks laid in sand offer a softer cottage garden look, as do spaced concrete pavers, especially if you plant ground cover between the pavers.

Raked gravel that imitates swirling water, carefully placed boulders, a fountain, and a hidden garden bench or bridge are all trademarks of a Japanese garden.

In desert climates, the patio can function as a retreat from heat and noise. To keep the air cool and moist, incorporate overheads and screens, as well as a fountain or a waterfall. Keep plants lush with drip or spray emitters.

landscaping principles

Whatever type of outdoor surface you choose, let the following basic landscaping principles—unity, variety, proportion, and balance—guide your thinking. You'll want to return to these principles repeatedly as your plan develops. On the following two pages is an introduction to these concepts. For

BELOW LEFT: The hanging stems of a grapevine cool the patio and keep the harsh sunlight from reaching under the overhang.

BELOW RIGHT: Flagstone pavers that support moss in the spaces between them blend naturally with their surroundings.

BOTTOM: One take on camping—for adults—is this patio that features a gas-fueled fire pit backed by a concrete wall to reflect heat back toward chairs.

more about them, see "Making Your Plan," beginning on page 170.

Here are examples of how some of these ideas apply to the design of your patio.

unity means that all the elements of your landscape look as if they belong together. Paving, overhead structures, and screens complement each other; furniture suits the patio's architectural style; and the plants relate to one another and to other plants in the landscape.

Unity between the patio and house is also an important consideration. If, for example, your patio is built off a casual-style kitchen, plan your patio so that it has the same feeling.

variety keeps unity from becoming monotonous. A good design offers an element of surprise: a path that leads from a large main terrace to a more intimate one, a plant display that brings the garden into the patio, a subtle wall fountain that gives dimension to a small space, or trees that provide varying degrees of light at different times of day.

You can also make use of variety on vertical planes. Patios that step up or step down, low walls, raised beds, privacy screens, and container plants of varying heights help reduce the visual impact of a vertical expanse.

proportion demands that the patio's structure be in scale with your house and garden. Keep in mind that as outdoor rooms, patios are built on a different scale than indoor rooms. Although many patios are scaled to the size of the living room, you can design something larger. Outdoor furniture usually takes up more room than indoor pieces, and you may want room for containers of plants as well. Choose plants with their mature sizes in mind.

There are sensible limits, however. If your lot is so big that you need a large patio to keep everything in scale, try to create a few smaller areas within the larger whole. For example, squares of plants inset in paving break up a monotonous surface. Use plantings or fences to divide one large area into two or more functional spaces.

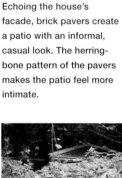

Echoing the house's facade, brick pavers create a patio with an informal, casual look. The herring-bone pattern of the pavers makes the patio feel more intimate.

To maintain proportion in a small patio, keep the design simple and uncluttered, as clean lines make elements seem larger. Stepped planting beds lead the eye up and out of a confined area. Tall screens used to enclose a small area actually make it appear larger, as does a solid paving material like brick, with its small-scale repetitive pattern.

balance occurs when elements are artfully combined to produce the same visual weight on both sides of a center of interest. For example, if a mature tree shades one side of your patio, balance the tree's weight with perimeter benches on the other side.

orientation to the sun

Your patio's exposure to the sun is one of the most important factors in your enjoyment of the outdoor space. Knowing the sun's path may prompt you to adjust the site of the patio, extend its dimensions, or change its design in order to add a few weeks or months of sun or shade to your outdoor room. Often the addition of a patio roof can moderate the sun's effects.

Typically, a north-facing patio is cold because it receives little direct sun, while a south-facing one is warm because, from sunrise to sunset, it is exposed to direct sun. Similarly, an east-facing exposure is cool because it receives only morning sun, while a west-facing is one hot because it is exposed to the full force of the sun's midafternoon rays. In addition, late-afternoon sun often creates a harsh glare.

Generally, the patio temperature will follow this north-south-east-west rule. Exceptions occur in climates where extreme summer or winter temperatures are predictable. For example, mid-July temperatures in Phoenix regularly climb above 100 degrees F (38 degrees C), and a north-facing patio there could hardly be considered cold. In San Francisco, on the other hand, a patio with a southern or western exposure would not be considered hot, because fog and ocean breezes are common in summer.

For useful diagrams about planning your landscape and its orientation to the sun, see pages 180–181.

ABOVE LEFT: Overhead timbers, supported on massive posts, harmonize with the natural surroundings, softening and shading the patio's hard surface.

ABOVE RIGHT: Furniture with spare, simple lines doesn't overwhelm this small patio.

patio paving
THERE ARE OPTIONS FOR EVERY SITUATION

PATIOS, STEPS, PATHS, AND OTHER PAVED AREAS ARE OFTEN DEFINED BY THEIR SURFACE MATERIAL, AND with good reason. Whether gentle, rustic adobe; warm, traditional brick; or sleek, stamped concrete, a patio's surface is its defining characteristic. The illustrations on the facing page show how the same patio area can take on a different look, depending on what material is used.

Although the surface is what most people first notice about a path or patio, there are other essential elements. Most patios have an edging, which serves both to visually define the borders and to physically contain the surface material. Edgings allow you, for instance, to subtly define the borders of a brick patio by using bricks placed on end or, to boldly emphasize the patio's outline, using wood stained in a color that contrasts with the bricks. Some materials, such as stone, allow a patio to blend seamlessly into the surrounding lawn or garden. For more on paving, see pages 228–229.

A proper foundation is essential to a well-built and long-lasting patio. Depending on the surface material you choose, an appropriate foundation may be a sand bed, compacted gravel, a concrete slab, or even stable, undisturbed soil. No matter the type of foundation, careful preparation is crucial for a long-lasting patio.

In some cases, steps and walkways are a necessary part of a plan. A walkway is basically just a long, narrow patio and may be all you need to unify other structural elements. For example, an existing deck near the house can connect with a new water garden planned in a far corner of the yard.

Steps may be crucial elements, especially on a sloping lot. If you decide to level an area for a patio, you may need steps to lead up or down to it. Sometimes the easiest way to tame a slope is to build a terraced walkway, which is a series of narrow patios connected by steps that rise up the slope one level at a time. See pages 112–113 for more on steps.

selecting the surface

The style of your patio depends a lot on the surface material. Choose a material that works with your house and landscape. Other factors to keep in mind include the following.

surface texture Smooth, shiny surfaces can be slippery when wet. Rougher surfaces are too absorbent where spills are likely, such as near a barbecue. Smooth surfaces are best for dancing, while games require materials with more traction. A soft surface is fine for foot traffic, but a hard-wearing one is a must if furniture may be dragged across it.

maintenance Most surfaces can be simply hosed down or swept, though some show dirt more than others and need more frequent attention. Large mortar joints may trap debris but have the advantage of shedding water easily. Sand joints are easy to maintain but may allow weeds to grow.

durability While bricks are extremely resistant to wear from normal use, consider the effects of climate. On stable soil where soil doesn't freeze, bricks set in sand make a permanent patio. But for similar durability in areas where soil freezes regularly, add a 4-inch-deep base of compacted gravel below the sand. Without that extra gravel base in cold climates, bricks will move in winter and need resetting in spring.

cost It's not just the price of materials that affects the cost of paving. If you want a material not common in your area, for example, you'll have to include the expense of having it shipped, a cost that can quickly become substantial. Labor costs may vary for the different installation methods. For some materials, doing all or some of the work yourself may cut labor costs.

There's more about these paving options later in this chapter on pages 100–109.

six paving options

In this corner of a hypothetical patio, you can see how paving is likely to affect a patio's look and feel. For the best effect, pave with materials that are local in origin (or that look like they might be). As you might imagine, many variations of each of these six types are available.

STONE Depending on the color and shape, stone can provide various effects, from rugged and rough-hewn to more formal.

BRICK Surfaces of brick, a classic patio paver, harmonize with many garden styles.

LOOSE MATERIALS Very casual in feel, loose materials such as gravel and wood chips are usually less expensive than other materials. They are also less permanent and harder to keep clean.

INTERLOCKING PAVERS These easy-to-install concrete units are available in contemporary patterns and colors.

CAST CONCRETE Modern finishing techniques, such as coloring and stamping, give concrete a variety of looks, from that of imitation stone to a sleek architectural finish.

ADOBE The rounded, massive blocks lend a casual feel, especially when softened with crevice plantings.

path and patio edges

BORDERS ARE BOTH FUNCTIONAL AND DECORATIVE

ALTHOUGH EDGINGS MAY NOT BE THE MOST OBVIOUS PART OF A PATH OR PATIO, THEY ARE AN important element. Edgings serve three main purposes. They literally contain the patio or path material, they serve as a transition between the paving and surrounding landscaping, and they're a decorative element in their own right.

Some surface materials, such as bricks or pavers laid in sand or loose surface materials, require an edging. But even when they're not structurally necessary, edgings add an attractive finish to a project. They can define borders and perhaps visually unify the area with other landscaping features.

Edgings can also visually link disparate elements in the landscape. For instance, using brick to edge a lawn, an exposed-aggregate patio, and a gravel path unifies the overall design. Edgings can also connect different areas of a garden. A brick-edged patio may taper off to a brick path that leads to another patio area that's also edged with brick.

wood edging The most common type of wood edging is made of dimension lumber, such as 2 by 4s or 2 by 6s. Wood that's resistant to rot, such as pressure-treated lumber or the heartwood of cedar or redwood, is your best choice for edgings that will last as long as the patio surface. To make curved edgings, use flexible benderboard.

Very tight curves can be formed with pieces of sheet metal or plastic.

Heavy timbers make strong, showy edgings and interior dividers, especially when drilled and held in place with steel pipe, as illustrated for railroad ties on this page.

In addition to rustic timbers, wood posts or logs in diameters ranging from 2 to 6 inches can form a series of miniature pilings. Set them vertically, butted tightly together, with their ends set underground in a concrete footing. Pack soil around the pilings. A horizontal 2-by-4 or 2-by-6 cap across the top prolongs the life of the edging by keeping water out of the end grain of the posts.

stone edging A rustic or woodsy landscape provides a good setting for edgings of cut flagstone, or a more informal edging of rocks and boulders. If your design includes a garden pond, a stone edging around both the patio and the edge of the pond can integrate the two areas, even if the project itself is surfaced with another material.

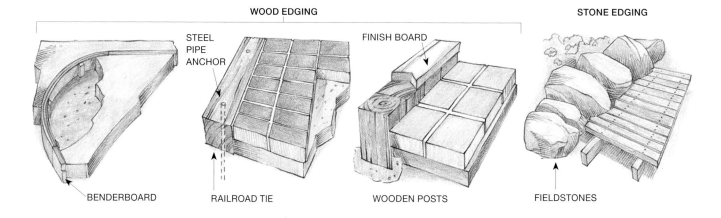

WOOD EDGING

STONE EDGING

STEEL PIPE ANCHOR

FINISH BOARD

BENDERBOARD   RAILROAD TIE   WOODEN POSTS   FIELDSTONES

Before laying flagstone or other small stones, arrange them in a pleasing pattern, cutting them if necessary. Lay the stones in a 1-inch-thick bed of mortar. Usually, large uncut rocks and boulders look best in edgings if they're at least partially buried; dig a hole to the appropriate depth for each stone. Otherwise, lay the stones directly on the soil, filling the spaces between them with smaller rocks. Pack the area with soil and add plantings for a more natural look. Irregularly shaped stones blend well with loose materials. More formal paving units will probably need to be cut to fit around the boulders.

brick edging The easiest masonry edgings to build consist of bricks in soil. Bricks are set in a narrow trench around the edges of the patio area. As much of the brick as possible should extend below the surface level of the patio. Set the bricks vertically, or angle them slightly for a toothed effect. Unfortunately, only very firm soil will hold the bricks in place without mortar, so brick-in-soil edgings are not possible everywhere.

Another option is invisible edging. It can be made with a small underground concrete footing that secures paving units without any visual support, or use a less expensive plastic edging. In both cases, paving units set into the surface conceal the edging material. The completed patio appears to have no edging at all.

When using bricks set in sand as the patio surface, you can create an invisible edging by simply setting the edge bricks in wet mortar. This makes it easier to maintain the brick pattern without going to the expense of installing an edging.

plastic edging Manufactured heavy plastic edgings are an easy-to-install option. The strips are secured to the ground with spikes and are easy to shape and cut. Brick or concrete pavers are held in place by the raised edge of the strip, which is set below the level of the finished paving. After the paving is completed, conceal the outside edge of the strips with soil or sod, creating a patio or path that has no visible edging. Flexible sections are available for tight curves, but rigid strips can be made to handle gentle curves if you kerf (partially cut) their edges. Secure plastic edgings with 10- to 12-inch spikes or follow the manufacturer's installation instructions.

concrete edging Similar to invisible edgings (see brick edging at left), these create a patio area with well-defined limits. These edgings might be a good choice if concrete is used elsewhere in the garden, such as on a path leading to the patio.

Concrete edging serves to retain the paving units, and it also functions as a mowing strip for a patio that's adjacent to a lawn. Running the lawn mower's wheels along the concrete edging allows you to cut the grass right up to the edge of the patio, reducing the need for edge trimming.

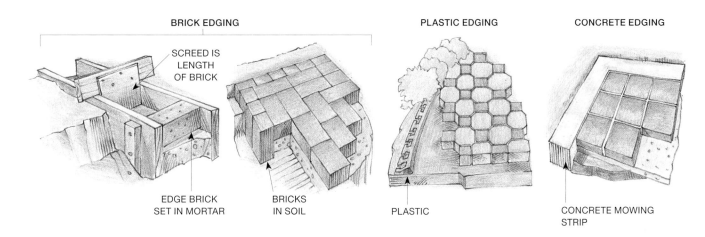

BRICK EDGING

SCREED IS LENGTH OF BRICK

EDGE BRICK SET IN MORTAR

BRICKS IN SOIL

PLASTIC EDGING

PLASTIC

CONCRETE EDGING

CONCRETE MOWING STRIP

anatomy of a deck

A SCHEMATIC FOR BUILDERS

TO HELP YOUR IDEAS TAKE SHAPE, YOU'LL NEED to understand a deck's structure. Even if you are not planning to build your deck yourself, it's good to know the name and purpose of each component so you can converse with a builder or architect. If you do intend to build your own deck, the right terms will be invaluable when you're talking to the people down at your local Lowe's store. The component names given here are common throughout much of the country, though some different terms may be used in your neck of the woods.

For details on building a basic deck, see pages 230–231.

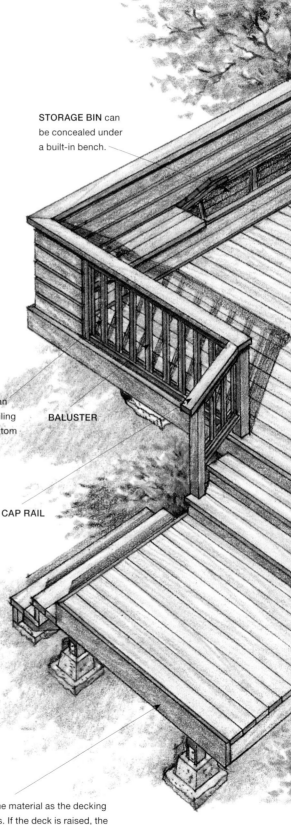

STORAGE BIN can be concealed under a built-in bench.

RAILINGS are needed if a deck is more than 18 inches above the ground. A standard railing consists of 4-by-4 railing posts, 2-by-4 bottom and top rails, 2-by-2 balusters (also called spindles or pickets), and a cap rail.

BALUSTER

CAP RAIL

FASCIA (trim) is made of the same material as the decking and covers visible framing pieces. If the deck is raised, the area under the joists may be covered with skirting.

PLANTERS on a deck require adequate drainage; the deck must support the weight of soil and plants.

DOORS to a deck lead from a dining or living room, kitchen, or bedrooms. French or sliding doors are the best choices.

ELECTRIC lighting and receptacles may be 120 volts or 12 volts and the former will likely require a permit to install.

LEDGER secures the deck to the house framing. Aluminum or vinyl flashing tucks up under the house's siding and folds over the ledger to keep water away from the house.

DECKING may be wood, pressure-treated wood, synthetic, or composite.

JOISTS are usually made of 2 by 6s, 2 by 8s, or 2 by 10s and spaced 16 or 24 inches (center to center). They sit on top of the beam. Joist hangers, hurricane ties, post anchors, and beam anchors tie the framing together.

BEAMS are supported by posts and are typically made of doubled 2-by lumber.

POSTS are made of 4 by 4s or 4 by 6s and rest on concrete footings (or piers), and they support parts of the deck not connected to the house.

PIERS are made of precast concrete and embedded in poured footings.

POURED CONCRETE FOOTINGS extend below the frostline.

RIM JOIST secures joist ends.

TREADS

RISER

decking materials

Decks are exposed to a wide range of elements, not only rain and snow but also radical temperature changes, ultraviolet rays, mildew, and wood-boring insects. Pressure-treated lumber is designed to stand up to the elements, making it the logical choice for a deck's structure. But when it comes to decking, railing, and fascia, you have an array of options, all of them with strong points in their favor.

structural lumber

Wood that has been factory-treated with preservatives will last far longer than untreated wood and is only marginally more expensive than untreated lumber, so most codes require it for all structural components. Don't skimp or assume that certain woods are equally long-lasting. Even many types of cedar and redwood will rot in only a few years.

Until recently, the most common preservative of wood was chromated copper arsenate (CCA). CCA-treated lumber that's rated for ground contact or has a treatment content (or retention level) of .40 or greater is nearly indestructible. However, because of concerns about its arsenic content, CCA has been banned for most residential use.

Newer treatments include ammoniacal copper quaternary (ACQ), copper azole (CA), and copper borate azole (CBA, or CA-B). Copper is the active ingredient in all of these treatments. Tests have confirmed that these treatments are very effective at eliminating rot.

Newer kinds of treated lumber cost more than CCA because of the higher copper content. But they area also much safer to use. To reduce costs, manufacturers produce boards with different levels of treatment. Decking typically receives the lowest chemical-retention level. Structural boards made for aboveground use—most 2-by lumber—contain more treatment, and structural members used for ground contact—4-by and 6-by material—have the highest levels.

pressure-treating and wood species

Treated Douglas fir is very strong and stable, but it is not available nationally and it is expensive. It does not readily accept treatment, so it typically has a grid of slits incised during the treating process. Southern pine is also strong, though a bit more likely to crack. It readily accepts treatment, so there are no incisions.

using the right fasteners Look for hardware that is clearly labeled as safe for your type of treated wood. Many new decking screws and nails are protected with both galvanizing and a polyester coat to make them safe to use with ACQ- or CA-treated lumber. You can also choose hardware with G-185 galvanizing, as opposed to the G-60 or G-90 galvanizing that was once common. Stainless-steel fasteners will not corrode, but they are expensive.

finishing pressure-treated wood Most treated lumber is a greenish color, which in time will fade to gray. You can buy stains designed to beautify pressure-treated lumber. Be sure to allow the wood's treatment to dry completely before you apply finishes. In arid areas, the wood may dry in a few weeks, while it may take up to half a year in humid climes.

decking and railing lumber

Pressure-treated is the least expensive choice. Treated wood goes on green and gradually turns a sort of gray if left untreated. However, properly stained treated lumber can be quite

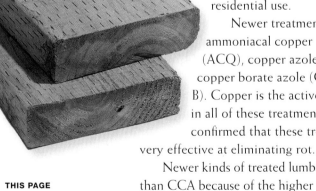

THIS PAGE CLOCKWISE FROM ABOVE Pressure-treated Douglas fir, Western red cedar, and redwood.

attractive. In fact, it may cost less to have a company refinish treated decking yearly for 15 years than it would to buy more expensive decking to begin with.

cedar This species is naturally good-looking and tends not to warp or crack too much. However, only the heartwood is reliably rot-resistant. The lighter-colored sapwood may rot within a few years if not sealed. Western red cedar is the most abundant type, but in some areas you can find northern white, Alaska yellow, and others. Most cedars are fairly soft, but that is usually not a concern unless you expect especially heavy traffic. Sealers add to the strength of the wood. Cedar is available in all sorts of dimensions, but 5/4 decking, which is 1 inch thick and 5½ inches wide, is most common for decks. It has rounded edges and is often installed butted tightly together. Once it dries, it will shrink, producing ⅛-inch gaps between the boards.

redwood This material has great beauty and stability. It can be stained to maintain rich wood tones or left unfinished to turn a silvery gray. As with cedar, only the dark heartwood is naturally resistant to rot. The biggest problem with redwood is its price, which continues to increase as sustainable supplies dwindle.

siberian larch is new to the American market, though it has been in use in Europe and Asia for decades. Siberian larch is naturally rot-resistant even though it is light in color. It is harder than pine but not as hard as ironwood, and most of the boards are straight and splinter-free.

ironwood is a collective term for various tropical hardwoods, the most common of which are ipé, cambara, pau lope, and meranti. These woods are very strong, so much so that a 1-by board can span the same distance as a 2-by softwood board. They look good and weather very well but are expensive. Also, working with them is not as straightforward as working with softer woods. For instance, before driving screws, you'll need to drill a pilot hole. Moreover,

some tropical woods are so full of natural oils that they will not accept a stain even after several months of exposure.

synthetic decking and railings In recent years many people have been drawn to decking products made in whole or in part of synthetic materials. These products range from composites of plastic and wood to "boards" made entirely of vinyl. Some products have a fairly smooth surface, while others have a deeply embossed wood-grain pattern. Still other products have variegated colors meant to further approximate the look of wood.

They are generally expensive, but the payoff is that they are virtually maintenance-free. Or at least some of them are. While it is certainly true that synthetics are easier to care for than wood, not all synthetics perform the same, and no synthetic is perfect. It's a good idea to talk with deck owners and Lowe's sales associates to learn how different products perform in your area.

THIS PAGE
CLOCKWISE FROM TOP:
Composite, synthetic, and tropical ironwoods.

composite lumber is the most common type of synthetic. Made of recycled plastic and ground-up waste wood, composites are an ecologically sound choice. At least three types of plastic are used in composite materials: standard polyethylene, which is fairly soft; polypropylene; and high-density polyethylene (HDPE). Composites engineered with the last two kinds of plastic are harder and more resistant to stains and scratches than are composites containing standard polyethylene. The wood particles in many composites are not, as you might expect, entirely shielded from moisture, which means many composites are still subject to mildew and fungus. To eliminate this problem, some products are made with a process that encapsulates the wood fibers.

IPÉ

CAMBARA

MERANTI

deck details

Don't forget the custom touches that can turn a deck into a comfortable outdoor room. Most decks require railings, and most will look better and be more comfortable if they include a table and chairs, sun and shade, and perhaps lighting. Planters make integrating nature easier, and furniture is essential.

railings The railing is probably the first thing people notice about a deck, and it is also an important safety feature. You can design your own railings using a variety of materials, and Lowe's offers various ready-made kinds.

Railings are usually required for decks that are more than 30 inches above ground level, and for flights of stairs 5 feet wide or narrower. However, rails are a good addition to any deck above ground level, especially if it will be used by small children or people who are less than steady on their feet.

You will need to make railings at least 36 inches high, but higher—up to 42 inches—feels safer. Code generally requires that the structure have no gaps big enough to accept a 4-inch sphere, ensuring that an infant can't slip through.

To detract from the view as little as possible, unobtrusive cables serve as safety railings around this elevated deck.

benches and furniture Outdoor patio furniture is the easiest way to provide seating on your deck, though built-in benches are space-efficient, can provide hidden storage, and are an opportunity to augment purchased furniture. If you're building a new deck, definitely plan on built-in benches. If you already have a deck, you can add benches. Choose materials that match the deck or other elements in your yard.

When arranging for seating on your deck, opt for portable patio furniture, built-ins, or both. Built-ins supplement portable patio furniture and free up floor space for other uses. Design benches into wide steps or transitions between levels, and make them from nonslip masonry, wood, or metal and allow for drainage. For fun, add overhead support for a porch swing or hammock.

lighting Safety, security, and decor can all be improved with good outdoor lighting. The only restriction is to keep both glare and wattage at a low level. Because the contrast between darkness and a light source is so great, glare can be a problem at night. Follow three rules: choose shielded fixtures, place fixtures out of sight lines, and lower overall light levels, because a little light goes a long way at night. You can choose standard 120-volt power or use a low-voltage system.

planters Portable containers can bring annuals and perennials, shrubs, and even vegetables to your most favorable location. Built-in planters, on the other hand, lend a custom look to your structure.

kitchens Over the past several years, the once ubiquitous barbecue has given way to the outdoor kitchen. Depending upon your interests and budget, outdoor kitchens may include not only grills and heating elements but also refrigerators, pizza ovens, sinks with running water, fireplaces, drawers and doors for storage, and sound systems.

The centerpiece of an outdoor kitchen is a counter. Many outdoor counters are made of heavy masonry, making them suitable for a patio but too heavy for a deck. However, you can build a fairly lightweight counter by framing it with wood or metal studs.

Before installing the counter, you will likely want to run electrical lines for a receptacle or two, and perhaps for lighting. Many counters have natural-gas lines for the grill, though you can also use a propane tank inside the counter. If there will be a sink, you will need to provide running water as well as a drain, which may tie into the house's drain or may simply run to a dry well (a large gravel-filled hole; see pages 206–207). When running any type of utility line, be sure to comply with local building codes. It's often a good idea to hire a professional plumber or electrician to rough in the lines.

For more about outdoor kitchens, see pages 56–57 and 278–283.

BELOW LEFT: A clematis vine uses the steel grid sheltering one end of a hot tub to climb up and over the redwood arbor.

BELOW CENTER: A low bench and deck made of composite wood jog around a focal-point tree.

BELOW RIGHT: Ready-made metal balusters are easy to install because they are simply screwed onto the top and bottom rails.

paths lead the way
DESIGN THEM FOR FUNCTION AND FOR FUN

PATHS GIVE STRUCTURE TO THE GARDEN AND DIRECTION TO ITS VISITORS. THEY ALSO INVITE YOU into a garden and through it, perhaps for a look at some roses that have just opened near the birdbath or for a sniff of the honeysuckle whose scent wafts from a sunny spot by the pond. And when tufts of moss or creeping thyme grow between pavers, paths urge you to slow down for a look underfoot.

Shaded by mature trees, this concrete-paver path and patio are an island of calm—a perfect place for weekend decompression.

Even if you do nothing, paths will eventually make themselves. Make a beeline across the lawn enough times to get to the mailbox, the compost pile, or the gate, and soon a path of flattened grass will mark the trail. A short time later the grass is gone and you have a path of packed earth. Before that

happens, map out the circulation patterns in your garden and draw a plan that allows just enough twists and turns to reveal the garden slowly, area by area. Every garden can do with a little mystery, which serpentine paths provide.

Keep the following guidelines in mind when planning and building paths.

FAR LEFT: The wide, even surface of this flagstone path eases walking through the landscape. Lighting ensures no nighttime missteps.

LEFT: Generous 2-by-2-foot pavers, flanked on the left by compact *Berberis × irwinii* and on the right by concrete spheres, make a narrow walkway appear wider than it is.

choose the right materials The most durable paths are designed for use in all weather. This means good drainage when it's wet and good traction when it's icy. Gravel and crushed rock are nearly perfect for varied conditions, as are loose-laid brick and pavers. Also consider slightly crowned paths, for drainage. Higher in the center, these can be made of textured concrete, brick, or stone.

make it wide enough Main paths should be wide enough for two people to walk on side by side; 4 to 5 feet is about right. Small subsidiary paths should be wide enough for a wheelbarrow (handles have a 24- to 30-inch spread). Two feet is a generous minimum,

as long as plants don't crowd the edges. Organize a network of paths like a river system, with smaller paths branching off larger ones.

add plants wherever possible Allow some space between pavers in which to plant thyme or other low creepers. Amend the soil well so that plants can establish roots. It should be on the sandy side so that it won't become packed down with foot traffic and kill the plants' roots. Don't tuck plants in paths used for main walkways or where snow removal will be necessary.

For details on how to build a basic path, see the instructions on pages 242–243.

PATHWAY CLEARANCE

SERVICE PATHWAY
2'–3'

MAIN PATHWAY
4'–5'

BENCH CLEARANCE

SITTING
3'

WALKING
3'

using concrete pavers

Once limited to gray or pinkish hues and plain rectangles, concrete pavers now come in an array of attractive colors and shapes. Though to some tastes they lack the charm of natural brick, concrete pavers are extremely durable and relatively inexpensive, two reasons they've become so popular in recent years.

Rectangular concrete pavers are installed much like bricks and can be arranged in the same patterns. Interlocking concrete pavers fit together like puzzle pieces. They may include only one shape or two or three shapes. Both interlocking and non-interlocking rectangular pavers make very stable patios.

Aside from the basic rectangular shape, you'll find circles, squares, triangles, hexagons, and specially shaped small pavers for complicated patterns. Small pavers with interesting shapes can be used in combination with larger ones. Simple squares can be part of a grid or even a gentle arc. Pavers can butt together to create broad, unbroken surfaces, or they can be spaced apart and surrounded with grass, ground cover, or gravel for interesting textural effects.

All concrete pavers are difficult to cut by hand, so use a masonry saw. They can be laid in mortar atop a concrete slab, or set in sand. Use

Standard rectangular pavers designed to mimic cut stone were used to form a network of paths through an herb garden. The paths converge in the center to form a planting bed, the garden's focal point.

coarse sand for the base and fine sand for stone dust to fill the joints between pavers. Lowe's sells patio paver base sand by the bag or in bulk.

Some concrete pavers are made to closely resemble natural stone; others come in pallets of several different sizes, shapes, and colors, resulting in what looks like a complicated pattern but actually takes no special planning to install. You can also buy concrete pavers that are made to look like bricks, as well as in replicated antique or used finishes. In many areas, they may be significantly less expensive than the real thing. Or try the circular or fan-shaped concrete paver ensembles, which typically use five or six different shapes. The manufacturer's instructions will show you which pavers go where.

Large pavers—up to 24 inches wide—enable you to create a patio surface quickly. You can set them in soil, sand, or dabs of mortar over a concrete slab. Because these larger pavers are so heavy, edging isn't needed to keep them in place.

There's more information about pavers and how to work with them on pages 228–229 and 242–243.

ABOVE LEFT: Pavers edged with recycled concrete make a pleasant corner for two.

ABOVE RIGHT: The rectangular paving grid near the house transitions to round pavers of varying size, partly to echo the circular lawn and partly just for fun.

LOWE'S QUICK TIP

The word "paver" refers to any masonry unit—such as a brick, tile, or flagstone—that is used to create a floor surface. A concrete paver is a specific type of paver manufactured from concrete. Lowe's stocks a wide variety of paver types.

HIDING THE EDGES

Concrete pavers range from precise geometric forms to the more casual look of tumbled stone. They also come in a range of colors. See the Web site of the Interlocking Concrete Pavement Institute (icpi.org) for more information. The Concrete Network (concretenetwork.com) includes listings of paving specialists.

using brick

Brick is a common patio-surfacing material. Set in sand or mortar, it provides a handsome surface that blends with nearly any architectural style and looks at ease in almost any setting.

Brick does have disadvantages, though. Cost per square foot runs higher than for most alternative materials. If you lay bricks in sand, you may have to rework the patio from time to time if frost heave (irregular buckling or swelling) raises some of the bricks. You may occasionally need to spend time pulling weeds that have pushed through the joints, though you can reduce this problem by laying landscaping fabric beneath the bricks. Also, bricks in moist, heavily shaded garden areas can become slick with moss. That said,

brick remains a popular paver, mostly for the charming way it ages.

People like the familiar color, texture, and density of common building brick. Bricks are familiar and reasonably uniform in size and color, though length may vary by as much as $1/4$ inch. The rough faces of common brick create a nonglare surface with good traction. And because the surface is porous and absorbs water, brick pavers cool the air as the water evaporates from them. Unfortunately, brick will just as readily absorb any spilled beverages, oil, grease, and paint—all of which are difficult to remove. In addition, wherever freezes are common, the moisture that the bricks absorb expands upon freezing and cracks the bricks.

Aged bricks randomly set in sand were used here to create a path with a wild and wacky spirit. Colorful plants line the path, such as yellow *Osteospermum*, violet petunias, and blue *Centaurea montana*.

brick types

Brick is produced with ground clay mixed with water. The clay is formed into the desired shape, then dried and fired—traditionally all accomplished by hand. Today brick is formed mechanically, usually by extrusion. After being formed, bricks are dried and fired in kilns. During firing, some clay bricks develop irregularities. Called clinkers, these bricks have an uneven surface and flashed patches from overburning. Use them for paving or as accents to give a rough cobblestone effect.

paver or clay bricks, also called building bricks, are kiln fired at a higher temperature for a longer time, making them very hard and strong. They make a metallic sound when struck by a hammer, as opposed to a dull, wooden sound. Only this type of brick is suitable for use as landscape pavers.

face bricks are more consistent in size and color, are more expensive, and are not as strong as paver bricks. Use them for their appearance, not structural qualities, on walls and similar exposed surfaces.

used bricks, which may be common or face, have uneven surfaces and streaks of old mortar that can make an attractive, informal pavement. Taken from old buildings and walls, these bricks are usually in short supply.

manufactured replica bricks are new bricks that are made to look like used bricks by chipping them and splashing them with mortar and paint. They cost about the same as the genuine article but are easier to find. They're also more consistent in quality than used bricks. Precut bricks in special shapes are a boon if you're venturing into more complicated patterns. Tacks, quoins, bats, sinkers, traps, and spikes are just some of the traditional names for these. Expect to pay about the same price per precut brick as for a full-size brick, but keep in mind that if you had to cut bricks to these shapes, you'd need the tools and expertise of a mason.

brick grades

All outdoor bricks are graded by their ability to withstand weathering. If you live where the ground freezes and thaws, or if the pavers are in direct contact with the ground, use only pavers graded SW. Other grades recognized by the Brick Industry of America are MW, for use where resistance to freezing or ground contact is not an issue, and NW, for interior applications.

A garden corridor of salvaged brick curves past oakleaf hydrangea, hostas, and lady's mantle, then under an arbor.

LOWE'S QUICK TIPS

- One hundred square feet of path or patio laid in running bond requires about 500 bricks.
- Running bond and jack-on-jack are the simplest patterns to lay. Experiment with patterns to check their look and installation.

cast concrete paths

A meandering 30-inch-wide path forms the major element of this side yard. The gentle curves of the path make the space seem wider than it is.

Sometimes the simplest paving options are the most effective. Cast concrete is inexpensive and can be customized to a wide variety of garden styles.

As a paving material, cast concrete is very adaptable. This mixture of sand, cement, gravel, and water is even more variable in appearance than brick. Cast in forms, it can take on almost any shape. It can be lightly smoothed or heavily brushed, surfaced with handsome pebbles, swirled, scored, tinted, painted, patterned, or cast into molds to resemble other paving materials. If you get tired of the concrete surface later on, it

provides an excellent foundation for brick, stone, or tile set in mortar.

Concrete does have some disadvantages. In some situations, it makes a harsh, hot, and glaring surface, and if it is troweled smooth, concrete is slick when wet. If you're thinking of pouring concrete yourself, remember that creating a top-quality, good-looking cast concrete patio that will wear well and not crack is more difficult than it may appear. The concrete must be mixed carefully to exact specifications, and there's little room for error. After the ingredients are combined and water is added, work must proceed quickly and

accurately. Mistakes will require costly removal and replacement. If the concrete isn't cured correctly or if drainage needs are ignored, the surface may buckle and crack.

Concrete paths are typically given some type of surface treatment, both for appearance and for traction. Washing or sandblasting concrete paving exposes the aggregate, or you can embed colorful pebbles and stones in it. Other ways to modify the standard smooth surface include color dusting, staining, masking, acid washing, and salt finishing. Concrete can also be stamped and tinted to resemble stone, tile, or brick (see page 223).

ABOVE LEFT: Black La Paz river stones were hand-set into concrete in an irregular pattern to achieve a water-like sense of motion.

ABOVE RIGHT: Slabs of poured concrete are set like pavers, with joints wide enough to support creeping plants.

FANCY FINISHES

Finish the surface of a concrete patio to give it a personalized look that is tailored to its function. Here are some options.

- A semismooth texture is achieved with a wooden float.
- A smooth, troweled surface is appropriate for covered areas that won't get wet and slippery.
- A broomed surface provides maximum traction.

Popular decorative finishes include rock salt, travertine, and seeded aggregate. Coloring concrete, either alone or in combination with other decorative finishes, adds a distinctive note. For more information, see the Concrete Network's Web site (concretenetwork.com).

LOWE'S QUICK TIP

In most areas, you need a permit to pour more than a very small concrete slab, so check with your building department. There are likely very specific requirements, and to pass inspection, you'll need to follow them to the letter. Doing so will produce a better result as well.

gravel and bark paths

For economy, good drainage, and a more casual look, gravel, bark, and wood chips are good alternatives.

You needn't opt for the large, uninteresting expanses that can give these materials a bad name. Gravel can be raked into patterns or used as a decorative element with other materials. You can set off different types of gravel with dividers. Or combine gravel or wood chips with concrete pads, concrete pavers, or other stepping-stones. Because gravel and other loose materials complement plants, they can also be used to good effect in transition zones between patios and gardens.

The main problem with loose paving materials is that they are loose—they move around, into planting beds and even indoors. Lightweight organic materials may wash away or relocate during downpours, and any organic material will need periodic replenishing.

wood chips and bark Wood chips and shredded bark, by-products of lumber mills, are springy and soft underfoot, generally inexpensive, and easy to apply. They're ideal for informal paths that get light use, and they can create an earthy, casual look. These come in a wide variety of colors and textures. To

A crunchy gravel surface is a clean, casual foil to the plant textures and colors that crowd this entry path, such as billowing Japanese silver grass (right), heuchera, and cotoneaster (both foreground).

work successfully on a path, wood chips and bark should be contained by a border. Wood chips also make a good cushion under swings and slides in children's play areas.

Choose a material that fits its situation—for example, a bark-mulch path in a woodland landscape or pine needles through a planting of evergreens.

gravel is collected or mined from natural deposits. With its rounded edges, it resists packing, making wheelbarrow navigation, and even walking, more awkward. Therefore, it's best used for its aesthetic value—

for instance, in dry streambeds or as a mulch around prized plants.

When making a choice, consider color, sheen, texture, and size. Take home samples, as you would paint chips. Keep in mind that gravel color, like paint color, looks more intense when spread over a large area.

crushed rock, such as decomposed granite, is mechanically fractured and graded to a uniform size. The irregular shapes of crushed rock allow it to pack down well and make a firm surface that can easily support a wheelbarrow.

TOP LEFT: Plants spill over a gravel path, obscuring the bed and path border.

TOP RIGHT: Square concrete pavers pair with gravel at key transition points.

ABOVE LEFT: Adobe-colored gravel echoes nearby structures.

ABOVE RIGHT: Shredded bark is an appropriate paving material in a woodland garden.

stone paths

Stone is a durable, natural material that comes in many forms and blends well in almost any paving project. Flat flagstones and cut stone tiles are ideal for formal paving, while irregularly shaped rocks or cobblestones create a more informal, relaxed setting.

Generally, preparing stone for use as paving is a labor-intensive process. It takes a lot of time and effort to quarry, trim, haul, and store it, so the price to cover a given area may be higher for stone than for other materials. However, stone's beauty, elegance, and—above all—permanence make it well worth the extra expense.

The selection of rock available depends on your area, one reason why imitation stones have become so popular. They come in many types and offer an inexpensive and attractive option where stone is hard to come by.

granite is an example of volcano-formed rock. Such rocks are usually the toughest, longest-wearing options. Granite cobblestones are roughly cut into squares or rectangles, generally from 6 to 12 inches on a side. They are stunning, but since they are expensive, they are often used just in borders, as accents, or for small walks.

flagstone is any flat stone that is either naturally thin or is cut from a rock that splits easily. Flagstone works in almost any setting. Its natural, unfinished look blends well with plants, and it's one of the few paving materials

Medium-size flagstones congregate in tight groups to form a patio, scatter to serve as stepping-stones, then recongregate to form another patio.

that can, if thick enough, be placed directly on stable soil. Its subdued colors—buff, yellow, brownish red, and gray—add warmth to a patio, and the irregularly shaped slabs contribute a pleasing texture.

Flagstones generally range in thickness from $1\frac{1}{2}$ to 2 inches. Test-fit them first so there are no uneven spots and the final pattern is pleasing. Without proper planning, including a test of their fit before you lay them, the finished look may be an unattractive patchwork.

Flagstone does have some less favorable attributes. It is much more expensive than brick or concrete are, and because of its irregularity, it's not a good surface for outdoor furniture, games, or wheeled toys. Snow removal can be challenging. Also, some types of flagstone are easily soiled and are difficult to clean. Ask your Lowe's sales associate about the characteristics of the flagstone you're considering.

stone tiles Many types are available, including ones machine-cut to specific shapes. You can also find hand-cut squares and rectangles in random sizes. Slate, which is available in many colors, and granite are both popular choices, though they are expensive.

limestone, sandstone, and others
Sedimentary stones such as limestone are more porous and usually have a chalky or gritty texture.

Fieldstone and river rock offer good alternatives to high-priced flagstone. These waterworn or glacier-ground stones produce rustic, uneven paving that makes up in charm for what it may lack in smoothness underfoot.

River rocks are available in a wide range of shapes and sizes. They are smooth, rounded, impervious to weather, and are virtually maintenance-free. Smaller stones can be set or seated in wet concrete, while large stones can be laid directly on the soil as raised stepping-stones. An entire surface can be paved solid with river rock set in concrete or tamped soil.

Keep in mind, however, that natural stones, such as river rock and smaller kinds, are smooth and can be slippery, especially in wet weather. Also, because of their irregular shapes, they may be difficult or unsafe to walk on.

Laying stones is a slow process, particularly when you're working with small pebbles and stones in mortar or concrete. For that reason most people confine this kind of surface to a limited area.

ABOVE LEFT: Stone slabs artfully placed to evoke a dry creek bed form a pathway from driveway to house. Pebbles fill in around the heavy slabs to reinforce the dry-creek look.

ABOVE RIGHT: Thick flagstones are like a chain of islands across a sea of flowers.

paths of wood

Few materials can match the natural, informal quality of wood. Its warm color and soft texture bring something of the forest into your landscape, and if stained or painted, wood can hold its own in even the most formal company.

A wooden pathway provides a solid, relatively durable surface requiring little or no grading and minimal maintenance. Because wood decking is raised above the ground and can dry quickly, it might be a good choice

wherever frequent rainfall or soil drainage is a problem. For even less maintenance and a lower environmental impact, consider decking that's made from recycled materials (see page 95). You'll still need wood or another material for structural members, but composite or synthetic decking is an option for pathways as well as for decks.

Whether new or old, natural or man-made, a wooden path feels right at home in almost any setting. Wood can link a house and garden

Spanning marshy ground amid a host of thriving plants, a boardwalk opens a corridor to a section of the garden otherwise difficult to access.

at flower-head height, smoothing out bumps and riding over drainage problems that would complicate if not preclude masonry paving.

Keep in mind that codes require any walkway more than 30 inches above the ground to have a railing or similar barrier. Beyond safety, railings also contribute an important design element. Use them to frame a beautiful view. Fill gaps with vertical slats, safety glass, or screening.

TOP LEFT: Cocker spaniels pause on an 18-inch-wide boardwalk of sunken landscape timbers that threads around stately trees.

TOP CENTER: In nature-center style, this boardwalk meanders over uneven ground in which ferns are thriving. Exposed posts remind walkers where the walk's edges are.

TOP RIGHT: The grain and warm colors of plantation-grown teak make otherwise ordinary steps a work of art.

ABOVE: This seaside boardwalk zigzags toward a driftwood-covered arbor.

landscape steps
EASING ELEVATION CHANGES

STEPS, WHICH SERVE AS A TRANSITION BETWEEN DIFFERENT LEVELS OR FROM ONE GARDEN FEATURE to another, can set the mood for an entire landscaping scheme. Most dramatic are wide, deep steps that lead the eye to a garden focal point. A set of stairs can also double as a retaining wall, a base for planters, or an additional garden seating space.

Materials influence step styles. Poured concrete and masonry block usually present a formal, substantial look. Unglazed tiles and concrete pavers have a similar effect. A natural, versatile material like wood adds a rustic informality to a garden.

Matching steps to the material used for a patio or wall helps unite a landscape. On the other hand, contrasting materials draw attention to the steps and the areas of the garden they serve. Combining materials can create a transition between unlike surfaces.

For example, steps of concrete treads (horizontals) and brick risers (verticals) can link a brick patio to a concrete walk.

To soften the edges of a series of steps and help walkers find them without difficulty, place containers or flower beds along their borders. You can even add planting pockets within a wide series of tiers, as long as the greenery won't impede smooth travel.

Regardless of the material you use, put safety first. Treads should give safe footing in wet weather, and steps should be adequately

The stairs linking the two levels of this Mediterranean garden feature risers of landscape timber and treads of decomposed granite.

lit at night with path lights or fixtures built into risers or adjacent step walls.

Your landscape layout and the steps' function will influence decisions about width. For instance, your home's entry requires steps that are inviting and that allow several people to climb them at one time. To allow two people to walk side by side, make steps at least 5 feet wide.

Conversely, service-yard steps can be scaled down to fit a more limited space. Simple utility steps can be as narrow as 2 feet, though a width of 4 feet is usually recommended.

To design your steps, work out a detailed plan on graph paper. For comfort and safety, make the sum of the tread depth and twice the riser height equal 25 to 27 inches. Common dimensions are a 6-inch riser and a 15-inch tread. You can vary these dimensions

somewhat, but don't make risers lower than 5 inches or higher than 8 inches, and don't make treads narrower than 11 inches.

Besides getting the tread-riser relationship right, for safety you also need to make the risers and treads in any one flight of steps the same. Try different combinations and configurations of risers and treads to achieve the necessary change of level. If your slope is too steep even for 8-inch risers, don't attack the slope head-on. Sometimes the most appealing solution is an L- or U-shaped series of multiple flights. In that case, place a wide landing between flights, using the transition for a reading nook, a rose bed, or a wall fountain.

If steps won't fit exactly into your slope, if you have questions about your site, or if your steps will be connected to a building or touch a public-access area, such as a sidewalk, check with your building department.

TOP LEFT: Steps of poured concrete navigate a steep slope. The stone wall and gray-foliaged plants blend the concrete into the landscape.

ABOVE LEFT: Broken concrete was recycled into a wall and steps. Gaps between chunks provide spaces for thyme to grow.

ABOVE RIGHT: These dry-stacked steps are made of 3-inch-thick slabs of tumbled flagstone doubled up to create 6-inch risers.

arbors and gazebos

PERMANENT OVERHEADS SUPPLEMENT LEAFY SHELTER

THERE'S NOTHING QUITE LIKE AN ARBOR OR GAZEBO TO ENHANCE YOUR ENJOYMENT OF THE GARDEN. Both structures provide shade during the day and shelter during cool evenings, yet they are always open to breezes and the enticing scent of flowers. Both give you a place to sit and relax, host a party, or simply mingle with family members and friends. And these garden structures play other, more practical roles as well. They link your house to the garden, define different areas of your landscape, direct foot traffic through the garden, mask an unattractive feature, or frame a spectacular view.

Weathered split rails perch atop solid pillars, defining and enclosing a private outdoor space.

Gazebos come in a variety of sizes and styles, from old-fashioned Victorian designs to ones with contemporary or rustic motifs.

You'll find a variety of arbors and gazebos, both ready-made and in kits, at your local Lowe's store.

Although typically built with open, airy framing, a gazebo has a solid roof that lends a feeling of enclosure to people sitting inside. By contrast, arbors frame the walls and ceiling of an outdoor room and can be embellished with fragrant or colorful vines. You can build an arbor in almost any style, using simple archways or elaborate neoclassical pavilions.

As you think about where to put a new gazebo or arbor, take a walk around your property under different weather conditions. Glance back at the house often. Look for a vantage point that marries a good view of the house with a view over the entire property. Also consider exposure. If your main deck or patio is in full sun, you may prefer to locate an arbor or gazebo in a shady corner. Finally, don't give up on a garden structure just because your yard is small. Tiny spaces often benefit from the focus created by a small arbor or gazebo.

TOP LEFT: This gazebo was assembled from a kit.

TOP RIGHT: Golden hop vine adorns a red arbor.

ABOVE LEFT: A barrel-vaulted arbor is covered with welded wire mesh.

ABOVE RIGHT: Protection from desert sun defines outdoor seating areas.

arbor basics

The first step in designing an arbor is taking a good, long look at your house. Repeating interesting architectural details you find there—a railing pattern, the pitch of a gable, or even a paint color—visually ties the house and arbor together and unifies the garden.

Arbors vary in height, but 8 to 10 feet is about right for most. This provides plenty of headroom but also makes it easy to prune any vines growing on the arbor. When deciding upon your arbor's length and width, remember that a roof overhead always makes the floor space below seem smaller than it is.

The key to arbor construction is to think of a crisscross of materials, with each new layer placed perpendicular to the one below

Simple arches give height to a colorful planting bed and frame a view of the pool beyond. The fastest climbers are annual vines, such as the morning glory shown here.

it. Whether freestanding or attached to a building, the structure is supported by posts or columns, which in turn support horizontal beams and rafters. (With an arbor attached to a house, a ledger takes the place of an end beam, and the rafters are laid directly on the ledger.) Although building an arbor starts from the bottom up, you'll need to design it from the top down. Decide first on the spacing and size of rafters, because these will dictate those of the support members. Wooden rafters can be as plain or fancy as you like, ending in curves, notches, or elaborate scrollwork. You can leave them uncovered or cover them with shade cloth, plants, lath, or lattice. Make sure your arbor can support the weight of any vines you plant for it. For added strength, add cross braces where the posts meet the beams.

Arbors are typically built from standard dimension lumber, though Lowe's offers ready-to-assemble arbors of long-lasting vinyl as well as wood.

ABOVE LEFT: An arbor over a side-yard path connects the house to the yard.

ABOVE CENTER: A substantial arbor frames the view of Adirondack chairs and highlights the path leading to them.

ABOVE RIGHT: A trumpet vine covers an arbor separating two small garden rooms.

a classic arbor

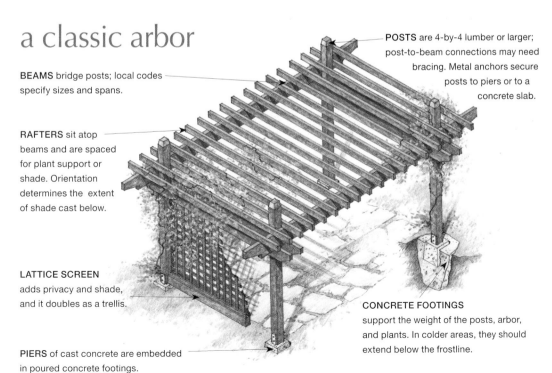

POSTS are 4-by-4 lumber or larger; post-to-beam connections may need bracing. Metal anchors secure posts to piers or to a concrete slab.

BEAMS bridge posts; local codes specify sizes and spans.

RAFTERS sit atop beams and are spaced for plant support or shade. Orientation determines the extent of shade cast below.

LATTICE SCREEN adds privacy and shade, and it doubles as a trellis.

CONCRETE FOOTINGS support the weight of the posts, arbor, and plants. In colder areas, they should extend below the frostline.

PIERS of cast concrete are embedded in poured concrete footings.

gazebo basics

Gazebos are also referred to as belvederes or summerhouses. While they can have many forms, most adhere to the same basic design. All require a foundation plus posts, beams, rafters, and some type of roofing. Make your gazebo at least 8 feet tall with enough floor space to accommodate several pieces of furniture—at least 8 feet wide and deep.

Nestled among pond lilies, this elegant gazebo boasts large screened bays and a cupola.

With few exceptions, support for a gazebo comes from a simple post-and-beam frame built of sturdy pressure-treated lumber. The roof may take a variety of forms. By far the trickiest shape to lay out is the most traditional one—a six- or eight-hub style. A roof with four sides is much simpler. Remember also that if the roof is

made of solid materials, as most are, it must be pitched to allow water to run off. If the structure is far from the house, it's a good idea to run electrical lines for lighting. Framing connections are most easily made with readily available prefabricated metal fasteners.

If building a gazebo from scratch is not a practical option, instead consider a ready-made one from Lowe's. Or build a gazebo from a kit. Kits include everything but the foundation (most gazebos sit on a concrete slab, a deck, concrete piers, or a bed of crushed stone). For most gazebos, assembly will take just a weekend or two and require only basic tools and skills, but it's a job for at least two people.

ABOVE LEFT: This ready-made gazebo comes with insect screening and installs in one day.

ABOVE RIGHT: A formal six-sided gazebo is nestled into a lush hillside. Its floor is made of brick pavers.

an elegant gazebo

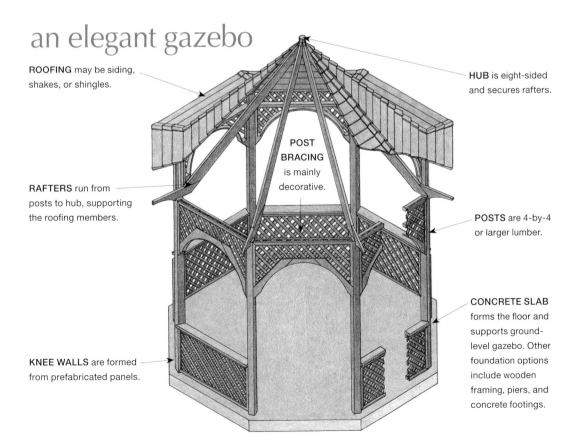

ROOFING may be siding, shakes, or shingles.

HUB is eight-sided and secures rafters.

POST BRACING is mainly decorative.

RAFTERS run from posts to hub, supporting the roofing members.

POSTS are 4-by-4 or larger lumber.

CONCRETE SLAB forms the floor and supports ground-level gazebo. Other foundation options include wooden framing, piers, and concrete footings.

KNEE WALLS are formed from prefabricated panels.

outdoor rooms

THERE'S MUCH TO BE SAID FOR TAKING A VACATION IN YOUR own backyard, beginning with no luggage, no traffic, and no airports. For the cost of one family vacation, you can convert your backyard into a destination that can be used much more often and cheaply. Your garden can be a private haven for relaxing, enjoying the view, gathering for a celebration, and generally recharging your batteries. If you plan to stay in your house for several years, the payback is significant. Yet it's an opportunity easily overlooked.

To create a spot of solitude, you may prefer man-made structures such as walls or fencing, or the natural screening of shrubs and trees. Beyond creating privacy, garden structures are highly efficient ways to define outdoor space, provide safe boundaries for children and pets, and dampen sound.

This chapter will help you make your own yard a place of comfort and solitude.

fences, walls, and screens

THEY OFFER PRIVACY AND SHAPE SPACE

FENCES AND WALLS ARE A PART OF MANY LANDSCAPE PLANS, ESPECIALLY IN NEIGHBORHOODS DEVOID of natural separations, such as in hills and woods, and in housing developments where one yard blends into the next. But wherever you live, you can create private spaces with a little careful planning.

Planting dense hedges or erecting tall fences around the entire perimeter of your yard will tend to make the space seem smaller as well as cast a deep shade. Instead, think about where you actually need privacy the most; in addition consider the seasonal use of each area. In many regions a patio needs screening only in summer because it's not used in the cooler seasons. Or maybe a vegetable garden needs no screening in summer because you've created a private seating area behind tall rows of corn or sunflowers.

A single row of bright pink crape myrtles creates a colorful partition between two driveways. Even in winter, when their branches are bare, screening trees and shrubs can provide shelter and privacy.

For each part of the garden, focus on what you're seeking to avoid. Are you trying to carve out a place away from the sights and sounds of traffic, your neighbors' backyard, or an unpleasant view much farther away? Do you need protection from sun and wind?

Solutions can be both natural and manufactured: tree canopies, awnings, umbrellas, potted plants, walls, fences, hedges, gates, pergolas, trellises, and vines. Deciduous plants are light screens in winter, fences can let the light through, and low walls allow views over them.

CREATE A SCREEN of clipped hedge to block wind and views of neighbors. Prune trunks to add height and still allow room for beds below.

USE A VINE-COVERED ARBOR for overhead protection and enclosure.

CREATE A BERM in front of your house to absorb noise and then cover it with low-growing shrubs, trees, and ground cover.

PLACE A SINGLE TREE at the front corner of your driveway to block a view of the entrance.

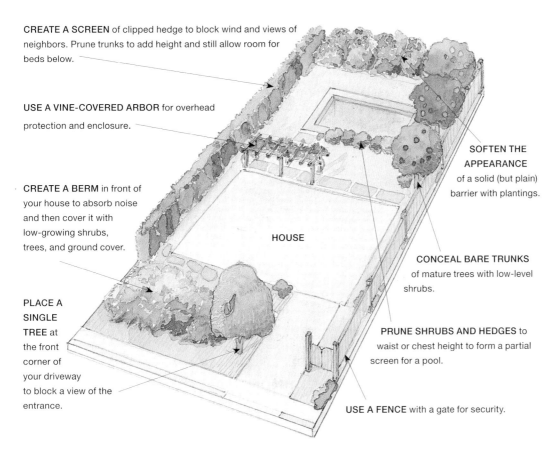

HOUSE

SOFTEN THE APPEARANCE of a solid (but plain) barrier with plantings.

CONCEAL BARE TRUNKS of mature trees with low-level shrubs.

PRUNE SHRUBS AND HEDGES to waist or chest height to form a partial screen for a pool.

USE A FENCE with a gate for security.

ABOVE LEFT: Maiden grass partially screens and softens the edges of a meandering path.

ABOVE RIGHT: Tall flowering perennials against a white picket fence separate this secluded yard from neighbors.

fence basics

STRUCTURES COME IN MANY STYLES AND SIZES

WHEN WELL DESIGNED, FENCES FILTER THE SUN'S GLARE, TURN A RAGING WIND INTO A PLEASANT breeze, and help muffle the cacophony of street traffic, noisy neighbors, and barking dogs. As partitions, they divide the yard into separate areas for recreation, relaxation, gardening, and storage. Although fences serve many of the same purposes as walls, they are generally less formal in appearance, easier to construct, and, when you calculate labor costs, less expensive to build.

Siding a fence on alternating faces provides visual screening and slows winds. Narrow, high-branched trees extend the height of the fence.

Most communities have regulations restricting fence height. In many places, the maximum is 42 inches for front-yard fences and 6 feet for backyard ones. In addition to city building codes, some communities have height and design covenants that may affect your project. Before you begin construction, check with the public works department of your city and community and, if necessary, obtain a building permit.

Beyond having to comply with codes and covenants, tall fences are also more difficult to build. An alternative way to gain some additional height beyond 6 feet is to clothe the top of the fence with a vine or to plant narrow shrubs adjacent to it and then

allow them to grow beyond the height of the fence.

Normally a boundary fence is owned and maintained by both neighbors. Make every effort to come to a friendly agreement with your neighbor on the location, design, and construction of the fence. One option is a "good neighbor" fence, with crosspieces mounted in alternating directions so that the fence looks the same from both sides.

Before installing your fence, check the terrain. Few lots are perfectly smooth, flat, and free of obstructions. If your fence line runs up a hill, build the fence so that it follows the contours of the land, or construct stepped panels that will maintain horizontal lines.

Most fences are built entirely of wood. Wood's versatility as a fencing material is reflected in its wide variety of forms—split rails, grape stakes, dimension lumber, poles, and manufactured wood products such as plywood and tempered hardboard.

Wooden fences have three parts: vertical posts, horizontal rails (or stringers), and

BELOW LEFT: A welded wire security fence provides little visual screen.

BELOW RIGHT: The picket fence is a visual barrier between front yard and driveway.

BOTTOM LEFT: Rounded, stuccoed pilasters contrast with rough logs.

BOTTOM RIGHT: An aged split-rail fence fits the woodland setting.

siding. Posts are usually 4 by 4s and should be made of pressure-treated or decay-resistant redwood or cedar heartwood. Redwood can be left to weather naturally, but fir or pine should be painted or stained. Rails are usually 2 by 4s. Fence siding can vary from preassembled picket sections to plywood panels.

Alternative materials beyond boards, slats, and timbers include vinyl, galvanized wire, plastic mesh, and ornamental iron. If wire fencing is the right choice but you don't like the look, plant annual vines, such as morning glories or climbing nasturtiums, for quick cover, or add permanent plantings for lasting cover.

Although the design possibilities are endless, wooden fences fall into one of three basic types: post-and-rail, picket, and solid-

board. Your choice depends on the fence's intended function (see facing page).

When you want to break up a large expanse in a solid-panel fence, a window or cutout lends a sense of mystery and discovery, especially when it frames a view.

For some degree of privacy that doesn't compromise ventilation, vertical lath (narrow strips of wood) is a good choice, as long as the space doesn't require complete visual protection. Likewise, vines trained onto lath trellises can block most of the unwanted wind and sun without destroying the airy, open feeling of your patio. Fences can also be designed to edit views. Louvers, slats, lattice, and see-through trellises that provide partial views of what lies within or beyond the garden are useful solutions.

The low fence encloses a vegetable garden on one side and backs a flower-filled perennial garden on the other.

fence styles

Some fences are wall-like and some are open, demarcating space without blocking a view. All kinds provide a background for plantings or support for climbing plants. Whatever your choice of fencing, coordinate it with the style and materials of your house.

SOLID-BOARD fence offers maximum privacy but requires more lumber and can create a boxed-in feeling.

POST-AND-BOARD fence encloses space with less wood and less privacy. The diagonal pattern adds visual interest.

PICKET FENCE is used with any style of house architecture, though traditionally it's associated with Colonial.

ALTERNATING-BOARD FENCE provides privacy without compromising ventilation, and it shows the same pattern on both sides.

POST-AND-RAIL fence encloses space with little wood. This one features mortised posts with overlapping rails (inset).

GRAPESTAKE fence is made of the rough-split redwood stakes traditionally used in vineyards. It's suitable for hillside and curved fencing.

gate basics

CREATING AN ENTRANCE TO YOUR YARD

PLACE A GATE FOR ACCESS, TO FRAME A VIEW, OR TO MAKE A DESIGN STATEMENT IN TANDEM WITH a fence. You may want to build the gate in a style and material that match the fence, but you can also choose a contrasting material or design, such as a wooden or wrought-iron gate within flanking brick columns or pilasters. A low picket gate or one made of airy lath invites people in with its open, friendly appearance. A high, solid gate guards the privacy and safety of the people within.

Bamboo poles affixed to sturdy wood frames convey solidity and suit the garden's Asian style.

The minimum width for a gate is usually 3 feet, but an extra foot creates a more gracious feeling. If you anticipate moving gardening or other equipment through the gate, make the opening wider to accommodate carts, wheelbarrows, tillers, or riding lawn mowers. For an extra-wide space, consider a two-part gate or even one on rollers that's designed to span a driveway.

The components of a gate are shown on the facing page: a rectangular frame of 2 by 4s and a brace running from the bottom corner of the hinge side to the top corner of the latch side. Complete it with the siding.

Use strong hinges and latches. Too hefty is better than too flimsy. Attach hinges and latches with long screws that won't pull out, and be sure to use rust-resistant hardware.

a basic gate

PICKETS may have decorative tops, and posts may be capped with decorative finials.

RAILS are 2-by-4 lumber.

SWING clearance between a gate and fence posts is usually ½ inch.

THE FOOTING (which the post sits in) is poured concrete, typically one-third the post depth.

A DIAGONAL BRACE prevents the gate from sagging.

HINGES must be strong enough to support the gate.

A GATE'S FRAME is generally built from 2 by 4s.

A GRAVEL BASE aids drainage; rock helps keep the posts from rotting.

TOP LEFT: The white picket gate is a pleasing contrast to the wall of heavy stones.

TOP RIGHT: Stacked decorative panels make an interesting gate detail.

ABOVE LEFT: A moon gate is an Asian style that blends well with cottage gardens.

ABOVE CENTER: A brightly painted gate marks the beginning of the garden and welcomes visitors.

ABOVE RIGHT: A wrought-iron gate maintains a sense of separation without seeming barrier-like.

wall basics

THEY ARE SUBSTANTIAL AND PERMANENT

WALLS BRING AN UNMATCHED SENSE OF PERMANENCE TO A GARDEN. IN FACT, SOME OF THE WORLD'S oldest structures are walls. After you've determined a wall's function and location, you can choose its height, width, and degree of openness. You'll also need to select materials that coordinate with the style and design of your house and existing garden structures.

Among the typical materials for garden walls are concrete blocks, uncut stone, and poured concrete. The easiest materials to use yourself are brick and concrete block, which are uniform units with modular proportions that you assemble piece by piece. You can choose a decorative pattern for laying the courses, incorporate a solid or openwork face, vary the thickness, and employ combinations of materials. Walls of concrete block can be covered with stucco or faced with stone.

In the hands of an experienced mason, stone creates walls that integrate with many landscapes. Native stone that's prominent in your region will look the most natural, but poured concrete offers more design possibilities because surface texture and shape are established by wooden forms. Most of the work goes into constructing and stabilizing these forms. The actual pour is accomplished quickly.

Consult a contractor for any poured concrete wall more than a few feet high.

This small garden is surrounded by a wall that's topped with a lattice screen for additional height.

Before beginning any wall, ask your building department about regulations that specify how high and how close to your property line you can build, what kind of foundation you'll need, and whether the wall requires steel reinforcement. Many municipalities require a building permit for any masonry wall more than 3 feet high. Some may also require that the wall be approved by an engineer.

retaining walls

You can tame a small, gentle slope with a low retaining wall or a series of garden steps that hold the surface soil in place. But if your slope is long and steep, consider building two or three substantial, professionally engineered walls to divide it into terraces, which you can then enhance with ornamental plants.

You can build a retaining wall from a variety of materials (see pages 224–225 and your local Lowe's). Wood is an option, whether boards of various sizes, railroad ties, or wood timbers set vertically or horizontally.

On a low slope, uncut stones or chunks of broken concrete can be laid without mortar

BELOW LEFT: The texture of this mortared stone wall blends well with the spreading flowers growing above it.

BELOW RIGHT: Succulents and grasses thrive in the crevices of a wall of concrete rubble.

BOTTOM: A colorful wall mirrors the curve of a meandering path.

BELOW LEFT: Open brick-work between columns makes the wall seem less imposing.

BELOW CENTER: Fieldstones were applied with mortar over a concrete block wall.

BELOW RIGHT: A low concrete seat wall borders a bed of flowers and a ground cover of thyme.

BOTTOM LEFT: Use a low wall to divide space and then let plants blur that division.

BOTTOM RIGHT: Soaking up heat from a south-facing wall is bougainvillea.

or footings. Fill the soil-lined crevices with colorful plantings.

There are new systems for building "concrete" retaining walls that do not require pouring actual concrete. These walls are built with precast concrete modules that stack or lock together with lips, pins, or friction. Ideal for low walls that are no higher than 2 to 3 feet, these are available in a variety of styles and colors at Lowe's.

Where a robust, engineered wall is especially critical, poured concrete is likely the best option. The labor required to excavate and form the wall can be costly. But if you take that step, make the concrete more interesting by forming it with rough boards to texture the

finish, or consider a surface veneer or other finish (see pages 224–227).

wall foundations

Regardless of the type of wall you plan to raise, it requires the support of a solid foundation. Poured concrete is about the best because it can be smoothed and leveled better than other materials can. As a general rule, wall foundations, also called footings, are twice the width of the wall and 12 inches deep, or as deep as the frostline. But, as always, consult local codes for exceptions before building.

For walls no more than 12 inches high or for low raised beds, the base of the wall can

rest directly on tamped, stable soil, or in a leveled trench.

In most cases, a freestanding wall more than 2 to 3 feet high should have some kind of reinforcement to tie portions of the wall together and to prevent it from collapsing. Steel reinforcement bars, laid with the mortar along the length of a wall, provide horizontal stiffening. Placed upright, such as between double rows of brick or within the hollow cores of concrete blocks, reinforcement adds vertical strength to a wall and so can keep it from toppling under its own weight.

Vertical masonry columns, called pilasters, can be tied into a wall to provide additional vertical support. Many building departments require that they be used at least every 12 feet. Also consider placing pilasters on each side of an entrance gate and at the ends of freestanding walls. When you're building the foundation, make the pilaster footing twice the width of the pilasters.

ABOVE LEFT: A curved, dry-stacked stone wall gracefully transitions through a grade change.

ABOVE RIGHT: The low retaining wall of landscape timbers has weathered enough to match the tone of the cut- stone paving.

a brick wall

HEADER COURSE (every fifth, sixth, or seventh course) spans front to back and helps lock the wall together.

CORNERS overlap with cut ¾ and ¼ closure bricks.

REINFORCEMENT BARS strengthen the structure (check local codes).

POURED FOOTING is typically twice the wall's width and 12 inches deep (or as deep as the frostline).

GRAVEL BASE ensures good drainage.

COMMON-BOND WALL has staggered joints from course to course. Double thickness is much stronger than a single row of bricks.

a concrete block wall

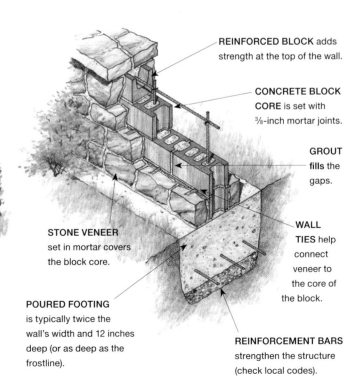

REINFORCED BLOCK adds strength at the top of the wall.

CONCRETE BLOCK CORE is set with ⅜-inch mortar joints.

GROUT fills the gaps.

WALL TIES help connect veneer to the core of the block.

STONE VENEER set in mortar covers the block core.

POURED FOOTING is typically twice the wall's width and 12 inches deep (or as deep as the frostline).

REINFORCEMENT BARS strengthen the structure (check local codes).

shrubs for enclosure

HEDGES MAKE WALLS OF LEAVES OR FLOWERS

HEDGES, TREES, AND VINES DEFINE GARDEN BOUNDARIES THE SAME WAY A FENCE OR WALL DOES, though less rigidly and at less expense. They can make a small space feel enclosed but also lush, and many can be sheared.

Shrubs are probably the most versatile group of landscape plants, given their variety in size, shape, and foliage. Some, such as roses and rhododendrons, are noted for their profusion of spectacular flowers; others, like yew and box, for their handsome foliage; and some, such as holly, cotoneaster, and pyracantha, for colorful berries.

The style and ambience of your house and garden should always factor into your planning. Massing large and small untrimmed shrubs can give your garden a sense of wild, untamed nature, while neatly shaped and clipped hedges have a much more controlled, formal appearance.

Think about your needs for privacy in particular areas of your garden. Must the plant barrier be solid, or would a light screen be enough? If you wish merely to obscure a direct view from the street to your front door,

A garden of any size seems larger if some of the space is defined within it. From walking height, this table and chairs are hidden from view by the sheared hedge.

a large, open shrub, such as rhododendron, may do well. But if you want to completely block a view, a closely sheared cedar, privet, or yew hedge may be your best bet.

Shrubs are either deciduous or evergreen. What kind of shrubs you choose depends on whether privacy is desirable year-round or just during the growing season. A patio that isn't used during the cold winter months could be sheltered from spring through fall by lilacs, which lose their leaves in winter. For screening

a view into a bedroom window, though, a fast-growing evergreen would be preferable.

using shrubs as hedges

Hedges are shrubs that have been planted to form a solid barrier or define a boundary. Although hedges have three dimensions, the primary emphasis in garden design is on their height and form. Besides transforming shrubs into a linear barrier, clipping can also increase the density of the planting. Trimming the

TOP LEFT: Shrubs sheared into columns contrast with the curve of a weeping larch.

TOP RIGHT: Sheared cedars enclose a patio space.

ABOVE LEFT: Mounding forsythia borders a path.

ABOVE RIGHT: The lowest boxwood branches are removed to allow a view.

growing shoots on both sides of the hedge encourages the shrubs to grow toward each other, knitting the plants into a continuous row that can effectively block the view into or out of your garden.

Hedges generally come in two forms: formal and informal. Formal hedges take up less space than informal ones, making them ideal for small lots. But to maintain their more rigid shape, formal hedges require regular pruning—a chore you may not want to deal with. In general, plants with small, tight branching habits are best for formal hedges. Boxwood, barberry, holly, privet, and yew are good choices.

Informal hedges, where plants are allowed to spread out naturally, are better suited to open spaces. Almost maintenance-free, they provide an effective easy-care screen. For an informal hedge, try viburnum, forsythia, honeysuckle, or spiraea. Higher hedges, especially dense ones, make very good insulators against street noise.

massing shrubs

Trees are often the most notable feature in a landscape, but shrubs usually provide organization, offer a sense of enclosure, and give a garden its form and structure. Think of shrubs as the skeleton of the garden.

Shrubs offer a tremendously wide and varied palette of leaf textures, growth habits, shapes, and seasonal leaf colors, as well as flower color and display. You may have to restrain yourself from choosing too many different kinds for your garden. Because shrubs are such strong structural elements, you'll want to maintain unity in the design by limiting your selections to a few species and varieties. Try to keep the same varieties together in clumps or stretches. If the same shrubs are dotted all over the garden, the eye will be busily drawn from one to another, leading to a choppy effect and cheating the shrubs of their chance to shine.

Think also of unity over time. You may wish to choose evergreen shrubs for your major plantings so that you will have a permanent green backdrop. This backdrop will give you visual privacy all year long and can be enlivened with plantings of annuals and perennials during the growing season. Deciduous shrubs can be used along with evergreens as accents for their flowers, autumn foliage, and interesting winter forms.

Like all plants, shrubs need plenty of room to grow. To ensure their future health, avoid the temptation to overplant, and be sure to take seriously the mature dimensions of your plants. (To judge their ultimate size, visit public parks and botanical gardens to see mature specimens.) Overcrowded shrubs will have a difficult time attaining their natural form and shape.

If planting in front of a hedge, allow 12 to 18 inches between the hedge and the foreground plantings. This allows some visual depth between the foreground and the hedge, and the play of light and shadow against the hedge can be very attractive.

BELOW LEFT: Billowy mountain laurel shields the house's front entrance from sidewalk traffic.

BELOW CENTER: Photinias growing in 24-inch-wide pots screen the view of the neighbor's roofline from this deck garden.

BELOW RIGHT: The color of screening evergreens is offset by brilliant gold-leaf barberry.

SHRUBS FOR HEDGES AND SCREENS

Plants with densely packed foliage from top to bottom serve best as living fences. Several large shrubs are good candidates; if grouped close together, they can block an objectionable view or direct attention to a garden focal point. Shearing can transform some plants into formal hedges.

One large shrub, planted off the lower, exposed side of this deck, rises high enough to provide a subtle sense of enclosure.

DECIDUOUS
Butterfly bush *(Buddleja)*
Crataegus, some
Dwarf purple osier *(Salix)*
European hornbeam *(Carpinus)*
Flowering quince *(Chaenomeles)*
Hedge maple *(Acer)*
Japanese barberry *(Berberis)*
Lilac *(Syringa)*
Mock orange *(Philadelphus)*
Osage orange *(Maclura)*

Privet *(Ligustrum)*
Roses, many
Silverberry *(Elaeagnus)*
Smoke tree *(Cotinus)*
Viburnum, some
Winterberry *(Ilex)*

EVERGREEN
Bamboo, many
Barberry *(Berberis)*
Boxwood *(Buxus)*

Camellia, many
Glossy abelia *(Abelia)*
Holly *(Ilex)*
Hop bush *(Dodonaea)*
Juniper, many
Lemon bottlebrush *(Callistemon)*
Oleander *(Nerium)*
Strawberry tree *(Arbutus)*
Sweet olive *(Osmanthus)*
Wax-leaf privet *(Ligustrum)*
Yew pine *(Taxus)*

trees for a canopy
THEY'RE TALL AND LEAFY SCREENS

IF YOU LIVE DEEP WITHIN A FOREST, PRIVACY is probably no problem. But even if space constraints don't allow you to surround your home with groves, you can use trees singly or in groups to create a sense of privacy and enclosure.

Use large trees to create a canopy, or smaller trees with shrubs to achieve a lush effect. Trees provide the vertical element in a garden design, while shrubs lend a lower, more horizontal feeling. Because most tree branches don't grow all the way to the ground, they provide a sense of enclosure from about eye level on up.

Trees contribute much more than a sense of enclosure. They can provide shade, fruit, and brilliant fall color. Some can withstand—or even require—freezing winters, while others enjoy baking summers. Some trees retain their foliage year-round, while others let winter sun through their bare branches.

Given the many kinds of trees that are available, deciding which one will best fill your needs is not an easy task.

Welcome in most cases, the cooling effect of trees can be overdone, especially in regions where summers are cool. For instance,

in coastal or northern areas too many trees might leave your garden too dark or cold. The same density of trees in the Southwest, though, would be clearly appreciated.

For more about choosing trees, see pages 308–315.

skyline trees

Trees that have a large mature size, such as sugar maple, coast redwood, or sycamore, will effectively create privacy. But they need a large area to grow in so they won't overwhelm their surroundings. If you're faced with a view of a freeway or multistory apartment complex at the end of your lot, one or two such trees may provide just the visual barrier you need. Again, use these big trees in your landscape with caution. Remember that trees grow out as well as up.

The shape of a mature tree depends on its branching structure and the rate of spread

Crape myrtle trees blaze with fall color while they frame the entrance to the house and shield the view into the courtyard.

relative to upward growth. Some trees remain narrow, and others become wide-spreading. There are named cultivars of many trees that might differ in shape or size from the regular species. An example is the 'Fairmount' ginkgo. It grows to 50 feet tall but only 15 feet wide, 10 to 15 feet less in diameter than is typical for other ginkgos.

groves of small trees

Groupings of moderately sized or small trees, such as redbud, ginkgo, or snowball, can be placed at appropriate spots to shelter the view from a neighbor's upstairs windows or to screen undesirable views. Smaller versions of these trees, particularly those with a smaller spread, give you more flexibility to design and plant around them, and they don't grow to dominate a garden.

hedges of trees

A row of small trees can achieve the effect of a hedge, although in most cases branches won't grow all the way to the ground. Good candidates for this treatment are hawthorn, crabapple, and flowering plum. You might use this kind of hedge along a boundary line or across the front property line.

If you're willing to routinely shear larger trees, you can also use them as a screen. A row of podocarpus makes an attractive lacy screen. Large, fast-growing trees, such as hemlock, can grow into a tall, dense screen in two or three years. Shearing will encourage the side branches to grow more densely than otherwise, and regular shearing is required. Skip a year and instead of forming a tall hedge the trees will revert to habit and stretch out to their full height.

ABOVE LEFT: River birch trees provide cooling shade and add texture and color with their flaking bark and dark green leaves.

ABOVE CENTER: At peak bloom a crape myrtle makes a colorful canopy over a porch.

ABOVE RIGHT: Mulberry trees provide an umbrella of shade over this French-style terrace in summer, then drop their leaves to admit winter sun.

SHAPES OF TREES

FASTIGIATE Thin and tapering at the top and bottom, like the Italian cypress (Cupressus semper-virens). A row of these could create a tall, elegant hedge to block or frame a view.

COLUMNAR The shape of a narrow cylinder, like the Lombardy poplar (Populus nigra 'Italica'). Trees of this shape can be planted to achieve a hedge effect, or a single one may block the view of a radio tower, utility pole, or other tall, slender eyesore.

CONE-SHAPED Tall-growing fir (Abies) or coast redwood (Sequoia sempervirens) fits this category. A small grove of these trees will conceal any large structures beyond them.

GLOBE Globe also means spherical, like beech (Fagus). Trees of this shape are best used singly.

WEEPING The pendulous branches of this form, such as the weeping willow (Salix babylonica), can create a soft visual screen that breaks up a view instead of blocking it.

LOWE'S QUICK TIPS

TREES FOR TALL SCREENS
Smaller, narrower trees can screen views without overwhelming the yard. But before planting any tree, double-check the mature height to confirm it won't grow too tall.
- American holly (E)
- Crape myrtle (D)
- English yew (E)
- Flowering pear (D)
- Japanese maple (D)
- Leyland cypress (E)
- Purple-leaf plum (D)
- Serviceberry (D)

vines for fast screening

USE SCRAMBLING PLANTS AS COVERS AND CLOAKS

THESE REMARKABLY VERSATILE PLANTS CAN BE A BOON TO ANY GARDENER. THE FAST GROWTH RATE of many vines makes them perfect candidates for temporary screens and permanent plantings.

A vine is simply a flexible shrub that doesn't stop extending its growth. It just keeps getting taller or longer, depending on whether you train it vertically or horizontally. If unsupported, it won't climb at all but will sprawl across the ground. Climbing plants are adaptable to gardens of any size. They can cover a broad area in a large garden or add their charm to a nook in a small plot.

Vines soften fences, walls, and freestanding screens, and they can be used to accentuate or

break up the horizontal line of these structures. A vine supported by a crisscross of wires or latticework can create a leafy screen to block the gaze of neighbors or passersby, or to set off or enclose different parts of your landscape. Many vines, such as Virginia creeper and American bittersweet, grow so rapidly that they cover a large expanse within a single season. Others, such as wisteria, grow slowly at first but in time are particularly effective when grown along a high trellis and

Rugged perennial vines, such as this clematis, grow larger and produce more flowers each year.

allowed to drape downward to create a light, delicate screen, as in the above right photo.

Some vines can provide a dense screen, completely covering a chain link fence, for instance, or add height to a fence. Equally rampant and densely growing vines, such as climbing hydrangea, soften the contours of a concrete block wall and integrate them with the rest of the plantings in the garden.

For help finding the right one for you, see the section about vines beginning on page 328.

evergreen or deciduous

A vine-covered arbor is the perfect way to obtain some overhead privacy and shade in summer. A deciduous vine allows more sunlight to penetrate during winter. Most deciduous vines have the added attraction of colorful foliage in fall, and the tracery of bare stems on a stone wall can also be attractive during winter.

annual or perennial

Annual vines, such as cup-and-saucer vine, sweet peas, and morning glory, start slowly in spring but are growing fast by midsummer. Use them to augment the screening effect of slower-growing plants. Because they die back naturally at the end of the growing season, you needn't worry that they'll overwhelm and stunt the growth of neighboring plants. Perennial vines do not require replanting each year, and they begin growing earlier in spring. But they are likely to need sturdier supports and occasional pruning. Examples of long-lived perennial vines are fiveleaf akebia, clematis, climbing roses, and wisteria.

flowers and fruit

Many vines serve as screens or adornments for fences, walls, or arbors, but they may also be grown for their flowers or fruit. Among those with desirable flowers are clematis, jasmine, morning glory, rose, and wisteria. The selection of vines with edible fruit is much smaller but well-known, grapes being the most outstanding example. Pole beans, such as 'Kentucky Wonder', create a lush annual screen with the bonus of delicious fresh produce.

ABOVE LEFT: This wrought-iron trellis, largely hidden by a vigorous 'Dortmund' rose, extends above the wall behind it.

ABOVE RIGHT: A wisteria-covered arbor transforms a simple wooden deck into a private retreat that's shielded from the summer sun.

before
and after

MOST OF US FACE TWO MAIN OBSTACLES WHEN IT COMES TO landscaping. The first is looking at a yard that is probably very familiar and seeing what it might be. The second is more prosaic and is the subject of this book: where to start what might be a fairly large and expensive project. It's mostly a matter of breaking the project down into small, discrete steps.

This chapter addresses both issues by sharing with you more than a dozen successful landscaping stories. Some of these projects are large and some are small. In some cases the homeowners did all the work, while in others professionals were enlisted for all or part of the project. Among these projects you should find a number of ideas that apply to your own situation.

There's one lesson you can take away from each of these case studies: they all began with good planning.

from predictable to posh

A BACKYARD IS TRANSFORMED INTO A SPA RETREAT

before When the owner of this house decided it was time to turn her nondescript backyard into a rejuvenating retreat, she called in a garden designer and gave him carte blanche—except for one request. She wanted him to fit a swimming pool into the 49-by-69-foot space.

after The sleek, dark pool gets star billing in the new garden, and rightfully so. Bordered on three sides by a rich array of bold foliage and sleek stone terraces, and adorned with a wall fountain, it could pass for a purely ornamental water feature. It's all that, but it also performs daily as a workout venue for a serious swimmer.

Continued ➤

ABOVE: The existing backyard was dominated by lawn. The small patio was too far from the house and was rarely used.

RIGHT: A ground cover of *Geranium macrorrhizum* spreads over the edges of a planter that bridges the pool and a walkway. Cut pavers of varying sizes are used for the walk and steps, then merge into same-size pavers set on a diagonal pattern.

A brilliant wall of vegetation spills into the water at the pool's shallow end, framing the flow from a spouting fountain. Leaves that fall into the water are quickly scooped up by an automatic floating skimmer.

ABOVE: Stone stairs rise in two stages, jogging to the left between levels. The steps lead to a sitting terrace, tucked away behind a thick hedge of heavenly bamboo.

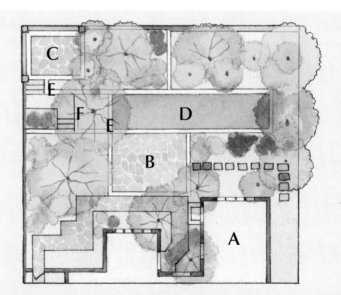

A HOUSE

B LOWER TERRACE

C UPPER TERRACE

D LAP POOL

E STONE WALLS

F RAISED BED WITH
   Geranium macrorrhizum
   and magnolia

New space for outdoor living was recovered from the front yard.

vintage remodel
CRAFTSMAN FLAIR ENHANCES A GARDEN MEANT FOR OUTDOOR LIVING

before The owners loved their neighborhood—they'd lived here 15 years—but not their 1940s house. They wanted it to have an older look, specifically that of vintage California Craftsman. So they remodeled it to incorporate the beautiful woodwork and other details that are common to that style. At the same time, they asked a landscape architect to design a garden that would complement the new-old Craftsman style of their house.

after To increase the amount of outdoor living space, they created an open-air "parlor" in the front yard. It has fairly private seating behind a low wall on the new porch, more public seating in front of it, and a neighborly perch on a seat wall. In the backyard is a new gravel-paved dining terrace. In front of the garage, which was turned into an office, a portion of the driveway became a lounge. The two areas are connected by a large landing with wide, deep steps.

LESSONS LEARNED

DETAILS, DETAILS Timeless materials and Craftsman styling give these spaces the illusion of age. The new driveway, for instance, is paved with broken concrete recycled from the old one, which provided instant patina. The same concrete is used in the entry courtyard. The new porch wall and seat walls look aged for several reasons: the inherent color variations in the buff-colored concrete, the textured surface, and rounded edges on the caps and steps.

GOODBYE TO LAWN While it can be hard to part with a lawn, for the sake of paved living spaces it is probably worth it.

NATURAL PLANT PALETTE The bark of the mature Chinese elm inspired the front yard's apricot, gray, and soft green plant color scheme. The designer took bark samples along on plant-hunting trips. House paint colors were also coordinated with this theme.

HAND-SEEDED AGGREGATE The beautiful finish of the lounge's paving (see facing page, bottom right) was created with colored pebbles embedded into buff-colored concrete.

STONE-FRAMED GRAVEL On the dining terrace, a 4-inch-high stone edging keeps the gravel neatly contained and creates an elegant finish.

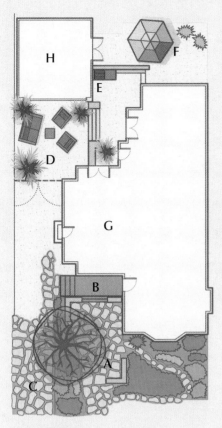

A FRONT PATIO E GRILL
B PORCH F DINING TERRACE
C DRIVEWAY G HOUSE
D LOUNGE H GARAGE OFFICE

TOP RIGHT: Broken chunks recycled from a concrete demolition replaced the lawn in the form of pavers. But a touch of the lawn remains where fescue grass and thyme grow between the concrete chunks.

ABOVE LEFT: The outdoor dining area in the backyard is covered in gravel.

ABOVE RIGHT: What had been the driveway was transformed into an outdoor room that features hand-seeded aggregate paving.

great escape

NARROW FRONT PATIO BECOMES A HANDSOME DINING AREA

before Bare concrete and a vine-covered fence offered little appeal.

after The east-facing outdoor space has become a favorite place for the owners to enjoy a sunny breakfast or escape the heat in the late afternoon.

Mediterranean-inspired accents enrich the surroundings, including details such as the stucco-clad exterior walls, matching caps of tumbled-flagstone on both the raised planter and walls, and the antique finish of the cast limestone fountain.

The 16-by-36-foot courtyard visually expands the ranch-style home, as it's now visible through larger kitchen windows and accessible through a set of French doors in the breakfast room. The doors face the fountain built into the wall, which was added to block the sight and sounds of street traffic. Terra-cotta pavers extend from the breakfast room into the courtyard.

ABOVE: The cramped and unappealing space was underutilized.

BELOW: Now a true outdoor room, the slightly expanded patio has a wall fountain as a focal point.

getting greener
RECYCLING WITH PANACHE

ABOVE: A staircase led from the house to an almost empty yard.

BELOW: The narrow space is divided into two areas: one for raised beds and vegetables, and the other for entertaining.

before The site was especially challenging: a small, irregular space hemmed in by houses, measuring only 12 feet wide at the rear, 20 feet wide close to the house, and 54 feet long.

after The designer treated the garden like an extension of the house and split it into two living areas or rooms—intimate spaces for relaxing and barbecuing.

Recycled-steel trellises planted with climbing *Asparagus retrofractus* and papyrus screen some of the views from neighboring windows. In front is a stroll-through garden also meant to be viewed from inside the house. Raised beds, framed with the same recycled steel used for the trellises, overflow with colorful foliage. To separate the front and rear areas, the designer created a divider from two boxlike steel-framed racks used to store firewood. The yard is paved with gravel, a permeable surface that allows rainwater to seep into the soil.

instant patio

A BACKYARD GOES FROM DREARY TO DREAMY

before It's a common situation: the deck looks tired and worn-out, and the landscape and lawn are overgrown. The trick here is seeing beyond the existing situation and realizing how a few relatively minor steps can make a big difference.

after The first step was cleaning the deck, in this case with a bio-degradable wood cleaner, to restore the Alaska cedar to its original yellow-orange color. The cleaner was allowed to soak into the wood as the directions specify, then washed with a rented power washer. Once dry, two coats of stain were applied with a roller and a brush. The rehabilitated deck provided inspiration for remaining tasks.

An 18-inch-wide gravel strip between the deck and the lawn was added for its framing effect and to make the lawn much easier to mow. The homeowners used string to delineate where the strip would go, removed 3 inches of sod and soil inside the marked area, then edged it with 2-by-4 composite decking and lined it with landscape fabric to prevent weed growth. Crushed-granite gravel fills the strip.

Circular concrete pavers supply visual punch and also act as an extension of the patio. Various sizes (20, 24, and 36 inches in diameter) were used, all sealed with water-base concrete stain. Once the placement was right, the pavers were lifted so that rounds of sod could be removed and the stepping-stones placed flush with the lawn.

Finishing touches, such as portable lighting and colorful furnishings, completed the backyard renewal. The owners chose a color palette to complement their house and deck, as well as nearby plants. Clustered pots in earth tones and shades of ocean and sky blue

ABOVE: The serviceable but plain backyard wasn't inviting to guests.

TOP RIGHT: Cleaning, creating edges and borders, and adding colorful accents did the trick.

BOTTOM RIGHT: Stepping-stones were laid out before they were sunk into the turf.

bring the look of a garden onto the deck. They're filled with easy-care plants, including golden sweet flag (*Acorus*), blue fescue, rosy-bronze New Zealand flax, and silvery echeverias.

The owners gave two faded wicker chairs a coat of deep red spray paint to accent the deck's golden tones and the soft green and deep plum French doors.

The string of lanterns makes the deck a festive place for evening barbecues and parties. The lanterns' string is supported by a $1/8$-inch steel cable suspended between an eave of the house and an 8-foot-long 4-by-4 post at one end of the deck.

Rounded stones, an antique watering can, and a decorative star of rusted metal nestle among potted plants on the deck.

INSTANT OUTDOOR DECORATING

FILL POTS WITH PLANTS For quick effect, slip potted nursery plants directly into decorative containers.

SET OUT LANTERNS Most of the ones used here (several are visible in the picture below) are fitted with light-diffusing frosted glass to cast a soft glow at step corners.

EMBELLISH THE LAWN WITH PAVERS Position concrete pavers as shown here, then trace around them with a serrated knife. Remove the pavers, dig up the circles of sod, and set the pavers so they're flush with the surrounding sod.

ADD PILLOWS The red wicker chairs got throw pillows. Garden steps can double as seating with their own scattering of cushions.

Lightweight glass lanterns hang from a seafoam green market umbrella, while a string of mini-lights stretches across the patio, creating a festive atmosphere.

open yard becomes
intimate

BUYERS LOVED THE HOME
BUT HATED THE YARD

before When the owners-to-be first saw this house, it was love at first sight. But that lasted only until they looked out the back door and realized that people in four surrounding houses had a bird's-eye view into the backyard. Not that anybody was ever out there, on its weed-choked lawn, ill-conceived deck, or skimpy brick patio. So the couple walked away and continued house hunting, ultimately touring more than 40 more houses before coming back to this one. What they decided was to buy the house and hire a landscape architect.

after Now that the backyard transformation is complete, they love the garden even more than the house. But then who wouldn't enjoy a secluded retreat complete with a gracious veranda, intimate dining terrace, exuberant flower garden, and four-hole putting green?

ABOVE: The existing patio was barely used because of its lack of shelter and privacy.

RIGHT: The veranda is now covered by an arbor and dressed up with Romanesque columns, brick pilasters, and a lattice deck skirt. Stairs from the veranda were redirected onto an intermediate-level dining terrace paved with bluestone.

TOP, FAR RIGHT: The path through the gate is paved with the same bluestone used on the dining terrace. *Mazus reptans* grows in the spaces between the pavers.

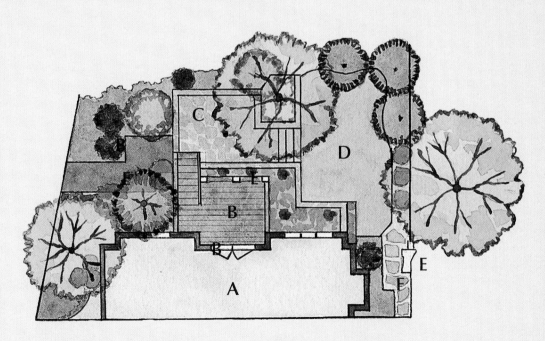

A HOUSE

B VERANDA

C DINING TERRACE

D PUTTING GREEN

E GATE

F STONE PATH

yard with a view

THE COURTYARD INVITES OUTDOOR RELAXATION

before The courtyard in the front had no privacy and no place to sit. And worse, a stunning view of San Francisco's skyline and the Golden Gate Bridge went begging as a result. Who'd want to admire the view from a walled-in patch of lawn and mud? So a landscape architect was tasked with transforming the unappealing area into a comfortable outdoor living space.

after The landscape architect began by removing the unused lawn and replacing it with pavers of square-cut Connecticut bluestone, leaving cutouts around the perimeter for plants and a water feature. The fountain of concrete and stainless steel, near one corner of the courtyard, has an attached redwood bench and serves as the focal point. Eyes are drawn to it from the front entrance and also from indoors. The fountain is inviting to visitors, who, once there, can't help but admire the view.

A steel-and-stucco arbor set atop the existing wall makes the space feel more enclosed, especially now that a wisteria vine grows over it. The arbor also improves how the house looks from the street.

On the upper slope just beyond the wall, near the redwood bench, the landscape architect concentrated the most colorful plantings. 'Garnet' penstemon, Pride of Madeira, and other flowering plants look like an extension of the courtyard. Across the rest of the slope, bamboo, miscanthus, and blue oat grass add texture. At the slope's base, a stepped retaining wall faced with Napa basalt and capped with bluestone minimizes the downward slope of the hill.

LEFT: Open space and a tire swing absorbed plenty of childhood energy, but otherwise the backyard was little used.

TOP RIGHT: The new patio is also an outdoor dining room, where curving beds frame the space and offer soothing views from every angle.

BOTTOM RIGHT: The pond is the focal point of the garden and is now the natural place to gather and recoup after a busy day.

a first landscape makeover

LESSONS FROM A FAMILY WHO DID IT THEMSELVES

before A patch of grass and a tree with a tire swing were fine as long as active kids were growing up. But as the family matured, needs changed.

after Today the same space is an oasis. To start, the family made a wish list. Their highest priority was to break up the roughly 2,900-square-foot backyard into a series of garden rooms. They also wanted more appealing views, a pond, a new patio, and drought-tolerant plants.

For help with the hardscape, the owners consulted a landscape architect, who provided conceptual drawings for the backyard. Once a master plan was complete, in came a jackhammer and a trash bin for tearing out brick paths and the concrete patio. Next, a concrete and masonry specialist installed the new patio. He made the paving look like slate by stamping texture onto colored concrete. He also built raised planters. Mediterranean plants that fit the region and the desired look were chosen for the planters.

SMART IDEAS

COOL COLORS Blue and green foliage around the pond enhances its serenity. Lime asparagus fern, pale variegated grass, blue fescue, and yellow Japanese forest grass are texturally diverse yet not overwhelming.

LAYERS For greatest impact, plant in layers: short plants and trailers in front, tall plants in back. Colorful, low-care plants here include artemisia, penstemon, rosemary, and salvia, with a Japanese maple as an accent.

EASY PATH Decorative and functional, a dry-laid flagstone path is bordered by ferns and red-flowered *Cuphea ignea*. A thick layer of mulch keeps soil moist. In the back planter, a tall mallow hedge screens a vegetable garden.

FAUX STONE Stone veneer (pages 228–229) is used to refine the raised planters. An affordable alternative to actual rock, it has the rustic, multitoned look of the real thing but is manufactured from Portland cement and bits of stone.

A POND
B VEGETABLE GARDEN
C DINING AREA
D FLAGSTONE PAVING
E CONCRETE PAVING
F SCREENING HEDGE

outdoor playroom
VARIED SURFACES AND USEFUL NEW SPACES DEFINE A FAMILY-FRIENDLY BACKYARD

MAKEOVER TIPS

START WITH A CLEAN SLATE If you've inherited or created a pool or spa that's in the wrong place, face up to the cost of demolition. The problem isn't going away otherwise.

INVEST IN HARDSCAPE Smooth surfaces that accommodate furniture turn a garden into a useful outdoor room, so they're worth the investment, especially compared to the cost of a room addition.

USE OFF-THE-SHELF MATERIALS TO REDUCE COSTS Though the patio was poured in place, the designer used precast pavers wherever possible for economy. The square concrete planters used throughout the garden are also ready-made rather than custom. Likewise, the decomposed granite and gravel are standard landscape supply materials.

USE PLANTS TO DEFINE, NOT DECORATE The purpose of plants in this garden is to emphasize the architecture of the house and garden. The designer used a small number of foliage plants, each planted en masse. Most of the plants—whether bronze New Zealand flax or tall, feathery papyrus—have a bold structure that complements the home.

before An oddly shaped slab of concrete used to be the only outdoor living space, and "uninviting" was an understatement. Just a few feet from the back door, a previous owner had installed a small lap pool, a feature the owners didn't use and found annoying. So they invested in new landscaping that would allow them to take full advantage of their best asset: the 3,000-square-foot, fully fenced, totally private outdoor living space.

after Now a crisply defined poured-concrete patio serves as another room. A green buffer of lawn on three sides both defines and softens the patio. Other plantings are simple but bold. For instance, an aged camellia was retained from the old yard, and new plantings of feathery papyrus and New Zealand flax were added.

The landscape architect removed the pool and in its place installed the simple concrete patio, which acts as an extension of the dining and living areas. She added a concrete bench at the end of the patio to provide built-in seating, and she placed a discreet water feature nearby (water bubbles up through gravel from a cistern hidden below). Because of its low-key nature, the water feature is safe enough for even a toddler to play around.

The lawn provides ample play space for young children. It slopes away from the patio in all directions, following the natural contours of the lot, and provides a softening contrast to the color and the hard geometry of the concrete forms. The rest of the landscaping consists of simple, low-maintenance plants planted en masse and used primarily to define space.

Squares of oversized concrete pavers accommodate small parties or additional seating space during larger parties, and a terrace of decomposed granite near the kitchen is for the barbecue.

ABOVE: Prior to the new landscaping, the backyard was mostly wasted space.
TOP RIGHT: A fountain burbles at one end of a low seat wall adjacent to the patio.
TOP, FAR RIGHT: A lawn for play and a patio replace the pool.
RIGHT: The new patio of poured concrete extends indoor living space.

scene stealer

A NEW LANDSCAPE EMBRACES ITS REGION

before A landscape of white picket fence, concrete entry path, lawn, and pruned foundation shrubs was neat enough but out of sync with its surroundings. It had a certain "Martha's Vineyard charm" in the middle of California chaparral.

after The white picket fence and concrete path were replaced by a wall and a path of blond stone; and plants like red-hot poker that blend in with the coastal chaparral replaced the lawn. Using stone, plants, and paint, the designer restored the Arts and Crafts character of the house and visually tied the garden to the tawny hills behind it.

Though the garden looks natural, there's order built in. Except for the existing locust tree, the two sides of the yard are symmetrical, much like the original landscape. Even the biennial tower of jewels—the showy, red-spired *Echium wildpretii* dominating the garden—is carefully placed to maintain the balance.

Working with a landscape architect, the homeowners began by removing the fence and digging up the yard. The garden's base was elevated, placing it behind a front retaining wall, in order to present it as though it were on a pedestal. Recessed mortar was used to create the illusion of a dry-stacked wall. To match the new front steps, the concrete ones near the front door were replaced with more flagstone, which was also used to create flanking piers. Finally, the house was painted to pick up tones in the flagstone and hillside.

ABOVE: Always neat and attractive, the previous landscape was plain and predictable.

TOP RIGHT: Now the landscape features colorful and drought-tolerant plants such as red-hot poker, *Kniphofia uvaria*.

TOP, FAR RIGHT: A stalwart perennial of the new garden is 'Moonshine' yarrow.

RIGHT: The new landscape blends into its surrounding environment in a far more natural way. It's also more colorful and requires much less water.

from scraggly to splendid

AN EYESORE NO MORE

before Filled with scraggly grass and a single dead fir tree, this backyard looked bleak, all right. In fact, the homeowners admit they used to leave the curtains closed all day long "because it was so gross out there."

after Bleakness has been banished. Now, flowering shrubs and colorful foliage plants cloak the board fence, lush turf carpets the yard, and stones ranging in size from pebbles to giant boulders provide a unifying theme. And the owners are no longer in a state of denial. In fact, they actually plan events around the garden.

ABOVE: Weeds and the neighbor's windows used to be the view from the backyard.

TOP RIGHT: Stone slabs cloaked in dwarf periwinkle lead to a bench below an old oak.

TOP, FAR RIGHT: A child's playhouse, fancifully painted, is now a garden focal point.

RIGHT: Multilayered plantings on mounds add both texture and height to the formerly flat landscape.

good-bye, blahs hello, stunning

THE HO-HUM LAWN IS GONE

before The young couple who bought this house had never gardened before, but they didn't let that discourage them. They studied enough pictures in books and magazines to know the look they wanted. In a nutshell, they sought a formal structure combined with loose and even wild-looking plantings. Their next step was to call a landscape architect.

after The architect kept the plan simple with a minimum of new structural features, primarily the new vine-covered arch over the entry walk. Reflecting the interests of the owners, a wide variety of plants were used, most of them low and mounding perennials that are well adapted to their environment and therefore low-maintenance.

ABOVE: The exterior of the bungalow-style house needed an updated look.

TOP RIGHT: The new arbor is covered with golden hops (*Humulus lupulus* 'Aureus') and clematis. Visitors pass under it moving from the sidewalk to the courtyard.

BOTTOM RIGHT: The corners of the courtyard are visually anchored by large planters of boxwood surrounded by blooming 'Snowstorm' bacopa.

FAR RIGHT: From the street, the positive impact of a lighter color paint on the shingle exterior coupled with the much more diverse landscape is clearly apparent.

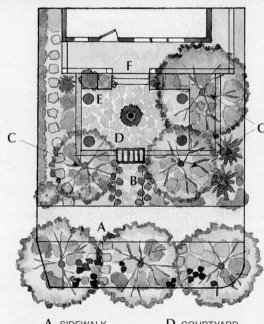

A SIDEWALK	**D** COURTYARD
B ARBOR	**E** PLANTERS
C TREES	**F** PORCH

the entry, revisited

ITS WALKWAY HAS BEEN MOVED AND WIDENED

before The owners of this house faced the same challenges that plague legions of their counterparts. Chief among them were noise and lack of privacy. On both sides, neighboring homes almost touch the property line, and the lots face a busy commuter road leading to a major city. The list went on. An asphalt driveway looked like a parking lot in front of the garage. To reach the house, visitors had to make their way over a narrow stone pathway that led from the street to the front door. Last but not least, there was just too much lawn.

after Now, dense plantings all but block the street from view, and they've lowered the decibel level considerably. A wide walkway curves gracefully from the front steps to the resurfaced, lower-key driveway. And the only lawn is a tidy semicircle of grass the owners cut in minutes with a manual reel mower.

ABOVE: A few shrubs, lawn, and a narrow path from the sidewalk across the lawn and to the front porch were the key elements of the existing landscape.

RIGHT: Exposed aggregate was chosen for the new driveway and a much wider walkway that now comfortably funnels visitors to the entry porch. A variety of perennials and shrubs provide some screening from the street. The blue flowers of *Verbena bonariensis* are at near right, while Oriental fountain grass and 'Casa Blanca' lilies are at far right.

making your plan

A PARTICULARLY BEAUTIFUL SPRING MORNING MAY FIND YOU sitting on your front or back steps, soaking up the sun and thinking how pleasant it is to be outdoors. With that thought in mind, you take a long look at your yard and begin to daydream: "What can I do to make the space I have a little more livable and a little more attractive?"

Take heart. Simply observing and dreaming about what you want is an important beginning. Next, read the following pages, where you'll find, step by step, a planning process that can turn your dream garden into a reality.

Developing a plan is critical. While the plan is still on paper, changing your mind is easy and cheap. A plan needn't look professional or fancy. If it's accurate and specific enough to suit your needs, it's fine. Working through the planning process will help you produce a more satisfying result, and save time and money, too.

beginning to plan
IT'S THE MOST IMPORTANT STAGE OF LANDSCAPING

ON PAGES 9–11 OF THIS BOOK, WE LAID OUT THE STEPS TO CREATING YOUR OWN LANDSCAPE FROM beginning to end. This stage, developing your plan, is about halfway through that process. At this point you can begin to play with specific choices and make some decisions.

Making a plan for a landscape is really a form of shorthand, an easy and effective way of notating ideas. In fact, you cannot make a workable design without a plan. As you record, study, and improve your ideas, the design develops. You may find yourself making notes, scrutinizing pictures of other landscapes, and making drawings of your own original ideas. All these are intermediate steps toward the final plan. The more possibilities you think out, the closer you are to an effective design.

There are three basic elements: a base map showing the specifics of your space, a bubble diagram that represents your general ideas, and your final plan, which merges the base map and bubble diagram and adds specifics.

Before you begin, collect precise information about the site, including its overall dimensions and the location of any permanent structures, utilities, and landforms, such as slopes. Once all of this information is available, begin to transfer it to paper. You will need a tape measure and an assistant.

planning tools
The tools you need are simple: pencil, eraser, graph paper, and tracing paper. Oversized paper may be helpful for a larger drawing that includes more details. Drafting tools such as a T square might also come in handy.

using your computer Visit Lowes.com and look for the interactive planning tools "Landscape & Garden Planner" and "Deck Planner," both of which feature click-and-drag simplicity. The landscape planner accounts for basics such as the size of your yard and planting zone, and it allows you to experiment with various layouts and combinations of plants and furnishings. When you think you've got it right, you can print out a shopping list.

There are also several software programs on the market to help homeowners plan their landscapes. Useful features include the ability to import your own photos; 3-D views, which enable you to move through the space and see it from different perspectives; and the

Lowe's "Landscape & Garden Planner" on the Web includes tools that can help you plan your deck, patio, and landscape.

You can draw your landscape either freehand or with the aid of mechanical drafting tools. Whichever method you choose, you'll still need to scale your plan. Working to a precise scale ensures accuracy when you're figuring how much you'll need in soil amendments, ground-cover plants, trees, shrubs, and so forth.

capacity to show plant growth over time. Some also help you plan decks, patios, and irrigation systems.

professional help

Begin by identifying the services you need. Be realistic in assessing the amount of work you want to do yourself. Collect names from friends and neighbors, and knock on doors when you spot a good design. Call the designers or contractors whose work you like in order to set up an interview either at your home or at their offices. Home consultations may be charged by the hour, while office visits are often free. Inquire about the nature of the designers' work, their availability, and their fees. Most important, ask for references—other residential clients whose gardens may give you an idea of the range and quality of a designer's work or the caliber of a contractor's construction.

Before the first visit, prepare a list of wishes, needs, and problems to deal with in the design, making sure everyone in the household has had a chance to participate in this step. Give serious consideration to your budget and schedule. When a design is complete, meet with the contractor and the designer to make certain the contractor understands the design and is comfortable working with the materials proposed. To protect yourself from any surprises, request a contract from any professionals you hire. This legal agreement should spell out the services to be provided, the schedule to be followed, and the fees to be charged.

landscape architect
Creating a landscape can call for the addition of patios, decks, dining areas, play yards, shade structures, drainage systems, and perhaps a pool or spa. Designing such structures and relating them to a coherent plan for your lot is the business of a landscape architect.

In addition to determining the most effective use of paving, planting, and lighting, licensed landscape architects design exterior structures and solve site problems such as poor drainage. Landscape architects are familiar with landscape and building materials and services and can suggest cost-saving options.

They can also advise on locating entries, driveways, parking areas, and service lines.

other professionals
Landscape architects aren't the only professionals involved in the creation of fine gardens. The terms "landscape designer" and "garden designer" apply to professionals who may be self-taught or may have the same academic credentials as landscape architects but lack a state license. The focus of their work is more likely to be residential gardens, and if you don't need a complex deck or high retaining wall, they may well serve your needs. Their fees may be lower than those of landscape architects.

A licensed contractor is trained in earth-moving, construction, and planting. You may work directly with a contractor, or your landscape architect or designer may select and supervise one.

Horticulturists are trained in the selection and care of garden plants, and many also have some design training. If you're looking merely for plants to complete a design, you can work with a horticulturist.

Making changes to a plan on paper is easier and quicker than making them on the ground. A plan also speeds communication with other contributors to the project.

moving from plan to reality

The landscape plan on the facing page was designed to incorporate the aspirations and goals of its owners. You can track the evolution of this plan from start to finish as it appears in various stages throughout this chapter. These homeowners had eight goals, noted here by letters A through H.

Irish moss adds texture to an entry path that is flanked by gently screening river birches. Creeping Jenny, yellow Japanese forest grass, campanula, and variegated boxwood mingle in the bed. The result is both inviting and visually stimulating.

A create privacy The walled patio is really an extension of the living room. It creates an enclosed space and conceals the front yard from passersby. A pond with a bubbler helps mask traffic noise.

B invite entertaining A broad deck that wraps around the house, specifically the family and dining rooms, offers plenty of outdoor space for dinner, parties, or relaxation within view of the pool.

C provide recreation The swimming pool is a great place to cool off on hot summer days. Solar water-heating panels on the roof extend the swimming season and help warm the spa under the arbor at minimal energy cost.

D modify the climate Clothed in vines, the arbor shades southern exposures from summer sun while allowing low winter sun to warm the house. Around the pool, screen plantings filter strong summer winds.

E beautify the property Lush plantings between the sidewalk and the front patio wall create an attractive view from the street, soften the lines of the house and wall, and add color.

F grow a kitchen garden Raised beds along the south side of the rear yard offer an ideal spot for raising herbs and vegetables. They are also convenient to both the kitchen and the garden work area next to the garage.

G attract wildlife Plantings—native and otherwise—and a birdbath lure butterflies and birds. The secluded deck makes a perfect viewing spot.

H reduce water use The simplest way to reduce landscape water use is to apply mulch liberally throughout the garden. Another tactic is to reduce the size of your lawn. Both steps will have an immediate and significantly positive impact on water use.

a well-designed landscape

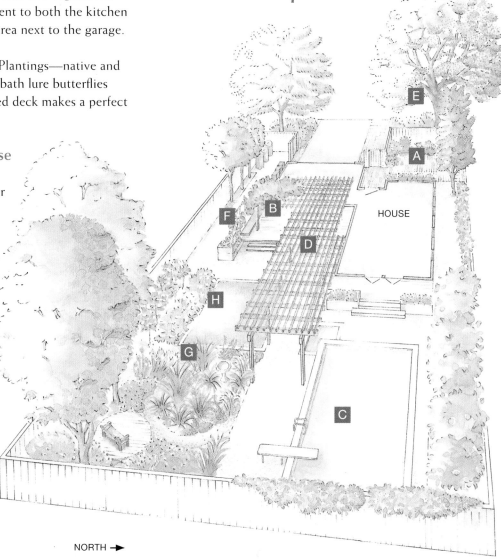

NORTH ➡

INCLUDE ON A BASE MAP

- Compass directions to help you identify exposures and patterns of sun and shade.
- Boundaries and dimensions of the lot and the location of the house and other structures.
- The location of all windows and doors. Note also the height of their sills above the exterior grade.
- Eaves, overhangs, downspouts, and drains.
- Existing paved areas, steps, and ramps.

- Location of utilities, easements, and setback boundaries.
- Existing plants, including the sizes, shapes, and general health of all plants, especially trees.
- Topography, including high and low points, slopes, and the direction of natural water drainage.
- Soil conditions, including areas that are typically dry or wet, or have been raised or filled; soil texture; fertility; and pH.
- Direction of prevailing winds throughout the year.

making a base map

Every property presents unique opportunities, but along with them come certain challenges. As you begin planning your landscape, you need to realistically assess both your yard's pluses and its minuses before finding a way to balance them with the features you want in your new landscape. You will also need to evaluate any man-made structures in your garden and any existing plantings, especially trees and large shrubs. Sketching these on paper gives you a base plan, a working document for the design stage.

You'll save hours of measuring if you can find any of the following: a deed map that gives actual dimensions and the orientation of your property; a topographical plan, with contour lines showing the exact shape of your site; or architectural plans that depict the site plan with the location of all buildings. If none of these is available, you will need to measure your property yourself and transfer the dimensions to the base plan, preferably on graph paper, using a scale of ¼ inch to 1 foot.

Later you can slip this base plan under a sheet of tracing paper and sketch designs to your heart's content. This gives you a chance to try out several ideas before laying out everything on-site—or, worse, installing a structure or planting and finding it doesn't suit the space, the property's microclimates, or your needs.

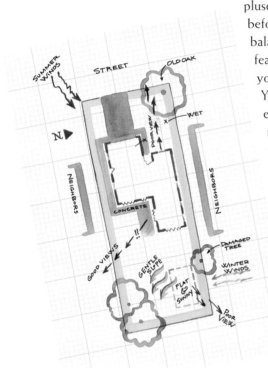

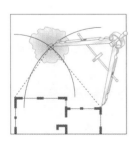

BELOW: To locate a tree or other feature, measure from two widely spaced fixed points to the feature. Working to scale, use a compass to draw two arcs based on the fixed points. Where the arcs intersect is the exact location.

starting to plan

Identify those aspects of the landscape that you wish to keep, as well as those you want to change. If you have just moved into your home, don't pick up a shovel and start digging just yet. Try to live with a new property for a full year, as you will get to know your garden through the seasons and can experiment with various plants. A design you make with a thorough knowledge of your property will fit your needs better.

After you have an intimate knowledge of the existing landscape, you can confidently go about removing or changing certain aspects. Don't feel you have to design your landscape around an existing feature, living or nonliving, just because it's there. If you're landscaping only one problem area of your garden, consider the impact the upgrade will have on the rest of the site. Keep in mind the landscape as a whole, for both the present and the future.

staying legal

Local zoning regulations or other laws may restrict or prohibit the construction you are planning. Consult the following documents, agencies, or individuals before proceeding, and note any relevant restrictions on your base plan.

your property deed
- Exact location of property lines
- Easements or rights-of-way
- Building restrictions
- Tree-removal restrictions

your building or planning department
- Setback requirements
- Height limitations for fences, buildings, or other structures
- Lot coverage guidelines
- Safety codes for pools and spas
- Open-burning restrictions for fire pits

- Requirements for fire walls between adjacent buildings
- Building codes for all construction
- Tree or historic-preservation ordinances
- Building permits for fences, retaining walls more than 30 inches high, other garden structures, and electrical or plumbing work

your utility company
- Location and depth of underground utility lines
- Building or planting limitations under power lines

your water company
- Restrictions on water use for irrigation, pools, and water features
- Limitations on lawn size

your neighbors
- Their views into your property (and your view into theirs) and your mutual need for privacy, quiet, sunlight, and airflow
- Homeowner association restrictions
- Neighbors' concerns about existing trees and other plants, structures, and shared walks or driveways

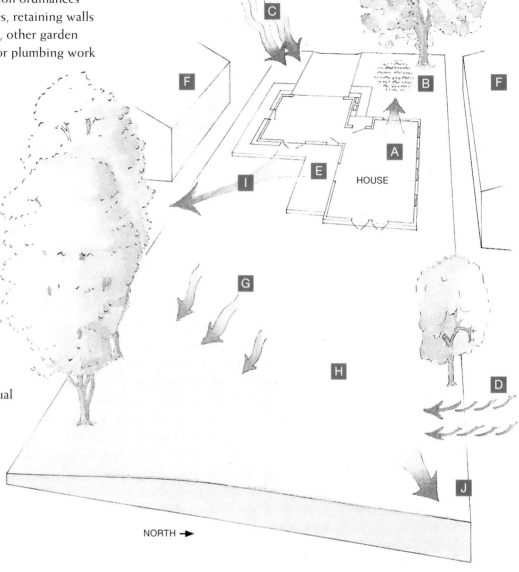

NORTH →

analyzing your property

A front view from the living room is of noisy street traffic, passersby, and parked cars.

B damp soil can limit plant choices.

C, **D** warm winds in summer are from the southwest (C), and winter winds blow from the north (D).

E concrete patio reflects heat into the home and is too small for entertaining.

F neighbors' homes are close to the property line, thus limiting privacy.

G gently sloping land and existing trees could be incorporated into the garden design.

H open, sunny areas in the rear and in the south side yard offer space for a swimming pool or for sun-loving plants.

I, **J** rear views from the patio are pleasant in one direction (I) but unpleasant in another (J).

using bubble diagrams

Now that you've identified the basic features of your garden, you're ready to put your creativity to work. The first step is site planning—creating and arranging the activity spaces in your garden. Carefully study how all these spaces relate to the rooms inside your house and try to plan the outdoor activity spaces near their indoor counterparts. For example, if you have young children, site their outdoor play space near a room in the house where you spend a lot of time, so that you can keep an eye on them. Organize vegetable and herb gardens near the kitchen, if possible, to make an easy chore of bringing the harvest to the table. Decide whether

some areas of the garden should serve multiple functions—for example, whether a sheltered walkway could include a composting area.

Look at your entire garden and lay out spaces that will flow logically and easily from one to the other. For instance, plan a path that won't require you to walk through a work area or past the trash cans to get from a sitting area to the swimming pool. Settle on an arrangement of planted areas that allows you to group plants according to their irrigation needs. As you sketch, you'll begin to make general decisions about the plants and structures you'll need and where they should go. Even if you don't use bubble

If a swimming pool is a part of your plan, consider sun exposure and wind patterns. Optimum placement can extend annual use of the pool by weeks or months.

Use bubble diagrams to try various sizes and shapes of spaces—both what you need and what you'd like.

planning to help you mock up some designs, refer frequently to your base map to remind yourself of site features and conditions.

bubble diagrams
Begin your landscape plan by making bubble diagrams. Known in some quarters less formally as "doodling," bubble diagrams are an essential step used by all professionals.

Bubble diagrams are quick studies drawn on tracing paper over the base map you've made of your property (pages 176–177). Each bubble (actually a rough oval, square, or circle) should represent a particular activity or outdoor space that you hope to incorporate into your design, and each should be approximately the size and shape needed. You can even make the bubbles different colors to distinguish them from each other—such as green for planting areas, blue for a pool, and brown for decks and patios.

Let the bubbles overlap where activity spaces will merge. Where spaces need to be separated, draw a line to suggest a screen or barrier. Simple cross-hatching can designate areas that need overhead protection from the sun. Show steps as sets of parallel lines and roughly indicate entrances to your house or front yard.

Bubble diagrams are helpful to amateurs because by oversimplification they rule out minor details that get in the way of the basic plan. They do not have the serious aspect of a full-on landscape plan. They are experiments in approach. They allow comparisons.

Sketch several versions, considering with each one the microclimates, views, and existing features. Note how well the placement of activities in each diagram takes advantage of the warm spots and shady areas in your garden. Look for smooth transitions from one space to the next and address practical issues by including spaces for work, storage, and service areas.

After you've completed several diagrams, lay them out and compare the arrangements, then settle on the one that will form the basis for your final design.

making the most of microclimates

In planning your landscape, consider the climate and weather in both your region and your own yard. The sun's path and angle, the seasons, and the wind patterns around your property all affect opportunities for outdoor living, the choice and placement of plants, and the overall design of the landscape.

Tender plants freeze in one garden, while the same plants thrive in a yard just a block away. A ground cover blooms heavily in the sun but is thin and wan a few feet away in the shade. Microclimates are responsible. Most gardens have areas that are a little warmer or cooler, wetter or drier than others. Microclimates are created by a combination of factors, including sun angle, wind direction, and the site's exposure and topography.

air temperature and movement

Because warm air rises and cold air sinks, cool air tends to pool in low places and back up behind obstacles, such as hedges and houses, creating frost pockets. Slopes are the last spots to freeze, because cold air constantly drains off them, mixing with nearby warmer air as it flows. Flat areas cool off quickly as heat radiates upward, especially during nights when the air is still and the sky is clear. Any barrier overhead slows this heat loss.

If you check your garden on a morning when the temperature reach just barely to freezing (32 degrees F or 0 degrees C), you will probably be able to see where frost has collected first. Keep tender plantings away from those areas or provide the plants with extra frost protection.

Wind can also be a factor. During the day, heated air rises, pulling in surrounding cooler air. At night, as the land cools off, airflow is reversed. Gardens near the ocean generally lie in the path of winds. If you live at the base of a canyon, the effects can be even more pronounced, leading to wind tunnels and strong breezes.

structural influences

Keep in mind that structures and materials influence the microclimates on your property. The presence of water—a swimming pool, pond, or other water feature—moderates the air temperature. Certain hardscape materials reflect sun and heat better than others. Light-colored masonry paving and walls spread sun and heat and can be uncomfortably bright, while wooden surfaces are a little cooler. On the other hand, dark materials, such as asphalt, will retain heat even after sundown. Plants and buildings filter or block wind.

cold-air pockets

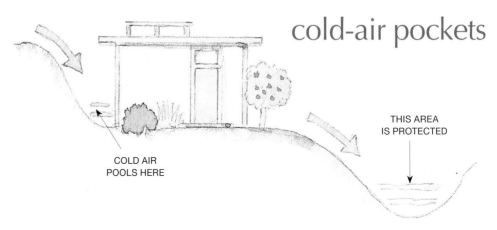

COLD AIR
POOLS HERE

THIS AREA
IS PROTECTED

sun angles

SUMMER SUN ANGLE

WINTER SUN ANGLE

sun and shade

In summer in the northern hemisphere, the sun rises in the northeast, arcs high across the southern sky, and sets in the evening to the northwest. This long passage means extra hours of daylight. By contrast, the winter sun rises in the southeast, passes low across the southern sky, and sets to the southwest. Days are much shorter.

The shifting sun angle means longer shadows in winter, more of your landscape in shade during the dormant season, and more of it in the sun when plants are growing. The pattern of sun and shade also varies depending on the time of day. The least shade is at noon, when the sun is highest.

exposure

In the northern hemisphere, slopes that drop to the south or southwest receive more sunlight and more heat than those that drop to the north or northeast. Similarly, walls that run east-west reflect more heat and sunlight onto plants from their south sides. Walls that run north-south will reflect more heat onto plants growing on their west sides, while the east side of a wall on the north-south axis is much cooler than normal for your area. While these varying exposures often determine why plants succeed or fail, they always dictate differences in care. For example, in sunny areas the soil dries out faster and plants will need more frequent watering.

shadows change with seasons

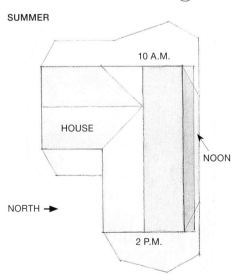

SUMMER

10 A.M.

HOUSE

NOON

NORTH →

2 P.M.

In summer, only those areas immediately beside the house are shaded. Note how features of the house, such as the roof, affect the shadows.

Winter shadows are much longer and can shift dramatically within a few hours. Compare the shadow cast at noon to that cast at 2 p.m.

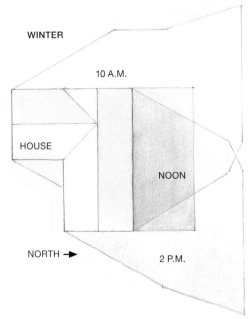

WINTER

10 A.M.

HOUSE

NOON

NORTH →

2 P.M.

making a final plan

When your experiments with bubble diagrams (see pages 178–179) have resulted in a rough sketch, lay a clean sheet of tracing paper on top of it. On this sheet, begin drawing in the various elements of the final design: hard-surfaced areas, walls or hedges, arbors or trees for shelter, gardening spaces, and perhaps a pool, hot tub, potting table, compost pile, or dog run. Rough at first, this schematic drawing will take shape as you continue.

At this point, keep in mind two tricks of the professional designer. Work with clear, simple shapes and relate those shapes to the lines of your house. Repeating a familiar shape brings simplicity and order to the design, unifying beds, borders, paving, walls, arbors, and other features. To add interest, vary the sizes of the shapes you work with and allow them to overlap or interlock. But don't use too many little shapes or you'll end up with a very busy design.

working with grids

After playing with simple geometric patterns, you may feel that a little more variety is necessary. A curving line may be needed to connect two rectangular spaces, or a diagonal line may emphasize the longest dimension in a small garden. As you become more adventurous in your design, you may find it easier to work with a grid module (4, 5, or 6 feet on a side) repeated over and over, like the squares on a checkerboard or the bricks in a wall. Fit the garden's structures and plantings to the dimensions of that module, allowing some elements to intersect or interlock with each other while letting others split a module in half. Also use the dimension of one or two modules to form the radius for a curved line.

The grid system speeds the decision-making process as you determine the dimensions of decks, pathways, and planting beds. It also allows you to quickly calculate quantities for paving, decking, or soil amendments, and it simplifies do-it-yourself installation by letting you pave, pour, or plow only one module at a time.

visualizing a grid

A Connect the garden to the architecture of your house with grid lines that run out to the landscape from major features of the house. Here, lines marking the doorways, windows, and corners of wings have been drawn on the garden plan. Placing various features in relationship to this grid, such as flowerbeds, paved terraces, and pools, lends a sense of organization and continuity to the garden.

one landscape four ways

B – **E** These simple plans were created for the same basic lot using one of four different geometric shapes—circle, rectangle, triangle, or square—to guide the design. Each design presents a similar arrangement of paved terrace, small lawn area, and planting beds with a mix of ground covers, shrubs, and trees. The repetition of a different geometric shape gives each design a distinct character, but all share a contemporary feeling.

To follow this approach in your own landscape, select a shape that appeals to you and use it for the largest element in your design—perhaps the terrace, lawn area, or swimming pool. Repeat the shape in smaller elements, such as the flowerbeds, vegetable garden, and pond. Shapes that emphasize the diagonal—offset squares or triangles—make a garden appear larger. Long rectangles or circles, especially when symmetrically placed, appear more formal. Whatever shape you use, play with the alignment and position of elements in a symmetrical or asymmetrical arrangement. Eventually, you'll settle on a balance that pleases you.

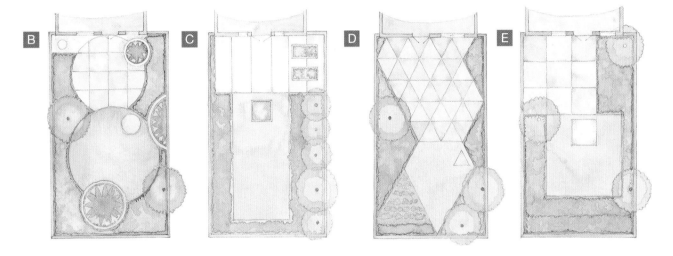

three plans for a rectangular lot

F – **H** These gardens use the simple 5-by-5-foot grid to show very different design solutions for the same rectangular property. Garden **F** incorporates a large overhead trellis or arbor to shade a portion of the paved terrace, while an L-shaped fence and planting bed screen a vegetable garden, compost area, and work space from view. In contrast, garden **G** allows more room for a sweeping lawn, which is backed by a curving line of trees to enclose the garden. A small round pond echoes the curve of the lawn. Garden **H** places a bold circular lawn just off-center, almost surrounded by a paved surface of varying width.

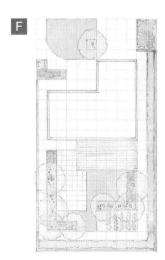

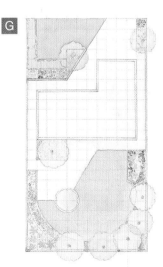

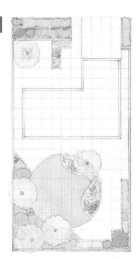

working with odd shapes

Don't be concerned if your property doesn't resemble the simple rectangle shown in the previous pages. Many properties, because of topography or the street pattern, have an irregular shape or are carved out of uneven terrain. A cul-de-sac subdivision, for example, results in pie-shaped lots with minimal street frontage and plenty of private backyard space, while in some older communities, deep, narrow lots are common.

Sloping lots present a different set of challenges than those on flat ground (see pages 186–187). Whatever your lot's size and shape, the tips and techniques described here will help you make the most of it.

Before you get carried away with the excitement of creating a whole new garden, now is a good time to consider the time, effort, and financial implications of your decisions. Like many homeowners, you may want to approach the landscaping process in stages. If so, identify features you'd like to have right away and those that can be added as time and money allow.

BELOW LEFT: By setting the pavers diagonally relative to the length of the lot, the designer has made this garden seem less narrow.

BELOW RIGHT: Along with low, sheared hedges, steps with broad landings create small but distinct spaces.

three lots, three solutions

Rarely is anyone blessed with a space and situation for which the design solution is obvious. It's always a matter of identifying a property's pluses and minuses followed by problem solving. Good solutions seem obvious only later, after all the work is done. Here are three hypothetical gardens, their design obstacles, and the solutions reached.

A avoid the feel of a bowling alley in a long space by dividing the area into smaller units; then focus each space on a different function. In this plan, a hedge separates a large dining terrace from a secluded bedroom retreat and from the swimming pool. The pool terrace then merges into a gravel-paved herb garden, and behind the pool house is a small vegetable patch with a work area under the arbor.

B don't be discouraged by a small lot. Make it seem larger by concealing the property line with dense shrubbery, emphasizing long diagonal lines, and hiding parts of the garden. Here, the focal point at the end of the angled deck is a bench that looks toward a curved bench beyond the pond, not visible from the main deck. A tall, angled hedge screens a vegetable garden, and the fences support berries and vines.

C opportunities abound in this lot with plenty of room for a series of different garden areas. Terracing the gentle slope of the fenced side yard makes space for vegetable, herb, and cutting gardens. A continuous patio area that unites all parts of the garden widens at the rear to provide space for entertaining. A small lawn nestles into one corner, and tucked into the narrow side yard is a sitting area.

A LONG, NARROW LOT

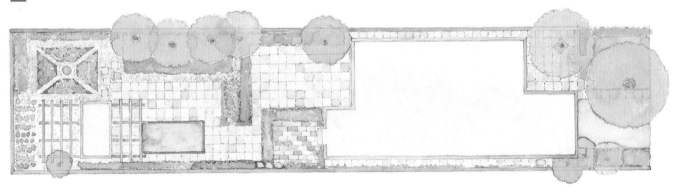

B SMALL LOT

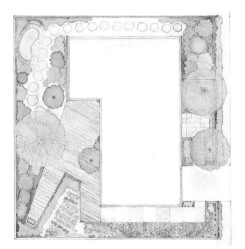

C IRREGULAR LOT

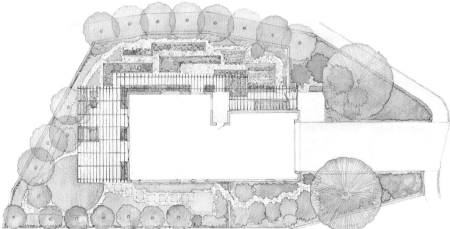

making the most of slopes

There's a good reason why real estate agents are eager to point out a flat lot when selling a home. The more steeply sloped a lot is, the less usable space it has. But that doesn't mean you can't turn a potentially negative situation into a positive one.

As the illustrations below demonstrate, how you go about dealing with a hillside depends on how much slope you have. A slightly sloped lot is actually advantageous because it's easy to direct rainwater away from the house and your usable space is almost the same as with a flat lot.

Steeply sloped lots, however, present a challenge. Creating level, usable spaces—such as lawns, play areas, a pool, and garden beds—requires liberal use of retaining walls. Construction costs can be considerable. An easier and less expensive alternative is to dedicate steep slopes to native vegetation that controls erosion, maintains privacy, and needs little upkeep. Forget about growing grass on steep slopes. Mowing on an angle is an easy way to hurt yourself.

RIGHT: A steep, unmowable slope is stabilized by native grasses and perennials.

TOP RIGHT: Contrasting colors of riser and tread make steps easier to navigate.

TOP, FAR RIGHT: The hidden entry here is signaled by the arbor.

BOTTOM RIGHT: Terraced plantings are linked by grass-covered paths.

THREE DEGREES OF SLOPE

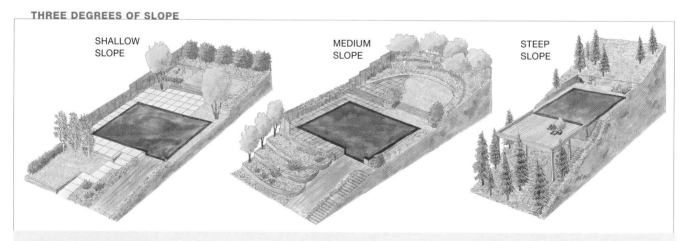

SHALLOW SLOPE

MEDIUM SLOPE

STEEP SLOPE

SHALLOW SLOPE To create a level lawn area in front, the grade has been raised at the street and lowered in front of the house. Ground cover has been planted on the slopes edging the driveway and entrance walk. In the backyard, terraces with steps between them create level areas for a lawn, play yard, and planting beds.

MEDIUM SLOPE Low retaining walls in front create five levels, while four levels solve the slope problem in the backyard. The lawn has a gentle slope, so the mower need not be lifted or pulled up and down steps.

STEEP SLOPE The simplest and least expensive way to create level space on a steep lot is to build a deck. Planting to bring foliage to deck height lessens your feeling of being perched above ground level.

learning from the pros
THESE ARE SIMPLE, PROVEN TECHNIQUES

LIKE ARTISTS AND INTERIOR DESIGNERS, LANDSCAPE PROFESSIONALS WORK WITH SEVERAL BASIC design techniques and principles to influence the way gardens are perceived and experienced. These principles apply to shaping and defining large spaces, designing plant compositions, and even placing cherished ornaments within a garden to best effect.

Two repeating elements—conical arborvitae and a row of white peonies—create visual unity in this formal garden.

unity is the guiding principle for a well-designed landscape. The plants, structures, and decorative objects all share one style and character, and all work together to convey the mood of the garden. There's contrast and drama, yet no element overwhelms or stands out too much. Instead, each component complements the others.

repetition of elements, such as plants, construction materials, shapes, and even colors serves to unify the look by forcing the eye to recognize similarities. Repetition organizes the garden and keeps it from being a hodgepodge. All landscape elements should be in proportion to the rest of the garden and to the size of the house and property.

TOP LEFT: The buff color of the flagstone stepping-stones is repeated here in the tan stalks of grass.

TOP RIGHT: Mass plantings of one type of plant, such as these hostas, are another way to create unity in a garden.

ABOVE: The yellow-pink color of the poolside paving is accented by the similarly toned perennials. The resulting landscape with its harmony of color gains a sense of unity.

focal points

A key design device exploited routinely by landscape professionals is the focal point. Plants or objects used as focal points create special interest for their size, shape, or color. Stra-tegically positioned, a focal point draws the eye through the garden, then gives it a place to rest. A favorite ornament or sculpture can make a focal point. So can a brightly painted garden chair or an architectural feature like a lattice screen. In a formal garden, place your focal point at the end of an axis, perhaps the centerline of a view or walk. Elsewhere, place it on the inside curve of a path or along some other line.

The teal lattice backdrop and purple chairs create a focal point, something that draws attention and brings order to the overall scene.

TOP: A focal point, such as this slightly raised jar positioned at the end of a path, draws the eye by its placement and distinction.

ABOVE LEFT: Centered between the two halves of this entry is the front door, which is also the focal point.

ABOVE RIGHT: This water feature is the garden's focal point, whether surrounded by blooming perennials in midsummer or front and center in winter when the garden is bare. The salvaged concrete planter was sealed to make it watertight, and holes were drilled in the three spherical finials by a local stone company to allow plumbing.

expert design tricks

In addition to basic design principles, professionals have an array of tools at their disposal that rely upon the fundamentals of human perception. These techniques help them overcome typical challenges or simply make the garden more attractive and livable.

An effective design draws you into the scene. For example, a large statue or a garden bench partially obscured by foliage extends a subtle but irresistible invitation to take a closer look. Likewise, if a splash of water can be heard but not seen, it will seem imperative

Drawing bold lines between grades, as the granite steps do here, serves to make both levels feel larger.

to discover its source. A change in the garden's elevation—even just a few steps up—makes a small garden feel larger by suggesting there is more to be explored at the top of the steps. Likewise, a curving path with no end in sight creates the illusion that there is more space beyond the bend.

The power of color to enhance a garden's look and feel cannot be overstated. Light colors tend to recede from the eye, creating an illusion of greater distance. Bold, saturated colors are attention getters and hence space definers. Red geraniums and orange cannas pack a strong visual punch, while the cool blues of delphinium and butterfly bush are soothing. White has its own special qualities. It offers a crisp, clean contrast to greenery during the day, and it glows with reflected moonlight at night. There's good reason white-variegated hostas and white-flowered astilbe are planted to brighten dark, shady corners.

BELOW LEFT: Planting a tree, a relatively large feature, in the foreground and smaller ones farther back creates the illusion of greater depth.

BELOW RIGHT: Wide steps and a white arch imply a more distant part of the garden, but in fact the garden ends at the hemlock hedge just beyond the arch.

BOTTOM: Concealing part of the garden makes a small space feel larger. Here, winding paths lead past a bed of colorful conifers that hide a granite basin fountain.

designing structures

Focus next on creating structure in your garden, defining spaces with horizontal and vertical planes, and establishing privacy.

enclosing your landscape

Just as the rooms in your house have walls and ceilings to give them form and function, so should the space in your landscape be designed with enclosing fences, walls, or hedges and with ceilings of tree canopies, arbors, or awnings.

walls and fences These serve several functions in a landscape. They can shade areas that are overly warm or reduce the chilling effects of strong winds. They can collect the sun's rays to warm a cozy spot or direct cooling breezes to moderate the temperature. A well-placed fence or wall can screen unsightly views while framing those you wish to enjoy. It can also enhance your feeling of privacy by blocking a neighbor's view into your landscape. Low walls, perhaps with built-in benches, define but don't confine a garden space. Both green and nonliving walls add beauty and expand the gardening space, and the latter can become green by supporting climbing plants.

ceilings and canopies Although it may seem odd to consider ceilings or roofs outdoors, they both create comfortable and functional spaces in a landscape. While a swimming pool or vegetable garden should have only the sky for a cover, other, more intimate activities benefit from overheads. Sitting and dining areas, in particular, need overhanging tree branches, arbors, or vines on taut wires to block sunlight.

Rain won't interrupt an otherwise perfect day if your dining terrace has a solid roof over it. A partial or retractable cover is ideal where the climate can change measurably in one day or through the seasons. Carefully placed, a

tree or an overhead structure can screen out a tall building nearby or block views from a neighbor's second-story windows into your private garden. An overhead can also support a collection of hanging potted plants, thereby increasing gardening space.

plants versus structures Structures such as walls, fences, and overheads are generally more expensive than hedges, shrub borders, or vines on trellises, but you should balance the additional cost against how quickly you want your landscape to take shape. Plants usually take several years to achieve as much screening and enclosure as a fence, and trees may take 10 years or more to provide the shade created by an arbor built in a weekend. If neither money nor time is an object, space may be. Hedges take up more room than a 6-inch-thick fence.

choosing enclosures

A A fence around the rear and side yards defines the garden's boundaries while supporting vertical plantings such as vines, espaliers, or hanging pots. To unify the garden with a common backdrop, maintain the same fence design throughout. Choose a material that suits your house's architecture.

B Extending the fence into the front yard creates a small, private sitting area next to the living room. Use the inside wall for a collection of interesting sculptures or hanging baskets filled with annuals. The large native oak provides a generous canopy overhead.

C Hedges and trellises along the property line are generally not subject to zoning restrictions. Here, a simple wire trellis for vines extends above the maximum fence height to increase privacy and the sense of enclosure. Citrus trees form a tall, unsheared hedge for the same purpose.

canopies and barriers

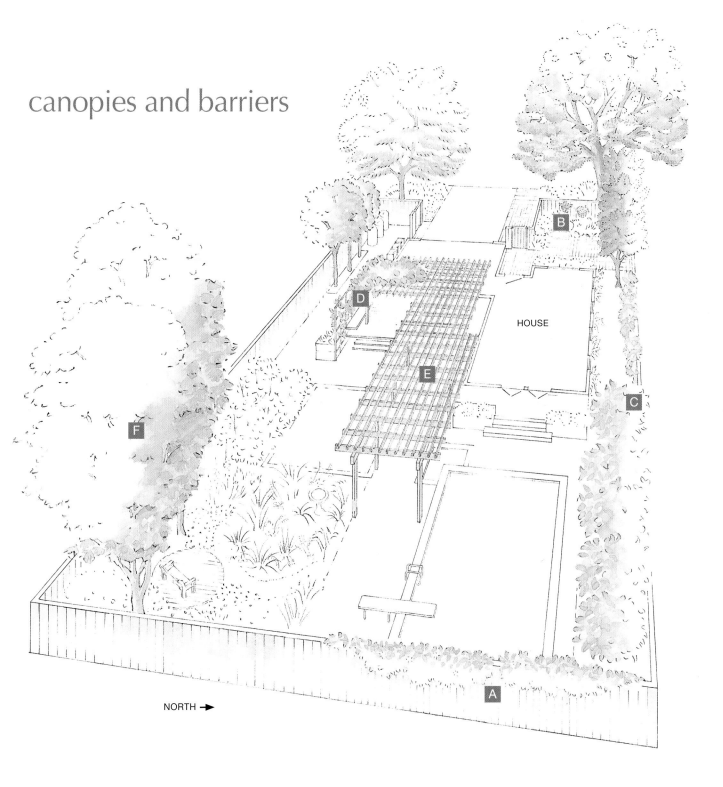

HOUSE

NORTH ➔

D Lattice screen along the south side of the main deck provides some seclusion from neighbors as well as a support for flowering vines. Its open structure allows cooling breezes to flow through.

E An arbor covering the deck protects people and plants from the heat of the

midday sun. The arbor's wooden crosspieces run from east to west to provide maximum shading.

F Existing deciduous trees create a shady roof over the tiny, wild garden retreat. Bare branches allow warming sunlight through in winter, encouraging year-round use.

outdoor flooring

Just as indoor floors serve many purposes, those in a landscape also meet different needs. The most obvious is as a surface for walking, playing, or placing furniture. Garden floors can also modify the climate. A large concrete slab will reflect the sun's heat into windows and under arbors, while dark pavement, such as asphalt, will collect heat during the day and release it at night. In contrast, a lush ground cover will reduce the air temperature by several degrees. Garden floors can be decorative as well as functional, providing an unbroken carpet of green foliage or an elaborate planting of brightly colored flowering plants. They also play a protective role, covering the soil and preventing erosion caused by rain and wind.

flooring materials

Outdoor floors are normally much more varied in character than those indoors. They can be permeable, or paved to make them impervious to water. In high-traffic areas, firm surfaces of concrete slabs, brick, block, or stone can be laid on sand or mortar. Wood is a serviceable material, particularly when raised above ground level as a deck. More flexible, water permeable materials able to handle fairly heavy traffic include gravel and crushed stone in varying grades, organic mulches of redwood bark, and sawn tree rounds.

living surfaces

Where a sports or play area calls for a soft but sturdy cushionlike floor, a turfgrass lawn is about the only solution. These grasses tolerate the often intense activity of children and athletes. To keep a well-used lawn in top condition, however, you'll need to schedule regular maintenance. Although other living ground covers will tolerate a small amount of foot traffic, most will not take more than occasional wear.

Turfgrasses most commonly used in lawns originated in regions with steady moisture, in either northern Europe or the subtropics. Most respond poorly to arid climates without tremendous amounts of water, which is often a limited resource. Give serious thought to the purpose of the lawn you are considering. If it is not to be used as an activity surface, investigate other ground covers or surfaces that will conserve water better than common turfgrasses.

choosing surfaces

A A main deck, raised above ground level, offers a generous and firm surface for outdoor entertaining. It serves well for games, parties, cooking, and simple relaxation.

B A tiny deck in a wild garden marks a quiet retreat, with just enough space for two or three chairs. But it is still within view of the pool and main deck. Rough wood for its surface suits the rustic corner.

C A flat lawn of dwarf tall fescue offers a soft surface for you to relax in the sun, for kids to play, or for a dog to cavort. It also serves as a low foreground to both the rose garden and the wild garden.

D A pool deck offers nonskid footing and has an easy-to-clean surface. It is broad enough for sunbathing without seeming to dominate the rear of the yard.

E A paved side yard is wide enough for moving equipment in and out of the rear yard. A general utility area, the smooth pavement is easy to keep clean—a desirable feature, especially around the compost pile and the potting table.

F A graveled side yard allows passage between the front courtyard and the rear

planting and paving

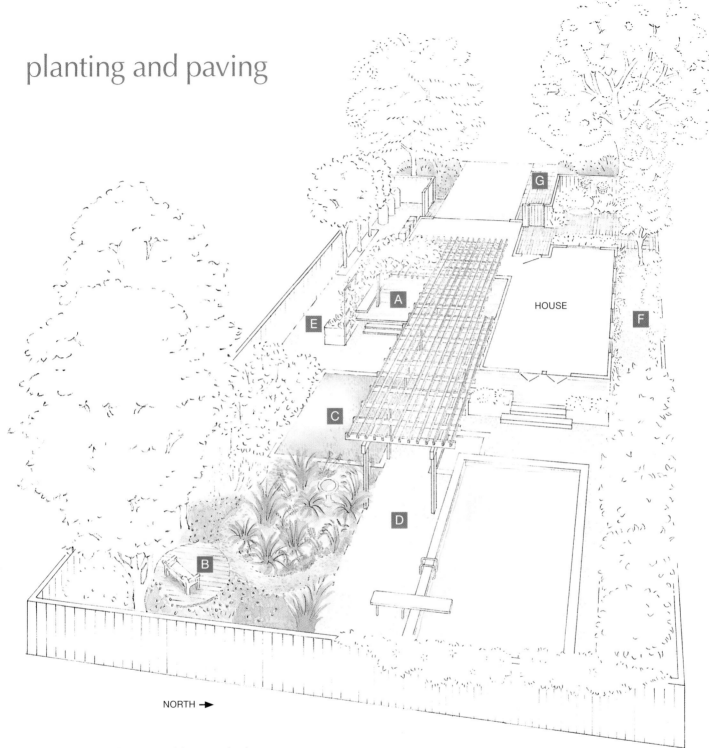

NORTH →

HOUSE

yard. Informal plantings of ferns and other shade-loving plants thrive here, as do vines that screen the bedroom windows.

G Brick paving in front makes a roomy entrance walk that extends into the private courtyard. Safe and stable in all weather conditions, the small pavers make the walk and courtyard appear bigger than they are.

moving from ideas to reality

CHECK YOUR PLAN BEFORE PUTTING SHOVEL TO SOIL

WHETHER YOU'VE COMPLETED YOUR GARDEN DESIGN YOURSELF OR HAVE A PROFESSIONALLY rendered landscape plan, the next step is to translate the design to your property. If you're having difficulty visualizing the finished landscape or can't quite decide on the specifics of certain elements, you may wish to mock up the design on your property. Seeing an approximation of the layout in the form of stakes, strings, and markings may help you determine the exact dimensions necessary for some features, such as decks, terraces, and walks. Even if you feel your paper plan is final, be prepared to make some adjustments as you lay out the design on your site, until the arrangement of spaces and elements feels just right.

Use landscape spray paint to mark out the elements of your new landscape. Here, a designer is marking out the shape of a new pond and waterfall.

Use any convenient method to stake out your design. The choice will likely depend on which features predominate: straight lines or curving lines, geometric forms or free forms. Materials that you have on hand or that can be found at Lowe's will work, such as bamboo or wooden stakes; string, clothesline, or garden hose; and lime or powdered gypsum.

Live with your design layout for a few days before beginning construction. Walk

through and sit in your mock garden to be sure it provides the spaces, comfortable circulation paths, and garden areas that suit your interests and the time you have to spend maintaining them.

Before construction, other mock-up techniques are also handy. Use stakes to mark an area of concrete to be poured, and colored powder to show the true boundaries of planting areas in borders and beds. Use a hose to outline the shape of a pathway.

TOP LEFT: Sanking a flexible garden hose on the ground is a convenient way to test the size and shape of planned elements, especially ones with curved lines.

TOP RIGHT: Once a curved edge is established, use land-scape spray paint to mark the location.

ABOVE LEFT: Use stakes and string to test the height of a new deck. Use newspaper or cardboard on the ground to represent the deck.

ABOVE RIGHT: Posts or tall stakes offer a handy way to test the height of a proposed fence or hedge. By checking at various times of day, you can also see shade patterns.

laying the foundation

BEGIN DESIGNING YOUR LANDSCAPE BY MAKING DECISIONS about the big things, like spaces and how to use them, color schemes, styles, materials, and plants. But before the digging starts, you'll also need to confront the mundane, and near the top of that list is your garden's plumbing: grading, drainage, and irrigation.

The majority of landscapes are managed without any grading beyond what the home builder has left. But there are situations in which reshaping the land is the one essential step, whether it's to ensure proper drainage or for aesthetic reasons.

Irrigation systems may seem an extra luxury, especially if you live where summer rains are usually sufficient for most plants. But considered as insurance for your plants and as a time saver for you, the investment begins to make a lot more sense. Moreover, well-planned irrigation is far more water-efficient, an increasingly important consideration.

getting started
WORKING WITH CODES, CONTRACTORS, AND RENTAL YARDS

BEFORE YOUR PLANS ARE TOO FAR ALONG, CONSULT THE LOCAL BUILDING DEPARTMENT FOR ANY legal restrictions. These include applying for a building permit and complying with building codes. Also be aware of zoning ordinances, which may govern other regulations, such as whether a deck can be built and where.

building permits Before you put shovel to soil, be sure to obtain any needed permits. Have the building department check the plans before construction begins, to ensure that you don't get off to a substandard start. Negligence may come back to haunt you. Officials can fine you and require you to bring an illegally built structure up to standard or dismantle it entirely.

building codes Requirements vary by region. Building codes set minimum safety standards for materials and construction techniques: depth of footings, sizes of beams, and proper fastening methods, for example. Codes help ensure that any structures you build will be well made and safe for your family and any future owners of the property.

zoning ordinances These municipal regulations restrict the height of residential buildings, limit the proportion of a lot that structures of any kind may cover, specify how close to the property lines you can build, and, in some areas, even stipulate architectural design standards.

variances If the zoning department rejects your plans, you can apply for a variance. In that case, it becomes your task to prove to the department that adhering to the zoning requirements would create "undue hardship" and that the structure you want to build will not negatively affect neighbors or the community. If you present your case confidently and convincingly, you will probably be allowed to build.

BUILDING A GOOD WORKING RELATIONSHIP

- Search for a contractor by collecting recommendations from friends and neighbors who are satisfied clients.
- Before you meet with a contractor, write down all your questions.
- If a magazine or brochure photograph captures what you're aiming for, take it to the meeting.
- Have some idea of your budget, both for consultations and for the entire project. Keep in mind that professional help need not be costly, especially if you hire on a short-term basis.
- Be as precise as you can about your expectations.
- Look for evidence that the contractor listens carefully to your ideas and respects your needs.
- Ask for references so you can see some of the person's work and talk to former clients.

Draft and sign a written contract with any landscape professional. You'll both be protected if the contract is specific, so make sure it includes the following:

THE PROJECT AND PARTICIPANTS Include a general description of the project, its location, and the names and addresses of both you and the professional.

CONSTRUCTION MATERIALS Identify the grade of materials, the quality of fasteners, and, in the case of lumber, the species and grade. Indicate the brand and model number of any accessories, such as lighting systems. Avoid the clause "or equal," which will allow for substitution of potentially inferior materials.

WORK TO BE PERFORMED Determine with your professional all major tasks required, from preliminary grading through planting and watering.

TIME SCHEDULE The contract should include both start and completion dates.

METHOD OF PAYMENT Payments are usually made in installments as phases of work are completed. If possible, insist on a fixed-price bid, although some contractors want a fee based on a percentage of labor and materials costs. Final payment is withheld until the job receives its final inspection and all liens are cleared.

WAIVER OF LIENS If subcontractors aren't paid for materials or services delivered to your home, in some states they can place a mechanic's lien on your property, tying up the title. Protect yourself with a waiver of liens, signed by the general contractor, subcontractors, and major materials suppliers.

EXHIBIT A It's a good idea to attach a copy of the property's site plan, drawn to scale.

---

deeds Your property deed can also restrict the project's design, construction, or location. Review the deed carefully, checking for easements, architectural restrictions, and other limitations.

Wet concrete and mortar are caustic to the skin, so wear heavy rubber gloves and tuck sleeves into them. If you must walk in the concrete to finish it off, wear knee-high rubber boots.

working safely

Although the garden is not generally a hazardous place, any time you climb a ladder, pick up a tool, or start moving heavy materials, you can injure yourself or someone else. If you plan to carry out any of the landscape projects shown in this book, follow the guidelines given here.

For protection from flying particles of dust or rock when you are cutting stone or brick, wear safety goggles or a full face mask. Look for goggles that fit comfortably, are fog-free, and are made of scratch-resistant,

shatterproof plastic. Portland cement irritates the eyes, nose, and mouth, so wear a dust mask when mixing concrete.

When working with lumber, protect your hands from wood splinters with all-leather or leather-reinforced work gloves. If you're sanding wood, wear a disposable painter's mask. For work with solvents, finishes, or adhesives, wear disposable rubber or plastic gloves. If you're using any rental equipment, ask the rental company's staff about safe operation first and read printed instructions carefully.

rental-yard savvy

Rental companies offer a wide range of specialized tools, allowing you to tackle projects you couldn't otherwise.

Don't rent more elaborate tools than you can safely handle. Rental companies will review the tools' proper operation, but they will assume you're capable and won't prevent you from renting any kind of equipment.

If you don't have a truck or a trailer hitch on your car, you may need large equipment delivered. Most rental yards will deliver and pick up tools for a fee—$50 is typical.

Expect to pay about $65 a day for a heavy garden tiller and $200 for a trencher.

To make sure the process goes well, assemble everything you need to complete the job. If you have to stop work and run out for supplies, you may not finish on time.

grading
RESHAPING THE LAND

MOVING SOIL FROM ONE PLACE TO ANOTHER SO IT'S AT THE PROPER HEIGHT AND SLOPE ENSURES adequate drainage. More specifically, grading adds contours to flat landscapes and provides the necessary foundation for walks and patios.

Start with a plan, taking into account drainage and any paving you're adding. If your house isn't connected to a sewer, locate the septic tank and drainage field.

three stages of grading

The work of grading progresses hand in hand with the other aspects of installing your landscape. The first step, rough grading, brings the areas of your yard to the desired finished level. Then, after the completion of underground systems and any construction projects, you'll need to reestablish the rough grade. The final stage is the finish grading.

rough grading The goal is to remove or add enough soil in each area of your lot to bring the surface to the height and slope you want. Rough grading can include reshaping the land and making mounds and berms, as well as digging foundations for patios and walks. Be advised, though, that it is always preferable to install paving of any kind on firm, undisturbed soil. Fill soil, no matter how carefully tamped, will settle.

Start by eliminating high and low spots. Save the soil you remove in two piles—one for topsoil (the top 2 to 6 inches) and the

The layer of crushed stone being spread here will form the base for pavers. The front-end loader makes moving the heavy material much faster.

other for subsoil—so that it can be reused. Then dig foundations for patios, walls, and other paving. You may be able to use the soil from these excavations as fill in other areas. After the rough grading is complete, tamp the soil. Also tamp each time you add a layer to a deeply filled area.

periodically reestablishing the rough grade You'll probably need to do this several times while you're installing your landscape. For example, you may have to fill trenches dug for underground systems or low spots caused by the movement of heavy equipment. Mound the soil over the trench and tamp it firmly until it's at the same level as the soil around it.

finish grading This is the last step after construction work is done, underground systems are installed, and the rough grade has been reestablished. The goal is to make the surface smooth enough for planting.

making the grade

You need a reliable method to ensure that you get the rough grade you need. Estimate the grade visually or, for greater accuracy, use a carpenter's level.

estimating visually Make sure the grade slopes away from structures and toward areas where water can drain away quickly. Establish the finish grade around permanent structures 6 inches below the finish elevation of the structure. Also check for high and low spots on the lawn and any other areas that require an even surface.

using a carpenter's level Set the level on an 8-foot-long 2 by 4 placed on the ground. With a tape measure, determine how far you have to raise one end of the board to center the bubble in the level. That will give you a rough idea of how much the ground slopes. A drop of ¾ inch over 8 feet is sufficient in most situations for adequate drainage.

grading a slope

If your property slopes so steeply that it remains unstable and virtually useless, consider constructing one or a series of retaining walls. The safest place to build a wall is at the bottom of a gentle slope, if space permits; fill behind it with soil. That way you won't disturb the stability of the soil. Otherwise the hill can be held either with a single high wall or with a series of low retaining walls that form terraces. All three options are shown below.

Whenever terracing or a high retaining wall is needed, contact an engineer or a landscape architect who can foresee problems, who is familiar with legal requirements, and who can calculate the strength needed.

LOWE'S QUICK TIP

Before you begin any excavation, check for underground utilities. The North American One Call Referral Service at (888) 258-0808 connects you to a national directory of utility companies.

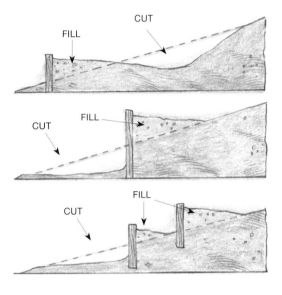

Grading a slope requires cutting and filling. The best solution for a specific situation depends upon the slope's grade, how much space is available, and the planned use.

MOUNDS AND BERMS

Mounds and berms are grading changes that can enhance privacy, reduce noise, deflect wind, and create attractive contours. The chief difference between them is their size. Mounds are small—perhaps just a few feet long and a foot or so tall. Berms can be several yards long and several feet tall.

- Anyone can construct a planting mound, but building a berm usually involves heavy machinery and professional skill. Both mounds and berms require lots of soil, and it's most economical to use dirt from an excavation in your own yard.

- To build a mound, take care that it won't interfere with good drainage channels and that it's back far enough from a patio, deck, or walk so water running off the mound won't flow onto the paving. Remove any sod covering the soil where you want the mound. Break the soil's surface crust before you bring in any new soil. Then spread a layer of soil for the mound and, using a shovel or tiller, mix it with the underlying soil to ensure good drainage. Continue this process as you shape the mound.

- Tamp the soil lightly and smooth the sides with the back of a rake. To prevent erosion, make sure the sides aren't too steep. Plant as you would on any other hillside. (See page 186 for more about landscaping slopes.)

drainage
MANAGING EXCESS WATER

YOU NEED TO PLAN FOR WAYS TO CHANNEL WATER away from your house foundation, patio, driveway, and low-lying garden areas. Drainage is obviously vital in high-rainfall areas. It's also important in arid regions, where you want to retain as much water as possible on the property in order to recharge the groundwater and reduce runoff.

Complex grading and drainage schemes, especially for slopes, are jobs for a professional. But with a shovel and some basic plumbing skills, you can likely handle some smaller tasks. A hypothetical drainage plan for a front yard is shown on the facing page.

choosing materials

Solid drainpipe directs water toward a dry well, storm drain, street, or other low spot where the water can be discharged safely. These plastic pipes may be rigid (typically PVC), or ribbed and flexible. Perforated drainpipe absorbs rising runoff from the areas around it and either channels water to a central point or gradually releases the excess as it travels through the pipe.

What size pipe do you need? The minimum sizes for both vertical pipes (like those for draining a roof) and horizontal pipes (those serving a lawn or patio) depend on three main factors: the square footage of the area to be drained, the pitch of the drainage pipe (you need about 1 inch per 10 feet), and the amount of rainfall expected (figured in terms of the worst 1-hour storm in a 100-year period). Plumbing codes may include charts specifying these values. If all this sounds confusing, check at Lowe's or with a qualified building inspector.

Lowe's carries couplings, elbows, Ys, and Ts that match and link each type of pipe. You'll also find a wide selection of both plastic and concrete drains, catch basins, matching grates, drainage channels, and various kinds of downspout fittings.

laying pipe

Place the pipe in a 12-inch-deep trench (deeper in frost areas), slanting it downward at least 1 inch for every 10 feet. Put coarse gravel or small stones about 2 inches deep in the trench and lay the pipe on top. If you use perforated pipe, lay it with the holes downward so soil won't seep in and clog it. Line the sides of the trench with landscaping fabric and then fill the trench with gravel. Cover the gravel with either soil or river rocks, whichever is more suitable to the site.

Simply laying a long perforated pipe in a trench will solve many drainage problems. To handle heavy runoff, or if there isn't room for a long pipe, have the pipe end in a dry well or drain it into a catch basin (facing page).

DRAINAGE CHANNEL

DOWNSPOUT COUPLER

DRAIN GRATE

CATCH BASIN

a sample drainage scheme

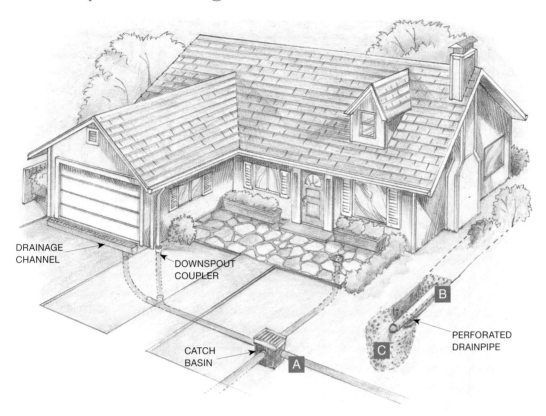

DRAINAGE
CHANNEL

DOWNSPOUT
COUPLER

CATCH
BASIN

A

B

C

PERFORATED
DRAINPIPE

A catch basins drain water from a low-lying area. Dig a hole at the lowest point and set a readymade plastic or concrete box into it (many sizes are available). Set a matching grate on top and dig a sloping trench for a drainpipe to direct water from the basin toward a storm drain (if permitted) or to a dry well.

B drainpipe and gravel-filled trenches are used to catch and deflect water where runoff is light, such as around a patio or swimming pool. Dig the trench 1 to 3 feet deep and 6 to 12 inches wide, depending on the volume of water the trench will have to handle. Fill it with gravel, not with soil.

C dry wells allow water to seep into the ground more quickly than it would into soil. To build a dry well, dig a hole 2 to 4 feet in diameter and at least 3 feet deep. Cover the hole's sides with landscaping fabric. Fill the well with coarse gravel or small rocks, then cover it with an impervious material, such as heavy roofing felt.

CATCH BASIN

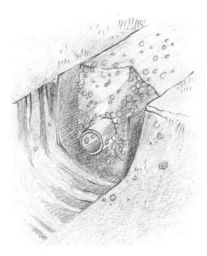

DRAINPIPE AND GRAVEL-FILLED TRENCH

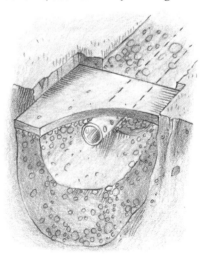

DRY WELL

planning watering systems
HEALTHIER PLANTS, LESS TIME, LESS WATER

WHAT SORT OF WATERING SYSTEM SHOULD YOU HAVE? THE CHOICES RANGE FROM SIMPLE TOOLS for applying water manually to sophisticated options such as an underground sprinkler system connected to soil-moisture and rain sensors, and a timer. Your decision depends upon your climate, the kinds of plants you're growing, your water supply, and your budget.

A cutaway of an underground sprinkler system shows the lateral sprinkler line that connects several sprinklers and the T-fitting that connects an individual sprinkler.

Watering with a hose and a portable sprinkler may be most practical for you, especially if you live where summer rains take care of most watering needs. Lowe's stocks a wide range of garden hoses, nozzles, and sprinklers, and finding the combination that works best for you should be simple. See pages 388–391 for more about basic watering techniques and systems.

However, while watering primarily with hoses and portable sprinklers has the advantage of simplicity, such systems are generally not very precise. It's easy to water either way too much or too little. Plus, this kind of watering takes time—often too much time. If you find yourself needing to either make more efficient use of the water you have or spend much less time spreading it around, you should consider installing a permanent system.

Assuming you're leaning toward a permanent system, the next question is whether to install underground sprinklers, a drip system, or both. The answer is, it depends. Conventional pop-up sprinklers are still the best way to water lawns and very closely spaced plants. Drip systems are optimal for plants that are more widely spaced and for situations that require maximum water efficiency. Following is a simplified explanation for installing an underground sprinkler system. See pages 214–215 for information on installing a drip watering system.

design Planning on paper helps you think the system through, guides you in ordering materials, and serves as a permanent record of where pipes are buried. Begin by gathering information.

You'll need a scale drawing showing all of the parts of your property to which your irrigation system will extend, including where the pipe will be buried and where the timer will be housed. Such a map typically includes at least a part of the house and garage, the driveway, walkways, fences, lawns, planting beds, trees and other large individual plants, outdoor faucets, your house water-service line, and any additional buried pipes (if you plan to trench). If you have a septic tank and leach field, note their locations and dimensions as

well. Measure the water pressure (below) and flow rate and add the information to the plan. Use the base map of your property (see page 176) and incorporate from it other pertinent details.

determine hydro-zones On an overlay of your drawing, such as at left, divide planted areas into hydrozones, which are groups of plants that have similar moisture needs. Take into account exposure, because plants in hot, sunny spots will need more frequent watering than those in cooler, shadier locations.

underground sprinkler systems

In order to purchase the right components for an underground system, you'll need to know the following about your water supply: water pressure in pounds per square inch (psi), and the water flow rate in gallons per minute (gpm). You'll also need to know the type of backflow prevention required by local code. Equipped with this information, you can choose the right equipment for your situation.

water pressure There are two measure-ments of water pressure—working (when the water supply is turned on) and static (when the water supply is shut off). You'll need to know your working water pressure number.

Checking your water pressure requires a pressure gauge. If you can't borrow one from a plumber, you can buy one. The gauge attaches to the outside faucet and provides a pressure reading in pounds per square inch (psi). Make sure all other water faucets (indoors and out) are turned off when you

components of a sprinkler system

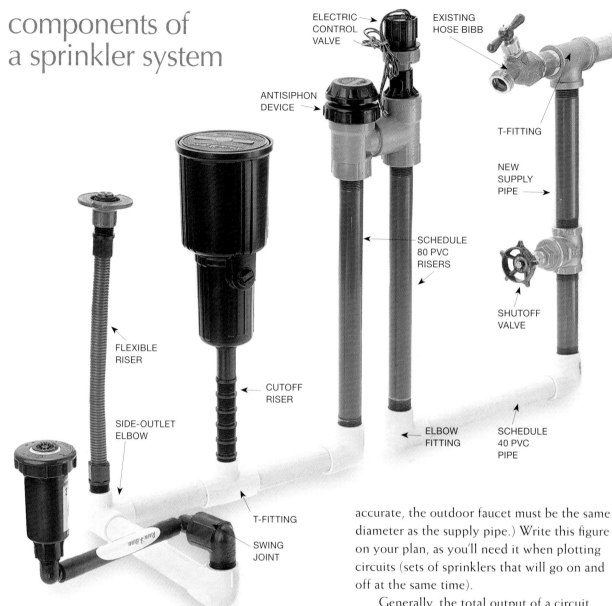

ELECTRIC CONTROL VALVE

EXISTING HOSE BIBB

ANTISIPHON DEVICE

T-FITTING

NEW SUPPLY PIPE

SCHEDULE 80 PVC RISERS

SHUTOFF VALVE

FLEXIBLE RISER

SIDE-OUTLET ELBOW

CUTOFF RISER

ELBOW FITTING

SCHEDULE 40 PVC PIPE

T-FITTING

SWING JOINT

take the reading. Record the psi at each outside faucet location (if you have more than one), taking several readings throughout the day. Use the lowest measure as a conservative basis when calculating sprinkler output.

flow rate The flow rate, the amount of water that moves through pipes in a given period, is measured in gallons per hour (gph) or gallons per minute (gpm). To determine flow rate, count how many seconds an outdoor faucet takes to fill a 5-gallon container. Divide the filled container size—5—by the time in seconds it took to fill it. Multiply this figure by 60 seconds to determine the gpm. (Note that for this method of measuring gpm to be

accurate, the outdoor faucet must be the same diameter as the supply pipe.) Write this figure on your plan, as you'll need it when plotting circuits (sets of sprinklers that will go on and off at the same time).

Generally, the total output of a circuit of sprinklers should not exceed 75 percent of the gpm. Otherwise, the heads won't work properly and household water pressure may dip. If the sprinkler circuit requires a higher flow rate, create several separate circuits, each directed by its own control valve.

valves The system begins at a cold-water service line, which is where you connect a T-fitting (see page 213) and the control valve supply line. Install a new shutoff valve on the new supply pipe (or at the end of the old pipe) so you can shut off the sprinkler system without turning off the water to your house.

The new supply pipe delivers water to control valves, usually valves with integral antisiphon devices. Each valve operates one circuit. Place the valves in a convenient, inconspicuous place, grouping them into what is called a manifold to avoid extra digging and to make operation easier.

In an automated system, low-voltage wires run from each valve to a timer. The timer directs the watering cycle by automatically activating the control valves for the different circuits so that they turn on for a pre-set period.

sprinkler heads The two broad categories of sprinkler heads are spray and rotary. Spray heads operate at relatively low water pressure—from 15 to 30 psi—so they're a good choice for the precise, controlled watering of shrubs, irregular landscaping, and fairly small lawns. For open lawn areas where foot traffic and mowing will occur, choose pop-up spray heads that automatically rise when the water comes on and drop when watering is finished.

Rotary heads need more pressure to operate—from 30 to 70 psi—but they throw water farther, up to 90 feet, which makes them economical for larger lawns and landscaped areas.

There are sprinkler heads that will throw water in various patterns, including full, half, and quarter circles. Some spray heads are adjustable rather than set to one pattern. Rather than spray, bubblers gently flood beds.

Low-flow nozzles reduce runoff, improve spray uniformity, and allow a larger area to be irrigated with a given amount of water.

Avoid placing rotary and spray sprinklers, shrub and lawn sprinklers, or low-flow and standard sprinklers on the same circuit.

CONNECTING VALVES AND TIMERS

The brain of an automated watering system is the timer. These are usually electronic clocks that regulate the operation of each sprinkler circuit connected to them. Dual- or multiple-program controllers allow for watering a lawn more frequently than ground covers, trees, and shrubs. Rain and moisture sensors override the program if a certain amount of rain has fallen or if the soil is moist.

Connect valves to a timer with low-voltage insulated cable (typically AWG-14 or -18) that's approved for direct burial. A different color wire joins each valve to a station on the timer, and another color wire (usually white) links all the valves to the timer. Thus, if you have four valves, you'll need five-strand wire. Run the wire underground to the timer, leaving plenty of slack. Loop the wire at each valve and at turns in the trench. At the timer, bring the wire above the ground and staple it along walls or joists as needed. Connect the wires to the timer as shown below.

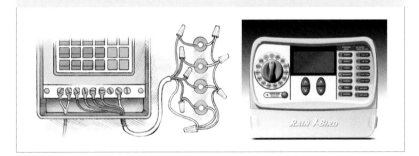

types of sprinkler heads

ROTARY HEAD

BUBBLER

SPRAY HEAD

POP-UP HEAD

installing lawn sprinklers

The installation procedure for a common permanent irrigation system—underground lawn sprinklers supplied by rigid PVC pipe—is shown below.

Most systems can be connected to an existing service-line pipe (1-inch diameter or larger is best). Pick out some possible locations for the valves. Consider how they

might be concealed (they can be unsightly) and, if your system will be automated, where to put the timer and how far it will be from an electrical connection.

Particularly if your system is automated and operates in the early morning, check it periodically for broken or clogged sprinklers or emitters.

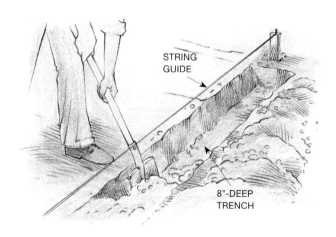

1 DIG 8-INCH-DEEP TRENCHES for pipes (deeper where soils freeze). To keep trench lines straight, run string between two stakes.

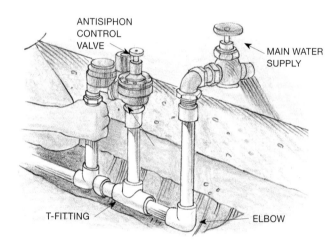

2 CONNECT PIPES to the water supply pipe, and then attach a control valve (with an antisiphon device) at least 6 inches above the ground. Use thick-walled ¾-inch PVC pipe.

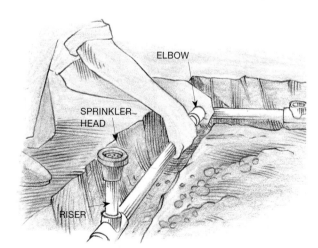

3 ASSEMBLE PIPES from the control valve outward, fitting risers and sprinkler heads to Ts and elbows. Joints may screw together or may require PVC cement.

4 FLUSH OUT pipes with heads removed. Replace heads. Fill in trenches, mounding loose soil along the center of the trench. Tamp the soil firmly. Avoid striking the sprinkler heads.

connecting to the water supply

A small drip system (see pages 214–215) can be connected directly to an outdoor faucet. But for larger, multi-circuit irrigation systems, you'll have to tap into the water pipes at a faucet or in the service line, either outdoors or at a basement meter. The best method is determined in part by your climate. Install a shutoff valve so that you can turn off water to the irrigation system without interrupting the water flow to the house. From the shutoff valve, run pipe to the control valves you'll be installing.

Remember to shut off the main water supply first, before the point of connection.

connecting to the service line outdoors

(above right) is often most convenient. After shutting off the water, remove a short section of pipe, leaving just enough of a gap to slide on a compression T (a T-shaped fitting). Slip the T over each end of the cut pipe, then tighten the compression nuts. Install a nipple of a convenient length in the stem of the T and attach a shutoff valve to it. For access to the valve, place it in a valve box.

all regions

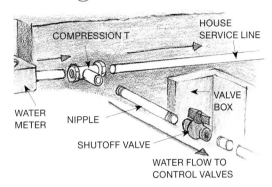

WATER METER — COMPRESSION T — HOUSE SERVICE LINE — VALVE BOX — NIPPLE — SHUTOFF VALVE — WATER FLOW TO CONTROL VALVES

connecting in the basement (below)

is necessary where frost reaches deep into the soil. Cut out a short piece of the service line just beyond the water meter. Install a compression T and a shutoff valve, as for the outdoor service-line connection (below left). Then drill a hole for the outgoing pipe through the basement wall above the foundation, making it just large enough to accommodate the pipe. To be able to drain the system before winter, install a drain cap at the lowest part of the assembly.

mild climates

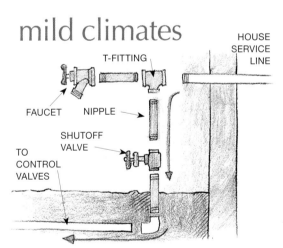

FAUCET — T-FITTING — HOUSE SERVICE LINE — NIPPLE — SHUTOFF VALVE — TO CONTROL VALVES

cold climates

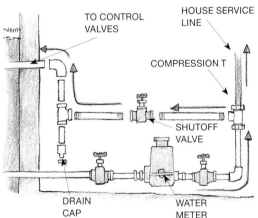

TO CONTROL VALVES — HOUSE SERVICE LINE — COMPRESSION T — SHUTOFF VALVE — DRAIN CAP — WATER METER

connecting at an outdoor faucet (above)

does not require you to cut any pipe. Remove the faucet and install a ½-inch or ¾-inch brass or galvanized T. Choose one with different size outlets if you want to connect ¾-inch irrigation pipe to ½-inch faucet pipe. Reattach the faucet and then install a nipple in the stem of the T and connect a shutoff valve to that.

PROTECT LINES FROM FREEZING

At the end of the growing season in colder regions, you may need to blow out residual water from the system before the ground freezes. Compressed air is the normal "tool" used. Find a pro to do this task. Exposed backflow preventers and valves may need to be protected from freezing.

installing a drip system

Drip irrigation is the most efficient way to water garden plants. Typically, water flows through lengths of flexible tubing and delivers water just where you want it and in a gradual flow adjusted for each plant's requirements. Because drip systems require only low water volume and pressure, you may be able to connect the system to a convenient outdoor faucet; check the manufacturer's literature.

head assembly

The components that connect the water source to the drip system are known collectively as the head assembly. This includes a manual or electric valve, backflow preventer, filter, and pressure regulator.

valves turn the water on and off. If you have a single drip line attached to an outdoor faucet, that faucet is the valve. If your drip line is attached to a battery-operated timer at a hose connection, the valve is built into the timer. If the drip line connects directly to your water line, a separate manual or remote-control valve is required for each circuit.

backflow preventers keep outside water from flowing back into the water supply. One type is an antisiphon valve, which creates an air gap at the high point in the system.

filters prevent the small openings on the emitters from becoming clogged. Small in-line filters are the least expensive and are usually fine for small systems and clean water supplies, but you have to take apart the lines to wash the screens. Larger Y-filters allow for easy cleaning.

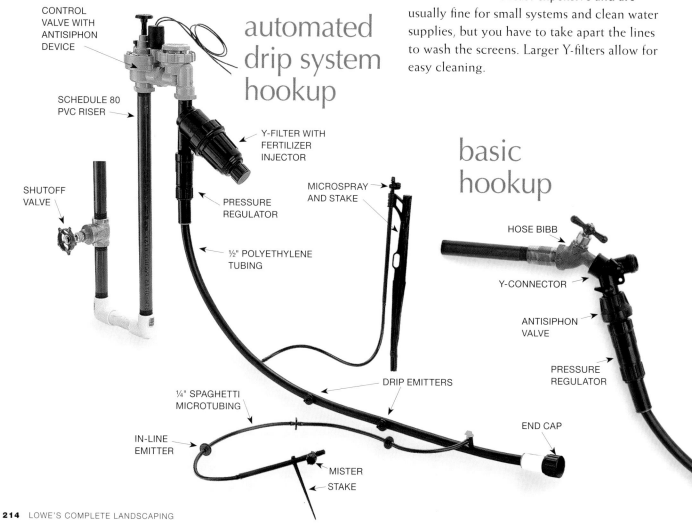

automated drip system hookup

CONTROL VALVE WITH ANTISIPHON DEVICE

SCHEDULE 80 PVC RISER

SHUTOFF VALVE

Y-FILTER WITH FERTILIZER INJECTOR

PRESSURE REGULATOR

½" POLYETHYLENE TUBING

MICROSPRAY AND STAKE

¼" SPAGHETTI MICROTUBING

IN-LINE EMITTER

DRIP EMITTERS

MISTER

STAKE

basic hookup

HOSE BIBB

Y-CONNECTOR

ANTISIPHON VALVE

PRESSURE REGULATOR

END CAP

pressure regulators reduce household water pressure, allowing your drip system to run at its ideal 15 to 30 psi.

tubing and fittings

These carry water from the head assembly to the different parts of the landscape.

drip tubing is made of flexible black polyethylene. It comes in ½-inch (standard) and ³/₈-inch diameters and is flexible enough to be snaked through plantings and looped around trees and shrubs, especially after being warmed in the sun. Insert emitters or microtubing directly into the drip tubing with a hole punch.

microtubing is small-diameter (usually ¼-inch), flexible polyethylene used to link individual sprayers or emitters to the larger pipe. Use stakes to hold microtubing in place.

fittings such as Ts let you branch off in different directions; L-shaped fittings are useful for making sharp turns. End caps close off the ends of drip tubing, and goof plugs are indispensable for sealing holes you've punched in the wrong place.

watering devices

Most emitters drip or ooze onto plants' root zones, while some spray water into the air like miniature sprinklers.

drip emitters drip water directly onto the soil. Most have barbed ends that snap into the wall of the drip tubing or that can be pushed into the ends of microtubing. Drip emitters typically dispense ½, 1, or 2 gallons per hour (gph), and manufacturers color-code them to make their output obvious. For help in choosing the right emitters for your soil type and plants, see the chart below.

microsprays are available in quarter-, half-, and full-circle patterns, as well as a bow-tie shape. These little heads are useful for covering tight or irregular spaces.

minisprinklers, also called spinners, cover larger areas than microsprays, throwing water in circles measuring from 10 to 30 feet across.

misters are used to raise the humidity or to water hanging plants or bonsai. Misters are often positioned above hanging plants so that the spray is directed downward.

SELECTING DRIP EMITTERS

This table provides general guidelines for the number and output of emitters for various types of plantings. The goal is to wet at least 60 percent of the root zone, so you may need to make adjustments depending on your soil type. Water tends to drip mainly downward in sandy soils but spreads wider before it goes deep in loam and clay soils (see page 390). Wherever a range is given for the emitters, choose the higher number if your soil is sandy, the lower one if it has a lot of clay. To avoid runoff on a slope, you may need more emitters with a lower output.

	OUTPUT RATE	NUMBER OF EMITTERS	EMITTER PLACEMENT
Vegetables, closely spaced	½–1 gph	1	Every 12"
Vegetables, widely spaced	1–2 gph	1	At base of plant
Flowerbeds	1 gph	1	At base of plant
Ground covers	1 gph	1	At base of plant
Shrubs (2'–3')	1 gph	1 or 2	At base of plant
Shrubs and trees (3'–5')	1 gph	2	6"–12" apart
Shrubs and trees (5'–10')	2 gph	2 or 3	2' from trunk
Shrubs and trees (10'–20')	2 gph	3 or 4	3' apart, at drip line
Trees (over 20')	2 gph	6 or more	4' apart, at drip line

landscape building

YOU'VE DREAMED AND PLANNED, YOU'VE GRADED AND DEALT with drainage and irrigation, and now it's time to lay some bricks and pound a few nails. How do you make a pathway or a low wall? How do you build a basic deck? And what about fences and gates?

On the following pages are directions for a variety of projects, all of them chosen for their utility in creating comfortable outdoor spaces.

The key structural materials to use outdoors are the classics—concrete, wood, and stone. If you are already experienced in working with them, the projects here will be second nature to you. If not, these pages can help you develop some basic literacy and skills regarding them. In addition, these pages will introduce some ways to customize their look, such as color tinting concrete. Remember that if you need help, you can ask for advice at Lowe's.

the basics of concrete

IT'S A VERSATILE, DURABLE, AND DECORATIVE MATERIAL

NO LONGER RELEGATED TO ONLY THE PLAINEST AND MOST UTILITARIAN USES, CONCRETE IS AN excellent decorative material. Adding color to it, using special sand or gravel in the mix, and varying the surface finish can alter its look in many ways. Concrete is strong, readily available, and relatively inexpensive.

Many people use the terms "cement" and "concrete" interchangeably, but the two materials are not the same. Cement is the glue. Concrete is what you get by mixing cement with aggregate (usually gravel and sand) and enough water to produce a workable consistency. Some concrete mixes also incorporate fibers, acrylic fortifiers, and other additives. Cement, a complex, finely ground substance, undergoes a chemical reaction called hydration when mixed with water, and in the process it binds everything together. It also gives the finished product its hardness. The sand and aggregate act as fillers and control shrinkage.

The standard slab for pathways and patios is 4 inches thick. In addition, allow for a

Concrete stained and embossed to look like flagstone makes a firm, stable surface that complements the Southwestern style of this patio.

base of 4 to 8 inches in most areas, though in frost-free areas, 2 inches is sufficient. Forms for concrete are built in the same way as for a path (pages 242–243). For standard paving, you will need 2 by 4s on edge for forms, and 12-inch 1 by 3s or 2 by 2s for stakes. If you plan to leave the lumber in place as permanent edgings and dividers, use rot-resistant cedar or pressure-treated lumber. For curved forms, choose tempered hardboard, plywood, or, if edgings will be permanent, metal.

using metal reinforcement Adding a few pieces of metal reinforcement may make all the difference in keeping your project intact. Reinforcement bar (rebar) or mesh plays a key role in fortifying structural features built of

concrete, but it is less common in decorative projects. Where concrete needs additional stiffness, rebar is often the best solution. Match the reinforcement to the thickness of your project so that 1 to 2 inches of concrete surrounds the metal. Note, however, that adding rebar to very thin slabs can actually cause the concrete to crack or break.

If your project is fairly large, order materials in bulk and mix them yourself, either by hand or with a power mixer. For small projects, hand mixing is less complicated than a power mixer, but it can be hard work. Use a power mixer, for large forms that must be filled in a single pour.

As with food, there are literally hundreds of different recipes for concrete. But for most landscaping projects the following basic formula works well. It contains gravel and so is suitable for projects that are at least 2 inches thick. With experience, you can adjust this formula to create special mixes.

basic concrete mix

$1/2$ part cement
1   part pea gravel ($3/8$ inch or less)
1   part sand
$1/4$ part water (approximately)

For larger projects that require a cubic yard or more of concrete, order it ready-mixed. (One cubic yard is enough for an 8-by-10-foot pad that's 4 inches thick.) Some dealers have trailers, designed to be hauled behind a car or small truck, with either a mixing drum or a simple metal box into which the concrete is placed. For larger pours, order a delivery by transit-mix truck. In both cases, have help on hand so that you can work quickly.

USING BAGGED CONCRETE MIXES

Concrete made from bagged mixes costs more per cubic foot than concrete you mix from scratch. But bags free you from searching for specialty ingredients, such as fiber reinforcement, and from buying them in greater quantities than you need. Manufacturers rarely reveal what's in their mixes, but you can look on the label or spec sheet for the strength (shown as psi, or pounds per square inch). Although this number refers specifically to crush resistance, you can use it as an overall indicator of durability and abrasion resistance. The standard 90-pound bag yields $2/3$ cubic foot of concrete, enough to fill one posthole or to cover a 16-inch-square area 4 inches deep.

working with concrete

For much more in-depth information about working with concrete, and for more patio ideas and projects, see *Lowe's Complete Patio & Deck Book*.

Pouring a small concrete slab is nothing magical as long as you make the proper preparations. But for more elaborate projects, you may need a contractor with a crew to achieve the desired results.

To start, lay out stakes and mason's lines to mark the outline of the slab. Plan for a slope of at least 1 inch per 10 feet away from the house for drainage. If the exposed soil is soft, wet it and then tamp it firmly.

If you need permanent partitions, use wood, steel, or copper dividers. They also serve as control joints to prevent cracking and help break up the job into several manageable pours. Before pouring, add any required reinforcement. Usually 6-inch-square welded wire mesh is the best choice for paving, but also check local codes.

Pour large areas in sections and be sure to have helpers on hand to assist with hauling and spreading the wet concrete. Wear gloves to protect your hands from the concrete's caustic ingredients, plus rubber boots if you have to walk in the wet mix.

how to pour a slab

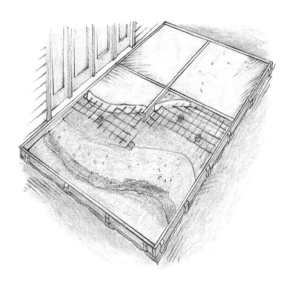

1 FOR ROUGH GRADING, dig deep enough to allow for 4 inches of concrete on top of 2 to 8 inches of gravel. Construct forms from 2 by 4s secured to 12-inch stakes, placing the form tops at finished slab height. Add welded wire mesh for reinforcement.

A brick-and-concrete terrace is sheltered by a lath arbor. The cedar breezeway is the bridge between house and garden.

2 BEGIN POURING concrete at one end of a form while a helper spreads it with a hoe. Work concrete up against the form and tamp it into corners, but don't press it down too hard. A splashboard or ramp lets you pour the concrete where you want.

3 WITH A HELPER, move a 2-by-4 screed across the form to level the concrete, using a rapid zigzag, sawing motion. A third person can shovel concrete into any hollows.

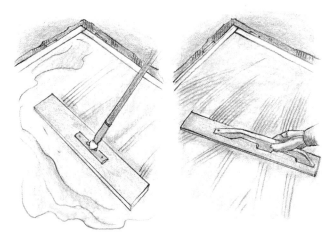

4 INITIAL FLOATING smooths high spots and fills small hollows left after screeding. Use a bull float with an extension handle for larger slabs.

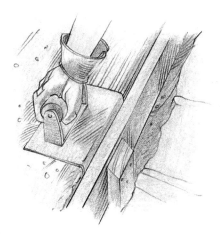

5 RUN THE EDGE of a trowel between the wet concrete and the form. Then run an edger back and forth to create a smooth, curved edge.

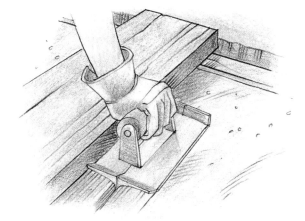

6 USE A JOINTER trowel to make grooves, called control joints, to reduce slab cracking. Joint spacing varies but is usually 12 times the slab's thickness, or every 4 feet for a 4-inch-thick slab.

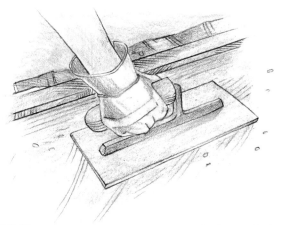

7 BEFORE THE SURFACE STIFFENS, give it a final pass with a wooden float. For a smoother surface, follow with a steel trowel. For a nonskid surface, drag a broom lightly across the concrete, without overlapping strokes.

concrete foundations

The great versatility of concrete makes it one of the most essential materials for outdoor construction. A strong concrete footing is basic to masonry walls whether they're built of stone or of manufactured bricks or blocks.

pouring a footing

Garden walls need a solid concrete base called a footing. Very low walls (ones no more than 12 inches tall), modular-block walls, and dry-stone walls may require only a leveled trench or a rubble base. Other walls require a footing made from concrete that's twice as wide and at least as deep as the wall's thickness. In cold-weather areas, extend the footing below the frostline. Add 6 inches to the trench depth for a bottom layer of gravel. To pour post footings for a deck, fence, arbor, or other similar small job, use bags of ready-mixed concrete.

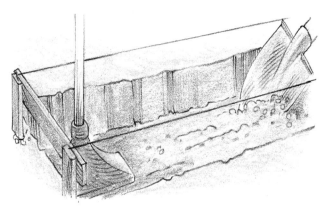

1 PREPARE A BASE for the foundation by leveling and tamping the bottom of the trench and adding a 6-inch layer of gravel.

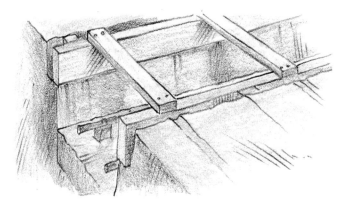

2 BUILD FORMS and set any required reinforcement bars on a layer of broken bricks or other rubble.

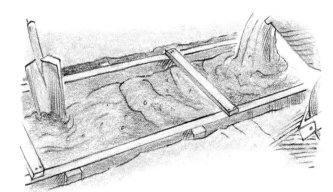

3 POUR CONCRETE and insert any vertical reinforcing bars required by code.

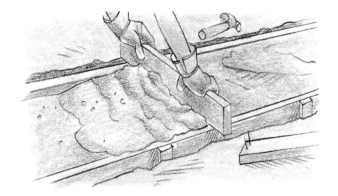

4 SMOOTH THE SURFACE until it is level with the tops of the forms, and cover with a plastic sheet. Let it cure for two days, and then strip the forms and start building the wall.

dressing up concrete

Perhaps the practicality of poured concrete appeals to you but the look does not. There are many ways to dress up poured concrete. One way is to embed stones in it, a technique used to good effect in the pathway shown at top left on page 59. But there are many other ways to use concrete creatively, such as the two shown below.

molding concrete

Molds simplify the process of forming concrete into attractive shapes. But don't expect perfect shapes to emerge automatically. After filling the mold, you'll need to spend time smoothing the rough edges. Also, consider tinting the concrete—an example is shown below—before you shape it.

1 POUR CONCRETE into the mold. Press the mold onto the gravel so that the concrete cannot seep out the sides. Mix a stiff batch of concrete. Shovel the concrete into the mold and take care to fill each cavity.

2 TROWEL with a magnesium or wood float to level the surface. Run the float across the form in at least two directions, fill in any voids, then level again. The float should scrape the plastic mold as you work.

3 REMOVE THE MOLD once all the surface water has disappeared, carefully lifting the mold straight up. Smooth rough edges with a brush. The resulting joints can be left as they are, or you can fill them with sand or mortar.

creating a flagstone look

A flagstone design like this is shown to best effect in tinted concrete. Add colorant to the wet concrete, or acid-etch and stain the concrete after it has cured. Depending upon your artistic ambition, you can also apply stains of several colors to various sections to duplicate the more irregular look of faux flagstone.

This refinement is easiest to execute on a narrow path that you can easily reach across. It is more difficult if you have to lay plywood on the concrete to kneel on.

1 TOOL A PATTERN with a bent piece of ½-inch copper pipe. Float the surface and edge the perimeter. Make joints after floating a second time, once surface water is gone.

2 TROWEL OVER THE PATTERN with a magnesium float to knock down most of the crumbs and to press any exposed gravel into the concrete.

3 BRUSH THE SURFACE with a paintbrush or a mason's brush to gently clear away any remaining crumbs and to produce a finely textured broom finish over the entire surface.

patio paver essentials
PAVING WITH CLAY AND CONCRETE BRICKS

THE AVERAGE PATIO HOSTS A WIDE VARIETY OF OUTDOOR ACTIVITIES. WITH THE RIGHT AMENITIES, IT can be a breakfast nook, living area, reading room, and play area all in one. Before you get to the stage of choosing amenities, however, you'll want to select the patio's more basic elements: its surface material, edging, and any stairs or walkways required to join the patio to the garden or to link different patio areas. Your decisions about these essentials will largely determine the style and cost of your project. For more about patio planning, see pages 82–91.

LOWE'S QUICK TIP

Buy pavers by the individual piece or by the pallet, enough to cover about 100 square feet. Prices vary by paver style, but doing the installation yourself will save as much as $10 per square foot.

Interlocking concrete pavers create an interesting pattern and provide a stable surface.

With careful preparation and installation, a brick-in-sand path or patio will prove as durable as bricks set in mortar. In addition, if you decide to change the surface later, you need only to chip out one brick to remove the rest in perfect condition.

Typically, you prepare a bed of 1½- to 2-inch-thick sand or rock fines (a mix of grain sizes) and lay the bricks tightly together. If your garden's drainage is poor, you may also need to add a 4-inch gravel base (in areas where the ground freezes, 6 to 8 inches is advisable). A layer of landscaping fabric will suppress the growth of weeds.

To hold both the bricks and the sand firmly in place, build permanent edgings around the perimeter. Install the edgings first, as they will serve as good leveling guides for preparing and laying the bricks. If you have to do a lot of cutting or shaping of complex angles (along curved edgings, for example), rent a brick saw from a tool-rental outlet.

Concrete pavers can also be laid in sand much like bricks. With interlocking types, alignment is easier. After laying, make several passes with a power-plate vibrator to settle them. You can probably rent one locally. If not, use a heavy drum roller instead. Spread damp, fine sand over the surface. When it dries, sweep it into the paver joints. Additional passes with either a plate vibrator or a roller will help lock the pavers together.

1 A BRICK-IN-SAND patio includes a gravel bed, a layer of landscaping fabric, packed sand, and rigid edgings, which hold the bricks in place. Install edgings first.

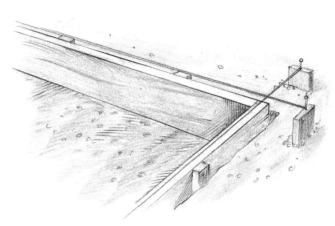

2 STRING MASON'S LINES from stakes to serve as guides, first to mark edgings at the desired level and slope. Later, edgings can serve as a reference for leveling sand and bricks.

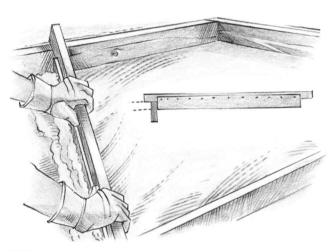

3 LAY DOWN a 1½- to 2-inch-thick layer of dampened sand and level it with a bladed screed, as shown. If necessary, use a temporary guide on which to rest one end of the screed.

4 ANOTHER MASON'S LINE will help align courses. Begin at one corner. Lay bricks tightly, tapping each into place with a hand sledge or mallet. Check the level frequently.

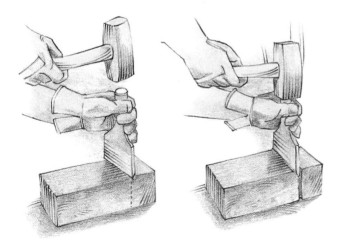

5 TO CUT BRICKS, score a line on all four sides (left) and make the cut with one sharp blow (right). To cut angles, nibble at the waste area, chipping away a little at a time.

6 SPREAD FINE SAND over finished pavement, let it dry for a few hours, and then sweep it with a stiff broom into joints. Spray lightly with water so that the sand settles completely.

surface-bonded block walls
THEY'RE STRONG, DURABLE, AND ATTRACTIVE

INTERLOCKING BLOCKS THAT FORM plumb vertical walls are relatively new to the market. Most are strong enough to function as a freestanding garden wall or a low retaining wall. This project shows how you can build an attractive garden wall of plain-faced interlocking blocks that are then stuccoed with surface-bonding mortar.

Like all masonry walls, inter-locking block walls must rest on a solid concrete footing. The first course typically is set in mortar or in a special bonding agent. The surface bonding adds strength as well as an attractive stucco surface.

1 POUR A CONCRETE FOOTING and allow it to cure (see page 222). Snap chalk lines on the footing to indicate the perimeter of the wall. Mix a batch of surface-bonding mortar. Lightly wet the concrete and then spread a bed of mortar, about ½ inch thick, to cover the area where the blocks will go. Set the first course of blocks in the mortar. Use a solid-faced block wherever the block end will be exposed. As you go, use a level to check that the blocks form an even surface.

2 STACK THE BLOCKS, once the bottom course is laid, so that vertical joints are staggered. If it's required by code, fill one or more of the cores with an approved grout. Unless you suspect a problem, there is no need to use a mason's line to check the wall for straightness and level.

3 IF A BLOCK FEELS WOBBLY, stack the next course. The weight of the blocks will probably set the block firmly. If it doesn't, pick up the upper course and the wobbly block. Trowel a small amount of mortar on top of the block below and set the wobbly block back into place. Tap it with a hammer and a scrap of wood to settle the block at the same height as its neighbors.

4 CAP THE WALL with cap blocks (shown here) for a squared-off look. If these are not available, spread surface-bonding mortar on the highest course and lay solid concrete blocks in the mortar.

5 APPLY SURFACE-BONDING CEMENT after moistening the wall. Mix a small batch and place it on a mortarboard. Hold the mortarboard against the wall as you scoop the mortar with a trowel and apply it, using upward-sweeping motions. Hold the trowel nearly flat and press firmly to ensure a tight bond.

6 SMOOTH AND MAKE CONTROL JOINTS once you have covered an area of about 4 square feet. Use long, sweeping strokes to smooth the surface. The mortar should be about ¼ inch thick, but minor variation in thickness is fine. Rinse the trowel regularly, as a clean trowel is easier to use. To control cracking, use a concrete jointer to cut vertical control joints spaced about twice as far apart as the wall is high. For example, if the wall is 3 feet high, space the joints 6 feet apart.

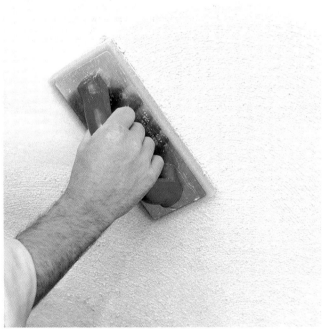

7 TEXTURE the surface-bonding mortar by running a trowel lightly over the surface in sweeping motions of approximately the same radius. Apply the texture lightly so that it does not alter or change the control joints. The mortar sets up quickly, so be ready to apply the texture of your choice.

facing a block wall
CHANGE THE LOOK WITH STONE

YOU CAN DRESS UP A WALL OF POURED CONCRETE OR CONCRETE BLOCK BY COVERING IT WITH flagstones. If possible, choose stones that are light and thin. They will be easy to cut and less likely to slide down the wall as you install them. The flatter the stones, the easier they will be to set. Use irregularly shaped stones, as shown here, or stones with roughly square corners for a more geometric look.

Lightweight faux-stone veneer is the easiest to work with. It is thin but gives the impression of large rubble stones. Special pieces that wrap around a corner complete the illusion. Set these stones using the same methods as for flagstones.

The wall itself should be in sound condition. Clean away any oily deposits. If a wall is flaking or producing white powder efflorescence, correct the problem before you apply face stones. Remove efflorescence by scraping, wire-brushing, and cleaning with detergent or with a pressure washer.

mortar and bonding agent

The three common types of mortar specified for new construction today are N, S, and M. They differ primarily in their adhesive strength. Type M is the highest strength, Type S is strong, and Type N is a moderate-strength mortar. Use Type N mortar for most exterior, above-grade uses. Use Type S for exterior applications such as this project, and for foundation or retaining walls.

Bonding agents are materials that increase the adhesion of a mortar to cement. They are either applied directly to a surface, mixed into the mortar, or both. Bonding agents are very effective on new block walls and on any concrete wall that is free of dirt, paint, and similar contaminants (see pages 226–227).

The same cut-stone pavers used for the patio become facing stones that cover a concrete block wall.

FACING WITH HEAVY STONES

If the stones are heavy, first install a sturdy shelf made of a staked 2 by 4 for the bottom row to rest on. Set the bottom row first and allow the mortar to harden before you set higher rows. Have on hand many short lumber scraps—1 by 4s, 1 by 2s, and shims—to use as supports. Have a helper hold a stone in place while you insert the lumber scraps to achieve the desired joint.

1 LAY STONES IN A DRY RUN on a sheet of plywood, as wide as the wall is tall, on the ground near the wall. Place it so that you can easily pick up stones from the plywood and apply them to the wall. Make adjustments as you would for a flagstone patio, by cutting with a hammer and chisel if necessary.

2 APPLY MORTAR, spreading a coat of latex bonding agent onto the wall. In a wheelbarrow, mix a batch of Type S mortar. It should be stiff but just wet enough to stick to the stones. Using a straight trowel, apply it about 3/8 inch thick, or thicker if the stones aren't flat. Cover an area of about 15 square feet.

3 SET THE BOTTOM ROW, pressing the stones into the mortar. Where necessary, use blocks of wood or small rocks to hold the stones in position. Make all adjustments as soon as possible. Avoid moving a stone after the mortar has begun to harden, which occurs in as little as 20 minutes.

4 SET UPPER STONES, if they are light enough, up to the top of the wall. But if the weight of the upper stones causes lower ones to move, wait for the mortar holding lower stones to set before installing upper ones. Use spacers to maintain fairly consistent joints.

5 FILL AND SHAPE JOINTS after the mortar has hardened. Go back and fill in the joints with mortar, using a pointed trowel or a mortar bag. When the mortar starts to stiffen, shape the joints and brush away any crumbs or flakes.

6 CAP AND CLEAN the top of the wall by placing large stones that overhang the wall by an inch or more on both sides. When the mortar has started to harden, wash the wall with water and a brush, then wipe it with a wet towel.

deck making

BUILDING A DECK ATTACHED TO THE HOUSE

A LOW-LEVEL DECK ATTACHED TO THE HOUSE EXTENDS THE INDOOR LIVING SPACE. IT IS ALSO A manageable and economical do-it-yourself project. Before you begin, review the advice on pages 92–97 and the diagram on pages 92–93, and check building codes. This type of deck can be completed in a few weekends, but it will require the work of at least two people.

Think ahead about benches or other items that may need to be integrated with the deck's framing. Be sure the completed deck will be at least 1 inch below adjacent access doors.

LOWE'S QUICK TIP

For complete and detailed directions on building a deck, see *Lowe's Complete Patio & Deck Book*. In addition to instructions, the book also includes plans and other helpful information.

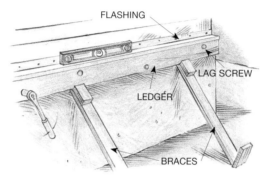

FLASHING
LAG SCREW
LEDGER
BRACES

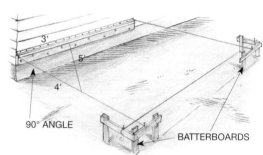

3'
5'
4'
90° ANGLE
BATTERBOARDS

Deck steps that fan out wide make moving in either direction easy and can double as extra seating.

1 POSITION the ledger and prop it in place with 2-by-4 blocks or braces. Drill staggered holes for lag screws every 16 inches, and then fasten the ledger in place, making sure it's level. To prevent rot, either space the ledger off the wall with blocks or washers or add metal flashing, as shown.

2 BATTERBOARDS MARK THE HEIGHT of the deck. Build them at outside corners, level with the ledger top. To mark the deck's edges, string mason's lines from the batterboards to the ledger. To make corners square, use the 3-4-5 triangle method shown.

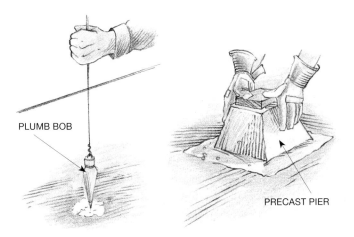

PLUMB BOB

PRECAST PIER

3 DANGLE A PLUMB BOB from the mason's lines to mark the footings. Dig holes to depths required by code, then add gravel and fill the holes with concrete. Push piers into the concrete, level their tops, and let the concrete set overnight.

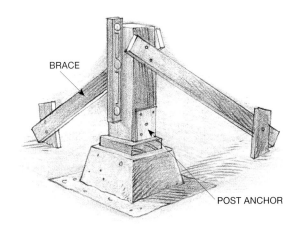

BRACE

POST ANCHOR

4 UNLESS PIERS HAVE INTEGRAL POST ANCHORS, add them now. Measure and cut posts—in this case, one joist's depth below the top of the ledger. Check plumb on two sides of each post, temporarily brace each in place, and fasten to piers.

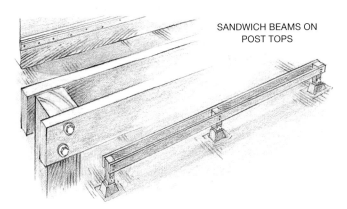

SANDWICH BEAMS ON POST TOPS

5 POSITION 2-BY BEAMS on each side of the post tops. After leveling them with the post tops, clamp them in place. Drill staggered holes and then fasten the beams to the posts with bolts or lag screws.

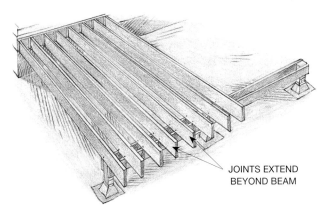

JOINTS EXTEND BEYOND BEAM

6 POSITION JOISTS at span intervals appropriate to decking (check with a Lowe's sales associate). Secure the joists to the ledger with framing connectors. Set one beam and toenail it in place. Brace the joists with spacers at open ends. Add posts for railings or benches or for an overhead anchored to the deck.

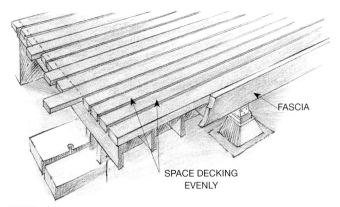

FASCIA

SPACE DECKING EVENLY

7 ALIGN DECKING BOARDS atop joists, staggering the joints (if any). Space the boards, leaving about $3/16$ inch—the thickness of a 16-penny nail—for drainage. Fasten the decking to the joists with the recommended nails or screws. Trim decking ends with a circular saw.

4 × 4 POST

8 FINISH DECKING ENDS and edges as desired with fascia boards or other trim. If you plan benches, planters, steps, or railings that aren't tied to the substructure, add them now.

deck finishing
PROTECTING NEW WOOD

WOODEN DECKS NEED A FINISH TO PROTECT THEM FROM SUN, rain, mildew, and insect damage. In the paint department at Lowe's you will find a variety of finishing products, some made specifically for decks and others that can be applied to exterior surfaces generally. Consult a Lowe's sales associate to see which products are best suited to your situation.

choosing a finish

Broadly speaking, there are two categories of wood finishes. Penetrating finishes provide protection by soaking through the surface of the wood. Film-forming finishes create a protective coating on the wood's surface.

penetrating finishes

Most products sold as deck finishes do not form a film on the wood, which means the deck can breathe and the surface of the wood will show through. Wood preservatives, water repellents, and pigmented deck stains are the major types of penetrating finishes.

Clear penetrating finishes are very popular. Readily available and affordable, they retain the natural color of the decking. But clear finishes are also the least durable and need to be reapplied every year. Many clear finishes contain mildewcide and ultraviolet (UV) stabilizers to provide added protection.

Semitransparent stains provide a degree of protection against sun damage that clear finishes, even those containing UV stabilizers, cannot match. Unless the sun really beats on your deck, you can expect these coatings to last approximately two to three years. Many colors are available.

film-forming finishes

Paint and solid-color stains are finishes that seal wood with a protective film on the surface. In general, latex exterior paints and stains work fine on trim and siding, and they can be good choices for railings, but no latex paint is hard enough for a surface people will walk on. Oil- or polyurethane-base porch and deck paint is much more durable but is banned in many areas because of environmental concerns.

If you want to apply latex paint or solid-color stain to your deck, restrict it to parts that are not often stepped on or handled, such as posts, rails, and balusters. Even there, be sure to coat the wood with a paintable water-repellent preservative first.

finishing a new deck

Once you have selected the right finish to put on your deck, applying it is a matter of getting the right tools, waiting for the right weather, and then allowing yourself the time to do it correctly.

Rollers, brushes, and pump sprayers are all application possibilities. Brushes are the most effective, however, as the finish is more likely to be worked into the wood. Whichever tool you use, you will need a

HOW SOON TO FINISH A NEW DECK

You may hear that you should let a deck weather in the sun awhile before applying the first coat of finish. However, unless the lumber has a factory-applied water repellent, this is wrong. Pressure-treated wood may need to dry for a week or two, but untreated wood should be finished right away. If you're not sure, test the wood for dryness by sprinkling it with some water. If the water soaks right in, the wood is ready to be finished.

brush to apply finish to railings and other smaller sections of the deck.

The ideal weather for applying deck finish is slightly overcast, with no rain in the immediate forecast. Avoid applying finish while the sun is beating down. Apply a fairly thin layer, let it dry, then apply a second coat soon afterward. Work plenty of finish into any exposed end grain and into joints where water could be trapped.

For best results, use a brush to apply at least the first coat to your new deck. Natural-bristle brushes are best for oil-base stains, but use synthetic-bristle brushes for water-base finishes.

1 NEW LUMBER often has a slight glaze on the surface. The wood will absorb finish better if you sand it lightly to remove the glaze before applying the first coat. A pole sander, with 120-grit sandpaper, allows you to sand while standing up.

2 SWEEP THE DECK thoroughly with a broom. Use a shop vacuum or a putty knife to clean out sawdust and other debris between boards. If you pick up dust when you run your hand over the wood surface, sweep again.

3 APPLY THE FINISH. If you are using a stain, try to minimize the lap marks that occur when you brush new finish over previously applied finish that has already begun to dry. For best results, apply the stain along the full length of a couple of boards at a time. Never let the stain puddle on the surface.

making landscape steps
USING TIMBER, WOOD, OR MASONRY

This formal brick patio echoes the traditional lines of the house. For instance, note how the handrails match the house trim.

MOST LANDSCAPES NEED STEPS. USUALLY THE HOUSE SITS ABOVE GROUND LEVEL, MAKING STEPS a necessity. Steps up a gentle slope may require no more than excavating a few level areas and positioning large stones onto them. A stairway of three or more steps is another matter.

Steps should be carefully planned so that they are a consistent and comfortable height. The most important aspect of step planning is the relationship of the tread, or step, to the rise. Make the depth of the tread plus twice the height of the riser equal 25 to 27 inches.

On average, the ideal outdoor step has a uniform 6-inch-high rise and a 15-inch-deep tread. Riser dimensions should not be less than 5 inches or more than 8 inches. Tread depth should not be less than 11 inches. For more, see pages 112–113.

LOWE'S QUICK TIP

To fit steps evenly, first measure the needed rise and the run. Divide an approximate riser height into the total rise of the slope (in inches), and round off so the answer is a whole number. Compare the estimated riser height to corresponding tread (far right), and then divide the number of treads into the total run. If it doesn't work out evenly, adjust the tread-riser relationship and try again.

MEASURING SLOPE RUN AND RISE

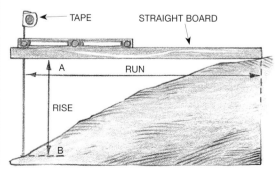

THE TREAD-RISER RELATIONSHIP

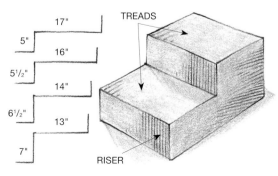

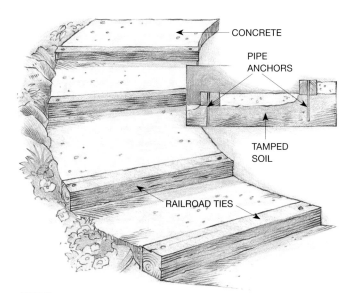

CONCRETE

PIPE ANCHORS

TAMPED SOIL

RAILROAD TIES

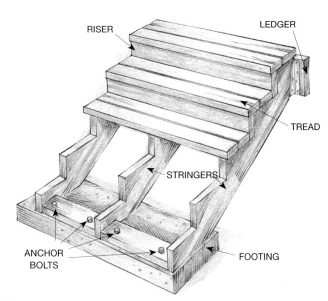

RISER

LEDGER

TREAD

STRINGERS

ANCHOR BOLTS

FOOTING

1 TIMBERS OR TIES: Both railroad ties and pressure-treated 6-by-6 timbers make simple but rugged steps. To begin, excavate the site and tamp the soil in the tread area firmly. Lay the ties or timbers on the soil and then drill a hole near each end of each tie or timber. With a sledge, drive 2-foot-long sections of either ½-inch galvanized steel pipe or ¾-inch reinforcement bars through the holes into the ground.

An alternative method that provides extra support involves pouring small concrete footings and setting anchor bolts in the slightly stiffened concrete. When the concrete has set (after about two days), secure the ties to the footings with the bolts.

After the tie or timber risers are in place, fill the tread surfaces behind them with concrete, brick-in-sand paving, gravel, soil, mulch, grass, or another material.

2 WOODEN STAIRS: Formal wooden steps are best for a low-level deck or for easy access to a doorway. Make stringers from 2 by 10s or 2 by 12s. If the steps are more than 4 feet wide, a third stringer will be needed in the middle.

Use galvanized bolts or metal joist hangers to secure stringers to a deck beam or joist. If you're running stringers off stucco siding or another masonry surface, hang them on a ledger, as shown. Note that when bolts are used, the first tread is below the surface of the house floor or deck. When joist hangers are the fasteners, however, the first tread must be level with the floor.

Attach the base of the stringers to wooden nailing blocks anchored in a concrete footing. Build risers and treads from 2-by or 5/4 decking material cut to width.

3 MASONRY STEPS: Steps can be built entirely of concrete, or, for a finished look, the concrete can be used as a base for mortared masonry units, as shown.

First, form rough steps in the earth. Allow space for at least a 6-inch gravel setting bed and a 4-inch thickness of concrete on both the treads and the risers. (In cold climates you will need 6 to 8 inches of concrete, plus a footing that reaches below the frostline.) Add the thickness of any masonry units to tread and riser dimensions. Tamp filled areas thoroughly.

With 2-by lumber, build forms like those shown on page 222. Lay the gravel bed, keeping it 4 inches back from the front of the steps. You will pour a thicker layer of concrete at that potentially weak point. Reinforce the concrete with 6-inch welded wire mesh.

Pour and screed the concrete as for a poured-concrete footing. To give treads more traction in wet weather, sweep the wet concrete with a broom to roughen its surface, then cure it.

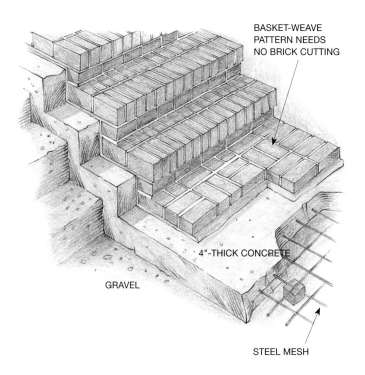

BASKET-WEAVE PATTERN NEEDS NO BRICK CUTTING

4"-THICK CONCRETE

GRAVEL

STEEL MESH

building fences

THE BASICS ARE SIMPLE, THE VARIATIONS MANY

FENCE BUILDING IS A STRAIGHTFORWARD TASK, AND THE HARDEST PART IS SINKING THE POSTS. BUT before you set a post or pound a nail, check local building and zoning codes.

Codes may dictate style, material, setback, and other requirements. Also review the advice provided on pages 124–127 of this book. Then tackle the building stages: plotting the fence, installing posts, adding rails and siding. For fences 3 to 6 feet tall, plan to set posts at least 2 feet deep—12 inches deeper for end and gate posts. For taller fences, the rule is one-third the entire post length. Dig postholes to a uniform depth. If you have a long fence run, use a power auger to make the job easier. Cut the posts to fit either before or after they are in the ground (see below).

There is also a wide variety of prefabricated fences available. At Lowe's stores, you can compare several kinds and arrange for professional installation.

SETTING POSTS

Installing posts is the most important part of fence building. Posts that aren't set firmly in the ground will be the bane of an otherwise solidly built fence. They must be plumb in their holes and perfectly aligned, or you'll run into trouble when you start adding rails and siding.

The post-setting process can be divided into three steps, shown below: digging the holes, setting the posts, and aligning the posts. Setting and aligning the posts is best done by two people—one to hold and align each post while the other fills the hole with concrete or earth and gravel.

Some fence designs call for post tops to be precisely level with one another. These include fences with rails attached to the post tops, and fences with rails recessed into the posts by means of a dado or mortise. You can cut the posts before setting them—which means you'll need to set all the posts to exactly the same height—or you can set the posts first and then cut them in place. If you choose the second option it's easier to align posts, but making the cuts will be more awkward.

Posts are generally set in concrete, but if the soil is stable (not subject to sliding, cracking, or frost heaving), earth-and-gravel fill is adequate for lightweight fences such as lattice, picket, and some post-and-board types no taller than 4 feet. For an overview of both techniques, see the drawings on the facing page. After setting the posts in fresh concrete, you have about 20 minutes to align them before the concrete hardens. Let the concrete cure for two days.

building a basic board fence

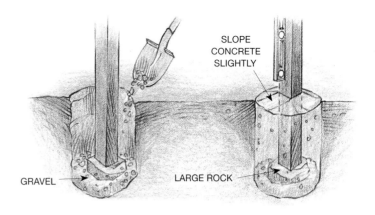

SLOPE CONCRETE SLIGHTLY

GRAVEL

LARGE ROCK

1 MARK EACH END OR CORNER POST LOCATION with a stake. Run a mason's line between the stakes, as shown. With chalk, mark the remaining post locations on the line. Using a level or plumb bob, transfer each mark to the ground and drive in additional stakes. Then dig holes 6 inches deeper than post depth and $2^{1}/_{2}$ to 3 times the post's diameter.

MASON'S LINE

PLUMB BOB

2 PLACE A ROCK AT THE BASE of each hole and add 4 to 6 inches of gravel. Place a post in a hole and shovel in concrete, tamping it down with a broomstick or a capped steel pipe. Adjust the post plumb with a level. Continue filling until the concrete extends 1 to 2 inches above ground level, and then slope it away from the post to divert water.

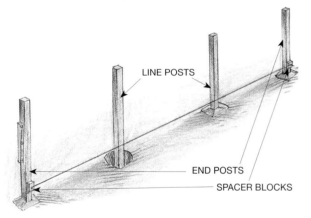

LINE POSTS

END POSTS

SPACER BLOCKS

3 TO ALIGN POSTS, first position two end or corner posts so their faces are parallel, then plumb them and set them permanently. Use spacer blocks and a mason's line to locate line posts, spacing each post a block's thickness from the line. After setting end posts in fresh concrete, you have about 20 minutes to align them before the concrete hardens. Let it cure for two days.

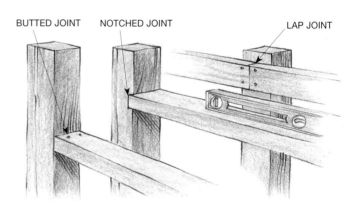

BUTTED JOINT   NOTCHED JOINT   LAP JOINT

4 BRUSH ON WOOD PRESERVATIVE where rails and posts will meet. Then fasten one end of each rail. Check level with a helper and secure the other end. You can butt rails against the post and toenail them, notch them in, or lap them over the sides or top of each post. If you're making lap joints, plan to span at least three posts for strength.

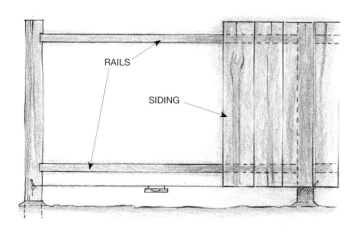

RAILS

SIDING

5 CUT SIDING BOARDS to the same length. Stretch and level a line from post to post to mark the bottom of the siding. Check the first board for plumb, and then secure it to rails with galvanized nails three times as long as the board's thickness. Secure additional boards, checking alignment as you go.

building a lattice fence

Lattice screens and fences are light, airy structures, commonly associated with Victorian architecture. They can serve several purposes. A tightly woven lattice can screen out an objectionable view while allowing a free flow of air into the yard. A widely spaced latticework can preserve a view, serve as a traffic director, or provide a backdrop for tall plantings. For details on how to build a lattice porch skirt, see pages 252–253.

Latticework usually consists of narrow strips of wood, crisscrossed either horizontally and vertically or diagonally, that are held within a frame. Because of their light weight and open design, lattice fences and screens can be built as tall as 8 feet without requiring heavy framing members or bracing.

The screen shown uses lath 1 1/2 inches wide and 1/4 inch thick. For every 8 feet of screen, you'll need 9 pieces 8 feet long and 17 pieces 65 1/2 inches long. The 2-by-4 posts are 8 feet long and set 2 feet into the ground, 4 feet on center. The top rails are 8-foot-long 2 by 4s nailed across three posts, and the bottom rails are 2 by 4s cut to length to butt

between the posts. Use galvanized nails three times as long as the thickness of the lath.

You can also buy preassembled 4-by-8-foot lattice panels, for which you simply need to build a frame. Use posts about 6 1/2 feet tall and set them 2 feet deep, leaving 6 inches of space between the ground and the bottom rail of the panel.

1 plot the fence line and lay out post locations (pages 236–237). Install the posts and join the rails to them. For a painted finish, paint the frame and individual lath strips before joining them. Cut lath to length with a backsaw and a miter box for square, clean cuts.

2 attach the first vertical lath strip to the face of the first post. Space successive vertical strips 6 1/2 inches apart, measuring and marking their locations on the top and bottom rails with a combination square a pencil. Attach each strip with a nail at the top and bottom.

3 attach the first horizontal lath strip along the face of the bottom rail, overlapping the vertical strips. Space successive horizontal strips 6 1/2 inches apart, measuring and marking their locations on the posts. Use one nail at each end to attach the strips to the posts. The last strip should end up directly over the face of the top rail, as shown at left.

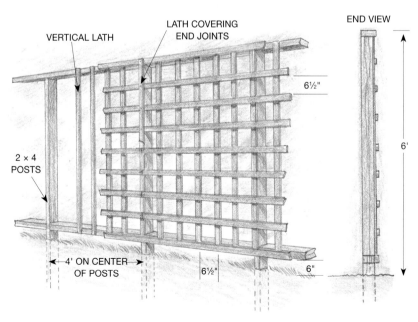

VERTICAL LATH

LATH COVERING END JOINTS

END VIEW

6 1/2"

6'

2 x 4 POSTS

4' ON CENTER OF POSTS

6 1/2"

6"

wood-and-wire fencing

Wire mesh has numerous applications in fencing. Heavy wire mesh provides security and offers support for plants without completely blocking a view. Chain-link fencing is popular for residential security.

Most wire and chain-link fences use metal posts and are best if professionally installed. However, using the instructions given here, you can construct a wood-and-wire fence with the aid of a strong helper. This fence consists of 2-by-4-inch welded-wire mesh attached to a wood frame of 4-by-4 posts and 2-by-4 rails.

Wire mesh comes in 50- and 100-foot rolls and in a number of widths, including 3, 4, and 6 feet. The width of the wire corresponds to the height of the fence. The fence shown here uses the 4-foot width, but you can adapt the design to a 3- or 6-foot fence. You may also want to substitute a tighter mesh.

Fasten framing members with galvanized nails three times as long as the thickness of the wood. Use ³/₄-inch galvanized staples to hold the wire to the posts and rails.

1 **to prepare the frame,** plot the fence line and post locations. Cut 6-foot lengths of 4 by 4s for the posts and set them 18 inches deep, 6 feet on center. For the top rail, use 2 by 4s about 12 feet long (they'll span three posts). For the bottom rails, cut 2 by 4s to butt between the posts, level them, and toenail them in place. Center a 1-by-6 cap rail over the top rail and nail it in place.

2 **attach wire** starting at one end of the fence and unrolling enough to cover two sections—about 12 feet. Align the top of the wire with the underside of the 1-by-6 cap rail. Tack the wire to the first post, hammering staples at the top, center, and bottom. While a helper stretches the wire taut, tack it to the next two posts at the top, center, and bottom, checking often to make sure that it stays in alignment. After the wire is tacked in place

over the first two sections, go back and secure it to the posts and rails by driving staples every 6 inches. Staple the wire in place as shown in the detail drawing (bottom left inset).

3 **repeat the process** until the fence is covered. If you run out of wire before reaching the end of the fence, splice a new roll by overlapping the meshes on a post. Cut the old piece so that it ends at the far edge of the post (bottom center inset). Lay the new piece on top of it, overlapping two vertical wires if possible. Fasten both pieces to the post with staples every 6 inches (bottom right inset). Finally, fasten 1-by-6 kickboards to the bottom of the fence. To give the fence a more finished appearance, cover the staples by nailing 1-by-4 boards to the posts and 1-by-2 strips to the top rail.

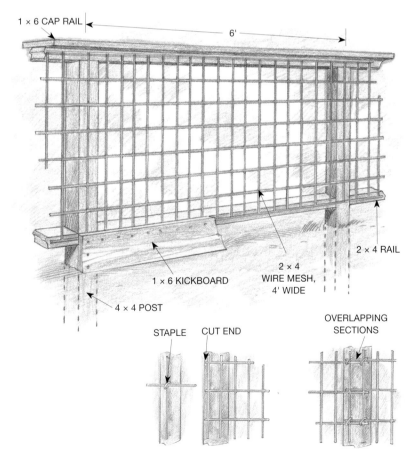

1 × 6 CAP RAIL

6'

1 × 6 KICKBOARD

4 × 4 POST

2 × 4 WIRE MESH, 4' WIDE

2 × 4 RAIL

STAPLE

CUT END

OVERLAPPING SECTIONS

building gates
HOW TO MAKE THEM STURDY AND STRONG

A GATE TAKES MUCH MORE ABUSE THAN THE REST OF A FENCE, SO MAKE SURE IT'S SOLIDLY constructed and attached with hardware that's sufficiently strong. The latches and hinges should be rust and corrosion resistant.

For the most part, gate-building procedures are quite simple, but they do require precise workmanship. A few miscalculations in gatepost alignment or in measuring, cutting, and assembling gate components will result in a gate that won't open and close smoothly. The gate must be built solidly and attached firmly to the post with heavy-duty hinges, or it will likely start to sag and bind soon after installation.

If you feel the required carpentry is beyond your ability, especially if your design calls for detailed joinery, you might prefer to have this part of your fence erected by a contractor or a professional carpenter.

Inadequate hinges are the usual cause of gate failure. It's better to use an overly strong hinge than one that's not strong enough. A lot of packaged hinges include fasteners that are too short for a heavy gate. Use screws that go as far into the wood as possible without coming out the other side. It's best to use

at least three hinges on gates taller than 5 feet or wider than 3 feet.

If a fence is used to confine small children or a pool, use hinges that will automatically close the gate with springs in the hinge mechanism. For more about gates, see pages 128–129.

building a basic wooden gate

The illustrations on the facing page show how to build a gate with board siding, but you can use whatever type of siding complements your fence. To build a basic gate, you must set and align the gateposts, build the frame, add the siding, hang the gate, and attach the latch. Finally, you'll also need to add a gate stop to keep the gate from swinging past its closed position (Step 6).

Unless you're using existing posts, your first job is to set the gateposts. Set these posts deeper into the ground than ordinary fence posts because of the added stress placed on

INSTALLING A LATCH

Latch designs and installation methods vary. Be sure that the latch design you choose aligns neatly with both the gate frame and the gatepost. Use screws or bolts that are as long as possible without coming out the other side.

To install a self-closing latch, first hold the latch in place on the gatepost and mark the screw holes. Drill pilot holes, and then the fasten the latch in place. Insert the strike into the latch and mark the screw holes on the gate. Again, drill pilot holes, then screw the strike to the gate frame, as shown at right.

them. The spacing of the posts determines the width of the gate.

Measure the distance between the gateposts at both top and bottom. If it varies greatly, straighten the posts, if possible, or else build a lopsided gate to fit. The gate-frame width should allow at least ¹/₂ to ³/₄ inch between the latch post and the gate frame to give the gate room to swing freely. Allow a ¼-inch space between the frame and the hinge post. The gate's height depends on its design and on the height of the fence.

Measure and cut the lumber carefully. Make sure you cut perfectly square corners when you saw, and check any ends that have been cut at the lumberyard to make sure they're also square. As you build, check corners carefully to see that they're square.

building a basic gate

1 SET 4-BY-4 GATEPOSTS at least 3 feet deep in concrete and gravel for extra stability. Add sloping concrete collars to direct water away from the wood. (For more information on installing posts, see page 236.) Carefully plumb and vertically align the posts.

2 BUILD THE FRAME OF 2 BY 4s, working on a table or other flat surface. You can use either simple butt joints or rabbet joints, as shown. Join pieces with water-resistant glue and galvanized nails. Use a square to keep the frame corners at right angles.

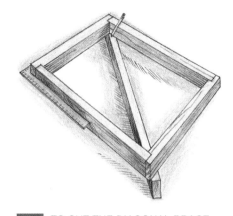

3 TO CUT THE DIAGONAL BRACE, place the frame on top of the 2-by-4 brace and mark sawing angles with a pencil. Saw just outside the pencil marks for a tight fit. Glue and nail the brace to the frame, and then nail on the siding of your choice.

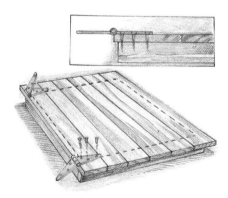

4 ATTACH THE HINGES firmly to the frame. Drill pilot screw holes with a bit slightly smaller than the diameter of the screws.

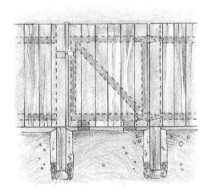

5 TO FIT THE GATE INTO PLACE, prop it on wood blocks to hold it in position. If it's too close to the posts to swing freely, trim the latch side until the gate fits. Attach the loose ends of the hinges to the hinge post. Attach the latch with long screws or bolts.

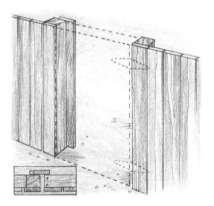

6 ATTACH A VERTICAL 1-by-1, 1-by-4, or 2-by-2 strip of wood to the latch post to stop the gate when it closes. The stop should run from top to bottom.

laying a pathway
WORKING WITH FLAGSTONE AND GRAVEL

IRREGULARLY SHAPED FLAGSTONE IS VERSATILE AND CAN BE LAID IN SEVERAL WAYS. THE MOST pleasing designs result from stones that are carefully fitted and trimmed.

Flagstones can be laid in a bed of sand with sand-packed or dry-mortared joints, in wet mortar over a concrete slab, or directly in stable soil. The last is the easiest but is an option only if the stones are large and thick and not prone to breaking.

Using a sand bed and sand-packed joints method provides a flexible surface that allows for easy repair should tree roots or frosts cause the underlying surface to buckle. The wet-mortar method provides the best protection against both weeds and fractures caused by frost heaves.

Before you begin, review pages 108–109 for ideas and tips on making stone paths.

flagstone basics

Because most flagstones have irregular shapes, they'll probably need trimming before they are set. Mark out the perimeter of the path, lay out the stones, and shift them around until you achieve a pleasing design that requires minimal cutting. If the stone is brittle or thin, don't step on it until it's bedded securely, or it may snap.

Chip off edges with a mason's hammer or a sharp brick set. It's often difficult to keep a stone from splitting or shattering beyond the cut line, so have some extra stones on hand.

The extra-wide gaps between these flagstones are filled with a gravel that has complementary colors. Clumps of blue fescue and petunias soften the edges.

fitting and cutting flagstone

1 LAY THE STONE under its neighbor and trace the cutting line with a pencil.

2 SCORE A ⅛-INCH-DEEP GROOVE along the line with a brick set (or a ⅜-inch-deep groove if you're using a portable circular saw or grinder).

3 PLACE A WOOD SCRAP or a metal pipe under the stone so that the waste portion and scored line overhang it. Strike sharply along the line.

laying a flagstone path

1 INSTALL BENDERBOARD EDGING, then lay landscaping fabric to prevent weeds. Secure fabric edges under edging.

2 SMOOTH A 2-INCH LAYER of sand over the landscaping fabric. Where soil freezes, lay 4 inches of gravel first.

3 AS YOU RAKE, moisten the sand with a fine spray of water.

4 FIRM THE SAND using a drum roller or a hand tamper. Pass over the moist sand several times to pack it down.

5 ADD FLAGSTONES and work them into place to ensure that they are firmly embedded.

6 FILL CRACKS between stones with gravel or, to hold the stones, use something smaller, like decomposed granite.

making a gravel pathway

Gravel, whether smooth river rock or more stable crushed rock, makes a low-cost, fast-draining path that can complement a wide variety of planting schemes. The first step is to install wooden or masonry edgings to hold the loose material in place (see pages 90–91). Lay landscaping fabric to discourage weeds. Gravel surfaces tend to shift when walked on, but the movement will be minimized if you use a compacted base of crushed rock or sand.

1 INSTALL EDGINGS FIRST, then land-scaping fabric or plastic sheeting. Pour decomposed granite or sand over the site, taking care not to dislodge the liner.

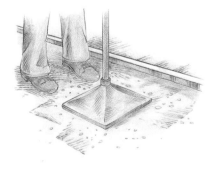

2 RAKE THE BASE MATERIAL evenly over the path until it is a nearly uniform 1 inch thick. Wet the material and then tamp it firmly into place.

3 SPREAD GRAVEL at least 2 inches thick and rake it evenly over the base. Use a drum roller, tamp, or vibrating compactor to press it into place.

laying cut stone

Cut stone laid on a bed of compacted sand makes a durable path or patio, provided the edgings are strong, the stone is laid in a tight pattern, and the joints are kept tightly packed with sand.

Sand-bedding the stones provides a flexible surface that allows for easy repair should tree roots or frosts cause the underlying surface to buckle. Also, if a stone is damaged, it can be replaced easily. To prevent weeds in the joints, lay landscaping fabric beneath the sand. Level and tamp the sand base—the firmer the base is, the more stable the finished surface will be.

Secure the edge of the path or patio by installing a 2-by-6 edging flush with the finish height of the cut-stone surface.

Dig out the area to be paved to a 4-inch depth—this assumes 2 inches of sand and 2-inch-thick stones—and install the edging. If your soil drains poorly, dig 4 inches deeper for a layer of compacted gravel below the sand. If your ground freezes, make the base 6 to 8 inches deep.

For invisible edgings, lay the stones around the edges of the path or patio on a concrete pad. To form the pad, build temporary forms around the path or patio perimeter as if for a concrete footing (page 222). Make the forms the width of one stone, and make the trench deep enough to allow for a 4-inch concrete bed. Pour in concrete and, using a bladed screed, level it one stone's thickness below the top of the forms. Set stones in the wet concrete. Remove the forms after the concrete dries.

Leave some corner and edge spaces unpaved so that a ground cover, such as the baby's tears here, can spread into them.

1 SET THE STONES IN POSITION, varying the size of the joints between stones to accommodate irregularities. Lightly tap each stone into place with a rubber mallet. Place a carpenter's level atop a straight 2 by 4 to check level.

2 WHEN ALL THE STONES ARE IN PLACE, spread sand over them and sweep it into the joints. Wet the area with a light spray to settle the sand. Repeat until the sand is completely settled and is about ¼ inch below the tops of the stones.

laying stepping-stones

Arrange stones in subtly different ways, spaced generously to quicken the pace through a storage area, or somewhat closer to slow the pace down. Raise the stones above grade to show them off, or set them flush in a lawn to eliminate the need to trim around them.

stepping-stones in gravel Set stepping-stones high enough above the surrounding gravel so that gravel doesn't spill over them. In an existing path, excavate holes for the stones and lay them as you would in soil, by exca-vating around the stone's shape 1 inch deeper than its thickness. If you're starting a path from scratch, excavate the area to the needed depth and lay landscaping fabric, followed by sand. Then settle the stones on the base before spreading the gravel. Be sure to buy stepping-stones that are at least 3 inches thick so they will rise above the minimum 2-inch layer of gravel.

A 1-inch-thick sand base is sufficient in most situations. In cold-winter climates or poorly draining soils, install 4 to 8 inches of gravel below the sand. Be especially careful to make a proper base if the path is used regularly throughout the year. You don't want to be continually resetting the stones. On sloping sites, consider setting them in mortar.

Large, heavy stepping-stones don't get dislodged as easily as small, thin ones. If the stones are large and the soil is stable, stepping-stones can sit directly on the soil.

stepping-stones in lawn or soil In flower or vegetable gardens or woodland paths, lay stepping-stones so that they sit 1 to 2 inches above grade. Water will drain off, and surrounding soil and fallen leaves won't wash onto them. They are also more handsome set above grade.

Set stepping-stones in a lawn flush with the soil so you can run the mower right over them. If you lay the stones raised, you'll need to trim the grass around each stone by hand.

Cut around each stone with a straight-edged spade, peel off the turf, and excavate to the full depth of the stone plus 1 inch. Spread 1 inch of sand in the hole and settle the stone until it's firmed seated into the sand and soil.

1 LAY OUT stepping-stones on top of the soil in a pleasing line. Arrange them so that the spaces between them allow for a comfortable, regular walking pace.

2 CUT AROUND each stone with a spade or a knife to mark its shape, then move the stone to one side.

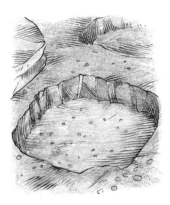

3 EXCAVATE A HOLE for the stone with a straight-edged spade as deep as the stone's thickness plus 1 to 2 inches.

4 SPREAD 2 INCHES OF sand in the hole and moisten it. Place the stone in the hole and twist it until the stone is level and firm.

landscape projects

ONCE THE BASIC STRUCTURE OF YOUR LANDSCAPE IS IN PLACE, you can begin personalizing it. Consider the particular qualities of your site, your family's interests and activities, and the functions you want the outdoor space to serve. You may want to add an overhead so you can use the patio on hot afternoons. Or you might build a trellis or pergola so you can be surrounded by the color and fragrance of climbing roses. A pond with a fountain adds a tranquil note.

In this chapter you'll find enhancements such as a window box and porch skirt, which add beauty and convenience to your outdoor space. Raised beds allow you to garden without straining your back, and they show off your plants. We also offer three compost-making options, a necessity in most gardens. And, finally, for your kids or grandkids, a play set provides hours of fun.

With the personal touches that make the most sense for your family, the yard will become a place that's really used, not just maintained.

building arbors

CREATE SHELTER FROM THE SUN AND SUPPORT FOR VINES

THERE IS NO MORE ROMANTIC WAY TO FRAME AN ENTRY—BE IT A SIDE GATE, A SECLUDED GARDEN path, or a front door—than with an arbor. Arbors are either freestanding or attached to the house with a ledger board. Many arbors are essentially three-dimensional trellises with crosspieces that allow plants to climb up the sides and perhaps overhead as well.

At Lowe's you can find a variety of arbors that are easy to assemble. Some simply stake into the ground. You can also customize a ready-made arbor or build your own as shown on the facing page.

For the uprights, use extra-high deck posts that rest in a concrete slab or are sunk in concrete-filled postholes. Overhead beams support rafters. If the arbor is attached to the house, the ledger takes the place of one beam. You may want to leave rafters open so that you can train a vine over them, or you can cover them with any one of a number of materials—lath, wire, bamboo, shade cloth, lattice, tree or grape stakes, woven reeds, or poles.

Building an arbor is as simple as sinking four posts into the ground and connecting them with crosspieces and beams. This one is dressed up with decorative corner brackets and a pair of window sashes.

choosing materials

A good design takes its cue from your house's architecture. Choose materials and colors that complement the style. If the arbor will be attached to the house, consider how it will affect the view from indoors. Beams that are too low may block a pleasing view. Generally, the lowest beam should not be less than 6 feet 8 inches above the outdoor floor surface. A taller arbor gives vines room to grow and lends a spacious feel to the area. If you plan to place an outdoor dining table under the arbor, allow at least 4½ feet of clearance all around the table and provide additional room for a barbecue area.

For the longest-lasting posts, beams, and rafters, choose pressure-treated wood or naturally decay-resistant materials, such as

ATTACHING AN ARBOR

Although most arbors employ the same basic components—posts, beams, rafters and joists, and some type of roofing—there are many ways to assemble them.

To attach an arbor to a house, install a ledger—much as for a deck, usually a 2 by 4 or a 2 by 6. Connect it with lag screws to wall studs, to second-story floor framing, or to the roof. If your house wall is brick or stone, drill holes and install expanding anchors to bolt the ledger in place.

Set rafters on top of the ledger or hang them from it with anchors, joist hangers, or rafter hangers. If the roof will be flat, square up the rafter ends. Sloped rafters require angled cuts at each end, plus a notch where rafters cross the beam.

LOWE'S QUICK TIP

Carriage bolts are used here to attach the beams, because they have a neat appearance.

redwood or cedar heartwood. You can use 4-by-4 posts for most arbors up to 12 feet tall. Use 2-by-6 beams for spans up to 6 feet, and 2 by 8s for spans up to 9 feet.

laying rafters and installing posts

The rafters control the amount of shade your arbor casts. For example, running them east to west provides midday shade. But if you plan to enjoy the arbor more in the early morning and the late afternoon, run the rafters north to south to maximize sun at those times.

How you attach the top boards also affects shade. If you stand 1 by 2s or 1 by 3s on edge, they will give little shade at midday, when the sun is overhead, but plenty of shade in the morning and afternoon, when the sun is at an angle. For the opposite result, lay them flat.

If you're including an arbor in a new deck, make the deck's posts tall enough to support the arbor. When adding an arbor to an existing deck, bolt the posts to the deck's substructure, placing them directly above or adjacent to the deck posts.

If the arbor will span an existing patio, set the posts in holes outside the edge of the patio or attach them to post anchors, as shown on page 231.

building a basic arbor

This arbor begins with two 4-by-4 posts sandwiched between pairs of 2-by-4 joists. Notched 2-by-6 beams connect the two ends and support eleven 2-by-2 rafters.

If you attach the joists before the posts are set, make sure that the tops of the posts are perfectly level and parallel with each other before setting them in concrete. Another method is to set the posts in concrete first, cut one or both at the top to make them level, and then install the joists.

In the arbor shown, the joists are cut at a 45-degree angle on each end, while the beams are cut more decoratively.

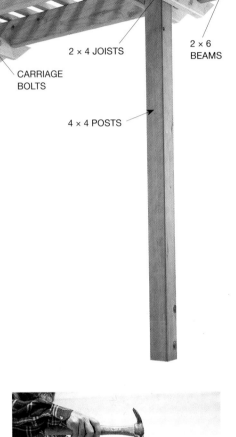

2 × 2 RAFTERS

2 × 4 JOISTS

2 × 6 BEAMS

CARRIAGE BOLTS

4 × 4 POSTS

1 CUT FOUR JOIST PIECES to the same size and shape. Clamp a pair of joists to each post and use a square to make sure they are square to the post and at the same height. Drill all the way through all three thicknesses. A larger countersunk hole, about ⅜ inch deep, helps conceal each carriage bolt's washer and nut. Use a ratchet-and-socket set to drive the nuts below the surface.

2 SET THE POSTS IN POSTHOLES. Use a post level to ensure they are plumb. Then measure to make sure the joists are parallel with each other. Brace the posts temporarily but securely. Cut two beams to the same length and shape, then mark and cut the 1½-inch-deep notches. On the inside faces, where they will be least visible, angle-drill pilot holes and drive screws to attach the beams to the joists.

3 COMPLETE THE ARBOR with 2-by-2 rafters that bridge both beams and are evenly spaced across the top. Nail the pieces from the top down, but if the wood tends to split, drill pilot holes first.

building a freestanding trellis

A SCREEN THAT DOESN'T OVERDO IT

A TRELLIS IS ESSENTIALLY A TWO-DIMENSIONAL FRAME FOR PLANTS, MADE WITH VERTICAL AND horizontal elements fastened together. The traditional model is a rectangular wooden grid that gives plants a good foothold and allows air circulation. But just about anything flat or round—for example, bamboo or wire mesh—that stands up to the elements, supports the weight of mature plants, and can be nailed, screwed, or wired together can serve as a lightweight trellis, especially if it will be supported by a wall or fence.

A freestanding trellis provides both a privacy screen for people and a growing place for vines, and it can be moved around the garden seasonally as needed.

In many cases, you can convert a two-dimensional trellis to a three-dimensional arbor simply by building one or more matching frames, placing them parallel to each other, and bridging them with horizontal braces that create "walls" and a "roof."

A permanent trellis, such as this one made of cedar and topped with decorative finials, becomes a focal point of the garden, even in winter.

choosing materials

Most trellises are made from milled wood: standard dimension lumber, lattice and lath, moldings, dowels, or tree stakes. Wood is easy to work with. It's strong and, if chosen and prepped properly, should stand up to many years of water, wind, and hot summer sun.

The most durable structures are made from naturally decay-resistant woods, such as redwood or cedar heartwoods, or from pressure-treated lumber. Most trellis pieces are lightweight—typically ½-by-1½-inch lath, 1 by 2s, 2 by 2s, and sometimes 2 by 4s. Occasionally, larger freestanding frames are held up with stout 4-by-4 posts or 6-inch-diameter poles. You can let redwood or cedar weather naturally, paint it, or seal it with an exterior finish (though you won't be able to repaint it once it is covered by vines). Pressure-treated lumber can be hard to find in small sizes; if you do use it, you'll probably want to paint or stain it.

Most trellis joinery is simple. Butt joints, such as those in the project on the facing page, are the norm. They are held together by nails, screws, or wire, and sometimes with waterproof glue as well. More formal projects call for more intricate lap joints. You'll want rust-resistant, galvanized fasteners and hardware for these outdoor projects.

1 LAY THE UPRIGHTS ON A FLAT SURFACE, facedown, and lay out crosspieces one at a time. The grid shown uses ⅝-by-1½-inch redwood pieces spaced 8 inches on center. Before assembly, add a dab of waterproof glue where pieces cross. Then nail or screw each intersection. When the finished grid is flipped over, the nail or screw heads are out of sight.

2 IF A SIMPLE STANDARD TRELLIS is all you're after, stop here. But if you'd like to add a frame, here's how. This frame has 1-by-3 verticals. The top piece was shaped from a 2 by 8. To be on the safe side, wait until you have built the grid before sizing the frame. Attach the sides to the top piece with counter-sunk deck screws and glue. Don't put the bottom rail on just yet.

3 SLIDE THE TRELLIS GRID inside the three-sided frame, and then snug the bottom 1-by-3 rail up against the grid's bottom edge. The grid is not as thick as the frame. For a nice de-sign touch, line up the backs, leaving a reveal at the front. Screws and glue hold the bottom rail in place. Add more screws, driven around the edges from the outside in, to keep the grid in place.

building a lattice porch skirt

IT'S A GROUND-LEVEL TRELLIS

IN BETWEEN COSMETIC TOUCHUPS AND MAJOR RENOVATIONS, YOU CAN TACKLE SMALL IMPROVE-
ments to keep a porch looking great. Here's how to handle one of the most common of all
porch projects: replacing or building a new lattice skirt. Keep in mind that these techniques
can also be adapted for replacing lattice on a deck, fence, gate, privacy screen, or trellis.

making the frame

If you are replacing a lattice screen, first remove the old one with a flat pry bar. Measure the openings between the columns or posts. To ensure clearance, make the

Hinged lattice panels dress up the skirt of this front porch while still allowing good air circulation and easy access.

completed frames $^1/_2$ inch narrower than the overall width and 1 inch shorter than the height of the opening. Since the porch shown here had five 26-inch-high openings ranging between $8^1/_2$ and $9^1/_2$ feet long. Because the lattice panels are 8 feet long, a vertical brace was installed in the middle of each frame to conceal the seam between the two lattice pieces and to add needed stability to the frame. If your porch has frames that are shorter than 8 feet, you can safely omit this center brace.

Make the four perimeter pieces of each frame out of a pressure-treated 1 by 6 ripped down to $4^1/_2$ inches wide. Use a pressure-treated 1 by 4 for the center brace. When buying the lumber, choose the straightest, driest boards with the fewest knots that you can find. If 1-by pressure-treated lumber isn't available, use 1-by-6 heart redwood or cedar or radius-edge 5/4 pressure-treated decking.

Cut the frame parts to length and as-semble them facedown on a flat surface. Strengthen the frame with steel reinforce-ment hardware. At each corner joint, install a 6-inch mending plate and a $3^1/_2$-inch flat corner brace (see Step 2, facing page). Posi-tion the hardware pieces about $^1/_4$ inch from the edge of the frame and secure them with $^3/_4$-inch-long flathead screws.

Connect the center brace to the frame with two 4-inch T-plates. Be sure the leg of the T-shaped plate is centered on the 1-by-4 brace. After the frames are assembled, apply a coat of primer, followed by two coats of stain/ sealer or gloss enamel trim paint to match your porch or deck.

attaching the lattice

Shown on the facing page is a forest green, diagonal-pattern plastic lattice. Made of high-density polyethylene, it resists decay, splitting, and mildew. This type of lattice is available at Lowe's in 4-by-8-foot sheets in six colors and three basic patterns: square and basket weave in addition to diagonal. Wood lattice is widely available and also paintable, which means it can more easily be matched to other colors.

First cut the lattice panels down to size using a jigsaw or circular saw. Lay the frames facedown and attach the lattice to them with 1-inch pan-head screws driven through washers (Step 4). Be sure to drill holes just slightly larger than the screw shanks so that the lattice can expand and contract without buckling. If a frame has a center brace, secure the seam between the lattice pieces with two rows of screws (Step 5).

installing the panels

Hang the framed lattice panels from the porch with a 3- or 4-inch strap hinges or T-hinges. Two hinges are sufficient for a panel 8 feet or shorter, bu t use three hinges on one longer than 8 feet. Step 6 shows the installation of 3-inch galvanized T-hinges.

Screw the hinges to the porch fascia first and then set the panels in the openings under the porch. Slip a pry bar under the panel and raise the panel up tight against the porch fascia and the hinge. Use a drill-driver to screw the hinges to the frames.

Finally, check to make sure that the panel swings up and down smoothly. If it drags on the ground, use a shovel or rake to remove some dirt from in front of the panel. Or, if there's a large, uneven gap beneath the panel, add some soil and then smooth it out to create a consistent space between the panel and the ground.

1 REMOVE THE OLD LATTICE SKIRT with a pry bar. If necessary, cut it into pieces with a reciprocating saw first.

2 HOLD TOGETHER EACH CORNER JOINT of the frame with a 6-inch mending plate and a flat corner brace.

3 USE TWO T-PLATES to secure the 1-by-4 center brace to the frame. Fasten the plates with ¾ inch screws.

4 SCREW THE PLASTIC LATTICE to the back of the frames after drilling oversized clearance holes.

5 SECURE THE SEAM between two lattice panels with pan-head screws that are driven through washers.

6 HANG THE LATTICE PANEL by screwing the hinges to the porch fascia first, then lifting the panels and attaching them to the hinges.

making a window box
IT'LL BE THE RIGHT SIZE AND STYLE FOR YOUR HOUSE

WHEN YOU WANT HERBS AND FLOWERS CLOSE AT HAND, TRY BUILDING A WINDOW BOX. ONE BIG advantage to making one yourself instead of buying one is that you get exactly the right size, plus you can stain or paint it to match your house or trim.

Designers recommend that a window box be as long as the width of the window where it will be installed, including trim. To allow enough room for plant roots, make the box about 8 inches high (slightly less for short-lived annuals) and 8 inches wide. To be sure the box has well-draining soil, drill holes in the bottom of the box.

A window box with flowers dresses up the exterior of a house and also improves the view looking out.

building the box
The box shown here is 32 inches long, 8 inches high, and about 8 inches wide. It is made from a single 10-foot 1-by-10 board of clear white pine. Although you'll pay a premium for clear pine, it's a pleasure not to deal with knots, which can bleed through paint finishes.

Boxes can be plain or elaborate, but remember that they are often mostly hidden once full of plants. This box is composed of only five pieces of wood: two sides, two ends, and a bottom. The ends of the outer side are tapered at a 10-degree angle, from 7 inches

HANGING A WINDOW BOX

Some houses may have windowsills wide enough to accommodate flower boxes. If yours does, set the box on spacers so water can drain freely from the bottom. More often, a window box must be attached directly to the side of the house or be held in place by wire attached to the window casing.

A pair of sturdy metal brackets should be enough to support most window boxes. On houses sided with wood, attach the brackets to the house with either galvanized or stainless-steel wood screws. For heavy boxes or when the house's siding is thin, drive screws 1½ inches into studs beneath the sheathing. For masonry walls, wedge or sleeve anchors will safely support the weight of the box. When installing a window box, be careful that it won't trap water against the house. A wood box in direct contact with wood siding is likely to encourage rot.

Vinyl-sided houses present a special problem. The siding needs to be free to move slightly with changes in temperature. When installing brackets on the wall, enlarge the screw hole, allowing ⅛ inch of clearance between the siding and the screw, and seal the gap with silicone caulk to keep water out. Instead of snugging the bracket tightly to the wall, allow a space of about ¹⁄₁₆ inch so the siding can move. Another method is to set the back edge of the window box on the sill and secure it with steel cable attached to the window casing. A third option is to attach the box to the front edge of the sill with T-shaped galvanized brackets: screw the long edge of each bracket to the back of the box, and attach the short leg to the sill.

at the bottom to $8^7/_{16}$ inches at the top. The dimensions aren't critical. But the taper does make the finished box much more interesting to look at.

After the pieces have been cut, they are assembled with an exterior-grade glue and $1^1/_2$-inch trim-head screws. The box could just as easily be nailed together with galvanized box or finish nails, or assembled with galvanized, stainless-steel, or brass screws. When set below the surface of the wood, however, trim-heads are easy to conceal with exterior putty. Choose a high-quality putty,

such as a two-part polyester filler, that holds up well outdoors.

One trick to making the box fit together well is to make sure that its edges are square and corners are 90 degrees.

If you want the box to last more than a couple of years, finishing it inside and out is crucial. A top-quality primer and two coats of 100 percent acrylic latex paint on the outside and a clear wood preservative inside protect this one. And don't forget the drain holes in the bottom. This window box has three pairs of $1/_2$-inch holes spaced along its length.

1 TAPERING THE FRONTS of the end pieces makes the box more interesting. Mark the line with a straight-edge, then cut along it. If necessary, smooth the cut with a block plane.

2 PREDRILL TO AVOID SPLITS. Make the hole in the top piece of wood the same size as, or slightly larger than, the screw shank.

3 GLUE AND SCREW PIECES together. Set screw heads slightly below the surface of the wood, and then conceal them with wood filler.

4 FILL SCREW COUNTERSINKS with an exterior-grade filler. After the filler has cured, sand it flush.

5 USE TOP-QUALITY PRIMER and paint to protect the wood from the elements. A finish coat of 100 percent acrylic latex is more durable than alkyd paint.

making a garden pond
USE A RIGID LINER AND A STONE BORDER

ADD A POND TO YOUR GARDEN IN A DAY OR LESS BY STARTING WITH A PREFORMED PLASTIC SHELL from Lowe's. Installing one is easy, but it does require gloves, a good shovel, and a strong back. You dig a hole, line it with sand, drop in the shell, and fill it with water and plants. Edged with stones and low-growing plants, the pond becomes graceful and inviting.

Preformed pond shells come in a variety of shapes, sizes, and depths. Some have smooth, vertical sides to discourage raccoons, while others have textured walls. Others feature shelves around the sides to hold containers of water plants. Despite their bulk, most shells are light-weight, made of a heavy-duty UV-stabilized polyethylene. Shapes range from tidy ovals to free-form varieties. Volume ranges from about 35 gallons to more than 100 gallons. Costs increase with size.

To help keep the pond clean, you'll need a pump. Submersible models are fine for a small pond like this one. Consider a pump powered by a small photovoltaic collector, but keep in mind that unless solar pumps include batteries, they'll operate only when exposed to sunlight.

Water plants also help keep ponds clean. As a rule, they should cover about two-thirds of the water's surface.

Stones cover the edge of the plastic shell, giving the pond a completely natural appearance. Water plants, low-growing grasses, and perennials also imitate nature's look.

1 SELECT THE SITE AND TRACE THE SHELL. Open areas are better than spots beneath trees whose leaves or needles will build up debris on the pond's bottom. To install a pond in a lawn, remove the sod and keep it moist and protected in a shady area so you can reuse it later. Set the pond shell on the cleared, level site, adjusting it to face the direction you want. Holding a yardstick vertically against the outside edge, trace around the pond shell to outline it in the soil.

2 REMOVE THE POND SHELL and mark the soil outline with sand (as shown), or use a hose or a length of rope. Estimate the location of interior contours that will require a different elevation, and mark them as well.

3 DIG THE HOLE INSIDE THE OUTLINE. Make the hole 2 inches deeper and wider than the shell to accommodate a layer of sand. With a carpenter's level, make sure the bottom of the hole is flat. Remove protruding stones or roots, then cover the bottom with 2 inches of packed, damp sand. Recheck flatness with a level.

4 PLACE THE POND SHELL IN THE HOLE slightly higher than the surrounding ground, with the top lip level. (Use a level to span the pond.) Adjust the shell as necessary. Start filling the pond, and as it fills, backfill around the shell with moist sand, tamping as you work. Periodically reconfirm that the shell is level. Use backfill to slope the soil away from the pond's edges, then cover the edges with stones and plants.

making a pebble fountain
ADD THE SOUND OF MOVING WATER TO YOUR GARDEN

IN A PEBBLE FOUNTAIN, WATER RISES FROM A RESERVOIR THROUGH A FOUNTAINHEAD NOZZLE ON a pump, spills over a tray of pebbles, and trickles back down to the reservoir.

Assembling a fountain that is accented with small rocks or pebbles such as the one shown here is relatively simple. Besides the rocks, you'll need a pump, a fountain jet, a grate to set over the basin to support the rocks, a small amount of builder's sand, and an underground basin, as shown on the facing page. The basin can be anywhere from 18 to 24 inches wide and should be at least 15 inches deep.

We made our fountain a 4-foot circle, but yours can be any shape you like. The spray jet sits just above the top of the stones, as shown. Add a valve so that you can fine-tune the flow. We used a sturdy plastic grate from a pond supplier to hold the rocks. You could also use heavy wire mesh, but it's not as strong. If you plan to add pebbles that are smaller than the grate openings, add a layer of hardware cloth on top to catch them.

A lively spray jet is at the center of this ground-level fountain, ringed by two colors of rock.

1 PREPARE THE SITE by first marking the outline of your fountain. Remove any sod with a shovel or spade. Then dig a deeper hole for the center basin where your fountain pump will sit, making it slightly wider and deeper than your chosen container.

2 INSTALL THE BASIN, pack sand or gravel around it, and tamp it level. Check that the rim is level, adding or removing sand as needed. To help support the sides, backfill the hole with some of the excavated soil or more sand. Tamp down the sides and check again to ensure that it is level.

3 ADD THE PUMP AND GRATE. Place the pump atop a clean brick inside the basin. Take the electrical cable out over the edge of the basin in the direction of a receptacle that's protected by a ground-fault circuit interrupter. For safety, bury the cable in PVC conduit.

4 PLACE A GRATE OVER the basin, making sure it overlaps the edges by at least 6 inches on all sides. Cut out an access hole big enough to put your hand through comfortably so you can reach the pump to adjust the water flow or clear the filter screen. Place a square

piece of mesh over the cutout, large enough not to sag through the hole once it's covered with rocks.

5 SET THE ROCKS after filling the basin with water. Place a few larger stones on the edges of the grate to secure it, then cover the rest of the grate with rocks and pebbles. Plug in the pump and check the jet spray. Adjust the water flow if necessary to ensure that the spray looks the way you want it to—and to be sure the water drips back into the basin.

building a raised bed
MAKE GARDENING EASIER, NEATER, AND MORE SUCCESSFUL

A RAISED BED IS JUST WHAT THE NAME IMPLIES: A PLANTING BED ELEVATED 8 TO 12 INCHES ABOVE soil level. In its most basic form, it's simply a raised plateau of soil. More often, though, you'll encounter raised beds surrounded by a low wall of wood (such as 2-by lumber or railroad ties), concrete, brick, or stone.

ultimate garden bed

You can build the basic raised bed pictured below in a few hours, then add versatility by mounting PVC pipes inside to hold hoops that elevate bird netting or row covers over your crops. Orient your bed north to south for maximum sun exposure.

Although making a raised bed takes a bit of effort, the advantages are many. If you have problem soil—impenetrable clay, nutrient-deficient sand, a soil that's highly acid or alkaline or that's compacted from construction—a raised bed filled with planting mix may be your best shot at raising healthy plants. Particularly where drainage is slow to nonexistent, a raised bed is the easiest way to provide well-drained soil for roots.

Even if your garden soil is good enough for what you want to grow, a raised bed may be worth having. It will help you prepare a

productive plot for intensive gardening, and it is a defined area where you can add topsoil, amendments, and fertilizer to make the finest possible soil.

In cold-winter regions, soil in raised beds warms earlier than that in regular garden plots, allowing you to plant earlier. When it comes time to pick flowers or veggies, the elevated soil level means less bending. And the fact that plants and soil are contained makes the entire operation neat and tidy. Water, fertilizer, and soil stay inside the bed.

When planning a raised bed, choose the site carefully. Most vegetable, flower, and herb plants love sun. For those kinds of plants, place the bed where it will receive at least 6 hours of sunlight daily.

Loosen the soil under the raised bed and amend the existing soil with the planting mix you'll use to fill the bed, creating some transition between the native soil and that of the bed.

To build this raised bed, you will need a table saw or other power saw to cut the wood. After cutting, treat the wood on all sides with an alkyd sealer. An electric drill is helpful for driving screws. The total cost is less than $200.

With a table saw or other power saw, cut four 16-inch-tall corner posts from a 6-foot 4 by 4. Cut two of six 8-foot-long 2 by 6s in half. Cut a 10-foot length of 1-inch PVC pipe into four 12-inch-long pieces, and cut two 10-foot lengths of $1/2$-inch PVC pipe into 6-foot-long pieces. Stain the lumber and let it dry overnight. Assemble the pieces on a hard, flat surface.

Holding lettuce and parsley, this raised bed is about 8 feet long and 4 feet wide.

1 BUILD THE BED UPSIDE DOWN. Begin by setting a 4-foot 2 by 6 on its thin edge on pavement and then place a 16-inch post at one end. Secure the post with two 3½-inch screws. Repeat at the other end of the board. Repeat with the other short board. Join the short sides with an 8-foot board and secure them with two screws. Add the other long side. Add a second layer of 2 by 6s.

2 FLIP THE BED RIGHT SIDE UP and move it into position, marking with a trowel each corner post's location. Move the bed aside. Dig a 5- to 6-inch-deep hole for each post. Put the bed back into place, with the posts in their holes. Fill around the posts with soil.

3 INSTALL THE LINING after leveling the existing soil at the bottom of the bed. Tamp soil smooth. Line the bed with a hardware cloth to keep out gophers and moles. Trim the hardware cloth with shears to fit around corner posts.

4 ATTACH THE PIPES that will support bird netting or a row cover. Attach four 12-inch pieces of 1-inch PVC pipe inside the bed on the long sides. Space pipes 4 feet apart, 2 feet from each end. Screw on two tube straps to secure each pipe. Fill the bed with planting mix, rake it smooth, and moisten it with a gentle spray from the hose.

5 INSERT THE HOOPS to form the frame for a protective cover. Simply bend two 6-foot pieces of ½-inch PVC pipe to form semicircles, then slip their ends into the 1-inch pipes inside the bed. Then drape the bird netting or row covers over them.

building compost bins
THREE TIME-TESTED SYSTEMS

THERE ARE NUMEROUS REFERENCES TO COMPOST IN THIS BOOK, AND FOR GOOD REASON. IT'S THE secret ingredient of many of the best gardens. Using it to amend soil prior to planting or spreading it around established plants as a mulch is one of the best things you can do for plants. Composting is also the most practical way to recycle garden and kitchen waste. You can read more about making compost and using it for mulch on pages 391–395. On these pages are directions for making three kinds of compost bins.

three-bin composter

This classic three-section container allows you to always have a bin for fresh material, and another bin for finished compost. The bin on the left holds new material, the one in the center contains the partially decomposed material, and the bin on the right holds compost that is ready to use. Material is forked from bin to bin as composting progresses. Side boards are spaced for air penetration and slide out for easy turning and removal of compost.

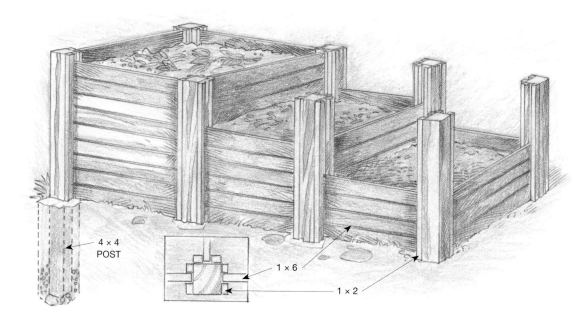

4 x 4 POST

1 x 6

1 x 2

1 DIG EIGHT POSTHOLES, about 3 feet deep, in two rows. The holes should be about 3 feet apart. Shovel a couple of inches of gravel into each hole and set a 6-foot-long 4-by-4 post in each hole. Use a level to check each post for plumb, then brace the posts temporarily. Mix and pour concrete into the holes. Allow a day for the concrete to set.

2 HAVE YOUR LUMBERYARD rip-cut pieces of 1-by-2 lumber to 1¼ inches wide, or rip it yourself with a table saw or radial-arm saw. Cut 40 pieces long enough to reach from the top of a post to the ground. Attach them to two or three sides of the posts, as shown, by drilling pilot holes and driving 1⅝-inch deck screws. Leave a 1-inch gap between the 1-by pieces.

3 CUT PIECES OF 1 BY 6 to fit loosely between the posts, so you can easily slide them in and out. Attach a 1-by-2 spacer to the bottom of each 1 by 6 to give the compost breathing room.

1 CUT TEN 1 BY 6s into 36-inch lengths and ten into 34½-inch lengths (see illustration below). Cut twenty 2 by 2s into 6-inch lengths. Lay each 34½-inch board over two 2 by 2s, with one 2 by 2 flush with each end but offset from the top edge by 1 inch. Drive two screws through the 1 by 6s into each 2 by 2.

2 PLACE ONE 34½-INCH BOARD upside down with 2 by 2s extending upward. Place a 36-inch board against one end, flush with the top, bottom, and outside edge. Connect them with two wood screws through the 1 by 6 into the 2 by 2. Add a second 34½-inch board at the other end of the 36-inch board. Complete the section with another 36-inch board, making a 36-inch square. Repeat the process for each of the remaining four sections. Apply two coats of wood sealer.

stackable compost bins

This design is simply five 36-inch-square boxes without bottoms. Set one box on the ground, perhaps with another box stacked on top, and start the compost pile by filling it. Stack on the other sections as you add more compostable material. You'll have about 20 cubic feet of finished compost after about six weeks.

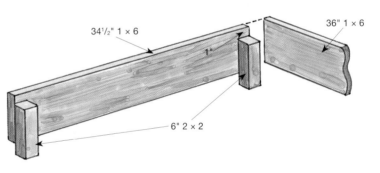

34½" 1 × 6   1"   36" 1 × 6   6" 2 × 2

single bin with removable frame

A compost maker need not be a complicated affair. All you really need for an annual collection of leaves, for instance, is a container with plenty of ventilation and a removable side so that you can easily add to the bin and then mix the ingredients with a shovel.

Construct four frames out of 2 by 2s, all cut to the desired height of the finished bin, usually 3 to 4 feet. Cut and attach a piece of chicken wire or hardware cloth to the inside of each frame. Fasten three of the frames together in overlapping fashion, as shown. Fasten the remaining frame with eyehook latches so that it can be removed easily. You can build a floor for this bin or simply rest it on the ground.

building a backyard play set
TWO KID FAVORITES COMBINED: SANDBOX AND SLIDE

THIS GYM PROVIDES A VARIETY OF ACTIVITIES FOR YOUNG ONES. NOT ONLY CAN THEY SLIDE, CLIMB, and play in the sandbox, but the area below the platform makes an ideal hideout.

A gang of kids turns this simple structure into a perpetual-motion machine. Fenced in, shaded, and surrounded by soft mulch, it is a space as comfortable for kids as for parents.

LOWE'S QUICK TIP

At Lowe's, you'll find an array of playground gym components, including slides (plastic or metal), ladders, rope swings, monkey bars, and net ladders. These parts can be bought separately or in kits that save you money and come with complete instructions.

POSTHOLE LAYOUT

In the plan, each square equals approximately 2 feet and the dimensions apply to the gym pictured. Your plan may vary—if you use a manufactured slide, for instance—or you may customize the gym in other ways. Once your own plan is established, carefully plot out post placement and mark each post's location with a stake before digging.

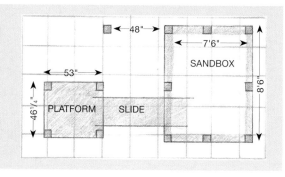

1 DETERMINE THE POSITIONS OF ALL THE POSTS (see the diagram on the facing page). Check that everything is square. Dig postholes at least 3 feet deep. Set the posts in the holes, brace them so that they are plumb, and check again that they are square in relation to each other. Pour concrete into the holes and allow it to set for two days. Use a level to mark the posts before cutting them to height. You may want to add a decorative post cap or adorn the post tops with bevel cuts.

2 TO BUILD THE PLATFORM, install the front and rear joists at the correct height for the slide you have chosen, using $3/8$-by-$3\frac{1}{2}$-inch lag screws with washers. Add the remaining joists and attach them with 3-inch deck screws. Cut 2-by-6 deck boards to fit, then anchor them with two 3-inch deck screws driven into each joist.

3 SET ONE 4-BY-4 RAMP SUPPORT against the platform at the desired angle, scribe the angle onto the face of the ramp support, and cut along this line. Cut a matching angle in the other 4-by-4 ramp support. Cut 12 or so 2-by-6 ramp boards to $46\frac{1}{2}$ inches and attach them from behind with $3/8$-by-$3\frac{1}{2}$-inch lag screws. Then attach three 2-by-6 ramp cleats for easy climbing.

4 FOR THE SANDBOX, attach 1-by-8 sides to each post with 3-inch deck screws. Miter-cut 2 by 6s for the caps, supported by 2-by-4 cleats. Attach the slide to the platform, following the manufacturer's instructions.

5 ATTACH 2-BY-6 horizontal rails about 3 feet above the platform. Taper-cut 2 by 4s to serve as railing uprights. Space them evenly, about 4 inches apart, and attach them with 3-inch screws.

6 FOR THE HANGING BAR, have a 1-inch galvanized pipe cut to length. Anchor it at the desired height (depending on the size of your children) with a pipe flange at each end.

7 SAND ALL THE EDGES smooth and apply a coat of waterproof sealer to all surfaces. Fill the sandbox with playground-grade sand.

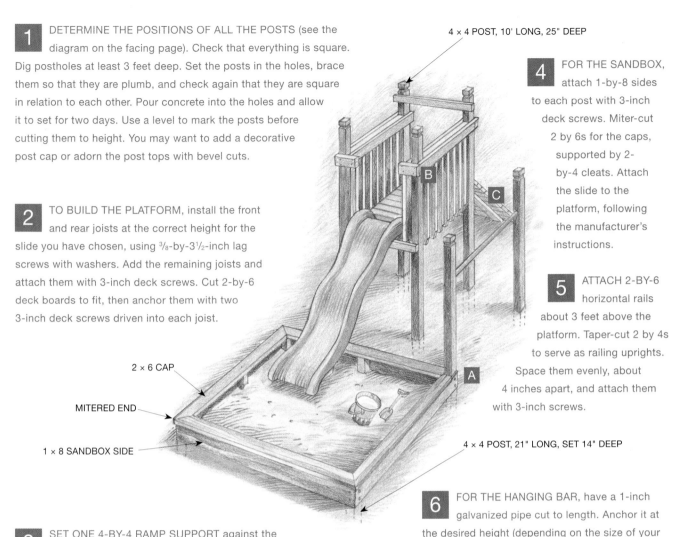

4 × 4 POST, 10' LONG, 25" DEEP

2 × 6 CAP

MITERED END

1 × 8 SANDBOX SIDE

4 × 4 POST, 21" LONG, SET 14" DEEP

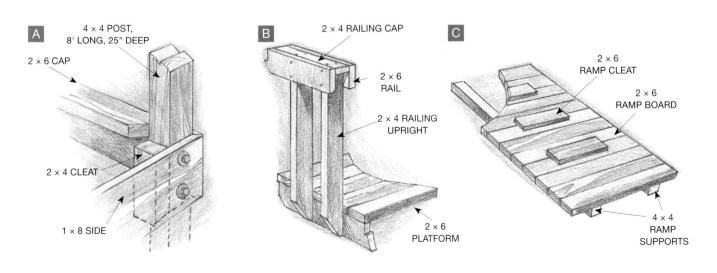

A

4 × 4 POST, 8' LONG, 25" DEEP

2 × 6 CAP

2 × 4 CLEAT

1 × 8 SIDE

B

2 × 4 RAILING CAP

2 × 6 RAIL

2 × 4 RAILING UPRIGHT

2 × 6 PLATFORM

C

2 × 6 RAMP CLEAT

2 × 6 RAMP BOARD

4 × 4 RAMP SUPPORTS

finishing touches

THE IDEAS IN THIS CHAPTER WILL HELP YOU PERSONALIZE YOUR outdoor room. Consider the particular qualities of your site, your or your family's interests and activities, and the functions you want the outdoor space to serve.

Create a natural outdoor retreat in your garden by adding seating, tables, and potted plants. With an ornament or two, an underused spot in the garden is transformed into a comfortable outdoor room—the perfect antidote to a busy day.

You may want to include lighting so you can use the patio in the evening, or an overhead that makes it pleasant to be outdoors even on sunny days. Perhaps you'd like a built-in grill. Or you might build a trellis so you can be surrounded by the color and fragrance of climbing roses. Add a fire pit, night lighting, the sound of water, and—most important—enjoy the space with family and friends.

furnishing the landscape

SEEK DURABILITY IN CHAIRS, TABLES, AND BUILT-INS

YOU CAN INSTANTLY ENHANCE THE LOOK OF YOUR OUTDOOR ROOM BY PURCHASING ATTRACTIVE patio chairs and tables. Choose high-quality furniture that holds up well under conditions in your area so it will still look great and provide comfort as much as 10 years later. Furniture that stays outdoors needs to be exceptionally durable.

New kinds of outdoor furniture offer the traditional look of wicker but in materials that are long lasting and weather resistant.

To save space, build in seating wherever you can. For example, put benches into a deck rail, cap a low wall or raised bed with planks wide enough to sit or place food trays on, and make garden steps wide enough for seating. An inexpensive folding table is useful if you have no space for something permanent. Simply store it in the garage when you're not using it and drape a pretty cloth over it when you need it for the garden.

furniture frames

The choice of furnishings for your yard depends on the style of your outdoor room and its exposure to the weather. Spaces in temperate climes or under a sheltering arbor or roof can accommodate more fragile materials than more exposed areas can.

Natural materials and textures are hallmarks of country and cottage styles. Wicker furniture recalls late-19th-century verandas

ADIRONDACK-STYLE
CHAIR

PORTABLE
HAMMOCK

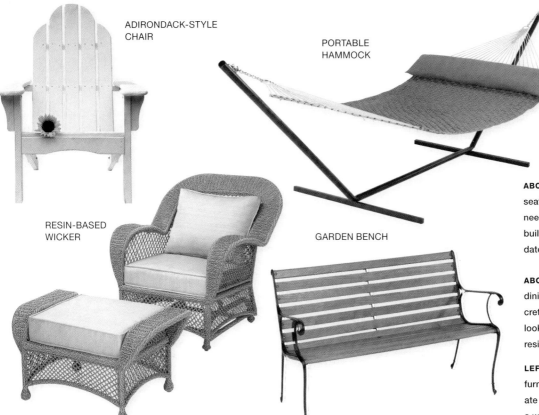

RESIN-BASED
WICKER

GARDEN BENCH

ABOVE LEFT: Portable seating handles everyday needs, and surrounding built-in benches accommodate the occasional crowd.

ABOVE RIGHT: This custom dining table of cast concrete has a rustic, country look and superior weather resistance.

LEFT: Portable outdoor furniture designed to tolerate the elements comes in a wide variety of styles.

and will never go out of style, though synthetic wicker can withstand more weather. Wrought-iron chairs and benches also have a suitably old-fashioned appearance. Or try a bentwood creation.

Aiming for a classic look? It's often anchored by a good, stout wooden chair or bench. Usually this kind of outdoor furniture is constructed from hardy, durable woods like teak or redwood. Adirondack chairs, sling chairs, and vintage metal chairs are also

classics. Matching sets remain popular, though some designers mix different kinds of furniture, combining wood and metal, for instance, just for the variety.

Modern designs call for furniture with bright colors, sensuous and sculptural shapes, and retro-modern style. These products are usually made of tough, all-weather materials like polypropylene or aluminum.

For maximum versatility, consider folding furniture, which can be stowed away when

ABOVE: Painted a bold red, a quartet of wicker chairs surrounds a low table.

RIGHT: A traditional-style but maintenance-free bench features a powder-coated aluminum frame and synthetic wood slats.

night falls. And don't forget another fair-weather friend, the hammock.

fabrics

Fabrics soften the hard lines of your furnishings, completing the "outdoor room" look, and padded seat cushions add comfort and color. Choose weatherproof fabrics if they'll be exposed for long periods. Synthetics like acrylic and, to a lesser degree, polyester are longest lasting. The best acrylics are coated to resist moisture and stains. Protected outdoor areas allow a broader range of natural fabrics. Both acrylic and polyester provide a wider range of accents and are easy to stash when stormy weather threatens.

protecting wooden furniture

Water and sunlight are your furniture's worst enemies. Penetrating oils, varnishes, and paints are the finishes most often chosen to prevent water damage. Paint offers the most

FURNITURE MATERIALS

ALUMINUM AND STEEL Strong, stand up well to years of harsh weather. Aluminum is rustproof. New finishes have increased versatility. Hand-forged wrought-aluminum frames and vinyl strap seating create furniture that is not only durable but also very comfortable. Powder-coat finishes are more durable than anodizing or paint.

RESIN By far the least expensive option. Stays cool in the sun and requires little maintenance. Store in the shade to enhance longevity.

WICKER AND RATTAN Not as long-lived as other materials but will last many years, especially if painted every other year or so. Inexpensive. Store indoors over winter.

WOOD Timeless appeal and long lasting if durable species such as teak or oak are used. Needs annual sealer and best if stored out of winter weather.

WROUGHT IRON Distinctive, formal look. Available in a wide array of styles. Touch up chipped paint to prevent rust.

protection from the sun, and generally the higher the gloss, the greater the sun protection. Some varnishes, such as spar and polyurethane varnishes, contain special UV blockers that protect the wood from the sun.

Furniture built from decay-resistant woods, such as cedar heartwood, redwood, teak, or tropical ironwoods, may be left unfinished. They will gradually fade to an attractive gray over time and require little maintenance other than removal of dirt and mildew. But exposure to weather will cause these woods to crack, however. To protect them and prevent graying and mildew, use a clear water repellent with UV protectors and a mildewcide. If you prefer the natural gray color, use a product with no UV protectors.

If you choose a typically decay-prone wood, finishing is essential to beautify, to conceal mismatched grains, and to protect from the elements. Use an alkyd primer prior to painting with either a latex or an alkyd paint, or use a stain that both colors and soaks into the wood.

TOP LEFT: A comfortable chair and an umbrella turn a special view into many special moments. In the container, 'La Jolla' bougainvillea blooms.

TOP RIGHT: A Victorian-style cast-iron bench lends its slightly antique, old-fashioned feel to a garden.

ABOVE LEFT: Resin furniture, now available in many styles, is an inexpensive option.

ABOVE RIGHT: A traditional porch rocker may be the right choice for a covered porch on a warm evening.

LOWE'S QUICK TIP

Clean wooden outdoor furniture that has been coated with an exterior-grade varnish with soapy water. Be sure to completely rinse the furniture with clean water. With the exception of cedar and teak, store wooden furniture indoors through winter.

the magic of paint
COLOR CAN TRANSFORM A GARDEN

"COLOR" AND "GARDEN" ARE NATURALLY PAIRED IDEAS WHETHER YOU PICTURE BEDS OF BLOOMING annuals or the many shades of green. But one of the quickest ways to add color to a garden is with paint. You can enliven the scenery with a single painted chair, brighten a path with vivid orange paving stones, or paint an entire wall pale pink or robin's egg blue. Color can highlight any area of the garden. Imagine painted pots tucked into a flower bed. Painting an ordinary door or gate a bright color turns it into a focal point.

Furniture painted in bold colors adds a funky ambience to a tiny backyard. The coordinated primary colors even match the color of the rust on the steel arbor.

As with any painting project, start with sample chips from Lowe's paint department. Then paint just a small portion of your project to gauge the effect. When in doubt, choose one shade lighter than you'd planned. That way, you can easily darken the color—or change it completely.

To achieve the best finish, paint in fair weather, out of direct sun, after morning dew, and at least 2 hours before evening dampness. Prepare the surface by removing dirt, grease, rust, and paint flakes. For new wood, prime the surface with one or two coats of latex or exterior wood primer. Then paint with flat latex, vinyl exterior enamel, or house paint in the desired sheen. For plaster and stucco, use exterior latex paint. A roller will apply the paint in a more uniform layer.

To paint cast-iron furniture, remove rust (using steel wool, sanding blocks, or a chemical rust remover), and then apply a paint that prohibits rust.

BELOW LEFT: Painted lattice, painted furniture, and painted artwork enliven this patio.

BELOW RIGHT: Fanciful colors jazz up the door and ramp of an old barn.

BOTTOM LEFT: Given a coat of paint, a zigzag seat wall becomes a statement.

BOTTOM RIGHT: A terra-cotta jar stained with a blue wash makes the green plants pop.

cooling and heating
HOW TO TAKE THE EDGE OFF WEATHER EXTREMES

SPENDING TIME OUTDOORS OFTEN MEANS CONTENDING WITH HEAT AND cold. While it makes no sense to try to make the outdoors like the indoors, if you can make the hottest days a little cooler or the cool ones a little warmer, you can enjoy much more time in your yard.

cooling

patio umbrellas may be the simplest and most flexible solution to keeping cool. They provide portable shelter from sun and rain, and they offer a convenient and affordable alternative to gazebos, pavilions, screened rooms, and awnings.

Umbrellas vary between 6 feet and 12 feet in height, and they unfurl up to 10 feet in diameter or more. Styles with variable tilt positions and a canopy that rotates on an offset arm

A polyester roll shade cuts 90 percent of the sun's glare. It is opaque from the outside, but from the inside looking out, visibility is not blocked.

allow constant shade without your having to move the base. In addition to classic market umbrellas, Lowe's offers an umbrella with solar-powered lights that keeps you cool by day and has enough light for dining at night.

solar screens that are designed to cut glare and reduce heat may be either retractable shades or stationary panels. In both cases, they attach to patio overhangs, arbors, and awnings. While some are custom designed and others improvised from items such as bamboo roller shades, ready-made exterior shades are increasing in popularity. Lowe's offers several options.

The exterior fabrics of commercial solar screens are woven from synthetic material, and the openings in the weave permit air circulation and outward visibility while providing visual privacy. In addition to keeping your outdoor room comfortable, exterior solar screens reduce heat transfer through windows, helping to keep your home cool and to reduce energy costs.

screened rooms protect you from the rain, provide filtered shade on hot days, and keep bugs out. Kids will build memories when they have a midsummer sleepover in a screened room. A screened room is often a rectangular space attached to the house, but you can also buy a gazebo kit that comes equipped with screens.

misters are worth considering if you live in an area with not only hot but also dry summers. In very dry air the mist evaporates almost instantly. Called flash evaporation, the process cools the surrounding air by as much as 20 degrees F.

Most are essentially sprinkler systems that spray a fine mist of water. One option is a kit that includes at least 30 feet of hose that can be attached to an overhead structure, and several nozzles that connect to the hose. Installed, it creates a mist over a large area. Or you can purchase a fan that attaches to a garden hose and directs a heavier mist over a specific area. Fog systems that operate at very high water pressures are also available.

TOP LEFT: A patio misting system attaches easily to an overhead structure.

TOP RIGHT: This steel-framed gazebo assembles in a day. The overhead fabric is weather resistant, and insect netting is easy to hang as needed.

ABOVE: Offset umbrellas move the pole out of the way for convenience and for improved sight lines.

Perhaps a grand, permanent fireplace like this one can be a part of your patio.

heating

To keep the party going when the weather turns cool, add heat. Portable stand-up patio heaters are practical in most situations. A commercial stainless-steel patio heater, sometimes known as an umbrella, radiates its warming rays from its top, producing a circle of heat as large as 20 feet in diameter. A gas-fired directional heater mounts to a house's eaves, allowing it to throw heat efficiently without being intrusive. Or choose an overhead infrared heater, which directs heat down to warm a more defined area. All of these types of heaters are powered by propane or natural gas.

portable firepits are the way to go if propane or natural gas aren't available. Old-fashioned–looking models are made of cast iron or clay, while modern-looking versions are generally made of powder-coated steel.

Portable firepits that burn wood are essentially elaborate versions of a camp-fire rock ring, and are popular for their ease of use and flexibility.

Use a portable firepit at home or take it on a picnic. Most are fueled by wood or compressed logs, though others run on propane or gel alcohol. While they are not intended for cooking, you can add an optional grill to some models. A sturdy wire-mesh spark screen is a sensible safety option for portable fireplaces.

If you opt to install a permanent firepit, consider making it at least 24 inches in diameter, though 36 inches is better, giving you more room to build a good fire. As an inexpensive alternative to a custom-built firepit, consider using a 24-inch-long section of large concrete pipe. Flip it up on end and sink it partially into the ground.

chimeneas are a popular option, especially where their Southwestern style looks right. Traditional versions are manufactured from clay, like a plant pot, and can be very fragile. Newer types are made of metal or iron. All types are designed to burn small logs.

Chimeneas often come in two components: the base or bowl, where the fire goes, and the neck or chimney. Because they have a small chimney, they direct smoke upward and away from your face. The characteristic chimney also may be integral to the base or sold separately. You can find chimeneas in unadorned terra-cotta or in more decorative finishes and colors. Chimeneas of cast iron, aluminum, steel, and copper are also available.

Add 3 to 4 inches of sand or fine gravel to the base before making your first fire in a chimenea. And for a clay chimenea, burn only small fires the first few

CHIMENEA

times you use it in order to temper the clay and help prevent it from cracking. Similarly, rain can crack a hot clay chimenea, so be wary making a fire in one if rain is forecast. Store a clay chimenea in a garage or other protected place for the winter if you live in a colder climate. Metal or iron chimeneas can be left outside year-round.

built-in fireplaces are the most permanent and also the most expensive outdoor heating option. Because these structures require a significant investment, they are usually designed to complement the architecture of the house and garden.

Outdoor fireplaces are just like indoor ones. They have a firebox, chimney, flue, and hearth. Because they are constructed just like an indoor fireplace, they have to meet local building regulations. And, unlike portable fireplaces and chimeneas, outdoor fireplaces can be built into a wooden deck. (Check with your local building officials and fire department about any codes governing outdoor fireplaces, fire pits, or chimeneas.)

BELOW LEFT: For your garden, consider a refined version of the classic campfire. Marshmallows are optional.

BELOW RIGHT: Move a portable fireplace like this steel one to exactly where it's needed.

BOTTOM LEFT: A homemade, and artfully adorned, steel fireplace is the center of this tiny patio.

BOTTOM CENTER: An elegant stone water feature with gas nozzles makes an instant conversation piece.

BOTTOM RIGHT: Propane-powered patio heaters come in various forms, such as this one that combines infrared heat with a gas light.

outdoor kitchens

DINING ALFRESCO MAKES YOUR YARD A RESORT

AN OUTDOOR COOKING SPACE CAN BE A FAIRLY SIMPLE AFFAIR—A GRILL UNIT AND A SMALL TABLE IN an area that has enough room for several people to converse while flipping burgers. Or it can be a full-blown kitchen complete with a sink, running water, spacious counters and cabinets, and even a small refrigerator. In fact, including multiple cooking units in an outdoor kitchen design including a pizza oven, a smoking chimney (for smoking meats), or a deep-fat cooker (for frying a turkey) has become increasingly popular, and for good reason: It makes sense to move the messiest and smokiest cooking operations out of the house, where they are fun rather than annoying for their heat and mess. Some families enjoy having a second gas-powered grill unit with a tight-fitting lid that can keep cooked food warm.

In some climates and situations, it makes more sense to move the formal dining room outdoors. This one has all the comforts of indoors but in the open air.

Before starting to design, learn where the sun will shine during the hours when you are most likely to cook. Place the outdoor kitchen in a comfortable spot so that you'll have plenty of shade during late afternoons in summer. If there is no tree nearby to provide shade, perhaps position a large umbrella. Plan the cooking area so that you'll have easy access to the kitchen. It should be near the kitchen door but 4 or 5 feet off to the side, out of the main traffic pattern. The outdoor dining area should be nearby.

Check manufacturers' guidelines for safe placement of your cooking unit. It should not be near anything flammable, such as a wooden railing. Make sure that food won't touch pressure-treated lumber, as the chemicals that treat the lumber can contaminate food.

Remember that no matter how well appointed your outdoor kitchen is, some of the food cooked or eaten outside will be prepared or stored inside. And the leftovers will be returned there. That is why it's a good idea to make sure the outdoor area has easy access to the indoor kitchen. Smooth, well-tended paths leading from the house are much appreciated by people shuttling back and forth. Use the base map you created (see page 176) to help place the outdoor kitchen, as well as dining and lounging areas, in the most practical locations.

All food preparation surface areas should be made from materials that are easy to sanitize and keep clean, so choose materials with that in mind. Glazed ceramic tiles, for example, are an excellent choice for countertops. Materials used for counters, fireplaces,

BELOW LEFT: Portable grills clad in stainless steel are weather resistant.

BELOW RIGHT: Built-in grills come in many sizes and styles and can fit into a variety of counters.

BOTTOM LEFT: A counter of cultured stone is the base of this grill.

BOTTOM RIGHT: This wooden counter has a tiled surface as well as an overhead shelter.

or fire pits should also complement house and patio building materials. For example, if you plan to build with bricks, match those used in walls and paving in other parts of your house and landscape.

climate considerations

Where winds are common, situate your outdoor kitchen on the lee side of the house, perhaps where the main house and a wing of the house join. Fences or other windscreens, such as hedges, can also reduce the influence of prevailing winds.

Where summer rains are common and unpredictable, some kind of overhead protection will very much extend the number of enjoyable days outdoors. Often, a small covered area you can retreat to if rains come is enough.

In sunny climates, make sure there's plenty of shade, whether from trees or an arbor, as well as areas that take full advantage of natural breezes.

planning your outdoor kitchen

A built-in propane or charcoal grill set into a 7-foot-long counter with storage below

provides a stable cooking appliance and plenty of counter space for preparing the salad and vegetables.

To take this simple setup a step or two further, add a raised counter with stools for dining. This arrangement brings family members and friends up close with the cook, turning grilling and dining into a seamless communal experience.

Here are descriptions of the basic components of an outdoor kitchen, along with some key considerations for planning.

counters Structures typically are made of concrete block, but you can also use steel or wood studs covered with concrete backerboard. You can face the counter with ceramic tile, stone tile, brick, or stucco. The countertop can be made of tile set atop a substructure of concrete backerboard, poured decorative concrete, a granite slab, or a rough stone slab.

If you build with concrete block or other heavy materials, check first with your building department to see if a poured foundation to support the counter is required.

Check at Lowe's on the dimensions of drawer units and doors made for outdoor kitchen counters to be sure you build the right size openings. There are also grills and other appliances that fit into counters.

grill The most popular outdoor cooking appliance is a built-in gas grill. For easy installation, use propane gas. The tank can fit in the cabinet below the grill. To save money over the long run and to avoid having to change tanks, connect the grill to a natural-gas line. Running a safe line may be a major project, however, so consult your building department or a plumber.

The alternative to a gas grill is a charcoal grill. Many people prefer the taste provided by a charcoal grill and enjoy the fire-building process as well.

Whichever type of grill you prefer, a host of accessories can greatly enlarge your cooking possibilities. These include rotisseries, infrared cookers, frying griddles that rest on the grill's grate, and a variety of racks designed to hold almost any cut of meat or vegetable.

From the waffle-like overhead to the stone paving, the line between indoors and outdoors, garden and living space, is erased.

sink If the sink will be near the house, running supply lines may not be too difficult and you may be able to connect into the kitchen drain. In many cases, you will need to have the sink drain into a dry well (see page 207). Before committing to a plan, check local plumbing codes. To supply hot water, it is usually easiest to install an instant-hot-water system under the sink.

refrigerator Adding a refrigerator is easy if you have or can find the space. Many people find an under-counter built-in to be convenient. In that case, make the counter height to fit. But in some cases, a full-size refrigerator makes the most sense.

side burner A gas-powered burner or two allows you to move more than just the grilling part of meal preparation outdoors, along with all of the accompanying heat. Several styles and versions of side burners are available, including ones that are permanently built in and ones that are portable.

Consider building a grill into preexisting outdoor features, the way this one is incorporated into a stone wall.

CHARCOAL GRILL AND SMOKER

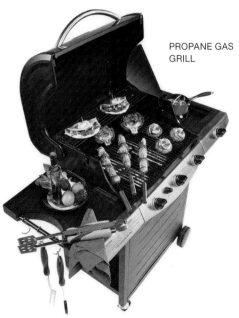

PROPANE GAS GRILL

Propane grills are popular for their convenience, but charcoal retains many fans who tout the superior flavor they impart.

pizza oven A pizza oven must heat to 750 degrees F to produce pizza and breads with crunchy crusts and roasts that are crisp on the outside and tender on the inside. The oven itself can be made of Italian clay or refractory concrete plus firebrick, and in either case is installed in a large masonry structure and insulated. Hire a pro to install one, or, if you're handy, build one from a kit.

ABOVE, FAR LEFT: Complete outdoor kitchens that include a grill, a refrigerator, storage, and a work top are available.

ABOVE LEFT: Built of concrete block and faced with replica used brick, this counter includes a grill and a side burner.

ABOVE: An outdoor kitchen or grill that mirrors the indoor one makes utility connections easier.

LEFT: Ready for any party, this outdoor kitchen includes a sink, plenty of counter space, a grill, a side burner, and even a pizza oven.

ALUMINUM TURKEY FRYER

ELECTRIC SMOKER

SINGLE-BURNER GAS GRILL

A variety of specialty grills, smokers, and cookers are available at Lowe's, several of which can add a new dimension to your outdoor culinary explorations.

light up the night
A LITTLE ILLUMINATION MAKES A BIG DIFFERENCE

A WELL-LIT FRONT YARD NOT ONLY WELCOMES GUESTS AND LEADS THEM SAFELY TO THE FRONT DOOR but also accentuates features—a graceful tree, a textured wall, or a bed of impatiens—that would otherwise be lost in the dark. Your garden becomes a stage set, the muted lighting giving it form, drama, and depth with unexpected silhouettes, highlighted shapes, and shadows that can be seen only at night.

design strategies

The four basic lighting techniques that a professional installer would use for a garden are illustrated on page 287. Each technique requires a slightly different placement and style of fixture.

Begin by noting the key features to highlight. You or the lighting designer should make a scale drawing of your garden to show pathways, trees, beds, walls, stairways, and decks that could be lit. Use the drawing to figure the type and number of fixtures required. Larger trees, for example, might need two up-lights to define the trunk and mantle of leaves.

Most lighting designers begin by dividing the garden into three zones: a foreground, which is usually given midlevel brightness; a middle ground, with low-level light where shadows interplay and overlap; and a background, often the brightest of all, to draw the eye through the garden.

Lighting should never be spotty. For example, uplighting gives the mantle of a tall tree a dramatic form, but it can also make the top appear to hover ghostlike above the ground. To visually anchor the trunk, have that light (or an additional one) illuminate the trunk near ground level. Also be aware of how your lights may affect your neighbors. Some communities

Low-voltage lights link together quickly and require no special wiring expertise.

GARDEN POST
LIGHT FIXTURE

even have ordinances regulating "light trespass."

Here are some common garden situations and how to light them.

walks and steps

Illuminate walkways with low fixtures that spread soft pools of light. Incorporate them into plantings along the edge of the path to both show off elements of your garden and to camouflage the fixtures themselves. Steps can also be lit by these same fixtures, or by ones built into the step risers or into a wall adjoining the steps.

OUTDOOR LIGHT TIMER

WEATHERPROOF JUNCTION BOX

OUTDOOR SWITCHES

DIRECT BURIAL CABLE

Avoiding glare, either through light placement or fixture selection, is important for both functional and decorative lighting.

placing fixtures

The best way to avoid glare is to place fixtures out of sight lines, either very low or very high—for example, along a walk or up in a tree. Direct the fixtures so that only the effect of the light is noticed. Avoid creating bright spots of light.

dining areas and living spaces

Dim lighting is most appropriate for quiet conversation or outdoor dining. Soft, indirect lighting provides enough visibility without robbing the evening of its mood. On the other hand, cooking and similar activity areas require small pools of bright light.

foliage

Uplighting, downlighting, and wash lighting are common techniques that utilize spotlights. To silhouette a tree or shrub, aim a spotlight or wall washer at a fence or a wall behind the plant.

For a dappled "moonlight" effect, place both up- and down-facing spotlights in a large tree to highlight some of the foliage and create shadows on the ground. To silhouette a tree or shrub, aim a spotlight or wall washer at a fence or a wall behind the plant.

Decorative minilights can be used to outline trees and other features while lending sparkle to the garden.

avoiding glare

Glare is responsible for the discomfort you feel when looking at a bright light that is aimed straight at your eyes. And if there's one important principle of good outdoor lighting, it's avoiding glare. You should never see an exposed lamp, only the light it is projecting.

using more fixtures

It's less glaring and more inviting to use a few strategically placed low-wattage lights outside a door than to use one high-wattage light.

using shielded fixtures

In a shielded fixture, the bulb area is completely hidden by a shroud that directs the light away from viewers' eyes. Only the warm glow of a lighted object is visible, not a spot of light.

Low-voltage lighting fixtures may be floodlights that you want to hide or fixtures that are decorative and designed to be prominent.

Three of the most common outdoor lighting techniques are illustrated here: the visible fixtures of path lights, uplighting (center), and downlighting (right). The inset shows the same perspective during daytime.

choosing lighting products

Once you've determined the areas that need lighting and the type, choose equipment. One of the first decisions to make is whether to use low-voltage or line current (120-volt household current).

Because low-voltage lights are safer, smaller, more energy efficient, and easier to install than 120-volt systems, they have become increasingly popular outdoors. Although they lack the brightness of line-current fixtures, their output is more than adequate for most outdoor applications.

Low-voltage systems use a transformer to step down household current to 12 volts and then thin, flexible cable sends the power to the fixtures. The cable can run along edgings

or fence lines, be buried a few inches deep, or simply be covered with mulch in a planting area. Transformers are available in different capacities. What you should get depends on the number and wattage of light fixtures in your setup. The more lights you have, the larger the transformer you need. A Lowe's sales associate can help you choose the right transformer, but the idea is to total the number of watts consumed by all your fixtures and then add 20 percent capacity in case you want to expand the system later.

The standard 120-volt system still has some advantages outdoors. The buried cable and metallic fixtures give the installation a look of permanence, light can be projected a greater distance, and 120-volt receptacles accept power tools and patio heaters.

fixtures and bulbs

Standard outdoor fixtures include uplights, path lights that spread pools of light, and downlights designed to be anchored to walls, eaves, or trees.

Most outdoor fixtures are made of bronze, cast or extruded aluminum, copper, or plastic. But you can also find decorative

LOW-VOLTAGE
LIGHTING KIT

stone, concrete, porcelain, and wooden fixtures (redwood, cedar, and teak weather best). Sizes vary. When evaluating fixtures, look for gaskets, high-quality components at joints and pivot points, and locking devices that hold the orientation of the lamp securely in place after you aim it.

Low-voltage halogen bulbs are popular for most uses, while larger halogen spotlights are best for lighting trees or wide areas. Floodlights, available in incandescent and mercury-vapor versions, are for security purposes only. They're too wide and too glare prone to be useful for garden lighting.

Some fixtures and bulbs are just for fun. Decorative rope lights help outline trees and structures and lend sparkle to your landscape. Strings of low-wattage party lights add a festive flair. And don't forget nonelectric sources, such as hurricane lamps, candle lanterns, and solar path lights.

take control

How can you set up landscape or security lights to take care of themselves? A timer is one solution. Two other options are daylight-sensitive photocells and motion-sensor fixtures and add-ons.

Daylight sensors are simply photocells that are sensitive to daylight. When it's dark, the photocell opens a switch that sends power to the light fixture it's connected to. Come dawn, the sensor breaks the circuit, shutting down the fixture. Like photocells, motion sensors can be purchased alone or

PATH LIGHTS These are the most decorative outdoor lights and are meant to be seen during the day. Some are available in copper, which will develop a patina over time, while others come in brass and more muted metal finishes. The best ones throw broad pools of light while shielding the lamp from view.

WASH OR HEDGE LIGHTS These fixtures use lamps with a broader beam to light expansive areas, such as hedges and walls, with a softer light. Some can be placed in the ground in cans, but most are installed low to the ground or on taller bases that elevate the light source above shrubs that would block light.

UPLIGHTS Aim these slender, stake-mounted fixtures upward at trees, shrubs, sculptures, and architectural features. Use them to cast shadows on walls. Many have hoods to help shield side views of the lamp inside. Remember to aim them away from the viewer.

DOWNLIGHTS These compact fixtures have deeply recessed lamps. Suspend them from overhead branches to "moonlight" areas below. You can use special brackets that mount the fixtures directly to thick trunks or that wrap around slender branches with straps.

can be integrated into a fixture that houses one or more floodlights. Sensors have adjustable ranges and can be set to remain on for varying lengths of time.

If your outdoor lighting circuit begins indoors, you can control it with the same switches and timers you'd use inside. If your system connects outdoors, choose a hardier outdoor timer.

SOLAR PATH LIGHT

LOW-VOLTAGE LIGHT

CANDLE LANTERN

PATH LIGHT FIXTURE

A wide range of fixtures is available for various lighting situations.

trellises support plants

THE VIRTUES OF SIMPLE SCREENS AND SUPPORTS

RUNNING OUT OF GARDEN SPACE? NEED TO FRAME A FAVORITE VIEW OR HIDE THE NEIGHBORS' peeling paint? Want to link disparate landscape elements, direct foot traffic, or define an outdoor retreat or entertaining area? Think trellises. Ranging from traditional to trendy to quirky, these familiar frames offer firm footholds for vines and vegetables while stretching garden space skyward. Trellises provide a whole new world of vertical expression: structures that are focal points, backdrops that add depth and layering, designs that shape a view and those that provide shade, screening, and style.

A lattice panel suspended in a sturdy frame makes a simple trellis for a raised-bed garden.

Whether it flanks a patio door, props up a riot of roses, cages tomatoes or pole beans, or livens up a large, boring lawn, a trellis can add a sense of drama to any garden. Walls, fences, and arbors perform this function too, but trellises do it with a superbly open

feel—the resulting dappled sunlight, breezes, and patches of blue sky counter any potential "prison wall" effect.

You can opt for a gridlike, symmetrical style or a more whimsical, gnarled look. What's more important is that the trellis suit the rest of the garden and easily support the weight of the plants you choose for it.

At Lowe's you are just as likely to find the one you want, already built. Most ready-made trellises come ready to install. Just push or pound the feet into soil beside a wall or in a planter box, plant a vine, and wrap the stems around the supports, using plant ties if needed. A few trellises need minor assembly, and some must be anchored to a wall.

ABOVE LEFT: Willow prunings make a rustic trellis for a rose and violet clematis.

TOP: Camouflage a shed with a trellis and vine.

ABOVE: This Gothic-arch trellis is one of many ready-made kinds available.

water features

THEY MAKE GARDENS COME ALIVE

A WATER FEATURE, SUCH AS A FOUNTAIN OR SMALL POOL, ADDS SOUND AND MOTION TO A GARDEN. It can be a mesmerizing focal point, a piece of garden art that delights both eyes and ears. And the quiet music of burbling, trickling, or splashing water brings a certain tranquility to a space. Even the smallest water feature can calm your surroundings and soothe the soul. As a bonus, the sounds of falling water can mask unwanted traffic noise and other neighborhood hubbub, creating a sense of the countryside in the middle of suburbia.

fountains

A pleasing water feature can be as modest as a wall-mounted fountain that trickles water into a basin, or as elaborate as a 6-foot granite sculpture that sends a graceful arc of water into a pool. You can convert a wooden planter box, metal basin, or large pot into a small, informal fountain (see the facing page for some examples). Coat the inside of a wooden container with asphalt emulsion or epoxy paint, or use a liner of heavy-gauge plastic sheeting. If you're using an unglazed pan or clay pot, coat the interior with asphalt emulsion, epoxy, or polyester resin. Then add a submersible pump and, of course, water.

pools

Any container that's watertight can make a reflection pool. For the most reflectivity, find a container with an extra-wide opening at the top and a dark interior. Aluminum and glazed ceramic containers are beautiful because they gleam when wet. Stone and unglazed bowls develop an interesting patina with age.

LOWE'S QUICK TIP

Ponds support fish and attract birds and a variety of other welcome creatures. The predators that feed on them—cats and raccoons are two common ones—follow shortly after. Deter them by forming the pond with sides that drop steeply to their full depth, rather than gradually sloping.

Gently recirculating water overflows the concrete container and falls into a tub hidden below stones.

Experiment to find the best places in your garden for water bowls. One way to do this is to look for interesting reflections. Set up a bowl and check the reflection as you approach it along a path or look down on it from a deck. Or, if it's too cumbersome to keep filling and emptying the bowl as you move it around the garden, test the reflection by putting a mirror across the top of the bowl to substitute for the water's surface.

After the bowl is in its final position, use a level to check that the rim is perfectly flat before you fill the bowl with water. Fill the bowl with water only then. When a bowl is full, even a slight tilt will be evident in the water line, and a large container will be too heavy and awkward to reposition.

See pages 256–259 for directions on how to build ponds and water features similar to the ones shown here.

HOW TO MAKE A WATER GARDEN IN A POT

A 30-inch glazed and watertight ceramic pot, such as the one pictured at right, makes a handsome water feature. Fill it about two-thirds full with water; then add plants, each in its own pot (set plants on bricks to raise them). The container's size dictates the number of plants you need. Start with water lilies and water irises. After they're in place, finish filling the tub. To control mosquitoes, add mosquito fish or goldfish, which also feed on algae. A 30-inch-diameter tub can accommodate about six fish. Once a year, without emptying the water, scrub the plant pots and the inside of the tub with a stiff brush. Remove loose algae. Drain when 2 inches of decomposed matter accumulates on the bottom (every few years). Scrub the inside surfaces and divide the plants.

BELOW LEFT: This fountain features a solar-powered pump, which makes set up especially convenient.

BELOW CENTER: This custom fountain is made of copper, which will develop an attractive patina.

BOTTOM CENTER: A fiberglass tub and an old water pump have an antique look.

BELOW RIGHT: Shade loving coleus and impatiens surround a fountain and basin designed to resemble an antique lead cistern.

artful touches

EXPRESS YOURSELF WITH FUN GARDEN ACCESSORIES

A GARDEN'S PERSONALITY COMES FROM MORE THAN ITS PLANTS AND STRUCTURES. MUCH DEPENDS on the gardener's knack for adding finishing touches—a copper lantern, a brightly glazed pot, a collection of folk-art birdhouses. From a teak bench to a lacy hammock or a well-placed boulder, these decorative elements can create a focal point, complement a grouping of foliage and flowers, or simply delight the eye.

BELOW LEFT: Decorative containers add charm to the simplest planting. Here, violas tumble over container edges.

BELOW RIGHT: Even an old bucket, when artfully composed, is a plant container of merit and charm.

The traditional pineapple symbol of welcome in Colonial Williamsburg still appears in many gardens, but you can opt for more obvious and personal invitations. Place a carved stone or a painted wooden or metal sign at the main entrance to your garden, or use a sign to point the way to a more hidden path. Don't be afraid to add a little humor or fun to your garden either. Just the right personal touch makes the space your own.

Fasteners on the garden gate, finials on the fence posts, or brass hose guides can add a pleasing touch. Or your details may be less evident, such as the careful selection of just the right flat stones to place at the end of a downspout, the use of a section of old iron fence as a trellis for a pea vine, or the choice of a translucent dragonfly that floats on a copper stake above a perennial bed.

By definition, details are not the focal point of the garden, but they can provide great pleasure when selected in thoughtful counterpoint to a garden's themes. Searching for just the right detail can continue the

adventure of gardening long after the main plan is accomplished.

Garden accessories have rarely been as plentiful and as varied as they are today. Furniture is available in a variety of styles, umbrellas come fitted with lights or with canvas walls that block the wind, and birdbaths range from rustic to sculptural in form. Resourceful gardeners are turning humble boulders into striking sculptures and adding flair to their gardens with birdhouses, statuary, outdoor lighting, and painted fences. Giving your garden a distinctive look is as simple as giving free rein to your imagination and letting it lead the way.

In style, spirit, and materials, you have a tremendous choice of garden decor. Whatever ornaments you use, they will look best if they're part of a unified and harmonious design based on principles similar to those for interior decor.

In a unified design, plants, structures, and decorative objects all share one style and character, and all work together to convey the garden's mood. No one plant, structure, or object stands out too much. Rather, all of the parts work together and thus establish a sense of unity.

Ornaments in the garden must also be to scale if they are to be blended attractively. A monumental sculpture will tend to overwhelm a small garden, just as a towering tree will. Conversely, a small stone figure will look lost in a spacious setting. Generally, the ornaments you choose should be in proportion to the house, the plantings, and any nearby garden structures. You can give a smaller object or statue more importance by placing it atop a pedestal or other support. This will usually look best if the support is surrounded by foliage or flowers that mask the distance between the ground and the ornament.

ABOVE LEFT: Secured atop a small Doric column, a gazing ball reflects the whole garden.

ABOVE RIGHT: Stones placed in a low bowl contrast with the lush foliage. Filled with water, the bowl is an ideal birdbath.

LEFT: Use cast concrete finials of classic Colonial style to complement formal gardens.

welcoming birds
ATTRACT THOSE SPECIAL GARDEN VISITORS

TO ENTICE BIRDS TO YOUR YARD, YOU'LL NEED TO PROVIDE THEM WITH THE THREE ELEMENTS THEY need most: food, water, and shelter. These necessities of life will be supplied in part by your selection of plants, but you can make your garden irresistible by supplementing the natural resources the plants provide.

feeder basics

Locate feeders at varying levels to attract different birds. Place them close enough to cover where they are safe from predators but not right next to hiding places for cats. Use feeders designed to protect seed from rain, snow, and garden sprinklers. Situate them where the wind won't blow seed away and birds will be protected from winter's chill. Keep suet out of direct sun, especially in warm weather, or it may turn rancid.

You can choose traditional feeders of wood, or more modern designs of sleek acrylic or lightweight metal—and all sorts of design styles, from whimsical to high-tech. Just keep in mind the kind of food you'll be offering and the species of birds you want to attract (or discourage). Some feeders are designed for certain birds. By offering more than one type of feeder, you're bound to attract a wider clientele.

When selecting a feeder, evaluate how easy it will be to fill and occasionally wash. Keeping feeders clean is important for the health of the birds, so you want feeders that open easily.

platforms The most basic kind of feeder is a platform or tray—a flat surface on which food is scattered. This is a good way to begin, because this type of feeder is quickly noticed by birds and appeals to many species, thus giving you a good snapshot of the birds in your neighborhood.

Platform feeders need frequent cleaning because seed hulls and bird droppings are deposited on the surface. Large birds tend to dominate these feeders, and birds are more vulnerable to predators on an open platform.

hoppers, tubes, and globes A longtime favorite, the hopper feeder has a storage bin

A shallow concrete bowl on a low pedestal offers seed to garden birds.

from which seed automatically flows as it is needed. This kind of feeder attracts a varied following of bird species. Some hoppers have separate bins for different kinds of seed or suet, or fruit holders in addition to seed bins.

Tube feeders are a popular way to dispense black oil sunflower seed or thistle (niger) seed, depending on the size of the holes. Tube feeders attract small birds, such as finches, chickadees, and nuthatches. Don't fill them with mixed birdseed, as unwanted seeds will just be discarded. Tube feeders with metal perches and openings are the most durable.

A globe feeder attracts small clinging species, like chickadees and titmice, giving them their own private diner, because larger birds can't get a toehold on the feeder.

other feeders Acrylic seed feeders that attach to windows with suction cups are fun to watch from indoors, although they usually have limited capacity. Most are best suited to small birds. Window feeders for suet and hummingbird nectar are also available. Some window feeders have one-way backs so that birds can't see through and won't be frightened away by indoor bird-watchers. Or you can buy a separate sheet of one-way screening material.

the lure of water

Water holds a powerful attraction for birds. By offering a place where they can drink and bathe, you'll greatly increase the number of resident and visiting birds in your garden. Birds will happily frolic in a puddle, but a birdbath in the right spot, kept full and clean, is the ultimate backyard watering hole for all kinds of feathered friends.

Birdbaths can be made of practically anything—concrete, glazed ceramic, metal, plastic, terra-cotta, stone, fiberglass, even wood. Plastic and metal withstand lots of weather variations, but surfaces can be slippery and some plastic cracks with age. Metal should be rust resistant.

Most birdbaths are quite shallow or deepen only slightly from the edges. If the bath has steep sides, position a flat rock or two in the center.

To allow room for more than one bird at a time, choose a bath that's at least 24 inches in diameter.

For your own enjoyment, position a birdbath where you can see it from your house or patio. For the birds' sake, choose a location sheltered from strong winds where the bath will get morning sun but midday shade so the water doesn't get too warm.

BELOW LEFT: Spring-loaded perches block large birds and squirrels from reaching seeds but are just right for cardinals.

BELOW CENTER: Peanut butter on a fake log brings in a Bullock's oriole.

BOTTOM LEFT: A brown-headed cowbird and an American robin share a drink and a bath.

BOTTOM CENTER: A tufted titmouse samples shelled peanuts.

BELOW RIGHT: American goldfinches feast on thistle seed in winter.

choosing plants

THIS CHAPTER INCLUDES OUR FAVORITE PLANTS, WHICH ARE

also some of the most beautiful and most reliable plants for

North American gardens. That's why this book, combined

with the expertise you'll find at your local Lowe's Garden

Center, leaves you well situated to choose the best plants

for your garden. Choosing plants involves more than just

making sure they're functional and pretty. They must also

be well adapted to the area where you live and the condi-

tions around your home, namely, low winter temperatures,

shade, hot and bright summers, rain, or drought. So that's

where this chapter begins—helping you choose plants that

will not only look good but also grow well after they're

planted. Then, properly placed, your plants can show off

their unique qualities—perennials that brighten beds and

borders, a redbud to cast dappled shade

on to a patio and a welcome

burst of

vibrant

color in spring.

where plants grow
LOW TEMPERATURES ARE KEY

WHEN YOU'RE TRYING TO DETERMINE WHETHER A CERTAIN PLANT WILL GROW IN YOUR GARDEN, begin by thinking about your typical winter minimum temperature. While it's not the only factor that affects a plant's hardiness, it's usually the most crucial.

what affects plant growth

Gardeners use a variety of maps and guides to determine whether plants are well adapted to their climates. While none are perfect, the system used most widely is the USDA Plant Hardiness Zone Map. Based on average annual minimum temperatures, it allows gardeners to identify the lowest temperatures a plant would commonly encounter in their area. The descriptions in this chapter include the USDA zones where the plants can be grown.

In addition to temperature, many other factors—such as heat, humidity, and intensity of summer sunshine—also determine how well a plant will grow in a given area. While most garden centers, including Lowe's, carry only plants that are adapted locally, you might want to look into local sources of information, such as cooperative extension bulletins, which offer details about plants in your area and the conditions under which they grow best.

Some areas are perpetually windy, while in others windy weather is seasonal. Wind dries out plants and soil, and it's hard on delicate foliage and flowers. You may be able to compensate by providing windbreaks and extra water and by choosing plants that withstand wind.

Many plants are adapted to a specific climate and the weather conditions that prevail in their native regions. In general, the eastern half of the United States has rainy summers, while summers in most of the West are dry (though early summer can be wet in the Pacific Northwest, as is the summer monsoon season in the Southwest). Plants native to the East need extra summer water if planted in the West. Conversely, some western plants will die in eastern gardens. For an example of these differences and how they affect zone recommendations, see "Plant Samplers Explained" on the facing page.

RIGHT: The characteristic plants of a region are the ones adapted to its climate. An example is the octopus cactus, which thrives in the Southwest but not elsewhere.

FAR RIGHT: Plants adapted to the north survive ice and temperatures far below freezing.

USDA Climate Zone Map

Average Annual Minimum Temperature		
Temperature (°C)	Zone	Temperature (°F)
-45.5 to -40.1	2	-50 to -40
-40.0 to -34.5	3	-40 to -30
-34.4 to -28.9	4	-30 to -20
-28.8 to -23.4	5	-20 to -10
-23.3 to -17.8	6	-10 to 0
-17.7 to -12.3	7	0 to 10
-12.2 to -6.7	8	10 to 20
-6.6 to -1.2	9	20 to 30
-1.1 to 4.4	10	30 to 40
4.5 and above	11	40 and above

Mountains interfere with basic wind patterns and the movement of air masses. Depending on their height and alignment, they either block the wind's progress or direct it. They also cause moist air to rise and cool, so more rain is deposited on one side of a mountain than on the other. If you live near hills or mountains, your climate may differ from that of a neighbor living on the opposite slope. You may live on the west side of a mountain and receive 40 inches of rain per year, for example, while a neighbor on the eastern side, just 20 miles away, receives significantly less.

If you live near the ocean or a large inland body of water, your climate will differ from that at the same latitude some miles inland. In Buffalo, New York, for example, Lake Erie causes very snowy winters, and the Pacific Ocean is the reason for those cool San Francisco summers. Accounting for such factors is what's involved in choosing plants.

PLANT SAMPLERS EXPLAINED

You'll find descriptions of plants and advice on their care in the plant sampler sections beginning on page 310. Each entry starts with the plant's common name (if it has one), followed by its botanical name in italics. Plants are listed alphabetically by their standard botanical names. The index, beginning on page 426, includes both common and botanical names.

The information varies slightly according to the characteristics of the particular group of plants. Usually you'll see a reference to the type of plant, such as "evergreen" (meaning it has green leaves all year) or "deciduous" (meaning leaves fall or the plant dies to the ground in winter). In all cases, you'll find a recommendation of USDA zones where the plant grows well. Those zone numbers, from 2 through 11, refer to the map shown above. Because zones 9 through 11 in the mild-winter West are different from the same zones in the South, the recommended zones for some plants in that region follow in parentheses. An example is the zone recommendations for Japanese maple on page 310: "Zones 5–8 (5–11W)."

improving your soil
START OFF RIGHT BY ADDING ORGANIC MATTER

WHILE YOU CAN'T DO MUCH TO CHANGE THE CLIMATE YOU LIVE IN, YOU CAN IMPROVE YOUR garden's soil. In fact, the most important task you can undertake to ensure the health and longevity of your new landscape is to properly prepare the soil before you plant.

amending soil

Most garden soil provides a less than ideal environment for many plants. Perhaps the soil is rocky or scraped bare from new construction. Perhaps it's too clay-like or too sandy to suit the plants you want to grow. While changing a soil's basic texture is very difficult, you can add amendments to improve its structure, making clay more porous or sand more water retentive.

The best amendment for any soil texture is organic matter, the decaying remains of plants and animals. As it decomposes, organic matter releases nutrients that are absorbed by soil-dwelling microorganisms and bacteria. The remains of these creatures, called humus, bind with soil particles. In clay, humus forces the tightly packed particles apart, so drainage is improved and the soil is easier for plant roots to penetrate. In sand, it lodges in the large pore spaces and acts as a sponge, slowing draining water so soil stays moist longer.

You want organic matter to make up at least 5 percent of your soil. Commonly available organic amendments include compost, well-rotted manure, and soil conditioners, which are composed of several ingredients. These and other amendments are sold in bags at every Lowe's, or in bulk, by the cubic yard, at supply centers. By-products of local industries, such as rice hulls, cocoa bean hulls, or mushroom compost, may also be available.

Finely ground tree trimmings (wood chips) and sawdust are also used, but because they are high in carbon they will use nitrogen as they decompose, taking much-needed nitrogen from the soil. To make sure your plants aren't deprived of the nitrogen they need, add a fast-acting nitrogen source, such as ammonium sulfate, along with the amendment. Use about 1 pound for each 1-inch layer of wood chips or sawdust spread over 100 square feet of ground.

Although the particular organic amendment you choose is often decided by what's available at the best price, many experts favor compost over all other choices.

Amend new beds before you put any plants into the ground. For long-term benefits, choose an amendment that breaks down slowly. Shredded bark holds its structure the longest, taking several years to decompose. Also include compost in the mix. Though it breaks down in just a few months, it bolsters the initial nutrient supply available to microorganisms. These microorganisms

LOWE'S QUICK TIP

Test soil before amending it, and then follow the recommendations provided. Doing so will likely save you time and money and result in superior plant growth.

Rich color, a fresh smell, and crumbly texture are all indications of good soil. The key ingredient is organic matter. Add it to your soil prior to planting and then periodically refresh it as needed.

amending soil

1 SPREAD AN AMENDMENT layer evenly over the soil surface.

2 MIX AMENDMENTS into the soil, using a rotary tiller or a spade.

3 RAKE TILLED SOIL smooth to remove stones and level the surface.

will contribute humus to the soil, increase the amount of air in the soil, and help protect your new plants from certain diseases.

In beds earmarked for vegetables and annual flowers, amend the soil before planting. Compost and well-rotted manure are preferred by most gardeners, as they dramatically improve the soil's structure, making it much more hospitable to the fine, tiny roots of seedlings. Unamended soil may dry into hard clods that small roots can't penetrate, and plants may grow slowly, be stunted, or die as a result. But manure and compost break down rapidly—manure in a few weeks, compost in several months.

To add amendments to unplanted beds, spread the material evenly over the soil and then work it in using a spade or a rotary tiller to a depth of about 9 inches. If your soil is mostly clay or sand, spread 4 to 5 inches of amendment over it. After you work this in,

the top 9 inches of soil will be about half original soil, half amendment. If the soil is loamy or has been amended each season, add just 2 to 3 inches of amendment. You'll have a 9-inch top layer of about three-quarters original soil, one-quarter amendment.

Permanent or semipermanent plantings of trees, shrubs, or perennials also benefit from soil amendments, but you need to do the job without damaging roots. Simply spread the amendment over the soil surface as mulch. Earthworms, microorganisms, and rain will all carry it downward over time. Around deep-rooted plants, you can speed up the process by working the amendment into the topsoil.

If your climate is generally mild and winters are rainy, amend the soil around established plantings annually after fall cleanup. In cold-winter regions with spring and summer rainfall, do the job as you begin spring gardening.

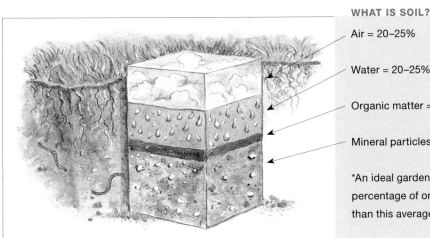

WHAT IS SOIL?

Air = 20–25%

Water = 20–25%

Organic matter = 5% or less*

Mineral particles = 45–50%

*An ideal garden soil has a higher percentage of organic matter than this average.

LOWE'S QUICK TIP

Of the many kinds of amendments and soil mixes available at Lowe's, the best for landscape plants is "planting mix" or "all-inclusive planting mix." You will also find lawn soils, garden soils, and starter soils, most of which contain fertilizers and are formulated for specific applications such as lawns or flowering plants.

solving soil problems
REMEDY POOR DRAINAGE AND ACID-ALKALINE IMBALANCE

IMPROVING SOIL STRUCTURE IS IMPORTANT, BUT YOU MAY ALSO NEED TO CORRECT OTHER PROBLEMS if your garden is to thrive. Soil may contain so much clay that it drains too slowly, or it may be too sandy and unable to retain water. Similarly, some soils are either too acid or too alkaline. This section describes these conditions and offers solutions.

BELOW LEFT: Checking the natural drainage of your soil is easy: Make a hole 2 feet deep, fill it with water, and let it drain. Once it is completely drained, refill the hole with water and note the time. If it takes longer than 24 hours to drain a second time, drainage is poor and most plants will not grow well.

BELOW RIGHT: Raising the soil above grade level and forming it into mounds improves water drainage.

poor drainage

Poor drainage causes myriad problems. If water stands in the soil's pore spaces instead of draining away, not enough air is available for roots and beneficial soil-dwelling micro-organisms and so both may die. The reduced root structure can't adequately support leaves and stems, and the resulting stress makes plants more susceptible to insect infestation or disease. Belowground, molds develop that disrupt the normal healthy balance of fungi, causing a weakened root structure to be more prone to invasion by water-mold fungi.

Fortunately, many drainage problems are easily solved once you become aware of them. Keep your soil's texture in mind. If the poor drainage is due to heavy clay soil, amend the soil thoroughly with organic matter. You may also want to mound the amended soil slightly and then grow plants on the mounds. This can be pleasing to the eye as well as beneficial to the plants.

Many gardens drain poorly only in some spots. To pinpoint problem areas, inspect your garden after a heavy rain to see where water is standing. You may be able to simply slope the soil in those areas so that water drains away. If that doesn't do the trick, you may need to dig a sloped trench, install drainage pipe perforated along the bottom sides, and refill the trench (see pages 206–207). When heavy rain comes, water should flow down through the soil, go into the pipe, and be carried away.

If certain areas in your garden are always slightly wet or boggy and don't lend themselves to structural change, your best tactic is to give in graciously. Accept the situation and choose water-loving plants for those locations.

acid or alkaline soil

The pH scale indicates acidity or alkalinity. A soil with a pH number below 7 is acidic, while one with a pH above 7 is alkaline. Garden plants typically grow best in neutral or slightly acidic soil, with a pH slightly below 7. Most won't thrive in highly acidic or highly alkaline soil, although a few have adapted to such extremes. Certain nutrients can't be efficiently absorbed by plant roots if the soil pH is too high or too low.

Local climate gives you a clue to the likely soil pH. In high-rainfall areas, soils are often acidic, and you tend to find acid-loving plants like azaleas, rhododendrons, camellias, and blueberries. Alkaline soils, in contrast, are found typically in low-rainfall areas. Many of the plants popular for water-wise gardens—those that need little water after they are established—do well in alkaline soil. The olive, native to the Mediterranean basin, is one example of a plant that thrives in alkaline soil. Oleander (*Nerium oleander*) and pomegranate also perform well.

If you're not sure about your soil's pH, you can test it yourself with a kit that tells whether your soil is alkaline, acidic, or neutral. Some also test for nutrients, such as nitrogen, phosphorus, and potassium.

To raise the pH of your soil, use ground dolomitic limestone. Look for the kind formulated into small pills, as it is much easier to handle and apply accurately. The amount needed depends on the soil texture and other factors. For example, more is needed for clay than for sandy soil.

Sulfur is the least expensive material available that will gradually lower pH. Other materials include aluminum sulfate and ferrous sulfate. Ferrous sulfate and iron chelates can enter plant leaves and correct the leaf yellowing that is common to iron chlorosis, a plant problem caused by a high pH. You can also lower the pH of alkaline soil very slowly by regularly applying organic amendments, such as compost and manure.

To know how much of these products to add, follow the advice included with your soil test results. But if you need to change the level by more than one point on the pH scale, check with a professional.

If correcting the soil's pH isn't feasible, either choose native plants that thrive in the kind of soil you have, or build raised beds and fill them with problem-free, well-amended topsoil (see pages 260–261).

the pH scale

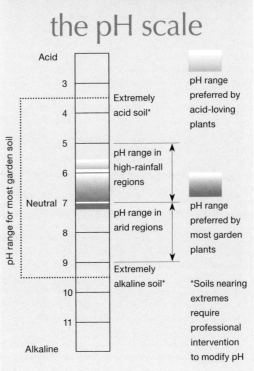

Use a pH test kit to measure the acid-alkaline balance of your soil. Mix a small amount of soil from the root depth with the provided solution, dip the strip of test paper into it, and compare the paper color to the kit's chart.

creating planting beds
START PLANTS THE RIGHT WAY

GARDEN BEDS COME IN TWO BASIC TYPES. SOME ARE DUG DIRECTLY IN THE GROUND, WHILE OTHERS are built in frames that sit on the soil surface (see pages 164–165 and 260–261 for examples).

When making new in-ground beds, some gardeners always raise them, even if just by a few inches, using decorative stones, bricks, or benderboard as an edging. These gardeners will tell you that by the time they amend the bed's soil, it's "fluffed up" higher than its original boundaries anyway. The raised soil gives plant roots a few more inches of growing room, and the edging keeps the soil in place.

Other gardeners make mounds as they dig. In this case, the bed's edges are close to the original soil surface, while the center is elevated. Plants can grow both on top of the mound and on its sides. You may want to

create several mounds, adding large stones for accents, so that the mounds form a part of the landscaping. As is true for slightly raised beds, the mounded soil ensures plenty of depth for root growth, as well as excellent water drainage.

When you're getting ready to dig, the soil should be neither too wet nor too dry. A handful squeezed in your fist should form a ball that crumbles apart yet still feels moist. If you work soil that's too wet, it becomes compacted (making it difficult for air to penetrate throughout the soil after it dries) and destroys beneficial microorganisms. You can't

Planting beds in which many different kinds of plants can thrive begin with good soil.

work amendments evenly into wet soil either. If the soil is too dry, water the area thoroughly.

When you dig, clear most of the debris from the soil. Then use a sharp, square-bladed spade or a spading fork to break up the soil to a spade's depth—typically 8 to 12 inches. Don't turn each spadeful completely over. If you do, roots and debris remaining on the surface may form a barrier that cuts off air and water. Instead, turn the loosened spadefuls only onto their sides. After you've broken up the soil, change to a round-point shovel for mixing in amendments and roughly evening the surface.

If you're digging a large bed, consider using a power-driven rotary tiller. If the soil hasn't been worked in a long time, go over it first with the blades set to a shallow depth. Spread amendments over the surface, then till again with the blades adjusted to reach as deep into the soil as possible.

After a bed is ready for planting, don't walk on it. Following this rule will be simpler if you can easily reach all parts of the bed from its borders. If it must be wider, add board paths or stepping-stones to control foot traffic.

If you select your plants wisely and plant them correctly, you'll be on your way to a successful landscape. Many kinds of plants— annuals, vegetables, and some perennials and ground covers—are sold as seedlings in small containers or in flats during the growing season. Larger plants, such as shrubs, trees, and certain vines and perennials, are offered in various ways: as bare-root plants during the dormant season; in 1-gallon, 5-gallon, or larger containers at any time during the growing season; or with the root-ball enclosed in burlap from late fall to early spring. In this section, you'll discover how to choose and plant each type.

selecting and planting seedlings

Nurseries offer young seedlings of both annuals and perennials, giving you a head start over sowing seeds yourself. Frost-tender summer annuals, such as marigolds and petunias, and warm-season vegetables, such as tomatoes and peppers, should be planted after the last spring frost in your area. Hardy annuals, including pansy and calendula, and cool-season vegetables, like lettuce and broccoli, can be set out three to four weeks before the last-frost date. They also can be planted in late summer and will provide flowers and vegetables in fall or, in mild climates, in winter. Plant perennials from pots or cell-packs in spring or early fall.

At the nursery, choose stocky plants that have good leaf color, and that are free of any leaf spots or visible pests. Choose younger in preference to older plants. It is always tempting to buy larger plants or ones that are already blooming. But because younger plants recover from transplanting more successfully, they quickly catch up with larger plants. Finally, until you're ready to plant, be sure to keep the plants moist but not soggy.

removing seedlings from containers

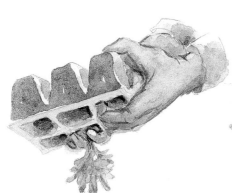

Turn cell-packs upside down and press on the bottom while holding the plant to push root-balls out.

Hold a root-ball around the stem with your fingers and turn individual pots over. Tap lightly if necessary.

Use a putty knife to cut through soil and roots of flat-grown plants and to lift them out.

container plants

Plants in containers are popular and convenient because they are available all season, are relatively easy to transport, and, unlike bare-root and balled-and-burlapped plants, don't have to be planted immediately. As a bonus, they can be purchased with their flowers, fruit, or autumn leaf color on display, letting you see exactly what you're getting before planting.

When selecting container plants, look for healthy foliage and strong shoots. Ask if you can slide the root-ball partially out of its pot, and avoid plants with root-balls either too small or too old and circling.

Container plants are available in several sizes, with 1- and 5-gallon the most common. Which of these you buy depends on how much immediate impact you want the plant to have and on how long you're willing to wait for it to grow. Keep in mind, though, that smaller plants grow quickly. Within three years, most 1-gallon plants will be the size of a 5-gallon one set out at the same time.

balled-and-burlapped plants

Some woody plants and evergreens have root systems that won't survive bare-root transplanting or just can't be bare-rooted. Such plants are dug from the growing field with a ball of soil around their roots, and the soil ball is then wrapped in burlap or a synthetic material. These are called balled-and-burlapped (or B-and-B) plants. Some deciduous trees and shrubs, and especially large ones; evergreen shrubs, such as rhododendrons and azaleas; and conifers are sold balled-and-burlapped, and primarily in fall and early spring.

When buying B-and-B plants, look for healthy foliage and an even branching structure. The covering should be intact so that the roots aren't exposed, and the root-ball should feel firm and moist. If you have any doubts about the condition of the root-ball, untie the covering and check for healthy roots and a solid, uncracked ball.

When moving the plant, always support the bottom of the root-ball. Don't pick the plant up by the trunk or drop it, which may shatter the root-ball. Because a B-and-B plant is usually quite heavy, it's best to have the nursery deliver it or have a friend help you load and unload it in a sling of stout canvas. At home, slide the plant onto a piece of plywood and pull it to the planting spot.

planting a container plant

1 DIG A ROUGH-SIDED planting hole twice as wide as the original root-ball. Fill the hole with water to check drainage (see page 302).

2 LAY A SHOVEL handle across the hole to check root-ball height. One-gallon plants should be about ½ inch above grade.

3 SOAK the surrounding soil; then knock the plant out of its container, loosen tightly knit roots, and set the plant in the hole.

4 FILL THE HOLE halfway with backfill, then water. Finish backfilling; water again. Double-check the elevation of the root-ball top.

planting balled-and-burlapped plants

1 MEASURE THE ROOT-BALL from top to bottom. The hole should be a bit shallower than this distance, so that the top of the root-ball is about 2 inches above the surrounding soil. Adjust the hole to the proper depth, then set the plant inside.

2 UNTIE THE COVERING. Burlap will eventually rot so need not be completely removed, but synthetic material must be removed entirely. If you are planting in a windy site, drive a stake beside the root-ball. Fill the hole to within 4 inches of the top, then water.

3 CONTINUE TO FILL THE HOLE, firming the soil as you go. Make a berm of soil to form a watering basin, then water the plant. If you staked the plant, tie it loosely to the stake. As the plant becomes established, keep the soil moist but not soggy.

bare-root plants

These plants are available in late winter and early spring. You can buy many deciduous plants this way, including fruit and shade trees, flowering shrubs, roses, grapes, and cane fruits. Look for strong stems and fresh-looking, well-formed root systems. Avoid plants with slimy or withered roots. Also avoid any bare-root plants that have begun to sprout leaves. Plant as soon as possible, or plant them temporarily in a shady spot and cover the roots with moist soil. Before planting, soak the roots for several hours or overnight in a bucket of water to rehydrate them. Just before planting, prune off any damaged roots.

planting bare-root plants

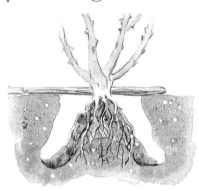

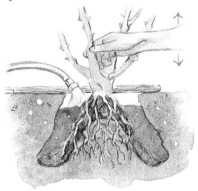

1 SPREAD ROOTS over a cone of soil, and position the plant at the same depth as, or slightly higher than, it was in the growing field; identify that level by the change in bark color. Use a shovel handle or yardstick to check the depth.

2 HOLD THE PLANT as you firm soil around its roots. When backfilling is almost complete, add water to settle the soil and eliminate any air pockets. If the plant settles too low, raise it to the proper level while the soil is saturated.

3 FINISH FILLING THE HOLE with soil, then water again. Don't water again until the soil dries. Later, make a ridge of soil around the hole to form a watering basin. Water only when the top 2 inches of soil is dry.

landscaping with trees

THEY PROVIDE BEAUTY, SHADE, AND PERMANENCE

WHETHER THEY ARE PALMS RUSTLING NEAR CALIFORNIA BEACHES OR SUGAR MAPLES COLORING NEW England mountain slopes, trees help define the character of a landscape. They serve so many purposes—both aesthetic and practical—that few homeowners would consider doing without them. Trees offer cooling shade, provide shelter, and establish perspective. They can also frame special vistas and block unattractive ones. Trees can make dramatic statements, enhance a garden with sculptural effects, and be the dominant feature of a landscape.

Although trees are often the most expensive individual plants to buy, they can be relied on to give permanence to any landscape. Not surprisingly, they are particularly valued in new housing developments.

It is easy to overlook the role trees play in a house's energy conservation. For example, a tree-shaded house will require less air-conditioning in summer than an exposed one. And if deciduous trees, which lose their leaves in winter, are planted around the

south side of a house, the warmth of winter sunshine will be able to penetrate to the interior of the house, helping reduce heating and lighting costs.

Your choice of trees will be determined largely by their purpose in your landscape. To block the sun, for example, select only trees that develop widely spreading branches. If you need a screen, look for trees that produce branches on their lower trunks, or combine shrubs or walls with trees that have bare

Deciduous sycamore trees on the south side of the house offer cooling shade in summer but let sunlight reach the house in winter.

lower trunks. For a focal point, choose a tree that displays flowers or fruits, one with attractive foliage or bark, or one with a striking winter silhouette.

Trees usually live for decades, even centuries. Each year, new growth springs from a framework of last year's branches to form a gradually enlarging structure. Tree silhouettes vary greatly from one species to another, and a tree's ultimate shape is usually not obvious in young nursery specimens.

Although the range of shapes is enormous, all trees are as either deciduous or evergreen. Most deciduous types produce new leaves in spring and retain most of them throughout summer. In fall, leaf color may change from green to warm autumnal tones, and the trees then drop their foliage for the winter, revealing bare limbs. Broadleaf evergreens, such as many magnolias, have wide leaves similar to those of many deciduous trees, but these cover the plant year-round (older leaves drop, however). Needle-leafed evergreens include trees with needlelike foliage—firs, spruces, and pines, for example—and those with leaves that are actually tiny scales, such as cypresses and junipers. Because they keep their foliage in winter, conifers retain their appearance throughout the year, although their colors may change slightly during cold months.

staking young trees

Avoid trees that are too weak to stand upright on their own. If you have such a tree, cut it back so that a new, stronger shoot is encouraged to develop. In general, staking prolongs the time a tree is too weak to stand on its own. The type of staking depends on the size of the tree. For trees with trunks up to 2 inches thick, place one stake on each side of the tree, then secure the tree to them at about breast height (as shown below left). Use three stakes to support trees that have trunks 2 to 4 inches thick.

In windy areas, a young tree's roots may need anchoring to keep them in firm contact with the soil. Use stakes and ties only a foot above ground level for this kind of staking (see illustration below left).

In both cases, sink stakes at right angles to the prevailing wind. Remove them after about a year, or as soon as the tree appears to be self-supporting.

staking

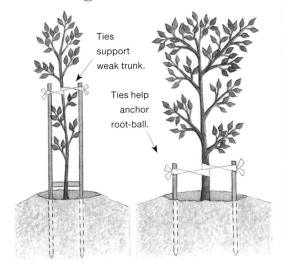

Ties support weak trunk.

Ties help anchor root-ball.

Stake a young tree if it is planted in an extremely windy location or if the main trunk is too thin to stay upright. Use wide strips of canvas or rubber that won't bind or cut into the bark, fastening them around the tree and the stakes in a figure-eight pattern. Tie the strips at the lowest height at which the tree's top remains upright and remove them once they are no longer necessary.

training

A young tree develops a strong trunk faster if its lower branches are removed gradually. At first, allow existing lower branches to grow (left). Gradually shorten lower branches as the tree matures (center) and then ultimately remove them (right). For more about pruning trees, see pages 400–405.

a sampler of deciduous shade trees

Japanese maple (Acer palmatum)

Red maple (Acer rubrum)

Eastern redbud (Cercis canadensis)

Japanese maple (*Acer palmatum*) Zones 5–8 (5–11W), 5–25 feet, depending on variety. Regular water. Small, graceful tree with diminutive habit and bright red, orange, or yellow fall color. Excellent for small spaces and pots. Prefers some shade in hot summer areas. Many named varieties are available, including those with lacy foliage, red or variegated leaves, or weeping habit.

Red maple (*Acer rubrum*) Zones 3–9, 50–70 feet. Regular to moderate water. Fast-growing, upright tree with red twigs and lobed leaves that turn glorious shades of red in fall. 'Armstrong', 'October Glory', and 'Red Sunset' are popular varieties. Good shade tree over a wide range of growing conditions.

Red horsechestnut (*Aesculus carnea*) Zones 4–8, 30–40 feet. Regular water. Round-headed with large dark green leaves that cast dense shade. Bears 8-inch-long plumes of soft pink to red flowers

in late spring. Useful as a showy tree. Popular varieties include 'Briotii' and 'O'Neill Red'.

Silk tree (*Albizia julibrissin*) Deciduous, zones 6–9 (6–10W), 30–40 feet. Regular water. Finely divided fernlike foliage folds up at night. Flat-topped, spreading canopy makes it a good patio tree. Fragrant fluffy pink flowers bloom from late spring through summer. Hardier variety 'Rosea' has darker flowers.

Serviceberry (*Amelanchier*) Zones 3–7, 20–40 feet. Regular to moderate water. A graceful, airy tree with drooping clusters of white or pinkish flowers in early spring followed by edible berries. Foliage casts light shade and turns fiery orange to red in autumn. Bark is smooth and silvery.

River birch (*Betula nigra*) Zones 3–9 (3–11W), 40–80 feet. Ample water. Bark is pinkish on young trees, brown and flaky on older

ones. Bright yellow autumn foliage. Tolerates poor or slow drainage and hot, humid climates. Good shade tree that is usually sold in multi-trunk clumps. 'Heritage' is a popular variety.

European white birch (*Betula pendula*) Zones 2–6 (2–11W), 30–40 feet. Ample water. Upright growth with weeping side branches on mature trees. Casts light shade and has yellow fall foliage. White bark on trunks and main limbs. 'Dalecarlica' has deeply cut leaves and a weeping habit, 'Purpurea' purplish twigs and leaves.

Eastern redbud (*Cercis canadensis*) Zones 5–9 (5–11W), 25–35 feet. Regular water. Attractive horizontal branching and round-headed habit. Depending on variety, pink to white early-spring flowers. Leaves turn bold yellow in fall. 'Forest Pansy' has purple foliage on reddish branches. An excellent patio or specimen tree.

Flowering dogwood (*Cornus florida*)

Hawthorn (*Crataegus viridis* 'Winter King')

Ginkgo (*Ginkgo biloba*)

Chitalpa tashkentensis Zones 6–9 (6–11W), 20–30 feet. Moderate to little water. Clusters of frilly pink, white, or lavender trumpet-shaped flowers from late spring to fall. Good in desert areas where it casts light shade. Varieties include 'Morning Cloud' and 'Pink Dawn'.

Flowering dogwood *(Cornus florida)* Zones 5–9, 20–30 feet. Regular water. Horizontal branching with a flat crown. White or pink flowers in spring followed by red berries. Red fall foliage. Many named varieties differing mostly in flower colors. Best in small spaces and in partial shade.

Hawthorn *(Crataegus)* Zones 4–8, 15–30 feet, depending on species. Moderate water. Small trees known for pretty white, pink, or red flower clusters in spring and for showy, small applelike fruit that persists into winter. Many species are available. Most are multitrunked and have thorny branches and orange to

red or purple autumn foliage. The eastern U.S. native green hawthorn (*C. viridis*) is one of the best.

Russian olive *(Elaeagnus angustifolia)* Zones 2–8, 20 feet. Regular to little water. Fast-growing tree with silvery green foliage that tolerates seashore and dry conditions. Often thorny and can be pruned into an excellent hedge or barrier. Fragrant, small greenish yellow flowers in early summer. Invasive in some regions.

Green ash *(Fraxinus pennsylvanica)* Zones 3–9, 50–60 feet. Regular to moderate water. Moderately fast-growing shade trees that tolerate hot summers and cold winters. Oval to upright pyramid shape and glossy divided leaves. Varieties include 'Marshall', 'Patmore', and 'Summit'. In the West, use *F. angustifolia oxycarpa* 'Raywood'.

Ginkgo *(Ginkgo biloba)* Zones 4–8 (4–11W), 35–80 feet. Regular to

moderate water. Fan-shaped leaves turn gold in autumn. Form and growth rate vary by variety from narrow and upright to broad and spreading. Trouble-free for use as a street tree or in lawns. Good varieties include 'Autumn Gold', 'Fairmount', and 'Princeton Sentry'.

Thornless honey locust *(Gleditsia triacanthos inermis)* Zones 4–9, 35–70 feet. Regular to moderate water. Grows quickly upright with spreading branches. Bright green fernlike leaves cast light shade. Tolerates many climates and growing conditions. Good varieties include 'Shademaster' and 'Skyline'.

Goldenrain tree *(Koelreuteria paniculata)* Zones 5–9, 30–40 feet. Regular to moderate water. Open branching pattern and 15-inch-long divided leaves provide light shade. Very showy, fragrant yellow flower clusters appear in early to midsummer followed by lanternlike fruits that mature from red to buff

a sampler of deciduous shade trees

Crape myrtle (*Lagerstroemia indica*)

Flowering crabapple (*Malus*)

Tupelo (*Nyssa sylvatica*)

or brown. Chinese flame tree (*K. bipinnata*) is showier and hardy to zone 8.

Crape myrtle (*Lagerstroemia indica*) Zones 6–9, 20 feet but variable. Moderate water. Habit varies from shrublike to tree depending on variety and pruning. All have dark green leaves, which often turn orange or red in fall, and clusters of crinkled, crepe-papery white, pink to purple, or red flowers. Smooth bark is attractively mottled.

American sweet gum (*Liquidambar styraciflua*) Zones 5–9 (5–11W), 60–75 feet. Regular to moderate water. Narrow and erect when young, becoming rounded with age. Leaves turn purple, yellow, or red in autumn. Attractive branching pattern and bristly fruits add winter interest. Plant where shallow roots won't interfere with lawn or raise pavement. 'Cherokee' doesn't make seedpods. 'Burgundy' and 'Palo Alto' offer bright red fall color.

Tulip tree (*Liriodendron tulipifera*) Zones 4–9 (4–11W), 60–90 feet. Regular water. Straight, columnar trunk with spreading branches that form a tall pyramidal head. Tuliplike flowers appear in the branches in late spring. Glossy green leaves turn bright yellow in autumn. Useful as a shade tree.

Saucer magnolia (*Magnolia soulangeana*) Zones 4–9, 20–30 feet. Regular water. White, pink, or purple goblet-shaped flowers bloom before large leaves unfurl in early spring. Late frosts frequently damage soft buds and blossoms. Choose late-blooming varieties such as 'Alexandrina' or 'Lennei'. Star magnolia (*M. stellata*) has spreading, star-shaped flowers and grows up to 20 feet tall. Many varieties exist.

Flowering crabapple (*Malus*) Zones 4–8, 6–40 feet, depending on variety. Regular to moderate water. White, pink, or red spring flowers and persistent red to yellow

fruit make these valuable for specimens, lawn trees, and street trees. Hundreds of varieties exist, some with reddish foliage. Growth habit ranges from weeping to round-headed to column-shaped. Varieties that are disease-tolerant include 'Donald Wyman', 'Profusion', and 'Snowdrift'. Both Sargent's crabapple and Japanese flowering crabapple are natural dwarfs, growing only about 8–10 feet tall and spreading up to twice as wide.

Tupelo (*Nyssa sylvatica*) Zones 4–9, 30–50 feet. Regular to moderate water. Pyramid-shaped when young, becoming spreading and dramatic with age. Glossy dark green leaves turn yellow and orange, and then bright red in autumn. Birds enjoy the small fruits. Excellent specimen or shade tree.

Chinese pistache (*Pistacia chinensis*) Zones 7–9 (7–10W), 30–60 feet. Moderate water. This broadly rounded tree has good

Flowering cherry *(Prunus serrulata)*

Pin oak *(Quercus palustris)*

Little-leaf linden *(Tilia cordata)*

orange to red fall color even in mild climates and tolerates a wide range of soils, including alkaline types. Very drought tolerant after it's established. A reliable choice for street, lawn, or patio plantings.

London plane tree *(Platanus acerifolia)* Zones 5–8 (5–11W), 30–70 feet. Regular water. Smooth, cream-colored bark on upper limbs and trunk looks handsome through winter. Grows somewhat slowly and tolerates city conditions but drops messy fruits. Disease-resistant varieties include 'Bloodgood', 'Columbia', 'Liberty', and 'Yarwood'.

Flowering cherry *(Prunus)* Zones 4–9 (varies with species), 10–50 feet (also variable). Regular to moderate water. Prized for glorious spring blossoms. Many also have very attractive horizontal branches and mahogany bark. Many kinds are available. Popular flowering cherries include sargent (*P. sargentii*), flowering (*P. serrulata*), and Higan (*P. subhirtella*).

Purple-leaf plum *(Prunus cerasifera* 'Atropurpurea')* Zones 5–9, 15–30 feet. Regular water. Popular for its purplish red leaves and small light pink to white flowers. Form varies from upright to round to spreading. Common varieties include the dwarf 'Purple Pony' and dark-leaved 'Krauter Vesuvius'.

Callery pear *(Pyrus calleryana)* Zones 5–8 (5–9W), 25–50 feet. Regular water. Horizontal branching, white flowers in early spring and glossy green leaves that turn purplish red in fall combine to make this a popular street and shade tree. Best varieties include 'Aristocrat' and 'Chanticleer'. Evergreen pear (*P. kawakamii*) has drooping branches and white flowers in late winter. Grows to 12–30 feet in zones 9–11.

White oak *(Quercus alba)* Zones 3–9, 50–80 feet. Regular water. Pyramidal in youth, then grows slowly to a round-headed or widely spreading form. Leaves with rounded lobes

turn red to brown in autumn. Other popular landscape oaks include red oak (*Q. rubra*); scarlet oak (*Q. coccinea*), which has bright red autumn foliage; pyramid-shaped pin oak (*Q. palustris*); and narrow-leaved willow oak (*Q. phellos*).

Golden trumpet tree *(Tabebuia chrysotricha)* Deciduous to partially evergreen, zones 9–11, 25–30 feet. Regular water. Showy, trumpet-shaped flowers in clusters appear in spring. Use as patio or specimen trees. Pink trumpet tree (*T. heterophylla*) blooms later and is sometimes grown as a large shrub.

Little-leaf linden *(Tilia cordata)* Zones 3–8, 60–70 feet. Regular water. A popular shade and street tree that forms a dense pyramid of deep green leaves. Fragrant white flowers in early summer. Very tolerant of city conditions. With pruning can form large hedges. Improved varieties include 'Chancellor', 'Glenleven', 'Greenspire', and 'June Bride'.

a sampler of evergreen trees

Deodar cedar *(Cedrus deodara)*

Leyland cypress *(Cupressocyparis leylandii)*

Southern magnolia *(Magnolia grandiflora)*

White fir *(Abies concolor)*
Needled evergreen, zones 4–8
(4–11W), 50–70 feet. A native of
Western mountains. Needs regular to
moderate water. Large, symmetrical,
pyramid-shaped tree with 2-inch-
long, bluish green needles. Good large
screen. Best in cold-winter climates.

Deodar cedar *(Cedrus deodara)*
Needled evergreen, zones 7–8 (7–
11W), 40–80 feet. Moderate water.
Fast growing with a spread of up
to 40 feet at ground level. Graceful
pyramid shape with soft texture.
Needles may be green or have a blue,
gray, or yellow cast. Suitable for hot,
humid climates.

Citrus *(Citrus)* Broadleaf evergreen,
zones 9–11, 6–20 feet, depending on
variety. Regular water; full sun. One
of the finest ornamental edibles for
mild climates. Fragrant white spring
flowers are followed by colorful,
edible fruit that hangs among deep
green foliage. Choose from oranges,
mandarins, grapefruit, lemons, and

limes, depending on local adaptation.
Excellent in containers, they are
useful small trees for the patio. Can
be clipped as hedges. Plant in well-
drained soil and fertilize regularly.

Leyland cypress *(Cupressocyparis leylandii)* Needled
evergreen, zones 6–10, 60–70 feet.
Needs regular to moderate water.
Very fast growing with an upright
form. Useful for hedges and screens.
Varieties offer differing foliage colors.

Arizona cypress *(Cupressus
arizonica)* Needled evergreen,
zones 7–9 (7–11W), 40–50 feet.
Moderate water. Broad pyramidal
shape with green to blue-gray or
silvery scalelike leaves. Thrives in
hot, dry climates. Useful windbreak
and screen. Italian cypress (*C. sempervirens*) grows tall and narrow and is
useful in formal gardens.

Gum *(Eucalyptus)* Broadleaf
evergreen, zones 9–11 (varies with
species), 20–80 feet (also varies).

Regular to little water. Fast-growing
trees good in hot climates. Many
are drought tolerant. Several species
have attractive flowers including
coral gum (*E. torquata*) and red-
flowering gum (*E. ficifolia*). Many
have aromatic ornamental foliage,
including silver dollar tree (*E. cinerea*
and *E. polyanthemos*) and willow-
leafed peppermint (*E. nicholii*).

American holly *(Ilex opaca)*
Broadleaf evergreen, zones 5–9
(5–10W), 40–50 feet. Regular water.
Slow-growing pyramidal to round-
headed tree has dark green leaves
with spiny margins. Bright red berries
appear on female trees and persist
into winter. Use as a specimen tree
or large screen. Hundreds of varieties
exist, some with variegated leaves or
yellow berries.

Southern magnolia *(Magnolia
grandiflora)* Broadleaf evergreen,
zones 6–9 (6–11W), 60–80 feet.
Regular water. Large, glossy green
leaves and huge, fragrant white

Colorado blue spruce *(Picea pungens glauca)*

Eastern white pine *(Pinus strobus)*

Japanese black pine *(Pinus thunbergii)*

flowers offer year-round beauty. A popular tree that varies in shape from spreading to upright, depending on variety. Its shallow roots and dense shade may defeat lawn grasses.

Colorado blue spruce *(Picea pungens glauca)* Needled evergreen, zones 3–7 (3–9W), 30–60 feet. Regular to moderate water. Stiff, horizontal branches spread to 20 feet across at the base, forming a broad pyramid. Needle color ranges from dark green to steely blue. The related dwarf Alberta spruce (*P. glauca albertiana* 'Conica') has softer, greener needles and grows to only 7 feet.

Eastern white pine *(Pinus strobus)* Needled evergreen, zones 3–7, 50–100 feet. Regular water. Fast growing with 4-inch-long blue-green needles and horizontal branching that give the tree a soft texture. Becomes broad and irregular with age. Intolerant of salt and air pollution. Some varieties remain dwarfs or have weeping habits.

Japanese black pine *(Pinus thunbergii)* Needled evergreen, zones 5–8 (5–10W), 20–40 feet or more. Regular to little water. Spreading branches form a broad, conical tree that becomes irregular and picturesque with age, often with a leaning trunk. Dwarf varieties are suitable for containers and bonsai. Tolerates seacoast conditions.

Southern live oak *(Quercus virginiana)* Broadleaf evergreen to partly deciduous, zones 8–10, 40–80 feet. Regular water. Heavy-limbed crown ultimately spreads twice as wide as the tree's height. Commonly used as a street tree and in parks and estates throughout the South. Sheds old leaves in spring before new leaves emerge. Tolerates salt spray.

Coast redwood *(Sequoia sempervirens)* Needled evergreen, zones 7–9 (7–11W), 60–90 feet or more. Regular water. Grows fast and forms a symmetrical pyramid of soft-looking, feathery foliage. The

straight trunk has horizontal limbs that curve up at tips and have many drooping branchlets.

English yew *(Taxus baccata)* Needled evergreen, zones 6–7, 25–40 feet. Regular to moderate water. Soft, flat dark green needles on wide-spreading branches that form a low crown. Tolerates shade and pruning; useful for hedges and screens. Other common yews include cold-hardy Japanese yew (*T. cuspidata*) and many hybrids. A tall and more narrow variety is 'Fastigiata'.

American arborvitae *(Thuja occidentalis)* Needled evergreen, zones 3–7, 40–60 feet. Regular to moderate water. Feathery juvenile foliage becomes flat and scalelike, forming sprays with age. Mature trees have scaly brown bark and an open, rounded canopy. Use for large screens or prune into tall hedges. Western red cedar (*T. plicata*) grows taller and retains the dark green color of its scaly leaves through winter.

palms

GROW THEM IN THE TROPICS AND BEYOND

FEW PLANTS REFLECT THE MILD CLIMATES OF FLORIDA AND CALIFORNIA THE WAY PALM TREES DO. BUT except for cabbage palm in the Southeast and a few others, most of the palms you see aren't native to the United States. Canary Island date palm, for example, comes from the islands off northern Africa.

The European fan palm naturally develops slowly expanding clumps.

Many palms are more cold hardy than you might expect. Windmill palm, one of the hardiest, tolerates temperatures as low as 5 degrees F. Many others can withstand brief periods of freezing temperatures, making them good candidates for milder areas of the South and West.

Palms shine in the right setting. Use them to shade a deck or form an evergreen backdrop. Some, such as lady palm and European fan palm, stay shrublike for many years and thrive under taller trees.

Palms are especially appreciated near swimming pools because they don't drop leaves and their roots don't buckle paving. Fronds, whether fanlike or feathery, reflect beautifully in the water. The curved trunks of the Senegal date palm, for example, create an exotic atmosphere that is very reminiscent of the tropics.

When carefully placed, palms produce dramatic effects. Night lighting in particular shows off their stateliness and spectacular leaves. You can backlight them, shine spotlights up on them from below, or direct lights to silhouette them against a pale wall. Even sunlight also casts their evocative daytime shadow patterns onto walls.

So many different palms exist for the garden that it's hard to keep up with them all. The modest array described here represents tried-and-true choices for just about anywhere palms can be grown.

Palms are one of the few plants that can be easily transplanted as large, mature specimens. Even tall plants can be dug up, placed in relatively small boxes, and transplanted with almost certain success. Planting specimen palms still usually requires heavy equipment and expert help, but it's one of the best ways to quickly convert an empty garden into a tropical paradise. Although expensive, transplanting may be worthwhile around a large new pool or patio or to create a stunning focal point in the front yard.

KING PALM

a sampler of palms

King palm (*Archontophoenix cunninghamiana*)

Canary Island date palm (*Phoenix canariensis*)

Windmill palm (*Trachycarpus fortunei*)

King palm (*Archontophoenix cunninghamiana*) Zones 10–11, 20–40 feet but may grow up to 60 feet in mildest climates. Eight- to 10-foot dark green leaves; purple flowers. Fast growing. Takes some frost when established. Grows best out of wind. Needs abundant water. Not suited to desert landscapes.

Bamboo palm (*Chamaedorea seifrizii*) Zones 10–11, 5–10 feet. Several species, most with clumping, bamboolike growth. All grow slowly. Frost tender. Needs ample water and a shady spot.

Mediterranean fan palm (*Chamaerops humilis*) Zones 8–11, 20 feet. Blue-green or silver-green leaves make this palm outstanding. Forms clumps if not pruned. Endures baking sun and drought. Grows slowly. Leaf stems carry sharp spines.

Chinese fountain palm (*Livistona chinensis*) Zones 9–11, 15 feet. Strongly drooping dark green leaf tips resemble a fountain. Remains trunkless for years, developing a broad head. Makes a fine patio palm when sheltered from the wind and hot afternoon sun.

Canary Island date palm (*Phoenix canariensis*) Zones 9–11, 60 feet. This big, heavy-trunked plant has long, gracefully arching fronds that form a crown up to 50 feet in diameter. When young the plant grows well in a pot.

Senegal date palm (*Phoenix reclinata*) Zones 9–11, 20–30 feet. Clumps grow from offshoots, with several curving trunks. Remove offshoots for a single-trunk tree.

Pygmy date palm (*Phoenix roebelenii*) Zones 9–11, 6–30 feet. Soft, feathery leaves. Stem grows slowly to 6 feet. Wind resistant but tender; suffers below 28 degrees F. Silver date palm (*P. sylvestris*) is similar in shape but is hardier and grows to 30 feet.

Lady palm (*Rhapis*) Zones 9–11, 5–18 feet. Multiple stems bear dark green, glossy leaves. Slowly makes a good screen. Requires little pruning. *R. excelsa* grows to 5–12 feet; *R. humilis* to 18 feet. Prefers rich, moist soil and protection from sun and winds.

Cabbage palm (*Sabal palmetto*) Zones 9–11, 90 feet. Single-trunked and slow growing. Dense, round head formed by leaves 5–8 feet across. Tolerates wind, salt spray, and sand. Ideal for coastal gardens in the South.

Queen palm (*Syagrus romanzoffianum*) Zones 9–11, 30–50 feet. Lush plumelike leaves 10–15 feet long. Grows quickly. Shelter from wind; water and fertilize generously.

Windmill palm (*Trachycarpus fortunei*) Zones 7–11, 30 feet. Stiff, upright shape and hairy brown trunk. Reaches 30 feet in warm-winter areas, shorter elsewhere. Looks best in groups of three or more. Fronds get shabby in wind and must be trimmed.

shrubs

THE BACKBONE OF A GARDEN

JUST AS A LARGE SOFA OR BULKY UPHOLSTERED CHAIR FILLS A ROOM, SHRUBS CAN ADD WEIGHT AND substance to a landscape. They are permanent fixtures, altering traffic flow and framing views. Planted near a wall, they create attractive backdrops; set close together, they form a living fence.

Like trees, shrubs are either deciduous or evergreen. They grow in a variety of shapes—rounded, tapered, or fountainlike. Many shrubs, with their showy flowers, fruits, or autumn foliage, offer seasonal appeal. Many, like camellias, have decorative foliage throughout the year. Still others, such as

daphnes, lilacs, and sweet box , are valued primarily for their fragrance.

With hundreds of shrubs available, one key to success is to select only ones that suit your landscape's climate, soil conditions, available sunlight, and water resources. Azaleas and rhododendrons, for example, thrive in

Deciduous azaleas and rhododendrons combine with spring bulbs in this Pacific Northwest garden.

pruning a mock orange

1 SHRUB IS OVERCROWDED and needs thinning to remain vigorous.

2 CUT OUT oldest and weakest stems in spring after flowering.

3 YOUNGEST canes and a desirable shape remain after pruning.

semishade and in acidic soil that both retains moisture and drains excess water fast.

maintaining shrubs

Prune most flowering shrubs after their blossoms fade. For example, prune a May-flowering lilac in June. Deciduous shrubs that produce long stems each year from the base benefit from an early-spring removal of some older stems. Most evergreens, however, can be pruned at any time of year. Exceptions are blooming shrubs, like camellia, and pines, such as mugho pine.

Rejuvenate overgrown shrubs that grow directly from their base by removing all or most of the existing stems. Shrubs that tolerate such treatment include glossy abelia (*Abelia grandiflora*), barberry (*Berberis*), forsythia, oleander, mock orange (*Philadelphus coronarius*), spiraea, and common privet (*Ligustrum vulgare*). Cut all stems back to the ground before new spring growth begins. If the treatment is successful, the plant will usually achieve its normal height within several years. If you're not sure whether a shrub can take such drastic pruning, carry out a four-year program. Do no cutting the first year; just water and fertilize well to make the plant as healthy as possible. Over the next three years, remove about a third of the oldest stems in spring, pruning them back to the ground just before growth begins.

salvaging an old shrub

If you move into a house with overgrown shrubs in the yard, try a salvage operation before taking them out.

If a shrub has one or more upright stems and a framework of side branches, convert it to a small tree by removing the lower side branches. Remove side stems on the trunk up to the point where you want the branching to begin, then thin those that remain to form an uncluttered crown. If the shrub has several good stems, you can leave them all.

If you don't want to transform an overgrown shrub into a tree, you can lower it. Each year, cut about a third of the highest branches back halfway. Most will sprout new growth at the lower level. After you've created a smaller shrub with vigorous young growth, thin out any weak, badly placed, or crowded shoots.

Transform a large shrub with upright main stems (left) into a multitrunked small tree (right) by removing side stems.

LOWE'S QUICK TIPS

- Maintain best flowering of most shrubs by selectively removing a few of the oldest stems each year.
- Prune spring-flowering shrubs after flowers fade.
- Prune summer-flowering shrubs in early spring.

a sampler of shrubs

Japanese barberry (*Berberis thunbergii*)

Butterfly bush (*Buddleja davidii*)

Lemon bottlebrush (*Callistemon citrinus*)

Glossy abelia (*Abelia grandi-flora*) Evergreen to semievergreen, zones 6–9 (6–11W), 5–10 feet. Regular water; full sun to light shade. White to light pink flowers in summer and fall. Small, oval, glossy leaves cover graceful, arching branches. Use in borders, for hedges, and near houses.

Japanese aucuba (*Aucuba japonica*) Evergreen, zones 7–10 (7–11W), 6–10 feet. Moderate water; shade to deep shade. Grown for its attractive green or variegated gold leaves and ability to grow in deep shade, even under trees. Useful in patio tubs or indoors. Popular varieties include 'Gold Dust' and 'Mr. Goldstrike'.

Japanese barberry (*Berberis thunbergii*) Deciduous, zones 4–8 (4–11W), 4–6 feet. Regular to moderate water; full sun to light shade. Slender arching branches are covered with sharp spines and small oval leaves that turn yellow

to crimson in autumn. Red berries persist into winter. Many varieties with differing leaf colors and growth habits, such as golden 'Aurea' and bronze 'Crimson Pygmy'.

Butterfly bush (*Buddleja davidii*) Deciduous, zones 5–9 (5–11W), 5–15 feet. Regular to moderate water; full sun to light shade. Spiky 6- to 12-inch clusters of small, fragrant white to purple blooms appear in midsummer, attracting many butterflies. Vigorous with willowlike leaves. Many varieties, including *B. d. nanhoensis*.

Japanese boxwood (*Buxus microphylla japonica*) Evergreen, zones 5–8 (5–11W), 15–20 feet. Regular water; sun or shade. One of the most widely planted shrubs for formal hedges and edging. Dense foliage of lustrous, dark green oval leaves. Many varieties and hybrids are available.

Lemon bottlebrush (*Callistemon citrinus*) Evergreen,

zones 8–11, 10–15 feet. Regular to moderate water; full sun. Massive shrub that can be trained into a small tree. Bright red, 6-inch-long brushy flower spikes attract hummingbirds throughout the year.

Scotch heather (*Calluna vulgaris*) Evergreen, zones 4–7, 1–3 feet. Regular water; full sun. Spikes of purple, pink, or white flowers from summer to fall. Foliage color is mostly dark green but can vary. Many varieties turn reddish in cold winters. Prefers cool, moist summers and acidic soils. Can be used as a ground cover.

Camellia (*Camellia japonica*) Evergreen, zones 7–9 (7–11W), 6–12 feet. Regular to moderate water; light shade. Large, showy blooms from autumn through spring and leathery, deep green glossy foliage make these very popular shrubs for patio containers and display gardens. Many species and thousands of varieties with differing flowers and

Wild lilac (*Ceanothus* 'Julia Phelps')

Flowering quince (*Chaenomeles*)

Redtwig dogwood (*Cornus stolonifera*)

growth habits. Especially useful are the sasanqua camellias (*C. sasanqua*). They are upright, spreading, sometimes vinelike plants that bloom from fall into winter. Flower form and color are similar to those of Japanese camellia. Use low-growing varieties as ground covers.

Natal plum *(Carissa macrocarpa)* Evergreen, zones 10–11, 2–7 feet. Little to regular water; full sun to light shade. Dependable flowering shrub for mild-winter areas. Star-shaped, fragrant white flowers bloom nearly year-round, followed by edible bright red fruit. Can be used as a low hedge or ground cover. Varieties differ in habit and height.

Blue mist *(Caryopteris clandonensis)* Deciduous, zones 4–9 (4–11W), 2–3 feet. Moderate water; full sun. Compact, mounding shrub with a long season of summer flower color in various shades of blue lasting into fall. Some varieties have grayish leaves. Fine grouped into a small

border or mixed with perennials. Keep plant compact by cutting back to 6 inches in winter.

Wild lilac *(Ceanothus)* Evergreen, zones 9–11W, 1–12 feet or more, depending on species. Little or no water; full sun. Mostly California natives valued for their blue or white spring flowers, dark green foliage, and ability to thrive with little water. Excellent for slopes and gardens of native plants. Many species and varieties to choose from. Shrubby types include 'Dark Star' (6 feet high, rich blue flowers), 'Joyce Coulter' (5 feet high), and 'Julia Phelps' (7 feet high, dark indigo flowers).

Flowering quince *(Chaenomeles)* Deciduous, zones 5–9, 3–10 feet. Regular water; full sun. One of the earliest shrubs to bloom in spring. Mostly red or pink flowers are borne on upright, thorny bare branches. Can be clipped as a hedge. Many varieties to choose from, varying in height and flower color.

Rockrose *(Cistus)* Evergreen, zones 9–11W, 2–5 feet, depending on species. Moderate to little water; full sun. Carefree shrubs that bloom profusely in spring and require little water to thrive. Tolerant of seaside and desert conditions.

Redtwig dogwood *(Cornus stolonifera)* Deciduous, zones 2–7 (2–9W), 7–9 feet. Regular water; full sun to light shade. Vigorous bright-red stems contrast in winter with snowy landscape. Creamy white flowers in summer, bluish fruits, red autumn foliage. Good for informal borders and barriers. Some varieties have yellow stems and some have variegated leaves.

Smoke tree *(Cotinus coggygria)* Deciduous, zones 4–10 (4–11W), 12–15 feet, sometimes taller. Moderate to little water; full sun. Tiny green flower clusters transform into purplish puffs, giving the whole plant the look of a cloud of smoke in summer; hence the name. Most

a sampler of shrubs

Parney cotoneaster (*Cotoneaster lacteus*)

Slender deutzia (*Deutzia gracilis*)

Twisted heath (*Erica cinerea*)

varieties also have purplish foliage that turns yellow, orange, or red in fall. Usually grown as a tall, upright shrub but can be kept small.

Parney cotoneaster (*Cotone-aster lacteus*) Evergreen, zones 7–9 (7–11W), 8–10 feet. Moderate water; full sun. Graceful, arching habit with dark green leaves. Clusters of white flowers are followed by red fruits that last well into winter. Use as an informal hedge or screen.

Winter daphne (*Daphne odora*) Evergreen, zones 7–9 (7–11W), 4–8 feet. Regular to moderate water; full sun with midday shade. Prized for its fragrant clusters of pink to red flowers and neat growth habit. The variety 'Aureo-marginata' has gold-edged foliage.

Slender deutzia (*Deutzia gra-cilis*) Deciduous, zones 5–8, 2–5 feet. Moderate water; full sun to light shade. Showy, fragrant white flowers on gracefully arching stems in spring.

Can be clipped as a hedge. 'Nikko' bears double flowers on a dwarf shrub and has burgundy fall color.

Hop bush (*Dodonaea viscosa*) Evergreen, zones 8–11W, 12–15 feet. Regular to little water; full sun to light shade. A rugged, dependable shrub that has a billowy habit. Most widely grown are purple-leafed varieties, such as 'Purpurea', which need full sun to retain color. Can get by with little water. Very useful screen or accent.

Silverberry (*Elaeagnus pungens*) Evergreen, zones 6–9 (6–11W), 6–15 feet. Regular to little water; full sun to part shade. Gray-green leaves with wavy edges on spiny branches. A tough shrub useful in containers and in hot, windy areas. Several varieties have variegated foliage.

Twisted heath (*Erica cinerea*) Evergreen, zones 4–8, 6–18 inches. Consistent, careful watering; full sun except in hottest climates. Small, needlelike leaves and abundant

small flowers throughout the year, depending on species. Many hardy, varieties are good for borders and ground covers. Larger species range in height up to 10 feet or more.

Escallonia (*Escallonia* 'Frades') Evergreen, zones 7–11W, 5–6 feet. Regular water; full sun in cool-summer climates, part shade in warmer areas. A colorful shrub particularly useful in coastal areas of the western United States. Rosy pink flowers appear among glossy, dark green leaves almost year-round. Can be trimmed as a hedge. Several other varieties that have a compact habit are available.

Winged euonymus (*Euonymus alatus*) Deciduous, zones 4–8, 15–20 feet. Regular to moderate water; full sun. Stems have corky ridges, and leaves turn flaming red in autumn. Growth is upright with horizontal branching. Use for hedge, screens, near houses. 'Compacta' stays smaller and more compact. Can be invasive.

Winged euonymus *(Euonymus alatus)*

Forsythia *(Forsythia intermedia)*

Oakleaf hydrangea *(Hydrangea quercifolia)*

Evergreen euonymus *(Euonymus japonicus)* Evergreen, zones 7–9, 8–10 feet. Regular to moderate water; full sun. Very glossy, small, leathery, deep green leaves. Upright growth often pruned into formal hedges. Many varieties with varying leaf color and size, such as 'Microphyllus Variegata' and 'Silver King'. Evergreen wintercreeper (*E. fortunei*) has a creeping or low shrublike habit and is hardy to zone 4. Many varieties are available that have yellow or white variegated leaves, such as 'Emerald 'n' Gold'. Some turn purplish in fall and winter.

Forsythia *(Forsythia intermedia)* Deciduous, zones 4–8 (4–9W), 7–10 feet. Regular to moderate water; full sun. Fountain-shaped shrubs cover themselves in bright yellow flowers in early spring. Use in informal borders and for screens. Many varieties with varying hardiness are available. Cold-hardy hybrids include 'Meadowlark' and 'Northern Sun'.

Gardenia *(Gardenia augusta)* Evergreen, zones 8–10 (8–11W), 1–8 feet. Regular water; light shade. White, very fragrant flowers contrast with shiny, dark green leaves. Grow in pots on patios and in greenhouses. Popular varieties include 'Golden Magic' and 'Mystery'.

Witch hazel *(Hamamelis intermedia)* Deciduous, zones 5–9, 12–15 feet or more. Regular water; sun to light shade. Delicate, wonderfully fragrant yellow to sometimes reddish flowers appear on bare branches very early in spring. Leaves turn gold in fall. Looks best with a dark green background. Plant where fragrance can be enjoyed.

Tropical hibiscus *(Hibiscus rosa-sinensis)* Evergreen, zones 10–11, 4–15 feet. Regular water; full sun. Showy trumpet-shaped flowers in all colors produced throughout summer. Glossy dark green foliage in all seasons. Use for hedge or accent planting. Hundreds of varieties.

Deciduous rose of sharon (*H. syriacus*) has smaller flowers and is hardy in zones 5–8.

Garden hydrangea *(Hydrangea macrophylla)* Deciduous, zones 6–9 (6–11W), 4–12 feet. Regular water; full sun to part shade. Large, thick, coarsely toothed leaves and rounded growth habit. Round or flat-topped pink, blue, or white flower clusters up to 12 inches across. Many varieties are available for containers and landscape accents. Oakleaf hydrangea (*H. quercifolia*) grows to 3–6 feet and has very attractive oaklike foliage that turns crimson in fall.

Chinese holly *(Ilex cornuta)* Evergreen, zones 7–9 (7–11W), 6–20 feet, depending on variety. Regular to moderate water; full sun to partial shade. Leathery, glossy leaves with spines and large, bright red, long-lasting berries. Varieties that produce berries without a male pollinator include 'Burfordii', 'Dazzler', and 'Dwarf Burford'. Many varieties and hybrids

a sampler of shrubs

Winterberry *(Ilex verticillata)*

Sargent juniper *(Juniperus chinensis sargentii)*

Wax-leaf privet *(Ligustrum japonicum)*

have differing growth habits, hard-iness, berry abundance and color, and foliage. Popular hybrids include 'Foster's', 'Nellie R. Stevens', and the Meserve varieties 'Blue Girl' and 'China Girl' (zone 4). Species that have smooth instead of spiny leaves, including Japanese holly (*I. crenata*), yaupon holly (*I. vomitoria*), and ink-berry (*I. glabra*).

Winterberry *(Ilex verticillata)*
Deciduous, zones 3–9 (3–8W), 6–10 feet. Regular water; full sun to light shade. Large crops of very showy red berries persist on female plants into winter and are prized by birds. Tidy oval, dark green leaves. Plant one male for every few female shrubs and choose varieties adapted to your climate. Good female varieties include 'Afterglow', 'Sparkleberry', and 'Winter Red'.

Juniper *(Juniperus)*
Needled evergreen, zones 2–9 (2–11W), 1–10 feet. Regular to moderate water; full sun to light shade. Widely used and

diverse group of landscape shrubs prized for use as ground covers, borders, plantings near houses, and large groupings. Many kinds have varying foliage color and growth habits. Popular varieties include the ground cover sargent juniper (*J. chinensis sargentii*). Shrub forms include *J. chinensis* 'Aurea', 'Kaizuka', and 'Sea Green'; the pfitzer juniper (*J. pfitzeriana*); *J. scopulorum* 'Wichita Blue'; and singleseed juniper (*J. squamata* 'Blue Star'). Columnar types include *J. chinensis* 'Spartan' and *J. scopulorum* 'Skyrocket'.

Wax-leaf privet *(Ligustrum japonicum)*
Evergreen, zones 7–9 (7–11W), 10–12 feet. Regular water; full sun to partial shade. Compact growth and thick, glossy leaves make it useful for hedges and screens. In zones 4–7, deciduous privets (*L. amurense*, *L. ovalifolium*, and *L. vulgare*) are popular hedge plants. Growth habit and leaf color is variable. Vicary golden privet (*L.* 'Vicaryi') develops yellow leaves when grown in full sun.

Chinese fringe flower *(Loropetalum chinense)*
Evergreen, zones 7–9 (7–11W), 5–10 feet. Regular water; full sun to partial shade. Neat, compact habit with arching tiered branches. Delicate-looking white flower clusters appear throughout bloom season, especially in spring. There are several varieties with pink flowers and purple leaves.

Oregon grape *(Mahonia aquifolium)*
Evergreen, zones 5–9 (5–11W), 3–6 feet. Moderate to little water; full sun to shade. Long, spiny-toothed leaves turn purplish to bronze in winter. Clusters of flowers mature to edible blue-black fruit. 'Compacta' grows to only 2 feet but spreads into broad colonies.

Wax myrtle *(Myrica cerifera)*
Evergreen, zones 8–11, 10–20 feet. Regular water; full sun to partial shade. Glossy, dark green leaves are aromatic. Waxy grayish white berries are used for candle making. Deciduous bayberry (*M. pensylvanica*)

Mock orange *(Philadelphus)*

Lily-of-the-valley shrub *(Pieris japonica)*

Mugho pine *(Pinus mugo)*

is similar but is hardy in zones 3–6. Use for hedges and screens.

Heavenly bamboo *(Nandina domestica)*

Evergreen, zones 6–9, 6–8 feet. Regular to moderate water; sun or shade. Lightly branched, cane-like stems and fine-textured, lacy foliage are reminiscent of bamboo. Clumps expand slowly via stolons. Excellent leaf color from pink to red when young, soft green changing to bronze and purple in fall. White flower clusters in early summer. Dwarf purple 'Nana' variety grows only 1–2 feet tall.

Oleander *(Nerium oleander)*

Evergreen, zones 8–11, 8–12 feet. Regular to little water; full sun. Narrow, 4- to 12-inch-long, dark green leathery leaves are attractive year-round. White, yellow, pink, and red flower clusters from spring into autumn. Many varieties. Use for screens, borders, and containers. All plant parts are highly toxic, including leaves, flowers, and stems.

Sweet olive *(Osmanthus fragrans)*

Evergreen, zones 9–10, 6–10 feet. Regular to moderate water; full sun to partial shade. Tiny white, powerfully fragrant flowers in spring to early summer. Glossy oval to holly-shaped 4-inch leaves. Forms a broad, dense hedge or screen with pruning. Also good in containers.

Mock orange *(Philadelphus)*

Deciduous, zones 4–8, 6–8 feet. Regular to moderate water; partial shade in hottest areas. White, very fragrant flowers in early summer. Fountain-shaped growth habit and medium green foliage. Use as a background plant, or choose a smaller variety, such as 'Dwarf Snowflake'.

Photinia *(Photinia fraseri)*

Evergreen, zones 7–9 (7–11W), 10–15 feet. Regular to moderate water; full sun. Five-inch bright bronzy, oval new leaves ma-ture to dark green. Highly valued as a foliage plant and for clusters of white flowers. 'Red Robin' has bright red new leaves.

Lily-of-the-valley shrub *(Pieris japonica)*

Evergreen, zones 5–8, 9–10 feet. Regular water; shade, especially in afternoon. Whorls of leathery, narrowly oval leaves are red to bronze when new, then mature to green. Drooping clusters of white to nearly red flowers emerge from red buds. Excellent as container plant as well as in shady woodland landscapes. Varieties include 'Mountain Fire' and 'Temple Bells'.

Mugho pine *(Pinus mugo)*

Needled evergreen, zones 3–7 (3–11W), 4–20 feet, depending on variety. Regular water; full sun. Stiff 1- to 2-inch-long needles densely cover the branches of this slow-growing mounded shrub. Use in containers and borders.

Tobira *(Pittosporum tobira)*

Evergreen, zones 8–11, 10–15 feet. Regular to moderate water; full sun to partial shade. Leathery, narrowly elliptical, shiny dark green leaves form dense whorls. White flower

a sampler of shrubs

Cinquefoil (*Potentilla fruticosa*)

Firethorn (*Pyracantha*)

Rhododendron (*Rhododendron* 'PJM')

clusters in spring. Tolerant of sea-coast conditions. 'Variegata' has gray-green, white-edged foliage.

Shrubby yew pine (*Podocarpus macrophyllus maki*) Evergreen, zones 8–11, 8–15 feet. Regular to moderate water; full sun or partial shade. Grows slowly into a dense, upright shape. Narrow 3-inch leaves. Excellent in containers and for low- to medium-height hedges.

Cinquefoil (*Potentilla fruticosa*) Deciduous, zones 2–6 (2–9W), 1–4 feet. Moderate water; afternoon shade in hot climates. Yellow, pink, or white single or double roselike flowers bloom from late spring to early fall. Trouble-free shrub has divided green to gray-green leaves. Popular varieties include 'Abbotswood' (white), 'Floppy Disc' (double pink), 'Goldfinger' (yellow), and 'Klondike' (yellow).

English laurel (*Prunus lauro-cerasus*) Evergreen, zones 7–10, 5–12 feet but often taller. Regular

water; full sun to partial shade (in hot summer areas). Very useful hedge, screen, or background plant with clusters of small, fragrant white flowers and rich green leaves. Bears small black fruit. Dwarf varieties, like 'Nana' and 'Otto Luyken', are most widely grown.

Firethorn (*Pyracantha*) Evergreen, zones 5–9 (5–11W), 2–15 feet (both zone and height depending upon variety). Moderate water; full sun. Grown for its spring flowers and bright red, orange, or yellow fruits and its deep green foliage. All forms have small, glossy leaves, and most have needlelike thorns. Cold hardiness varies, so ask before purchase. Grow or train against a wall or fence.

Indian hawthorn (*Rhaphiolepis indica*) Evergreen, zones 8–9 (8–11W), 3–5 feet. Regular to moderate water; full sun to light shade. Clusters of small white to pinkish blooms from early winter to late

spring. New growth is bronzy red, then matures to glossy dark green. Grow as a low hedge.

Azaleas and rhododendrons (*Rhododendron*) Evergreen and deciduous, zones 3–9 (3–10W), 2–15 feet. Regular water; filtered shade. A large and variable group that includes more than 800 species and several thousand named varieties. All are grown for their spectacular clusters of blooms in white and many shades of pink, red, purple, yellow, salmon, and peach. Evergreen types have thick, glossy leaves. Deciduous species often have red to orange fall foliage. Nearly all require moist, acidic soil, though specific varieties are more tolerant of extremes. Grow in containers, near houses, and in woodland landscapes.

Roses (*Rosa*) Many roses make excellent landscape shrubs that are useful in borders and as edgings and hedges. For more information, see pages 354–357.

Bridal wreath spirea *(Spiraea vanhouttei)*

Common lilac *(Syringa vulgaris)*

Doublefile viburnum *(V. plicatum tomentosum)*

Rosemary *(Rosmarinus officinalis)* Evergreen, zones 7–8 (7–11W), 2–8 feet. Moderate to little water; full sun. Dense, needlelike, highly aromatic 1-inch-long leaves are useful in cooking. Trailing to upright growth habit varies with variety. Use it in a container or as a ground cover, low border, or hedge, depending upon variety.

Sweet box *(Sarcococca)* Evergreen, zones 6–8 (6–11W), 1–5 feet. Regular to moderate water; partial to full shade. Prized for handsome dark green, waxy foliage and tiny but very fragrant white flowers that bloom in late winter to early spring. Slow growing and needs rich soil. Useful in shaded areas under trees and house overhangs, or on the north side of a house.

Spirea *(Spiraea)* Deciduous, zones 3–8 (3–10W), 1–6 feet, variable. Regular to moderate water; full sun to light shade. Popular for clusters of white, pink, or reddish flowers in spring, summer, or some-times fall. "Bridal wreath" forms have long, arching branches covered with white flowers. Mounding types form lower, rounded shrubs. Most common is *S. japonica.* Popular varieties include 'Anthony Waterer', 'Froebel', 'Goldflame', 'Little Princess', and 'Shirobana'. For the classic bridal wreath, plant *S. vanhouttei.*

Lilac *(Syringa)* Deciduous, zones 3–9, 6–20 feet. Regular water; light shade in hot areas. Very popular and highly regarded anywhere winters are cold. Multistemmed and hardy shrubs are cherished for showy, usually fragrant flowers clustered at stem tips in early to late spring. Common lilac *(S. vulgaris)* has hundreds of varieties differing in cold and heat hardiness, flower color, and bloom period. Lilacs with smaller leaves and more compact habits include meyer *(S. meyeri)*, littleleaf lilac *(S. microphylla)*, and 'Miss Kim' *(S. patula)*. In mild-winter regions of California, choose Descanso hybrids.

Viburnum *(Viburnum)* Deciduous and evergreen; zones and height variable. Regular water; full sun or partial shade. A large and diverse group including more than 150 evergreen and deciduous species and countless varieties. All bear clustered, sometimes fragrant flowers often followed by brightly colored fruits, most of which are sought out by birds. Some have attractive horizontal branching or colorful autumn foliage. Useful near patios and as screens, hedges, and specimens. (Species immune to the viburnum leaf beetle are noted with "I".) Popular deciduous kinds include Burkwood viburnum *(V. burkwoodii)*; Korean spice viburnum, I *(V. carlesii)*; Japanese snowball viburnum, I *(V. plicatum)*; doublefile viburnum, I *(V. plicatum tomentosum)*; tea viburnum, I *(V. setigerum)*; and dwarf cranberry viburnum *(V. trilobum 'Compactum')*. Evergreen species include sweet viburnum *(V. awabuki)*, leather-leaf viburnum, I *(V. rhytidophyllum)*, and laurustinus *(V. tinus)*.

vines

THEY COVER TRELLISES, ARBORS, AND WALLS

WHETHER FRAMING AN ENTRY, DRAPING A PILLAR, OR JUST RAMBLING ALONG THE GROUND, VINES can bring dazzling color to any landscape. The fast growth of many vines makes them ideal plants for temporary screens and permanent structures alike. They can cover a large area, such as a fence, or weave a delicate tracery on a wall in a small garden. Trailing vines can be planted in hanging containers on a small deck or balcony to shield the space from view. And because many vines are evergreen or feature variegated foliage and decorative fruits, they can provide year-round interest.

Not only do vines have a softening effect on walls, but they also greatly improve the appearance of other landscape structures, such as arbors, gazebos, and spa surrounds. Keep in mind that plants climbing on vertical supports need less frequent pruning than those that are growing horizontally. The latter tend to bloom more heavily, however, in part because their stems are more exposed to sunlight.

Other than the fact that all have long, pliable stems (at least when they're young), vines differ greatly. They may be evergreen, semievergreen, or deciduous. They may be modest in size or rampant enough to engulf trees or scale high walls. Many grow well in ordinary garden soil with an annual springtime application of fertilizer, but a few need rich, well-amended soil and regular fertilizer throughout the growing season. Some require ample moisture, but a great many perform well with little additional water after they're established.

Climate preferences vary as well, so always match your climate zone (see page 299) to the vines you want to grow. Many are native to semitropical parts of the world and cannot tolerate low temperatures. Some remain lush and green all year where winters are mild but drop their foliage or die to the ground during winter in colder areas. Some vines are well behaved in temperate zones but grow with great vigor in warmer regions, overwhelming their support and possibly the entire garden.

how vines climb

The particular way each vine climbs is what primarily determines the sort of support you'll need to provide.

Trumpet honeysuckle covers itself with orange-yellow to red flowers in late spring.

TWINING STEM TENDRILS CLINGING WITH HOLDFASTS CLINGING WITH AERIAL ROOTS SCRAMBLES, AND LACKS ANY MEANS OF ATTACHMENT

twining vines As these vines grow, their stems twist and spiral. They coil too tightly to grasp large supports like posts, so give them something slender, such as cord or wire. To cover a wooden fence with fiveleaf akebia (*Akebia quinata*), for example, string wire through screw eyes set at 6- to 8-inch intervals along the fence.

vines with tendrils or coiling leafstalks Tendrils are specialized plant parts growing from the end of a leaf or the side of a stem. They grow straight until they contact something they can grasp—wire or cord, another stem on the same vine, another plant—then reflexively contract into a spiral and wrap around the support. Vines that climb by tendrils include grape and sweet pea (*Lathyrus odoratus*).

clinging vines If any kind of vine gives the whole group a bad name, it's the clinging sort, which adhere tenaciously to almost any flat surface. Specialized structures let them grip their supports. Some, such as trumpet vine (*Campsis*) and ivy (*Hedera*), have stems equipped with aerial rootlets. Others, like Boston ivy (*Parthenocissus tricuspidata*), have tendrils that terminate in tiny suction-cup–like disks called holdfasts.

scrambling vines Some vines have no means of attachment. They climb only in the sense that their stems will proceed on a vertical path if the vines are secured to a support. Left to themselves, they'll simply mound, sprawl, and scramble, although a few, such as climbing roses and most bou-

gainvilleas, can hook their thorns through adjacent shrubs or trees. To attach this type of vine to a wall, attach screw eyes and wire to the wall, then tie the plant in place at various points as it grows.

training and pruning vines
Until a vine gets a firm hold on its support, you may need to tie it in place with twine or plastic garden tape. For heavy vines, you can use thin rope or strips of canvas or rubber. For clinging vines, you might tack plastic mesh over the stems until you see the aerial rootlets or holdfast discs adhering. After the stems of twining and scrambling vines gain some length, weave them through any openwork support, such as a trellis or wire fence.

To encourage bushy growth on young vines, pinch out the stems' terminal buds. If you want just a few vertical stems, as for a tracery of growth around a column, don't pinch. Instead, remove all but one or two long stems at the base.

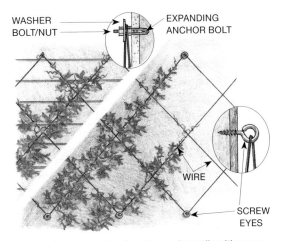

WASHER BOLT/NUT
EXPANDING ANCHOR BOLT
WIRE
SCREW EYES

Attach wires for training vines to wooden walls with screw eyes, to masonry walls with expanding anchor bolts.

a sampler of vines

Bougainvillea

Deciduous clematis *(Clematis)*

Carolina jessamine *(Gelsemium sempervirens)*

Fiveleaf akebia *(Akebia quinata)* Semievergreen or deciduous, zones 5–11. Regular water; full sun or partial shade. A lush yet delicate clinging vine. Foliage is fine textured, with each leaf consisting of five small leaflets radiating from the stem tip. Small, purplish spring flowers are a bonus (to some people they smell like chocolate). The vine ascends rapidly to 15–30 feet, providing shade and hiding less than lovely structures from view.

Bougainvillea Evergreen, zones 10–11 and protected parts of zone 9. Regular to moderate water; full sun or partial shade. Gloriously colorful, shrubby vine. Summer blooms in bright shades of purple, red, orange, yellow, and white. Must be tied to a strong support. Vigorous varieties will grow to over 15 feet. Train to a warm, sunny wall or sturdy fence. Can also be used as a sprawling ground cover.

'Mme Galen' trumpet creeper (*Campsis tagliabuana* 'Mme Galen') Deciduous, zones 5–11.

Regular to moderate water; full sun to light shade. Vigorous climber uses its rootlets to attach to almost anything. Can reach 30 feet tall, so it's suitable for large areas. Large salmon red flowers are held in loose clusters. Prune to keep compact and within bounds.

Deciduous clematis *(Clematis)* Zones 4–10. Regular water; leaves in sun, roots in shade. Huge family of lovely, delicate vines. Large-flowered hybrids, most widely grown, bloom in every shade but green. Clings by tendrils, climbing about 10 feet. Grow on a trellis or allow it to sprawl among other plants.

Evergreen clematis *(Clematis armandii)* Evergreen, zones 8–11. Regular water; leaves in sun, roots in shade. Clusters of shiny white, fragrant flowers in spring. Attractive deep green, divided foliage. Clings with tendrils, climbing to 20 feet. Perfect growing on eaves, trellises, fences, or a small arbor.

Silver lace vine *(Fallopia baldschuanica)* Deciduous to partially evergreen, zones 5–9 (5–11W). Regular water; full sun to partial shade. Silver white, frothy flower clusters from spring to fall. Attractive glossy foliage on twining stems. Incredibly vigorous. Grow only on sturdy fences or a large arbor. Prune heavily to maintain size.

Creeping fig *(Ficus pumila)* Evergreen, zones 8–11. Regular water; full sun, partial shade. Clean-looking, leathery foliage will attach to anything it touches and will also damage any surface—other than stone or masonry—in the process.

Carolina jessamine *(Gelsemium sempervirens)* Evergreen, zones 7–9 (7–11W). Regular water; full sun to partial shade. Cascading clusters of fragrant yellow flowers in late winter to early spring. Glossy green foliage on a shrubby, twining plant that grows up to 20 feet. Train to a sunny trellis, arbor, fence, or wall.

Lilac vine (*Hardenbergia violacea* 'Happy Wanderer')   Chinese jasmine *(Jasminum polyanthum)*   Goldflame honeysuckle *(Lonicera heckrottii)*

Lilac vine (*Hardenbergia violacea* 'Happy Wanderer') Evergreen, zones 9–11W. Moderate water; full sun to partial shade. Long clusters of sweet pea–shaped, small pinkish purple flowers from late winter to early spring. Handsome divided leaves. Twines to 10 feet. Ideal for a trellis and in large containers. Cut back after bloom.

Chinese jasmine *(Jasminum polyanthum)* Evergreen (partially deciduous in cold areas), zones 8–11. Regular water; partial shade. Intensely fragrant white and pink flowers in spring. Bright green leaves on twining stems up to 20 feet tall. Best in hot-summer areas. Grow on a trellis, an arbor, or a fence, or let it sprawl over a bank.

Honeysuckle *(Lonicera)* Evergreen and deciduous, zones vary by species. Regular water; full sun to partial shade. Tubular white to yellow, fragrant flowers mostly in summer. Rampant twining plants that can grow over 40 feet, depending on species. The most popular are goldflame honeysuckle (*L. heckrottii*) and trumpet honeysuckle (*L. sempervirens*). The worst is *L. japonica*, a seriously invasive plant, and should be avoided. All need sturdy support, lots of room, and heavy pruning, and all can be used as ground covers.

Boston ivy *(Parthenocissus tricuspidata)* Deciduous, zones 4–9 (4–11W). Regular water; full sun, partial shade, or full shade. Glossy green, lobed leaves up to 8 inches wide turn to red, yellow, or orange in autumn. Stems cling tightly with rootlike holdfasts, quickly climbing as high as 30 to 50 feet and beyond. For a finer-textured, smaller-leafed vine, look for *P. t.* 'Veitchii'. Its foliage is burgundy red when new, and many people believe it has the finest fall color. Virginia creeper (*P. quinquefolia*) is similar but has more open growth.

Climbing roses *(Rosa)* The large and diverse rose family includes many climbing roses. For more information, see pages 354–357 in this chapter.

Star jasmine *(Trachelospermum jasminoides)* Evergreen, zones 8–10 (8–11W). Regular water; full sun to partial shade. White, sweetly scented summer flowers borne in showy clusters. Lustrous dark green leaves. Twines to 20 feet high. Excellent on fences, trellises, and posts. Widely used as ground cover.

Chinese wisteria *(Wisteria sinensis)* Deciduous, zones 5–10 (5–11W). Regular water; full sun. Grapelike clusters of fragrant violet-blue flowers in spring. Twining branches eventually become woody and classically gnarled. Can climb over 50 feet. Needs annual pruning for best flowering. Delicate divided leaves cast wonderful shade when grown on an arbor. Also beautiful when trained to eaves. Japanese wisteria (*W. floribunda*) is more cold-hardy but less showy.

ground covers
THEY BLANKET THE GARDEN'S FLOOR

A tapestry of color results from a mixed planting of flowering ground covers.

YOU CAN COUNT ON THESE PLANTS TO BLANKET THE SOIL WITH DENSE FOLIAGE, ADDING BEAUTY and variety to the landscape while holding soil in place and suppressing weeds. Where foot traffic is infrequent and sites are inhospitable—in the shade under large trees or on hot, steep banks, for instance—ground covers are the likely solution. The variety of heights, textures, foliage and flower colors is huge. Some are low mats, while others are knee-high. Some spread by underground runners, and others root on top of the ground as they grow.

planting ground covers

Where winters are cold, plant in spring to give the ground cover an entire season to become established before it must face the rigors of winter. In areas with hot, dry summers and mild winters, plant in fall.

Ground covers are tough, but they'll grow and spread faster if you prepare the planting area. Dig out weeds, amend the soil with compost or well-rotted manure, and broadcast a complete fertilizer over the area, following package directions for amounts. Work in amendments and fertilizer with a shovel or tiller, then rake to level the soil. (Shrubby plants from gallon containers are an exception. They are often planted in the native soil, without amendments.)

Plant ground covers in a diamond pattern. This spreads the plants efficiently and gives any size bed a neat, natural look as plants fill in.

ground cover maintenance

SHEARING
Use hedge shears to cut back vigorous ground covers. This removes old growth and keeps plants from spreading out of bounds. Rake up and compost clippings.

MOWING
A mower set to cut 3 to 4 inches high makes fast work of trimming expanses of spreading ground covers, such as English ivy, creeping St. Johnswort, and periwinkle.

spacing ground covers

How much space to allow between ground-cover plants depends on the growth rate of the particular plant and, to some extent, on how quickly you want the growth to cover the area. As a general guide, space fast-growing plants farther apart, and slow-growing ones closer.

When planting ground covers from smaller pots or flats, set them in holes just deep enough for and slightly wider than the root-ball. To plant from gallon containers, dig a hole that tapers outward at the bottom to accommodate the loosened roots, leaving a plateau of undisturbed soil in the middle. The root-ball rests on the plateau. Set the crown of each plant slightly above the soil surface to prevent rot (see pages 306–307).

Set the plants in staggered rows when planting on a slope where erosion is likely. Make an individual terrace for each plant and create a basin or low spot behind each one to catch water.

After planting, water thoroughly. As your ground cover becomes established over the next several weeks, water every few days, keeping the soil moist but not soggy. To help maintain soil moisture and prevent weed seeds from growing, spread a 2- to 4-inch-thick layer of organic mulch between the young plants, taking care not to cover the plants' crowns.

caring for ground covers

Most ground covers require little attention beyond routine watering, mulching, fertilizing, and grooming. In many cases, maintenance takes very little time, especially compared to the hours typically invested in lawn care. However, in a few cases, some special attention pays off.

weeding A primary reason for planting a ground cover is to eliminate weeding. However, don't expect to be freed from the job starting from the moment the plants are in the ground. Until they fill in, some weeding is usually necessary. Getting rid of weeds before they set seed is important to prevent ongoing problems. Replenishing the mulch as it decomposes also aids in weed control. For serious weed problems, you may be able to use a selective herbicide—one that will kill weeds but not your ground cover. For more on weed control, see pages 424–425.

edging If not restricted, many ground covers will advance beyond the area you've allotted for them. If the plant spreads by underground stems or by rooting along stems that touch the soil, you may be able to control it by trimming the planting's edges with pruning or hedge shears or with a mower.

pruning Some shrubby ground covers that are normally low growing may occasionally send out upright stems that spoil the evenness of the planting (cotoneaster is one example). When you see such stems, cut them back to their point of origin or to a horizontally growing stem within the foliage mass.

Rejuvenate perennial ground covers by digging them up, dividing each clump, and then replanting the strongest and most vigorous divisions.

a sampler of ground covers

Carpet bugle (*Ajuga reptans 'Variegata'*)

Bearberry (*Arctostaphylos uva-ursi*)

Scotch heather (*Calluna vulgaris*)

Bishop's weed (*Aegopodium podagraria*) Zones 4–9 (4–11W), 12 inches. Moderate water; sun or shade. Divided leaves are light green or variegated with white edges. Spreads vigorously—often too vigorously— by underground stems, forming dense colonies. Contain with underground barriers of wood or concrete.

Carpet bugle (*Ajuga reptans*) Evergreen perennial, zones 3–9 (3–11W), 4–5 inches. Regular water; full sun or partial shade. Spreads quickly by runners covered in dark green leaves and 4- to 5-inch blue flower spikes in spring to early summer. Can invade lawns. Some varieties have purplish or yellow variegated leaves or white flowers.

Bearberry (*Arctostaphylos uva-ursi*) Evergreen shrub, zones 2–6 (2–11W), 6–12 inches. Moderate water; sun or light shade. Small, glossy oval leaves on spreading stems that root as they grow. Leaves turn red or purplish in winter. White flowers

are followed by attractive red or pink fruits. Use bearberry on banks and near seashores, especially in sandy to gravelly soil.

Cape weed (*Arctotheca calendula*) Zones 10–11W, 20 inches. Moderate water; full sun. Spreads by underground runners. Six-inch leaves with woolly undersides form rosettes. Yellow flowers come in spring to early summer. Plant on banks and areas where it has room to spread.

Scotch heather (*Calluna vulgaris*) Evergreen shrub, zones 5–7 (5–8W), 4–24 inches. Moderate water; full sun. Neat clump-forming shrubs with tiny scalelike leaves and very showy spikes of bell-shaped flowers in summer to fall. Many varieties with differing flower and foliage colors, hardiness, and growth habits. Heather grows best in cool, moist climates.

Carmel creeper (*Ceanothus griseus horizontalis*) Evergreen shrub, zones 9–11W, 18–30 inches.

Little water; full sun or light shade. Glossy leaves on stems that spread 5–15 feet wide. Light blue flowers. Point Reyes ceanothus (*C. gloriosus*) is similar but has spiny leaves.

Dwarf plumbago (*Ceratostigma plumbaginoides*) Deciduous, zones 5–10 (6–11W), 6–12 inches. Moderate water; sun to partial shade. Dwarf plumbago provides a spot of vivid blue from midsummer to mid-autumn, when cool tones are most welcome in the garden. Loose clusters of intense blue flowers top wiry stems. Leaves turn bronzy red with frost. Shear after bloom.

Chamomile (*Chamaemelum nobile*) Evergreen, zones 3–10 (3–11W), 3–10 inches. Moderate water; full sun to partial shade. Soft-textured, spreading mat of bright, light green, aromatic foliage. Button-like yellow flowers in summer used to make tea. Useful as a lawn substitute or between stepping-stones. Mow or shear to keep compact.

Bearberry cotoneaster (Cotoneaster dammeri)

Ice plant (Delosperma floribundum)

Epimedium (Epimedium rubrum)

Bearberry cotoneaster *(Cotoneaster dammeri)* Evergreen shrub, zones 5–7 (5–11W), 3–6 inches. Moderate water; full sun. Bright glossy green leaves with bright red fruit. Prostrate branches spread 10 feet wide, rooting as they grow. Creeping cotoneaster *(C. adpressus)* is deciduous and spreads to 6 feet. Rock cotoneaster *(C. horizontalis)* grows quickly to 2–3 feet tall and 15 feet wide. Its stiff, horizontal branches form a flat herringbone pattern.

Ice plant *(Delosperma floribundum)* Succulent perennial, zones 6–10 (6–11W), 1–5 inches, depending on species. Little water; full sun. Fleshy, bright green leaves. Brilliant white, golden yellow or purple flowers in spring or summer. Plant in rock gardens and areas with excellent drainage.

Indian mock strawberry *(Duchesnea indica)* Evergreen to semievergreen perennial, zones

4–9, 6 inches. Moderate water; sun or shade. Looks and grows like strawberry, with trailing, rooting stems. Produces yellow flowers and ornamental red fruit carried above the leaves and enjoyed by birds. Useful under trees and open shrubs. Alpine strawberry *(Fragaria chiloensis)* is similar with white flowers.

Epimedium *(Epimedium)* Perennials, zones 4–9, 6–12 inches. Moderate water; partial shade. Creeping underground roots support thin, wiry stems holding leathery, divided heart-shaped leaves. Foliage is pinkish in spring, turning green, then bronze in autumn. Airy spikes of white to yellow or pink to red flowers in spring. Excellent under trees and open shrubs.

Winter creeper *(Euonymus fortunei)* Evergreen shrub or vine, zones 4–9, 1–3 feet. Regular to moderate water; sun or shade. Spreads up to 20 feet and climbs by rooting, clinging stems. Dark green, oval 1- to

2-inch leaves with scalloped edges attractive in all seasons. Many varieties with white or yellow variegated foliage, including 'Colorata', 'Emerald Gaiety', and 'Emerald 'n Gold'. Use to cover banks or to control erosion, spacing 3 feet apart.

Common blue fescue *(Festuca glauca)* Zones 4–8 (4–11W), 10 inches. Moderate to little water; full sun. Fine, threadlike blue-green leaves form mounds. Pale gold flowers come in summer. 'Elija Blue' is an improved, darker blue variety.

Sweet woodruff *(Galium odoratum)* Zones 4–8, 6–12 inches. Partial to full shade; regular water. Quickly forms a mat of stems bearing whorls of dark green leaves. Clusters of tiny white flowers appear from spring into summer. Use under trees and tall shrubs. Space plants 1 foot apart.

Trailing gazania *(Gazania)* Evergreen perennial, zones 8–10 (8–11W), 6–10 inches. Regular to

a sampler of ground covers

English ivy (*Hedera helix* 'Buttercup')

Dead nettle (*Lamium maculatum*)

Lantana (*Lantana montevidensis*)

moderate water; full sun. Spreads rapidly by trailing stems and has clean silvery gray leaves. Flowers in yellow, white, orange, and bronze. Varieties have larger flowers, greener leaves, more clumping habit. Use on banks and cascading over walls.

Bigroot cranesbill *(Geranium macrorrhizum)* Zones 4–8 (4–11W), 8–10 inches. Regular to moderate water; full sun, afternoon shade in hot regions. Large, fragrant lobed leaves smother weeds. Spreads by underground stems, forming tidy clumps. One-inch-wide magenta, pink, or white flowers come in spring, depending on variety. Deer resistant.

English ivy *(Hedera helix)* Evergreen vine, zones 5–8 (4–11W), 4–6 inches. Regular to moderate water; partial to full shade. Lobed leaves on long, trailing stems that root deeply as they grow. May climb trees and buildings, clinging with aerial rootlets. Trim to control spread and density. Many varieties, some

with variegated leaves and differing foliage shapes and sizes. Good on banks to control erosion.

Creeping St. Johnswort *(Hypericum calycinum)* Evergreen shrublet, zones 5–9 (5–11W), 12 inches. Regular to moderate water; sun to partial shade in hot areas. Spreads vigorously by underground stems to form large colonies of medium yellow green leaves. Bright yellow blooms throughout summer. Use to control erosion, and also underneath trees. Mow every two to three years to renew.

Juniper *(Juniperus)* Needled evergreen shrub, zones 4–9 (4–11W), 6–24 inches. Regular to moderate water; sun to light shade. Widely used for mass plantings on level ground and banks. Many species and varieties. Creeping types grow low, root along their stems, and include varieties of blue carpet juniper (*J. horizontalis* 'Wiltonii'); shore juniper (*J. rigida conferta*), such as 'Blue

Pacific'; and *J. horizontalis* 'Bar Harbor', 'Blue Rug', 'Plumosa', and 'Prince of Wales'. Spreading types grow low, produce horizontal branches, and include varieties of sargent juniper (*J. chinensis sargentii*), tamarix juniper (*J. sabina* 'Tamariscifolia'), and Virginia juniper (*J. virginiana* 'Silver Spreader').

Dead nettle *(Lamium maculatum)* Zones 4–8 (4–11W), 6–12 inches. Regular water; partial to full shade. Gray-green to white or silvery variegated leaves light up shady areas. Short spikes of small pink or white flowers in early summer. Popular varieties include 'Beacon Silver', 'Pink Pewter', and 'White Nancy'.

Lantana *(Lantana montevidensis)* Evergreen shrub, zones 10–11, 2–3 feet. Moderate water; full sun. Branches trail to 3–6 feet. Dark green toothed leaves, often red-tinged in cold weather. One-inch clusters of white, pink, lavender, purple, or orange flowers. Many varieties are available.

Lily turf (*Liriope* and *Ophiopogon*)

Trailing African daisy (*Osteospermum fruticosum*)

Japanese spurge (*Pachysandra terminalis*)

Lily turf (*Liriope* and *Ophiopogon*)

Evergreen perennials, zones 5–10 (5–11W), 6–12 inches. Regular to moderate water; partial sun or shade. Clump-forming perennials with grasslike leaves and spikes of white or lavender flowers in summer. Especially useful in borders and around pools and trees. Mow or cut back old foliage in winter to rejuvenate ragged plantings. Many varieties with differing leaf and flower colors.

Trailing African daisy (*Osteospermum fruticosum*)

Zones 10–11, 6–12 inches. Regular to moderate water; full sun. Spreads rapidly by rooting branches, covering 2–4 feet per year. Lilac to purple daisylike flowers appear throughout the year, most heavily in fall and winter. Good in mass plantings and on slopes.

Japanese spurge (*Pachysandra terminalis*)

Evergreen perennial, zones 4–8 (4–9W), 8–12 inches. Regular water; partial to full shade.

Shiny, toothed dark green leaves in neat whorls form large colonies under trees and near buildings. Spreads by underground runners.

Cinquefoil (*Potentilla*)

Evergreen perennial, zones 3–8 (3–11W), 4–12 inches. Moderate water; sun, shade in hot climates. Bright green to gray-green divided leaves form low-growing carpets. Roselike 1-inch flowers in white, yellow, or pink to red bloom in spring and summer. Many species and varieties thrive, especially in cool climates.

Roses (*Rosa*)

Among the many rose varieties are several that make useful ground covers. For a listing of them, see page 356.

Baby's tears (*Soleirolia soleirolii*)

Zones 9–11, 1–4 inches. Regular water; partial to full shade. Creeping plant with tiny round leaves spreads aggressively to form large mats. Use under ferns and other shade-loving plants.

Star jasmine (*Trachelospermum jasminoides*)

Evergreen vine, zones 9–10 (9–11W), 18–24 inches (as a ground cover). Regular water; sun, shade in hot areas. Glossy green foliage on spreading, twining branches. Will climb supports. Profuse, 1-inch sweet-scented white flower clusters attract bees. Use as edging or under trees and shrubs, pruning frequently to control growth.

Dwarf periwinkle (*Vinca minor*)

Evergreen perennial, zones 4–9 (4–11W), 6 inches. Moderate water; sun or partial shade. Trailing, arching stems with shiny 1-inch oval leaves and bright blue, lavender, or white flowers in spring to summer. Excellent under trees and for edging. Varieties have various flower and leaf colors, including white-flowering 'Alba' and variegated 'Ralph Shugert'. Greater periwinkle (*V. major*) has larger leaves to 3 inches long. It spreads rapidly in zones 7–11 and is extremely invasive in sheltered, wooded areas.

lawns

THEY ARE THE ULTIMATE GARDEN CARPET

ALTHOUGH THE LAWN IS USUALLY THE MOST CONSPICUOUS FEATURE OF A HOME LANDSCAPE, IT need not be large to enhance the overall beauty of the property. A well-designed small lawn can be just as functional and handsome as a big expanse of grass, and because both must be regularly fertilized, irrigated, and mowed, a small lawn requires much less work.

New lightweight push mowers make it easy to keep a small lawn trimmed. Hybrid grasses being developed for every climate grow more slowly than their predecessors and thus require less frequent mowing.

Some water-conscious gardeners question the need for a grass lawn at all, but it does have advantages. Grass is one of the best planting materials to keep the ground attractively covered, and it provides a uniquely safe and inviting surface for children's play and for recreational activities.

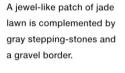

A jewel-like patch of jade lawn is complemented by gray stepping-stones and a gravel border.

the lawn in your landscape

Lawns combine handsomely with flower borders, informal plantings, and paved entertainment areas. Don't think of a lawn as a simple rectangle or square. A small circle of lawn ringed by trees and flowers, for example, can be the centerpiece of a formal garden, while a curved or kidney-shaped lawn can direct the eye to a focal point, such as a tree or sculpture. A grassy pathway can lure a visitor around a stand of shrubs to a secret garden waiting beyond. Squares of turf alternated with paving can create a cool and interesting space for patio tables and chaises.

When designing or redesigning a lawn area, give some thought to the amount of care the grass will need. A shady spot under a tree may be better planted with a ground cover, such as sweet woodruff. To eliminate tedious hand trimming, install mowing strips along the perimeter of your lawn. A ribbon of concrete, brick, or flat pavers, just wide enough to accommodate the wheels of a mower, will allow you to cut right to the edge of the grass. Lawns with rounded or simple geometric shapes are quicker to mow than ones with irregular or rectangular shapes.

If you don't use mowing strips, use an edging of plastic, metal, or wood bender-board to contain your lawn, as well as any plantings on the other side. If you plant a grass that spreads by runners, 8-inch-deep edging will keep it from invading nearby flower beds.

Especially in the arid West, make sure you have a plan for irrigating your lawn. Will a simple hose and hose-end sprinkler serve your purposes? Do you have an existing system that needs upgrading or repair? If you want a built-in automatic sprinkler system, it is simplest to install it before the turf is planted (see pages 208–211).

grass zones

Lawn grasses fall into two general categories: cool-season grasses for the north, and warm-season grasses for the south. Fertilizer and water needs differ between the two groups, and susceptibility to some pests and diseases varies as well. Where you live usually dictates the type of grass you can grow.

The map at right is divided into seven regions, each characterized by particular climate conditions. Grasses that grow well in each zone are listed below.

Keep in mind that the map is only a guide. Specific areas within a zone vary in rainfall, temperature, altitude, terrain, and soil. Areas adjacent to the map's dividing lines are transitional, meaning that grasses that flourish in those areas may be different from those that do well throughout most of the region. For further clarification, consult a Lowe's sales associate.

west, pacific northwest, and western canada
Climate is cool and humid along the coast but hot and dry in inland valleys. Rain falls in winter, while summers are dry. Lawns seeded from cool-season grasses—bent, fine and tall fescue, Kentucky blue, and perennial rye—do well throughout the region. Use tall fescue or Bermuda in inland areas.

southwest
Most grasses require supplemental irrigation. Bermuda is the primary lawn grass, with some zoysia and St. Augustine. Perennial rye is used for a winter lawn.

mountains, great plains, and central plains of canada
Climate is dry and semiarid, with wide temperature fluctuations. Drought-tolerant native grasses—buffalo, crested wheatgrass, and blue grama—do well. With irrigation, fine fescues and Kentucky and rough-stalk bluegrasses succeed in northern areas, while tall fescue, Bermuda, and zoysia do well in the south.

a climate map for lawns

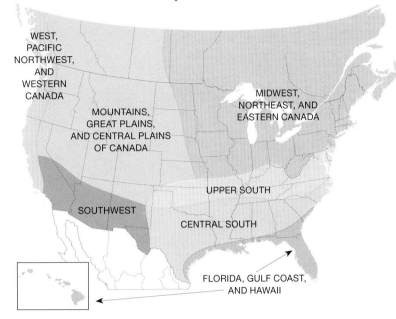

WEST, PACIFIC NORTHWEST, AND WESTERN CANADA

MOUNTAINS, GREAT PLAINS, AND CENTRAL PLAINS OF CANADA

MIDWEST, NORTHEAST, AND EASTERN CANADA

SOUTHWEST

UPPER SOUTH

CENTRAL SOUTH

FLORIDA, GULF COAST, AND HAWAII

midwest, northeast, and eastern canada
Summers are hot and humid, winters cold and snowy. Rainfall is abundant, and soils are often acidic. Kentucky bluegrasses, perennial and annual ryegrasses, and fine fescues are common throughout this region.

upper south
Summers are typically warm and humid, with abundant rainfall throughout the growing season. Winters are usually mild but can be severe. Bermuda, tall fescue, and zoysia grasses are generally best adapted. Kentucky and rough-stalk bluegrasses and perennial and annual ryegrasses are also widely planted.

central south
Climate is warm and humid in summer, usually with abundant rainfall, and winters are mild. Bermuda, centipede, tall fescue, and zoysia grasses do well. Kentucky bluegrass is used in cooler areas, St. Augustine in southern areas.

florida, gulf coast, and hawaii
Climate is subtropical to tropical, and the growing season is year-round. Rainfall is generally very high. Bahia, Bermuda, centipede, St. Augustine, and zoysia grasses grow well throughout most of the region. Use cool-season grasses for winter overseeding of dormant warm-season lawns.

Spread organic amendments over the soil and then work them into the soil as deeply as possible. After tilling, remove any large stones, level, and rake the soil smooth.

planting a new lawn

Establishing a lawn takes planning and a fair amount of effort. Sowing seed or laying sod is only the final step.

When preparing the area to be planted, make sure it has a gentle slope away from buildings and other areas that could be damaged by water. If possible, create basins where runoff from the lawn can collect. Allow 1 inch of slope for every 10 feet, or 1 foot for every 100 feet (see pages 206–207). As you measure for slope, you may find that some areas are higher or lower than others. Grade those for an overall even appearance. If you need to bring in additional soil, buy the same type as your existing soil (to the extent possible) and mix it with the existing soil as you prepare for planting.

If you are installing an underground sprinkler system, allow enough time in your schedule to design it carefully for complete, even coverage (see pages 208–209). Otherwise have a landscape contractor do the design, installation, or both.

test the soil See page 303 for information on how to determine your soil's acidity or alkalinity. If tests indicate a highly acid soil (pH below 6.0), add ground limestone.

If the soil is highly alkaline (pH above 8.0), add iron sulfate or elemental sulfur.

HULLED BERMUDA   UNHULLED BERMUDA

UNCOATED
TALL FESCUE

FESCUE
COATED WITH
FUNGICIDE

For Bermuda and buffalo grass, always sow hulled seed, because it will germinate much better than unhulled seed. Seed treated with fungicide protects disease-prone seedlings from failing.

Iron sulfate acts fast and will provide iron that is lacking in alkaline soils. Check with a Lowe's Garden Center sales associate for recommended amounts and types of amendments for adjusting soil pH that are available and effective in your area.

add organic soil amendments Nitrogen-stabilized soil amendments that are derived from sawdust and ground bark are available at Lowe's and most other garden supply stores. Although more costly, these materials are easier to use than raw sawdust or bark products, because you don't need to add additional nitrogen to hasten breakdown.

smooth the seedbed Usually you have to conform to surrounding paving, but if you have a choice, try to have a slight pitch away from the house. Grass forms a thick mat about 1 inch high, so the prepared planting area should finish out about an inch lower than surrounding areas. After raking and leveling, firm the seedbed with a full roller, making passes in two directions. If necessary, level the area again.

A small, pool-like circular lawn is easy to mow and care for but packs the visual punch of a much larger one.

how to sow grass seed

1 SCATTER SEED and starter fertilizer after the site is prepared.

2 LIGHTLY RAKE the seed into the soil enough to ensure seed-soil contact.

3 SPREAD MULCH and then press it into the soil with an empty roller.

starting from seed

Seeding applies most often to cool-season grasses. (Warm-season kinds are most often started from sprigs or plugs.) Lawns started from seed are best planted in fall, and early enough in the season to give the grass time to establish itself before cold weather. The next best time, for cool-season grasses, is in spring. To plant warm-season grasses from seed, wait until all danger of frost is past but before hot weather arrives.

When you prepare the soil, don't cultivate it too finely, as it then may form a hard crust that emerging seedlings cannot penetrate. Ideally, aim for pea-size to marble-size soil particles. Do the final leveling with a garden rake. Choose a wind-less day and sow the seeds evenly, using a drop or rotary spreader. Apply a complete dry granular fertilizer, also using a spreader. Several manufacturers offer fertilizers formulated for starting new lawns.

Water thoroughly, taking care not to wash away the seed. Keep the seeded area moist for about three weeks or until all grass is sprouted, watering briefly but frequently—5 to 10 minutes at a time. During warm periods, you may need to water three, four, or more times a day.

Mow for the first time when the grass is one-third taller than its optimum height. Mow slowly to keep from disturbing the barely set roots. After the initial mowing, continue to water frequently. The top inch of soil should not be allowed to dry out until the lawn is well established, usually after about six weeks and four mowings.

If weeds emerge, don't attempt to control them until the young lawn has been mowed four times. By this stage, many weeds will have been killed by mowing or crowded out by the growing lawn. If weeds are still a problem after four mowings, many gardeners prefer to treat the lawn with an herbicide. Unlike hand pulling, it kills weeds without the risk of disturbing the root systems of the grass.

Try to avoid walking on the lawn too much during the initial four to six weeks.

how to plant plugs and sprigs

Many warm-season grasses are sold as sprigs or plugs. Early spring is the best time to plant.

A sprig is a piece of grass stem with roots and blades. A plug is a small square or circle cut from sod.

Plugs are usually 2 to 3 inches across and are often sold 18 to a tray—enough to plant 15 square feet on 8-inch centers. Plant in

BERMUDA GRASS SPRIG

BUFFALO GRASS PLUG

Two-inch plugs of buffalo grass, planted at 8-inch intervals, will grow together in a year.

Torn into pieces by a machine, sprigs of hybrid Bermuda grass will root and spread quickly in well-prepared soil.

the prepared area, spacing them 8 inches apart. Sprigs are usually sold by the bushel, and the supplier can tell you how much area a bushel will cover. The fastest way to plant sprigs is to scatter them evenly by hand over the prepared area, then go over them with a cleated roller.

how to plant sod

Sod lawns can be started almost any time of year, except when weather is very cold or very wet. It's best to avoid installation during a summer heat wave, though it can be done. Here are the basic steps.

Water the planting area thoroughly the day before the sod is delivered. Time the delivery of sod so you can cover the whole area in a single day, beginning early in the morning. When you lay out strips, stagger them so the ends aren't adjacent. Butt the sides tightly together. With a sharp knife, cut the sod to fit it into oddly shaped areas. Roll the entire lawn with a roller half-filled with water to smooth out rough spots and to press the roots of the sod firmly against the soil. Water once a day (more often if the weather is hot), keeping the area thoroughly moist for at least six weeks.

Mow for the first time when the grass is a third taller than its optimum height. When mowing during the initial six weeks, be very careful not to disturb the seams.

how to plant sod

1 UNROLL STRIPS of sod over moist prepared soil, overlapping them so seams don't align.

2 TRIM THE SOD with a heavy knife until it fits snugly around paving, borders, and obstacles.

3 PRESS NEW SOD with a roller so that roots are in firm contact with the soil. Water frequently for six weeks.

a sampler of lawn grasses

Creeping bent *(Agrostis stolonifera)*

Buffalo grass *(Buchloe dactyloides)*

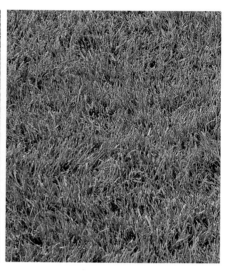

Tall fescue *(Festuca arundinacea)*

Creeping bent *(Agrostis stolonifera)* Cool-season. Fine-textured grass that requires more water and care than other lawn grasses. Grow in acidic soil, in sun or light shade. Mow at $1/2$ to $3/4$ inch. Sold as seed, sod. Varieties include 'Penneagle', 'Penncross', and 'Seaside'.

Blue grama *(Bouteloua gracilis)* Warm-season. Tolerates drought, extremes of temperature, and a wide range of soils. Does best in sun. Makes a higher-quality turf when blended with buffalo grass. Mow at 2 to 3 inches, three or four times a year. Sold as seed.

Buffalo grass *(Buchloe dactyloides)* Warm-season. Very drought-tolerant lawn for sun; slow upright growth. Mow at 3 inches, four or five times a year. Sold as seed, sod, plugs. Several improved varieties are available. Best sod varieties are '609', 'Prairie', and 'Stampede'. The best seed varieties are 'Cody', 'Tatanka', and 'Topgun'. Often sold as plugs.

Bermuda grass *(Cynodon dactylon)* Warm-season. Fine-textured; spreads via runners. Hybrid Bermuda is similar to common Bermuda, but it's finer textured and does not self-sow. Mow at $1/2$ to $3/4$ inch. Sold as sod, sprigs, plugs. Varieties available as seed include 'Cheyenne', 'NuMex Sahara', and 'Sundevil'. The softest- and finest-blade Bermudas are sterile hybrids that come as sod, plugs, or sprigs, including 'Tifgreen', 'Tiflawn', and 'Tifway'. Use them for golf or putting greens in southern regions. Plant 'Santa Ana' sod for a hardy, attractive play lawn.

Centipede grass *(Eremochloa ophiuroides)* Warm-season. Light green medium- to fine-textured grass spreads by underground stems. A chief virtue is its ability to thrive in acidic, poor soils. Very little maintenance is required, and it's resistant even to chinch bugs. But low temperatures push it into dormancy, and below 5 degrees F, it dies. Look for the varieties 'Centennial', 'Centiseed', and 'Oklawn'.

Tall fescue *(Festuca arundinacea)* Cool-season. Tolerates heat and some drought and flourishes in sun or shade. It freezes out in the coldest climates. Newer selections (dwarf tall fescue) are finer bladed and deeper green. Mow at 2 to 4 inches. Sold as seed, sod. A few varieties—such as 'Rebel III', 'Earth Save', 'Shenandoah', 'Titan II', and 'Tarheel'—have endophytes, a pest-repelling fungus, bred into them. The many named varieties include 'Aztec II', 'Bonsai 2000', 'Cochise', 'Crewcut', 'Falcon III', 'Guardian', 'Jaguar 3', 'Millennium', 'Mustang II', 'Ninja', 'Pixie', 'Plantation', 'Rebel IV', 'Rembrandt', 'Shenandoah II', and 'Tar Heel II'.

Fine fescues *(Festuca)* Cool-season. Fine-bladed grasses succeed in well-drained soil in shaded sites. Fairly drought-tolerant Mow at $1 1/2$ to 2 inches high. Sold as seed. There are there types of fine fescue. Chewings fescues include 'Ambassador', 'Jamestown II', and

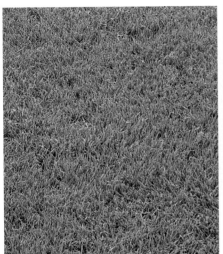

Perennial ryegrass (*Lolium perenne*)

Kentucky bluegrass (*Poa pratensis*)

St. Augustine grass (*Stenotaphrum secundatum*)

'Longfellow II'. Hard fescues include 'Bighorn', 'Defiant', and 'Scaldis'. Creeping red fescues include 'Boreal' and 'Shademaster'. All are often mixed with Kentucky bluegrass and perennial ryegrass, adding greater shade and drought tolerance, and sometimes used to overseed warm-season grasses.

Perennial ryegrass (*Lolium perenne*) Cool-season. Deep green grass that does best in sun. Needs frequent watering. Used as year-round lawn in cooler regions or to overseed winter-dormant grasses. Mow at 2 to 3 inches. Sold as seed or sod. Look for 'Applaud', 'Charismatic', 'Exacta', 'Dimension', 'Manhattan II', 'Palmer', 'Pennant', 'Pick 715', 'Pizzazz', 'Riviera', and 'SR-4100'. 'Manhattan II' has pest-repelling endophytes, just like some of the tall fescues.

Bahia grass (*Paspalum notatum*) Warm-season. A tough, low-growing, coarse grass used in the Southeast for a low-maintenance lawn. It is

drought and shade tolerant but requires frequent mowing. Improved varieties include 'Argentine', 'Paraguay', and 'Pensacola'.

Seashore paspalum (*Paspalum vaginatum*) Warm-season. A glossy, deep green, medium-textured grass. An alternative to Bermuda in coastal areas where soil is too salty. It takes heat, drought, and salty soil in stride, and it shrugs off pests. Plant it in sprigs, plugs, or sod. Usually sold as sod by names Adalayd or Excalibre and Sea Isle 2000.

Kentucky bluegrass (*Poa pratensis*) Cool-season. Classic grass for cooler, northern regions. Needs regular water. Takes sun, light shade. Mow at 1 to 3 inches. Widely available as seed or sod. Usually mixed with other cool-season grasses. Top varieties include 'A-34', 'America', 'Award', 'Blacksburg', 'Chateau', 'Eclipse', 'Glade', 'Liberator', 'Midnight', 'Princeton 104', 'Rugby II', and 'Showcase'.

St. Augustine grass (*Stenotaphrum secundatum*) Warm-season. Coarse-textured grass is adapted to a wide range of soils but does best along the coast. Dark green blades have rounded tips. Grows best in sun but tolerates shade. Needs regular water. Spreads fast by surface runners that root at joints. If it invades other parts of the garden, the shallow roots pull up easily. Mow 1½ to 3 inches high. Sold as sod, sprigs, plugs. Top varieties are 'Bitterblue', 'Floratine', 'Floralawn', 'Jade', 'Palmetto', 'Raleigh', and 'Seville'.

Zoysia (*Zoysia*) Warm-season. Tolerates drought and heat and takes sun or shade. Mow at 1 to 2 inches. Sold as sod, sprigs, plugs. Fine-textured with stiff, wiry blades. It's deep rooted and slow to spread. A tough grass, though a downside is its long winter dormant season. Varieties such as 'Cashmere', 'De Anza', 'Emerald', and 'Victoria' minimize dormancy. Plant 'Zen 300' and 'Zenith' from seed.

perennial flowers
COLOR AND CHARACTER YEAR AFTER YEAR

LONG-LIVED BLOOMERS, PERENNIAL FLOWERS ARE PRIZED BECAUSE THEY COME BACK EACH YEAR. Most are easy to grow, although it may take a few years to get them established. They also vary in the length of time they can grow in one spot without revitalization.

Classic perennials—lavender, Russian sage, purple coneflower, and sedum 'Autumn Joy'—combine to colorful effect.

You can find perennials suitable for every location and condition. Some are hardy in the snowiest mountain areas, while others live in the driest deserts. Some die down to the ground after blooming and reappear the following year. Others, including Russian sage and some daylilies, are evergreen in mild-winter climates. A few, such as coral bells, live most of the year as low-key foliage plants and then explode in brilliant color. With deadheading (removing old flowers), many perennials offer repeat shows throughout the season. Becoming familiar with the various characteristics of perennials will help guide your selections.

Many gardeners like to create a mixed border, which can include small trees and shrubs, bulbs, roses, ornamental grasses, and annual flowers in addition to perennials. The perennials supply successive waves of color throughout the year, lengthening the border's period of attraction and lending it enormous variety in color and form.

Before buying, always consider how wide and high a perennial will ultimately grow. Some reach 7 to 8 feet tall, while others are quite low. Plants only a few inches across when brought home from the nursery may eventually form mounds 3 to 4 feet wide. To avoid crowding problems, space plants and choose planting locations with an eye toward each plant's mature size.

planting and caring for perennials

Perennials are purchased in 4-inch to 1-gallon containers. Mail-order sources often also ship them bare-root. Plant them as directed on pages 306–307.

soil, water, and fertilizer In general, perennials prefer soil that is well amended with organic matter, but a surprising number do well in ordinary or even poor garden soil. Some thrive in full sun, while others need some shade, especially in hot-summer climates. Water needs also differ. Some perennials are thirsty, while others succeed with little water. Most perennials appreciate an annual feeding, in the form of either organic amendments worked into the soil in spring or fall, or a complete fertilizer applied in spring. Some, however, need regular fertilizing throughout the growing season.

growing-season care

Perennials look their best with regular maintenance during the growing season.

deadheading This habit keeps the landscape looking neat and can prolong blooms for several weeks. For many flowering perennials, trimming and pinching also improve appearance. After a spring-flowering plant's blooming period ends, cut back all stems and foliage by a third. A healthy mound of new growth soon fills in and remains throughout the growing season. To prevent lanky, floppy growth on some summer- and fall-blooming perennials, control growth early in the season. Pinch individual terminal buds to encourage bushier growth (see the illustration above). To make plants bushier still, cut back entire branches by a few inches rather than just pinching the top bud.

pruning techniques

Pinch growing tips to make plants more compact and bushy.

Cut back to improve appearance and promote continued flowering.

dividing Divide perennials for at least one of two reasons: to improve the health and flower production of overgrown, crowded plantings, or to gain new divisions to increase a planting. Note that this kind of rejuvenation/propagation is usually feasible only for perennials that grow in clumps with an expanding root mass. It is not practical to divide those that grow from a taproot. Check the following pages for recommendations about specific perennials.

how to divide clumping perennials

1 LIFT THE OVERGROWN PLANT from the ground after loosening soil around and under the clump with a spading fork.

2 SLICE THROUGH THE CLUMP with a trowel, dividing it into four sections. Break each section by hand into 4-by-4-inch pieces.

3 IMMEDIATELY PLANT DIVISIONS in a prepared bed. Water the new divisions regularly until they are established.

a sampler of perennials

Lady's-mantle *(Alchemilla mollis)*

Columbine *(Aquilegia)*

New England aster *(Aster novae-angliae)*

Common yarrow *(Achillea millefolium)* Zones 3–9 (3–11W), 24 inches. Moderate water; full sun. Large, flat-topped flower clusters on 1- to 3-foot stalks from clumps of lower-growing fernlike foliage. White, yellow, pink to red flowers throughout summer. Choices include Summer Pastels and Debutante strains. Other yarrows include fernleaf yarrow *(A. filipendulina)*, *A.* 'Moonshine', and *A. taygetea*.

Lady's-mantle *(Alchemilla mollis)* Zones 4–7 (4–11W), 12 inches. Regular water; sun to deep shade. Neat mounds of rounded, scallop-edged pale green leaves appear silvery, especially after rain or dew. Airy clusters of tiny yellow-green flowers above the foliage in summer. Excellent for edging, front of borders, lightly shaded landscapes.

Columbine *(Aquilegia)* Zones 3–9 (3–11W), 6–30 inches. Moderate water; full sun to filtered shade. Lacy, divided gray-green leaves and colorful spurred flowers in nodding or upright clusters. Single and double yellow, red, white, purple, blue, or pink, flowers, often bicolored. Self-sows. McKana Giants are a popular hybrid strain.

Wormwood *(Artemisia)* Zones 4–9 (4–11W), 6–60 inches. Moderate water; full sun. Many species and varieties, all prized for silvery gray to white aromatic foliage. Feathery 'Silver Mound' and deeply lobed, white-leafed 'Silver Brocade' are good for edging. 'Silver Queen' and 'Powis Castle' grow to 3 feet.

Butterfly weed *(Asclepias tuberosa)* Zones 4–9 (4–11W), 3 feet. Moderate water; full sun. Clusters of bright orange to yellow flowers in summer. Narrow lance-shaped leaves on straight, unbranched stems. Monarch butterflies lay eggs on the leaves.

New England aster *(Aster novae-angliae)* Zones 4–8 (4–11W), 1–5 feet. Regular water; full sun. Forms clumps of strong, hairy stems topped by brightly colored clusters or plumes of flowers in late summer to autumn. Hundreds of varieties of varying growth habits and with flower colors ranging from white to blue to deep purple, most with yellow centers.

Astilbe *(Astilbe arendsii)* Zones 4–8 (4–11W), 1–4 feet. Regular water; full sun to partial shade. Deeply divided fernlike leaves are attractive in all seasons. White, pink, red, purple flower plumes grow above the foliage in summer. A mainstay in shady borders and near water. Varieties include white 'Deutschland', dark red 'Fanal', and pink 'Glow', and *A. simplicifolia* 'Sprite'.

Bergenia *(Bergenia)* Zones 3–8 (3–11W), 12–18 inches. Regular water; full sun in cool climates or partial shade. Large, glossy evergreen leaves form attractive colonies in borders, in edges, under trees. White, pink, or rose flowers in spring.

Painted daisy *(Chrysanthemum coccineum)*

Lanceleaf coreopsis *(Coreopsis lanceolata)*

Common bleeding heart *(Dicentra spectabilis)*

Tussock bellflower *(Campanula carpatica)* Zones 3–7 (3–11W), 4–12 inches. Regular to moderate water; full sun to partial shade. Small heart-shaped, toothed leaves form neat mounds. Covered with white or blue to violet bell-shaped flowers in summer. Varieties include 'Blue Clips' and 'White Clips'. More than 300 other campanula species and many varieties vary widely in height, form, and flower habit. Varieties include spreading clustered bellflower (*C. glomerata*), trailing Italian bellflower (*C. isophylla*), up-right peach-leafed bell-flower (*C. persicifolia*), and Dalmation bellflower (*C. portenschlagiana*).

Painted daisy *(Chrysanthemum coccineum)* Zones 4–9 (4–11W), 18–30 inches. Regular to moderate water; full sun. Upright clumps of stems with finely divided leaves, topped by brightly colored pink, crimson, or white daisy flowers with yellow centers. Varieties include 'James Kelway', 'Snow Cloud'. Shasta daisy (*C. maximum*) is similar and has large white flowers with yellow centers. Use it in mixed borders.

Lanceleaf coreopsis *(Coreopsis lanceolata)* Zones 4–9 (4–11W), 12–24 inches. Moderate water; full sun. Profuse 1½- to 2-inch yellow daisylike blooms all summer. Narrow, often lobed leaves form a loose clump. Thread-leaf coreopsis (*C. verticillata*) has finely divided leaves on clumps of erect 18- to 30-inch stems topped by bright yellow flowers summer through fall.

Candle delphinium *(Delphinium elatum)* Zones 3–6 (3–11W), 3–7 feet. Regular water; full sun to partial shade. Tall spires of showy white, pink, blue to purple flowers for the back of the border. Divided to lobed foliage clumps at base and partway up flower spikes. Give support in wind-prone areas. Popular strains include Belladonna, Magic Fountains, and Pacific Giants. Easiest in cool climates.

Cottage pink *(Dianthus plumarius)* Zones 3–9 (3–11W), 12–16 inches. Regular water; full sun to light shade. Flowering stems hold fragrant single or double fringed blooms in shades of white, red, or pink above narrow gray-green foliage. Hundreds of species and varieties, including maiden pinks (*D. deltoides*), cheddar pinks (*D. gratianopolitanus*), and biennial sweet William (*D. barbatus*). Plant under open shrubs, in rock gardens, and along edges.

Common bleeding heart *(Dicentra spectabilis)* Zones 3–9 (3–11W), 2–3 feet. Regular water; partial shade. Stems bearing pendulous pink and white, heart-shaped flowers in spring. Soft green fernlike foliage dies down by mid- to late summer. Long-time favorite 'Alba' has white flowers. Other popular species and varieties include 'Adrian Bloom', 'Luxuriant', fringed bleeding heart (*D. eximia*), and western bleeding heart (*D. formosa*).

a sampler of perennials

Purple coneflower (*Echinacea purpurea*)

Blanket flower (*Gaillardia grandiflora*)

Daylily (*Hemerocallis* 'Tahitian Sunrise')

Purple coneflower (*Echinacea purpurea*) Zones 3–9 (3–11W), 3–5 feet. Moderate water; full sun. Very showy daisylike flowers with drooping purple petals and bristly cone-shaped centers from mid- to late summer. Large, stiff, coarse-textured plant with hairy leaves and stems. 'Bright Star' has rosy pink flowers, 'Magnus' grows to 3 feet, and 'White Swan' has white flowers.

Blanket flower (*Gaillardia grandiflora*) Zones 3–8 (3–11W), 8–18 inches. Moderate water; full sun. Flowers in warm shades of red and yellow with maroon or orange markings bloom from early spring to autumn frost. Rough gray-green foliage. Often short-lived but also self-sowing. Many varieties with differing flowers and habits.

Cranesbill (*Geranium*) Zones 3–9 (4–11W), 6–36 inches. Regular water; sun to afternoon shade. More than 300 species and many varieties. Rounded, lobed, or divided leaves form neat mounds to sprawling carpets, depending on species. Five-petaled flowers in white, blue, pink to purple in spring to fall. Popular cranesbills include 'Claridge Druce', 'Johnson's Blue', 'Rozanne', 'Salome', and 'Wargrave Pink'.

Baby's breath (*Gypsophila paniculata*) Zones 4–9, 2–4 feet. Moderate water; full sun. Many-branched sprays of small white flowers used in bouquets. Slender, pointed leaves. Varieties include 'Bristol Fairy' and 'Pink Star'. Creeping baby's breath (*G. repens*) forms a 6- to 10-inch-tall mat of white to pink flowers.

Hellebore (*Helleborus*) Zones 4–9 (4–11W), 12–30 inches. Regular to moderate water; partial to full shade. Many species and varieties form clumps of thick, long-stalked divided leaves. Large green to pink or purple flowers bloom over a long period from winter through spring. Elegant woodland plant.

Daylily (*Hemerocallis*) Zones 3–10 (3–11W), 1–4 feet. Regular to moderate water; full sun to light shade. Long, arching, straplike leaves form spreading clumps. Branched stalks in summer hold trumpet-shaped blooms in shades of yellow, orange, red, pink, and cream. Use for borders and edges. Thousands of varieties, including 'Eenie Weenie', 'Mary Todd', 'Pardon Me', 'Stella de Oro', and 'Tahitian Sunrise'. 'Hyperion' has fragrant flowers. Lemon daylily (*H. lilioasphodelus*) has fragrant yellow flowers in early summer.

Coral bells (*Heuchera*) Zones 4–8 (4–11W), 12–24 inches. Regular water; sun to light shade in hot areas. Prized for low mounds of ornamental foliage and tall stalks of airy white, pink, or red flowers. Leaves vary from round with scalloped edges to maple-leaf shapes, colors from glossy green to purple to silvery gray. Many varieties, including 'Chocolate Ruffles', 'Palace Purple', 'Persian Carpet', and 'Pewter Moon'.

Plantain lily (Hosta)

Bee balm (Monarda didyma 'Cambridge Scarlet')

Peony (Paeonia)

Plantain lily (Hosta) Zones 3–8 (3–11W), 3–36 inches. Regular water; partial to full shade. Hundreds of varieties with wide range of foliage colors, shapes, and sizes. Heart-shaped to rounded to lance-shaped leaves form neat, spreading clumps; renew by division. Colors vary from yellow to all shades of green to blue gray, many variegated white or yellow. Often showy stalks of white to purple flowers in summer. Popular varieties include 'August Moon', 'Aureo-marginata', 'Francee', 'Frances Williams', 'Golden Tiara', 'Gold Standard', 'Halcyon', 'Honeybells', 'On Stage', 'Sum and Substance', and 'Wide Brim'.

Lavender (Lavandula) Zones 5–9 (5–11W), 12–36 inches. Moderate water; full sun. Prized for fragrant lavender or purple flowers used for soaps and perfumes. Aromatic gray to gray-green needlelike foliage forms spiky clumps. Use for edging, massing, mixed borders. Many varieties and species.

Gayfeather (Liatris spicata) Zones 4–9 (4–11W), 3–5 feet. Regular to moderate water; full sun. Tall stalks of fluffy purple flowers emerge from tufts of narrow, grass-like leaves in late summer. Very showy in mixed borders, good for bouquets. 'Kobold' has magenta flowers, 'Alba' white flowers.

Virginia bluebells (Mertensia pulmonarioides) Zones 3–7 (3–9W), 18–24 inches. Regular water; partial to full shade. Loose clusters of nodding 1-inch pink to blue flowers in early spring. Leaves die back by midsummer. Plant with spring bulbs and ferns in woodland landscapes.

Bee balm (Monarda didyma) Zones 3–9, 2–4 feet. Regular to ample water; full sun to light shade in hot areas. Fragrant, dark green leaves in vigorously spreading clumps. Tubular flowers of red, pink, white, or purple attract hummingbirds in summer. Many varieties, including 'Cambridge Scarlet' and 'Marshall's Delight'.

Catmint (Nepeta faassenii) Zones 3–9 (3–11W), 12–36 inches. Moderate water; sun to light shade in hot areas. Clump-forming to spreading, aromatic-leaf plants with blue to purple, pink, or white flower spikes. Downy foliage, often gray-green. Use in mixed borders and along edges. Popular catmints include 'Dropmore' and 'Select Blue'.

Peony (Paeonia) Zones 3–8 (4–10W), 20–40 inches. Regular water; full sun to light shade in hot areas. Large, showy, often fragrant blossoms, white to pink to deep red, in early summer. Several flower forms, from single with prominent yellow centers to double with many crowded petals. Divided leaves on long stalks form attractive, shrub-like clumps that die to the ground in autumn. Hundreds of varieties. Tree peonies have woody stems and flower colors that include yellow and apricot. Plants need at least 2 to 3 years in the garden to reach flowering size.

a sampler of perennials

Russian sage *(Perovskia)*

Summer phlox *(Phlox paniculata)*

Black-eyed Susan *(Rudbeckia hirta)*

Oriental poppy *(Papaver orientale)* Zones 3–9, 2–4 feet. Regular to moderate water; full sun. Bowl-shaped flowers with silky petals on leafy stalks above a low mound of long, narrow, notched foliage. Red, orange, white, or pink flowers with black centers bloom in early summer, followed by attractive seedpods.

Beard tongue *(Penstemon)* Zones 3–10 (3–11W), 12–30 inches. Regular to moderate water; sun to afternoon shade. Spikes of tube-shaped flowers in white, pink to red in summer above sprawling clumps of narrow, pointed foliage. Many varieties, including 'Elfin Pink' and 'Husker Red'. Useful in mixed borders and hummingbird gardens.

Russian sage *(Perovskia)* Zones 4–10 (4–11W), 3–4 feet. Drought resistant; full sun. Woody-based clump with many grayish white, upright-growing stems clothed in gray-green foliage. Lavender-blue flowers come in late spring and summer in sprays atop branched stems, creating a soft purple haze above foliage. Varieties include 'Blue Spire' (also sold as 'Superba' and 'Longin'), lighter blue 'Blue Mist' and 'Blue Haze', and silver-leafed 'Filagran'.

Summer phlox *(Phlox paniculata)* Zones 3–8 (4–9W), 3–4 feet. Regular water; full sun. Showy dome-shaped clusters of fragrant flowers atop tall, leafy stems in mid- to late summer. Colors from white to deep pink to blue to orange, often with contrasting centers. Other popular phlox include spring-blooming moss pink (*P. subulata*) and thick-leaf phlox (*P. maculata*), which blooms in early summer.

Primrose *(Primula)* Zones 2–8 (2–11W), 4–18 inches. Regular to ample water; full sun to shade in hot climates. Rosettes of rounded to tongue-shaped foliage, often toothed or puckered. Leafless stalks carry clusters of rounded five-petaled flowers in many differing colors, usually in spring. Use at front of borders, in woodland landscapes, near water, or in rock gardens. Hundreds of species and hybrids.

Lungwort *(Pulmonaria)* Zones 4–8 (4–11W), 12–18 inches. Regular water; partial to full shade. Hairy, ornamental foliage, often spotted with silver, forms neat, spreading clumps. Drooping clusters of funnel-shaped blue or pink flowers in spring. Excellent with spring bulbs, in shady borders, and under trees. Varieties include 'Mrs. Moon', with blooms that turn from pink to blue.

Black-eyed Susan *(Rudbeckia hirta)* Zones 3–9 (3–11W), 1–4 feet. Regular to moderate water; full sun. Masses of large bright yellow to orange or rust daisylike flowers with brown, black, or green centers in summer to fall. Useful in mixed borders and bouquets. Many popular species and varieties, including *R. fulgida sullivantii* 'Goldsturm'.

Spiderwort *(Tradescantia virginiana)*

Speedwell (*Veronica* 'Crater Lake Blue')

Violet *(Viola)*

Sage *(Salvia)* Zones 4–10 (4–11W), 1–8 feet. Regular water; full sun. More than 60 species and many varieties of prized landscape perennials, annuals, and shrubs. Very showy spikes of white, blue, scarlet, or pink flowers in summer. Foliage varies widely, from smooth to hairy, lance-shaped to rounded, green to purple to silvery. Excellent for borders, edges, and massing. Most need full sun, good drainage, and little pruning. Popular perennials include pineapple sage (*S. elegans*), *S. nemorosa* 'East Friesland', common sage (*S. officinalis* 'Tricolor'), and the often short-lived clary sage (*S. sclarea*).

Stonecrop *(Sedum)* Zones 3–11, 2–24 inches. Moderate to little water; full sun to light shade. Growth habits vary from creeping or spreading to upright. Fleshy leaves from bright green to blue green or gray green to red or plum. Many species and varieties have brightly colored, showy flower clusters. Favorites include hybrids 'Autumn Joy' and its

improved version, 'Autumn Fire'. Others include trailing goldmoss sedum (*S. acre*), two-row stonecrop (*S. spurium* 'Tricolor'), and spreading *S.* 'Vera Jameson'.

Lamb's ears *(Stachys byzantina)* Zones 4–8 (4–11W), 12–18 inches. Moderate water; sun to light shade in hot areas. Popular for its tongue-shaped, silvery green to white, woolly leaves that form clumps of rosettes. Flower stalks bear small purple flowers in early summer. Foliage contrasts nicely with more brightly colored perennials. Use in borders, as edging, and for ground cover.

Spiderwort *(Tradescantia virginiana)* Zones 4–9 (4–11W), 18–36 inches. Tough plants with long stems. Ample water; sun or shade. Long, deep green, arching, grasslike foliage; three-petaled flowers in clusters. Bloom varies from white to pink to purple in spring through summer. Many varieties and other species. Use for edging and ground cover.

Speedwell *(Veronica)* Zones 3–8 (3–9W), 6–18 inches. Regular to moderate water; full sun. Spikes of small bright blue, white, or purple to pink flowers bloom over a long period in summer. Shapes range from upright clumps to creeping mats. Narrow to rounded, toothed foliage varies from bright glossy green to silvery gray. Varieties include 'Blue Giant', 'Crater Lake Blue', 'Goodness Grows', 'Royal Candles', 'Tickled Pink', and creeping *V. prostrata* 'Heavenly Blue'.

Violet *(Viola)* Zones 4–9 (4–11W), 2–12 inches. Regular water; sun to shade. Scalloped round to heart-shaped or narrow leaves. Smooth stalks hold colorful, often fragrant flowers in spring through fall, depending on species. Blooms in all colors, including bicolors. Popular violas include Australian violet (*V. hederacea*), sweet violet (*V. odorata*), and hybrids known as Parma violets, which include 'Marie Louise'. Use all kinds in borders or containers.

roses

THEY'RE THE QUEEN OF FLOWERS

LONG A GARDENER'S FAVORITE, AND AMERICA'S NATIONAL FLOWER, ROSES STILL SUFFER FROM A reputation of being difficult to grow. In reality, roses are tough and long-lived. No plant is more flexible or more versatile than this flowering shrub.

roses in the landscape

Roses offer much more than simple beauty. For example, climbing roses on trellises can form the walls of outdoor rooms or create a passageway underneath a series of arched arbors. Thorny shrub roses can function as protective hedges. Roses clambering atop an arbor can supply needed summer shade. And roses that form colorful hips can attract birds and other wildlife.

There's a rose for every garden situation and for any climate. Miniature roses can be used to edge beds and pathways. Use climbing roses to take the place of vines, standard roses as accents or focal points in place of flowering shrubs or ornamental grasses, and shrub roses mixed in with other plants to form spectacular borders or foundation plantings. Use drifts of roses in place of annuals and long-flowering perennials, or mix them with a single plant, such as lavender or clematis, for dramatic contrasts. Roses can even bring color into a vegetable or herb garden.

Continuous, season-long bloom and easy care are hallmarks of modern shrub roses. This one is 'Pink Meidiland'.

planting and caring for roses

The best time to buy roses is in late winter, when they're available as dormant bare-root plants, or in mid-spring during the first flush of bloom. At that time they are growing in containers and you can see the flowers before buying. Shop early for the widest selection.

Roses need well-amended soil. If you know you'll be planting bare-root roses in late winter, clean up the area and amend the soil in fall. That will leave you with less work to do come planting time, when the weather is often cold and unpredictable and when planting may have to be rushed in during brief periods of good weather.

Because most modern roses put out new growth and flowers throughout the growing season, they need regular water and consistent fertilizing during that time. In general, keep soil moist (but not soggy) to the full depth of the roots. This can take up to 5 gallons of water per rose bush in sandy soil, almost 8 gallons in loam, and up to 13 gallons in clay. Water again when the top several inches of soil are dry—usually within a week for sandy soil, 10 days for loam, and up to two weeks for clay. To save water, mulch around plants.

Most roses respond well to fertilizer. Many gardeners prefer to work a controlled-release complete fertilizer into the top few inches of soil at the start of the growing season, before applying a mulch. If you don't use a controlled-release kind, feed repeat-flowering roses every six weeks with a dry granular fertilizer or every month with a liquid fertilizer. Stop fertilizing about six weeks before the first-frost date. Or if you live where winters are frost free or nearly so, stop fertilizing in September.

With repeat-flowering roses, remove old flowers from spent blooms regularly, cutting back several inches to a five-leaflet leaf. If the rose bears attractive hips, stop deadheading in September. You'll be able to enjoy the brightly colored hips during autumn, and you will also be sending a signal to the plant that it's time to slow down and prepare for dormancy. There's no need to deadhead roses that flower just once a year.

pruning

Prune repeat-blooming roses just before dormancy ends, in late winter or early spring. But prune roses that bloom only once per season, which include most of the old-fashioned types of roses, just after their bloom period ends. Strong new growth produced after bloom will then bear flowers the following spring.

Large red flowers and growth naturally limited to about 10 feet have earned 'Altissimo' a top spot on most rose lists.

The amount of pruning needed depends on the rose. Most old and modern shrub roses need relatively little pruning. Prune them to remove dead or damaged limbs or to lightly control growth. Other roses, such as hybrid teas and grandifloras, usually need more extensive pruning. They tend to produce larger blooms on longer, stronger stems if a portion of the previous year's growth is shortened and if weak and old wood is removed regularly.

When you prune, first remove any weakened or winter-damaged stems, then cut out stems growing at odd angles (see the illustrations below). After you have removed all unwanted growth, reduce the length of the remaining stems. In mild-winter regions, cut them back by about a third to a half. In cold-winter regions, cut out dead and damaged stems after you remove any winter protection. The final size of the bush depends on the severity of the past winter.

pruning roses

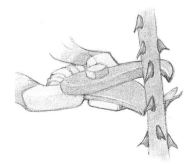

Use shears with scissorlike bypass blades for clean cuts. Hold them with the cutting blade below and the hook above.

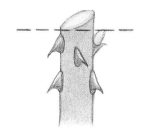

Make a sloping cut so that the lowest point is opposite and just above a growth bud (see page 404).

Remove old canes by cutting them flush with the bud union or larger stem from which they originated.

a sampler of roses

'Margo Koster'

'Ballerina'

'Double Delight'

shrubs

red 'Alexander Mackenzie', 'Henry Kelsey', 'Home Run', 'Knock Out', 'Red Meidiland', 'Will Scarlet', 'William Shakespeare' 2000

pink 'All That Jazz', 'Aunt Honey', 'Ballerina', 'Belle Story', 'Betty Prior', 'Bonica', 'Carefree Delight', 'Carefree Wonder', 'Cornelia', 'Country Dancer', 'Erfurt', 'Felicia', 'First Light', 'Gertrude Jekyll', 'Heritage', 'John Cabot', 'Kathleen', 'Mary Rose', 'Maytime', 'Penelope', 'Pink Meidiland', 'Queen Margrethe', 'William Baffin'

orange/warm blend 'Abraham Darby', 'Alchymist', 'Buff Beauty', 'Kaleidoscope', 'Margo Koster', 'Paul Bocuse', 'Prairie Princess', 'Westerland'

yellow 'Autumn Sunset', 'Baby Love', 'Golden Celebration', 'Graham Thomas', 'Molineux', 'Yellow Jacket'

white 'Hawkeye Belle', 'Pearl Drift', 'Sally Holmes', 'Sea Foam', 'Starry Night', 'White Meidiland'

lavender/mauve 'Outta the Blue'

ground covers

red 'Fire Meidiland', 'Ralph's Creeper', 'Red Flower Carpet', 'Ruby Meidiland', 'Scarlet Flower Carpet'

pink 'Appleblossom Flower Carpet', 'Coral Flower Carpet', 'Pink Supreme Flower Carpet'

yellow 'Yellow Flower Carpet'

white 'Blossom Blanket', 'White Flower Carpet', 'White Meidiland'

climbers

red 'Altissimo', 'Blaze', 'Cl. Étoile de Hollande', 'Don Juan', 'Dortmund', 'Dublin Bay', 'Fourth of July'

pink 'Cl. Cécile Brunner', 'Cl. First Prize', 'Cl. Queen Elizabeth', 'Eden', 'Jeanne Lajoie' (miniature), 'New Dawn', 'Nozomi', 'Pearly Gates'

orange/warm blend 'America', 'Cl. Earthquake' (miniature),

'Cl. Peace', 'Cl. Rainbow's End' (miniature), 'Handel', 'Joseph's Coat', 'Polka', 'Royal Sunset'

yellow 'Garden Sun', 'Golden Showers', 'Royal Gold'

white 'Cl. Iceberg', 'Lace Cascade', 'White Dawn'

hardy in zones 3–5

red 'Champlain' (shrub), 'Dortmund' (shrub), 'F. J. Grootendorst', 'Hansa', 'Roseraie de l'Hay', 'Rugosa Magnifica', (all hybrid rugosas)

pink 'Belle Poitevine' (hybrid rugosa), 'Celestial' (alba), 'Delicata' (hybrid rugosa), 'Frau Dagmar Hartopp' (hybrid rugosa), 'Great Maiden's Blush' (alba), 'John Cabot' (shrub), 'Morden Blush' (shrub), 'The Fairy' (polyantha), 'Thérèse Bugnet' (hybrid rugosa), 'William Baffin' (shrub)

yellow 'Autumn Sunset', Golden Wings' (shrub), 'Graham Thomas' (shrub), 'Sun Flare' (floribunda)

'Abraham Darby'

'Heritage'

'Graham Thomas'

white 'Blanc Double de Coubert' and 'Henry Hudson' (both hybrid rugosas), 'Madame Plantier' (alba), *Rosa rugosa alba* (species)

fragrant
red 'Cl. Étoile de Hollande', 'Don Juan', 'Double Delight' (red and white), 'Firefighter', 'Mister Lincoln', 'Oklahoma', 'Polka', 'Royal Sunset'

pink 'Bayse's Blueberry', 'Clotilde Soupert', 'Erfurt', 'Felicia', 'Gertrude Jekyll', 'Heritage', 'Hermosa', 'La France', 'New Zealand', 'Rose de Rescht', 'Secret', 'Souvenir de la Malmaison', 'Tiffany', 'Yves Piaget'

orange/warm blend 'Alchymist', 'America', 'Ambridge Rose', 'Belle Story', 'Folklore', 'Fragrant Cloud', 'Just Joey', 'Mrs. Oakley Fisher'

yellow 'Autumn Sunset', 'Golden Celebration', 'Molineux', 'Sun Flare'

white 'Fair Bianca', 'Kronprincessin Viktoria', 'White Dawn'

lavender/mauve 'Angel Face', 'Barbra Streisand', 'Fragrant Plum', 'Neptune', 'Stainless Steel'

thornless
red 'Smooth Prince'

pink 'Climbing Pinkie' (climber), 'Heritage', 'Paul Neyron', 'Zépherine Drouhin' (climber)

orange/warm blend 'Crépuscule' (climber)

yellow Lady Banks' (climber), 'Mrs. Dudley Cross'

white 'Aimée Vibert' (climber), Lady Banks' (climber), 'Marie Pavié'

lavender/mauve 'Reine des Violettes', 'Veilchenblau'

shade tolerant
red 'Eutin'

pink 'Cl. Cécile Brunner' (climber), 'Old Blush'

orange/warm blend 'Penelope'

white 'Marie Pavié'

cut flowers
red 'Firefighter', 'Ingrid Bergman', 'Mister Lincoln', 'Olympiad', 'Opening Night', 'Veterans' Honor'

pink 'Bewitched', 'Bride's Dream', 'Brigadoon', 'Color Magic', 'Dainty Bess', 'First Prize', 'Gemini', 'Memorial Day', 'Miss All-American Beauty', 'New Zealand', 'Royal Highness', 'Secret', 'Sheer Bliss', 'Tiffany', 'Timeless', 'Touch of Class', 'Yves Piaget'

orange/warm blend 'Abbaye de Cluny', 'Artistry', 'Brandy', 'Cary Grant', 'Chicago Peace', 'Double Delight', 'Folklore', 'Fragrant Cloud', 'Just Joey', 'Medallion', 'Perfect Moment', 'Remember Me', 'Rio Sam', 'Sunset Celebration', 'Tropicana', 'Voodoo'

lavender/mauve 'Barbra Streisand', 'Fragrant Plum', 'Neptune', 'Paradise', 'Stainless Steel'

annual and biennial flowers

BLOOMS FAST AND FURIOUS

ANNUALS FILL THE LANDSCAPE WITH QUICK, DEPENDABLE COLOR IN EVERY IMAGINABLE HUE. These are plants that germinate, flower profusely, set seed, and die, all in a single growing season. In contrast, biennials take two seasons to complete their life cycle, while perennials (pages 346–353) can live and bloom for many years. Although the annual-biennial-perennial distinction seems clear on paper, it's somewhat blurred in the garden. For example, some tender perennials—such as geranium (*Pelargonium*), some kinds of salvia, and verbena—flower year after year in mild-winter climates but are grown as annuals where winters are cold.

using annuals

Flowering annuals provide quick and showy color that can bring instant drama to an otherwise quiet corner of the landscape. Use annuals to fill spaces between shrubs in mixed borders, set them out for temporary color in a newly planted rose garden or perennial flower border, and put them in containers or window boxes where you want continuous color.

Rose-colored 'Dreamland' zinnias bloom from mid-summer to frost.

Where you would like broad sheets of color, limit annuals to a single shade and species. A long, sweeping bed of pink petunias or bright red salvias can be an attention-getter in front of an evergreen hedge or along a brick patio.

Consider seeding annuals in a kitchen garden, as they will add color and fragrance. And many annuals provide a supply of cut flowers for indoor arrangements. Those that keep their color when dried—for example, sea lavender (*Limonium*)—are ideal for floral crafts.

planting annuals

The best time to plant annuals depends on the specific plant and your climate. Annuals are designated as cool-season or warm-season, based on the temperatures they prefer. Cool-season annuals, such as pansy (*Viola*), primrose (*Primula*), and calendula, grow best in the cool soils and mild temperatures of spring and fall. Most withstand fairly heavy frosts. When the weather turns hot, they set seed and deteriorate. If you live in a cold-winter area (zones 3 through 7), plant these annuals in very early spring, as soon as the soil can be worked. To bloom vigorously, they have to develop roots and foliage during cool weather. In mild-winter regions (zones 8 through 11), plant cool-season annuals in fall for bloom in winter and early spring.

Warm-season annuals include marigold (*Tagetes*), zinnia, and impatiens. These plants grow and flower best in the warm months of late spring, summer, and early fall. They're cold-tender and may perish in a late frost if planted too early in spring. In cold-winter climates, set out warm-season annuals after the danger of frost has passed. In warm-winter areas, plant them in midspring.

Careful soil preparation helps get annuals off to a good start so they'll grow well all season. Dig out any weeds on the site and add a 3-inch layer of compost, well-rotted manure, or another organic amendment. It's also a good idea to add a complete fertilizer (follow the package directions for amounts). Dig or till amendments and fertilizer into the soil and then rake the bed smooth.

Start annuals from seed sown in pots or directly in the garden (the steps for this are outlined at right). Or buy started plants at a nursery. For best results, choose relatively small plants with healthy foliage. Plants with yellowing leaves and those that are leggy, root-bound, or too big for their pots will establish slowly in your garden, and they'll usually bloom poorly.

For even spacing, measure the distance between plants with a piece of wood of the desired length. The table of recommended spacing below shows the area that will be covered by a particular number of plants set out at various spacings. Space plants in a diamond pattern, as shown for ground covers on page 332, so they look natural.

After planting, water thoroughly. Apply a 2- to 4-inch layer of mulch (such as compost, ground bark, or pine needles) to conserve moisture and help prevent weeds from becoming established.

HOW MANY PLANTS DO YOU NEED?

RECOMMENDED SPACING BETWEEN PLANTS	AREA PLANTS WILL COVER	
	48 Plants*	64 Plants*
4 in.	4½ sq. ft.	6 sq. ft.
6 in.	10 sq. ft.	13½ sq. ft.
8 in.	18 sq. ft.	24½ sq. ft.
10 in.	28½ sq. ft.	38½ sq. ft.
12 in.	41½ sq. ft.	55½ sq. ft.

*Typical number of plants in a nursery flat

broadcasting seeds in a prepared bed

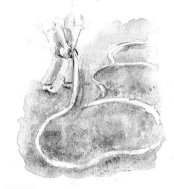

1 OUTLINE THE AREA for each kind of seed with gypsum, flour, or stakes and string.

2 FOR EVEN COVER of tiny seeds, shake each kind of seed in a covered can with several times its bulk of sand.

3 SCATTER THE SEED (or seed-sand mixture) evenly over planting areas. Rake lightly, barely covering the seeds with soil.

4 SPREAD A THIN LAYER of mulch over the bed to keep seeds moist and to hide the seeds from birds.

5 WATER with a fine spray to keep the soil surface barely damp until the seeds sprout. Gradually decrease watering frequency after they sprout.

6 THIN ANY SEEDLINGS that are too close together once they have two sets of true leaves. Transplant thinned seedlings to fill empty spaces in beds.

a sampler of annuals

Floss flower (*Ageratum houstonianum*)

Madagascar periwinkle (*Catharanthus roseus*)

Yellow cosmos (*Cosmos sulphureus*)

warm-season annuals

Floss flower (*Ageratum houstonianum*) Full sun or partial shade. Fluffy flower tassels come in azure blue, lavender, pink, or white on plants 1–2½ feet tall. Blooms in early summer to fall. Space dwarf varieties 6 inches apart, tall ones 1–1½ feet apart.

Amethyst flower (*Browallia*) Partial shade. Choice plants for connoisseurs of blue flowers. Bears one-sided clusters of lobelia-like blooms in brilliant blue, violet, or white. Blue and violet flowers are accented by contrasting white centers. Grows 1–2 feet tall. Easy from seed. Plant 9–12 inches apart.

Madagascar periwinkle (*Catharanthus roseus*) Full sun or partial shade. Phloxlike flowers bloom in shades of pink, rose, lavender, and white on plants 4–24 inches tall, depending on the variety. Thrives in hot conditions, whether dry or humid. Space 8–12 inches apart.

Cockscomb (*Celosia argentea*) Full sun. Unusual blooms in electric shades of yellow, orange, pink, red, and purple. Flowers come in two forms: C. 'Plumosa' has blossoms resembling ostrich plumes, while C. 'Cristata' has velvety crested flowers that resemble the vivid combs of a rooster. Both types make excellent dried flowers. Plants range in height from 1 to 3 feet, depending on variety. Space plants 9–12 inches apart.

Annual coreopsis (*Coreopsis tinctoria*) Full sun. Daisylike flowers in yellow, orange, and coppery reds. Some forms are banded with contrasting colors. Grows 1½–3 feet tall. May need staking. Easy to grow from seed. Thin seedlings to 6–8 inches apart. Thrives in heat, and plants can tolerate some dryness.

Cosmos (*Cosmos*) Full sun or partial shade. Showy daisylike flowers nod above lacy foliage from summer through fall. Fast-growing plants range from 2 to 7 feet. Tall

kinds are good for background planting. *Cosmos bipinnatus* has flowers in white, bicolors, and shades of pink, lavender, purple, and crimson. Yellow cosmos (*C. sulphureus*) has bold yellow to deep orange blossoms. Both grow best in soil that is dry and not very fertile. Space plants 1 foot apart.

Globe amaranth (*Gomphrena globosa*) Full sun. Rounded, papery, cloverlike blossoms in red, pink, orange, purple, and white on plants 9–24 inches tall. Easy to dry for winter bouquets. Narrow, oval leaves. Space plants 8–12 inches apart.

Common sunflower (*Helianthus annuus*) Full sun. Huge radiant blooms in yellow, orange, maroon, creamy white, and bicolors. Depending on variety, plants grow 2–15 feet tall, with flower heads 4–12 inches across. The flowers are followed by edible seeds that birds relish. Stake the tallest varieties, such as 'Russian Giant' and 'Kong'. 'Sunspot' grows 2 feet tall. Plant 1½ feet apart.

Busy Lizzie *(Impatiens walleriana)*

Monkey flower *(Mimulus hybridus)*

Petunia *(Petunia)*

Strawflower *(Helichrysum bracteatum)* Full sun. Flowers have strawlike petals with velvety centers in shades of yellow, orange, red, pink, and white. They hold their color indefinitely when dried. Grows 12–36 inches tall, depending on variety. Easy from seed or transplants. Space 12 inches apart.

Busy Lizzie *(Impatiens walleriana)* Partial to full shade. Invaluable for providing months of color in sites too shady for most other annuals. Single or double flowers come in every color but blue. Dwarf varieties grow 4–12 inches tall; space these 6 inches apart. Tall kinds reach 2 feet; space 1 foot apart.

Morning glory *(Ipomoea tricolor)* Full sun. Large trumpet-shaped flowers, mostly in shades of blue, pink, and white, are borne on a fast-growing, climbing vine. Individual flowers last only one day. Needs a trellis or fence to climb on. Can also be grown among corn or

sunflower stalks. Grow from seed, which should be nicked and soaked overnight before sowing. Reseeds easily and can become weedy. Space plants 12 inches apart.

Sweet alyssum *(Lobularia maritima)* Full sun to partial shade. Masses of tiny flowers in white, pink, or violet. Low-growing, spreading plants reach 6–12 inches tall. Use as a quick ground cover in bulb bed or as a low border. Space 6–8 inches apart. Easy to grow from seed.

Monkey flower *(Mimulus hybridus)* Partial to full shade. Showy, velvety blooms in bright shades of red, yellow, and orange. The two-lipped flowers are often spotted and give the impression of a smiling monkey's face. Neatly mounded plants grow 12–18 inches high. Space plants 6–8 inches apart.

Flowering tobacco *(Nicotiana alata)* Full sun to light shade. Upright, open plants topped with

tubular flowers in shades of white, pink, red, purple, and green. Some are fragrant at night. Height from 12 to 48 inches. Space seedlings 12–24 inches apart, depending on ultimate height of variety.

Petunia *(Petunia)* Full sun. Richly colored flowers come in red, pink, blue, purple, yellow, cream, white, and bicolors. Single blossoms are simple trumpets, while double ones are ruffled blooms resembling carnations. There are several types, such as Hybrid Grandiflora, but flower size is the key distinction. Plants range from 8 to 27 inches tall. Space 7–10 inches apart.

Annual phlox *(Phlox drummondii)* Full sun. Clusters of colorful, slightly fragrant 1-inch flowers in shades of lavender, pink, red, white, and yellow. Profuse bloom is best used in masses and is great in containers. Flowers are also ideal for cutting. Grows 6–20 inches tall. Space transplants 10 inches apart.

a sampler of annuals

Scarlet sage *(Salvia splendens)*

Marigold *(Tagetes)*

Black-eyed Susan vine *(Thunbergia alata)*

Rose moss *(Portulaca grandiflora)* Full sun. An old-fashioned favorite that flourishes in sunny, dry areas. Silky-petaled roselike blossoms in shades of white, yellow, orange, red, and pink cover the sprawling, succulent plants. Flowers open in sun and close in late afternoon. Excellent in pots and hanging baskets. Start from seed or transplants, spacing plants 9–12 inches apart.

Painted tongue *(Salpiglossis sinuata)* Full sun. Brilliant display of trumpet-shaped flowers in an unusual combination of velvety texture, delicate veining, and muted, rich colors. Blooms in shades of white, yellow, pink, red, purple, and brown are held in loose clusters on wiry stems. Grows 12–36 inches tall, depending on variety. Does best in cool-summer climates. Space transplants 12 inches apart.

Scarlet sage *(Salvia splendens)* Full sun or partial shade. Red, yellow-pink, purple, lavender, or white flowers on gray-green plants 8–30 inches tall. Use as a tall border or background plant. Space transplants 8–12 inches apart. Perennial mealy-cup sage (*S. farinacea*) is usually grown as an annual. Tall spikes of deep blue or silvery white flowers bloom from spring until fall.

Creeping zinnia *(Sanvitalia procumbens)* Full sun. Tiny, bright, zinnialike flowers and creeping habit are prized virtues. Use as an edging for a border, clumped in a rock garden, or cascading from a window box or hanging basket. Produces masses of single or double blooms in warm shades of orange, yellow, and white with purplish brown centers. Easy to grow from seed. Space plants 3–6 inches apart.

Marigold *(Tagetes)* Full sun. Robust, fast growing, and virtually trouble-free, with flowers in vibrant shades of yellow, orange, and orange red, as well as white and bicolors. Foliage has a pungent scent. *T. erecta,* called American marigold (although all garden marigolds are descended from species native to Mexico), has large blossoms—fully double in most varieties—on plants 20–36 inches tall. *T. patula,* the French marigold, bears single or double flowers and grows 6–18 inches tall. Space dwarf varieties about 6 inches apart, taller kinds 1–2 feet apart. Plant tall types deeply, and stake them early in the season to keep them from toppling. Avoid watering them from overhead, which often damages flowers.

Black-eyed Susan vine *(Thunbergia alata)* Full sun to light shade. This twining vine is studded with flaring 1-inch flowers in shades of white, yellow, and orange with the namesake dark center. A perennial in mild-winter climates, it is usually grown as an annual. Grow on fences and trellises; dwarf types are attractive when trailing from hanging baskets and window boxes. Can climb up to 10 feet high. Space transplants 12 inches apart.

Zinnia *(Zinnia elegans)*

Snapdragon *(Antirrhinum majus)*

Calendula *(Calendula officinalis)*

Garden verbena *(Verbena hybrida)* Full sun. Small, richly colored flowers may be white, pink, red, purple, blue, or bicolor and are borne in flat clusters 2–3 inches wide. Available in mounded, trailing, and dwarf forms, plants cover themselves with bloom. Leaves are bright green and serrated. Can be used as a small-scale ground cover. Perennial in mild-winter climates. Space transplants 12–18 inches apart.

Zinnia *(Zinnia elegans)* Full sun. On plants 1–3 feet tall, colorful daisylike flowers bloom in yellow, orange, red, pink, and purple, as well as white. Excellent cut flowers. These are hot-weather plants that don't benefit from early planting. Easy from seeds sown where you want plants to grow. Space 6–12 inches apart, according to the size of the variety. A favorite cutting variety is the 4-foot-tall Blue Point strain. Zinnias are susceptible to mildew. To prevent it, water at ground level rather than sprinkling.

cool-season annuals

Snapdragon *(Antirrhinum majus)* Full sun. Bright colors, pastel shades, and white flowers bloom on plants that range from 6- to 8-inch dwarfs to 3-foot-tall giants. Several flower forms including double, bell-shaped, and azalea-shaped flowers. Space dwarf plants 9 inches apart, taller kinds 15 inches apart. Choose rust-resistant varieties.

Calendula *(Calendula officinalis)* Full sun. Bushy, upright plants with pungently scented foliage reach 1–1¹⁄₂ feet tall and bear abundant blossoms reminiscent of double daisies. Common colors are orange and bright yellow. Also look for white and subtle shades of cream, apricot, and soft yellow. The edible petals have a slightly tangy flavor. Space plants 12–14 inches apart.

Bachelor's button *(Centaurea cyanus)* Full sun. Lovely blue, red, or white flowers atop wiry stems 1–2 feet tall. Great fresh or dried cut flower. Blue is the classic boutonniere. Easy from seed, and self-sows. Thin seedlings to 12 inches apart.

Miniature marguerite *(Chrysanthemum paludosum)* Full sun. Perfect miniature daisylike flowers on compact, mounded plants 6–12 inches high. Ideal edging or potted plant. Grow from seed or transplants, spacing 12 inches apart.

Larkspur *(Consolida ajacis)* Partial shade. Delicate flowers in blue, lilac, rose, and white on 4-foot-tall stalks. May need staking. Chill seeds in refrigerator for a week or two before sowing. Thin seedlings to 1–2 feet apart.

California poppy *(Eschscholzia californica)* Full sun. California state flower. Brilliant-colored silky flowers in shades of gold, orange, pink, red, and white dance above ferny foliage. Easy from seed. Grows 8–24 inches tall. Thin seedlings to 6–8 inches apart.

a sampler of annuals

Sweet pea *(Lathyrus odoratus)*

Stock *(Matthiola incana)*

Forget-me-not *(Myosotis sylvatica)*

Globe candytuft *(Iberis umbellata)* Full sun to partial shade in hot areas. Clusters of white and pastel blooms on compact plants reaching 6–15 inches tall. Edging or cover for spring-blooming bulbs. Easy from seed. Thin to 6–9 inches apart.

Sweet pea *(Lathyrus odoratus)* Full sun. Fragrant blooms are pink, purple, blue, salmon, red, white, cream, and bicolor. Bush types grow 1–3 feet high, and vines can reach 5 feet or taller. Space seeds or plants 6–12 inches apart. Provide a trellis for climbing types at planting time.

Lobelia *(Lobelia erinus)* Full sun to partial shade. Tiny white or blue flowers on low-growing to trailing plants. Plants reach 6–8 inches tall. Excellent low border. Space plants 6–8 inches apart.

Stock *(Matthiola incana)* Full sun or partial shade. These old-fashioned favorites bear 1- to 3-foot spikes of clustered single or double flowers with a wonderful spicy-sweet scent. Colors include white, cream, pink, lavender, purple, and red. Long, narrow leaves are soft gray-green. Space plants 9–12 inches apart.

Forget-me-not *(Myosotis sylvatica)* Partial shade. Sprays of tiny blue or white flowers on plants to 2 feet tall. Good planted under shrubs or as a bulb cover. Best sown directly where you want plants to bloom. Comes back year after year.

Nemesia *(Nemesia)* Full sun. Wide range of brightly colored flowers on sprawling 10- to 18-inch-tall plants. Great in hanging baskets. Start from seed or transplants. Space seedlings 6–8 inches apart.

Iceland poppy *(Papaver nudicaule)* Full sun. Cupped, slightly fragrant flowers up to 4 inches wide come in shades of white, cream, yellow, and pink. The blooms come on hairy stalks 1–2 feet tall. Space transplants 12 inches apart.

Garden nasturtium *(Tropaeolum majus)* Full sun to partial shade. Distinctive, easy, and fast growing. Broad, $2\frac{1}{2}$-inch-wide flowers in shades of red, orange, maroon, and white are lightly fragrant and have spurs. Roundish dark green leaves are edible (as are flowers). Climbing varieties reach about 6 feet high, and there are also smaller bush varieties. Climbs on string or wire. Can also be used as a sprawling ground cover in full sun or partial shade. Sow seeds where you want plants to grow.

Pansy and viola *(Viola)* Full sun or partial shade. Pansies (*V. wittrockiana*) are much hybridized, and numerous strains are available. Most have 2- to 4-inch flowers in white, blue, mahogany, rose, yellow, apricot, and purple. Petals are often striped or blotched. Viola (*V. cornuta*) has blossoms about $\frac{1}{2}$ inch across, in bicolors as well as in many clear solid colors. Both pansy and viola grow 8–10 inches tall. Space both 6–8 inches apart.

a sampler of biennials

Hollyhock *(Alcea rosea)*

Canterbury bell *(Campanula medium)*

Common foxglove *(Digitalis purpurea)*

Hollyhock *(Alcea rosea)* Full sun. Old-fashioned favorite has 3- to 6-inch-wide single to double flowers on stems that range from 2½ feet to a towering 9 feet tall. Blossoms appear in summer. Colors include yellow, cream, white, pink, red, and purple. Rust can be a serious problem, so choose rust-resistant varieties, remove any infected leaves you see, and avoid overhead watering, which can spread rust spores. Plants self-sow freely. Space 1½ feet apart.

Canterbury bell *(Campanula medium)* Full sun or partial shade. Another choice for an old-fashioned garden, plants send up leafy 2½- to 4-foot stems bearing loose clusters of bell-shaped flowers 1–2 inches across. Blossoms come in late spring or early summer. Besides the traditional blue, colors include purple, violet, lavender, pink, and white. Space 15–18 inches apart.

Sweet William *(Dianthus barbatus)* Full sun. With clumps of narrow leaves and fringed flowers, sweet William bears an obvious resemblance to its perennial relative, cottage pinks *(D. plumarius)*. But its leaves are green rather than blue-gray, and ½-inch flowers come in large, dense clusters rather than singly. A number of named strains are available, including some with double flowers. Heights range from 6 to 18 inches. Flowers come in white, pink shades, red, and purple, and in striking bicolor combinations, usually with concentric bands of color. Space transplants 12–18 inches apart.

Common foxglove *(Digitalis purpurea)* Light shade. This staple of cottage-gardens forms clumps of large, furry leaves from which tall flowering spikes (to 4 feet or taller) emerge in spring to early summer. Pendulous, tubular 2- to 3-inch-long flowers bloom in white, lavender, pink, or purple, are attractive to hummingbirds. Volunteer seedlings often have white or light-colored blossoms. The leaves are the source of digitalis, a valuable (and potent) medicinal drug. But all parts of the plant are poisonous if ingested. Space plants 1½ feet apart.

Money plant *(Lunaria annua)* Full sun to partial shade in hottest areas. Old-fashioned plant grown for coinlike, translucent seedpods that hang on flower stalks. Small white to purple flowers appear in spring on 1½- to 3-foot stalks. Best used in an out-of-the-way area. Reseeds and can become weedy. Space plants about 12 inches apart.

Silver sage *(Salvia argentea)* Full sun. Silver sage provides highly ornamental foliage to admire even when it's out of bloom. Each plant is a 2-foot-wide rosette of 6- to 8-inch-long gray-white leaves covered with silvery, woolly hairs. In the summer of the plant's second year, branched white, woolly flowers rise to 3 feet, bearing pink- or yellow-tinted white flowers that are 1½ inches long. Space plants 12–24 inches apart.

flowering bulbs
BIG COLOR FROM SMALL PACKAGES

SOME OF THE BEST-LOVED GARDEN FLOWERS, SUCH AS TULIPS AND DAFFODILS, ARISE FROM bulbs—or from corms, tubers, rhizomes, or tuberous roots. Although bulbs are traditionally associated with spring, some bloom in late winter, summer, or fall, making them ideal for single displays and for mixed borders.

Tulips, dark blue grape hyacinths, and lofty yellow-and-orange crown imperial fritillaria reach peak bloom in spring.

Bulbs are inexpensive, and to get a good splash of color, you should plant them by the dozens. Bulbs that multiply and spread from year to year, such as grape hyacinths, can be naturalized under trees or in meadows.

In naturalized settings, grassy cover disguises bulb foliage, which must be left until it has yellowed and can easily be pulled away. In formal landscapes, plant annuals over newly planted bulbs. The flowers will usually bloom simultaneously, but the longer-blooming annuals will camouflage the wilting bulb foliage.

In fall, plant bulbs in containers, in flower boxes, or along a walkway or path for spring color. Spring-planted bulbs, such as gladiolus, can be set out at four-week intervals to provide an ongoing source of cut flowers. Autumn-blooming bulbs, such as autumn crocus, saffron crocus, and spider lily, offer special bursts of late-season color.

how bulbs grow

All bulbs grow from underground structures that serve as energy reservoirs. They enable the plant to survive winter or drought and to resume growth and bloom once weather conditions are favorable again. Although gardeners typically call all such structures bulbs, botanists divide them into five types according to specific features: true bulb, corm, tuber, rhizome, and tuberous root.

buying bulbs

When you shop, look for plump, firm bulbs that feel heavy for their size. Avoid soft or squashy bulbs, as they may have some sort of rot. Also steer clear of lightweight or shriveled bulbs, because these may have lost too much moisture to recover well.

Large bulbs are likely to give the most impressive performance. The biggest tulip and daffodil bulbs, for example, produce larger flowers on taller, thicker stems. But if you're willing to give bulbs a year or two to build themselves up in your garden, you'll get fine results with smaller sizes of most kinds of bulbs. Their lower cost also makes them a good buy.

planting bulbs

Like most plants, bulbs need good drainage. If your soil drains very poorly, it is best to plant on a slope or in raised beds.

To speed up planting, use a bulb planter (left) or excavate the entire planting area to the correct depth (right).

You can prepare an entire bed for bulbs alone or intersperse bulbs among existing plants. To plant a bed, remove weeds and other vegetation. Spread 1 to 3 inches of an organic amendment over the soil and sprinkle on a complete fertilizer, following the label directions for amounts. Dig or till in these additions, rake the soil smooth, and you're ready to plant.

In most soils, bulbs should be planted about three times as deep as the bulb is wide. In hot climates or sandy soils, plant slightly deeper; in heavy soils, slightly shallower. Most bulbs can be set quite close together to provide a mass of blooms, but keep in mind that closely spaced bulbs will need dividing sooner than those given more room to grow. For spacing, see the individual descriptions starting on page 368.

To plant bulbs among other plants, use a trowel or bulb planter to dig a hole for each bulb, making the hole a couple of inches deeper than the recommended planting depth. Add a handful of compost, set the bulb in, and cover it with soil. After planting, water thoroughly to establish good contact between the bulb and soil and to provide the moisture necessary to initiate root growth.

five types of bulbs

TRUE BULB
(Leucojum)

CORM
(Watsonia)

TUBER
(Tuberous begonia)

RHIZOME
(Calla lily)

TUBEROUS ROOT
(Dahlia)

NATURALIZING BULBS

Some bulbs, corms, and tubers can be planted once—in lawns, in perennial gardens, or on hillsides—and they'll come back year after year as though they were wildflowers. By choosing bulbs that adapt to naturalizing and that thrive in your climate and location, you can enjoy an annual display without much work.

To start bulbs, plant in small clusters of five or so. Because most bulbs grow in expanding clumps, the planting will look natural the first year it blooms. Expand the planting by continuing to add bulbs to established clumps, imitating the way bulbs gradually spread outward from a main clump. Once the pattern you want is established, you can continue adding bulbs, expanding the planting. After they bloom, fertilize the bulbs and allow the foliage to remain until it withers. After a number of years, overcrowding may cause a decrease in the number of flowers. When this happens, it's time to dig, divide, and replant.

a sampler of bulbs

Ornamental onion *(Allium)*

Anemone *(Anemone blanda)*

Crocus

Ornamental onion *(Allium)* Bulb, zones 3–11, depending on species. Regular water during growth and bloom; full sun or partial shade. Bears roundish clusters of small flowers at ends of leafless stems that range in height from 6 inches to 5 feet. Many are delightfully fragrant. Blooms in spring or summer with flowers in white and shades of pink, rose, violet, red, blue, and yellow. In spring or fall, plant as deep as their height or width, whichever is greater. Space smaller ones 4–6 inches apart, larger ones 8–12 inches apart.

Belladonna lily *(Amaryllis belladonna)* Bulb, zones 8–11. Regular water while leaves grow in winter; dry during summer. Best in areas with warm, dry summers and wet winters. Straplike leaves grow from clump that becomes about 1 foot tall and 2 feet wide. Leaves die back by early summer. About six weeks later, 2- to 3-foot flower stalks rise from bare earth, each topped by a cluster of 4 to 12 fragrant, trumpet-shaped pink

flowers. Plant dormant bulbs after bloom, about 1 foot apart. All parts of this plant are poisonous if consumed.

Anemone *(Anemone blanda)* Tuber, zones 6–10. Regular water; partial shade. Sky blue flowers held above a low mat of soft, hairy leaves in spring. In spring, each 2- to 8-inch stem bears one sky blue flower that is 1–1½ inches cross. Plant in fall or spring, setting tubers 1–2 inches deep and 8–12 inches apart. Great ground cover under trees.

Tuberous begonia *(Begonia)* Tuber, zones 9–11, or dig and store over winter. Regular water; light shade. Spectacular summer- to fall-blooming tubers most often grown in pots. Available in every flower color but blue, including many multicolored types. Flower form varies, from single to double and from frilly to roselike. Plant form is upright to pendulous (ideal for hanging baskets), 12–18 inches tall. Upright kinds produce the largest flowers. Plant in early spring.

Fancy-leafed caladium *(Caladium bicolor)* Tuber, zones 10–11, or dig and store over winter. Regular water during growth. Grown for large and colorful leaves, especially in southern United States and Hawaii. Many varieties; most are 2 feet high and wide. All need rich soil, warmth (rarely below 60 degrees F), and humidity. Outdoors, plant in spring, knobby side up so tops are level with soil surface. Keep plants moist and fertilized.

Crocus *(Crocus)* Corm, zones 3–11. Regular water during growth and bloom; full sun or partial shade. Most crocuses bloom in late winter or early spring, bearing tubular 1½- to 3-inch-long flowers in a rainbow of colors. Others, including saffron crocus (*Crocus sativus*) and C. *speciosus*, bloom in fall, with flowers rising from bare earth days after planting. Plant corms of both spring- and fall-blooming types as soon as they are available in autumn, setting them 2–3 inches deep and 3–4 inches apart in light, porous soil.

Freesia

Common snowdrop *(Galanthus nivalis)*

Common hyacinth *(Hyacinthus orientalis)*

Dahlia *(Dahlia)* Tuberous root, all zones. Regular water during growth and bloom; full sun, partial shade where the summers are hot. Blooming from summer through fall, dahlias are available in numerous colors and floral forms. Flowers range from 2 to 12 inches across. Plant height varies from 1 to 7 feet or more. Stake varieties that grow more than 4 feet tall. Plant after the last frost in spring, setting roots 4–6 inches deep. Space tall varieties 4–5 feet apart, shorter ones 1–1¹/₂ feet apart. Roots can be left in the ground where winter temperatures remain above 20 degrees F; most gardeners dig and store them over winter.

Freesia *(Freesia)* Corm, zones 8–11. Regular water during growth and bloom; full sun or partial shade. In spring, wiry 1- to 1¹/₂-foot stems bear spikes of richly perfumed, tubular flowers in almost all shades but green. Narrow, sword-shaped leaves grow 1 foot long. Plant in fall, 2 inches deep and 2 inches apart. Naturalizes readily.

Common snowdrop *(Galanthus nivalis)* Bulb, zones 3–9. Regular water during growth and bloom; full sun or partial shade. Among the first bulbs to bloom as winter draws to a close. Plants grow 6–8 inches tall, bearing one nodding, bell-shaped white flower on each stalk. Best suited to cold-winter climates. Plant bulbs in fall, setting them 3–4 inches deep and 3 inches apart.

Gladiolus *(Gladiolus)* Corm, zones 6–11. Regular water during growth and bloom; full sun. These longtime favorites have sword-shaped leaves and flaring flowers that are shaped like funnels. Large summer-flowering garden kinds (grandiflora hybrids) grow 3–6 feet tall and come in a wide variety of colors. Plant corms in spring after soil has warmed; they'll bloom in 65–100 days. To enjoy an extended flowering season, plant corms at one- to two-week intervals over a period of four to six weeks. Set each corm about four times deeper than

it is thick and space them 4–6 inches apart. In the zones listed, corms can overwinter in the ground, although many gardeners prefer to dig them up. In colder regions, they must be dug and stored in a frost-free location and replanted in spring.

Common hyacinth *(Hyacinthus orientalis)* Bulb, zones 4–11. Regular water during growth and bloom. Dutch hyacinth blooms in spring producing 1-foot-tall spikes densely packed with waxy, fragrant flowers in shades of blue, purple, red, pink, buff, and white. Largest, exhibition-size bulbs produce the largest spikes and are the best choice for containers or forced flowers. Next-largest-size bulbs are good for massing in beds and borders. Grow best in cold-winter areas, where they last from year to year. In those zones, plant in September or October. In mild areas, bulbs will not persist and are best treated as annuals. Plant from October to December. Set bulbs 4–5 inches deep and 4–5 inches apart.

a sampler of bulbs

Bearded iris *(Iris)*

Summer snowflake *(Leucojum aestivum)*

Hybrid lilies *(Lilium)*

Bearded iris *(Iris)* Rhizome, zones 3–11, depending upon type. Full sun or light shade. Regular water during growing season. The most widely grown irises are bearded kinds that grow from rhizomes. Bearded irises come in a dazzling array of colors and color combinations. Plant sizes also vary widely. Plant in July or August in cold-winter zones, in September or October where summers are hot. Space rhizomes 1–2 feet apart, setting them with their tops just beneath the soil surface and spreading out the roots.

African corn lily *(Ixia maculata)* Corm, zones 8–11. Regular water during growth; keep dry once leaves begin to fade. Leaves are narrow and grasslike. Spikes bearing 2-inch flowers come on wiry stems in late spring. Plant in fall, setting corms 4 inches deep, then mulch.

Summer snowflake *(Leucojum aestivum)* Bulb, zones 3–11. Regular water during growth and bloom; full sun to light shade. Small, nodding white flowers with green-tipped segments reach about 1¹⁄₂ feet tall in late winter to spring. Prefers shade in hot climates. Great for naturalizing under trees. Plant in fall, 3–4 inches deep and 4 inches apart.

Hybrid lilies *(Lilium)* Bulb, zones 4–11. Keep soil moist; full sun or partial shade. Many species and hybrids are available. Asiatic hybrid lilies bloom in early summer on strong stems 1¹⁄₂ –4¹⁄₂ feet tall. The 4- to 6-inch blossoms come in colors ranging from white to yellow and orange to pink and red. Oriental hybrids bloom later, in midsummer to early fall. Their 2- to 6-foot stems bear fragrant flowers up to 9 inches wide with pink or white petals marked with center stripes and speckles. Plant as soon as possible after you get them. Space bulbs 1 foot apart. Cover smaller bulbs with 2–3 inches of soil, medium-size ones with 3–4 inches, and larger ones with 4–6 inches.

Grape hyacinth *(Muscari armeniacum)* Bulb, zones 3–11. Regular water during growth and bloom; full sun or light shade. Grape hyacinth's narrow, grassy leaves emerge in fall and live through winter's cold and snow. Small, urn-shaped blue flowers with the scent of grape juice are carried on 8-inch spikes, blooming in spring. Plant bulbs in fall, setting them 2 inches deep and 3 inches apart.

Daffodil and narcissus *(Narcissus)* Bulb, zones 3–11. Regular water during growth and bloom; full sun to partial shade. Easy to grow and generous with their spring flowers, daffodils are classified into 12 divisions, based in part on differences in flower form. Divisions include the familiar trumpet daffodils, large- and small-cupped types, and double forms. Besides yellow and white, colors include shades of orange, apricot, pink, and cream. Plant bulbs twice as deep as they are tall, spacing them 6–8 inches apart.

Persian ranunculus *(Ranunculus asiaticus)*

Tulip *(Tulipa)*

Common calla *(Zantedeschia aethiopica)*

Persian ranunculus (*Ranunculus asiaticus*) Tuber, zones 8–11. Regular water during growth and bloom; full sun. Peony-like blooms held above fresh fernlike foliage on 1½-foot stems in early spring. Many shades of white, cream, yellow, orange, red, and pink. Plant in fall, 2 inches deep and 6–8 inches apart. In cold-winter areas, plant in spring and grow as an annual, or dig and store in the fall.

Harlequin flower (*Sparaxis tricolor*) Corm, zones 9–10. Regular water during growth and bloom, dry afterward; full sun. Brilliant blooms above clumps of swordlike leaves over a long period in late spring; 12- to 18-inch-tall flower stems bear spikelike clusters of small, funnel-shaped blossoms. Each flower has a yellow center surrounded by a dark color, and another color—red, pink, orange, or purple—on the rest of the petals. Plant corms 2 inches deep and 3–4 inches apart. Plant in fall where corms are hardy in the ground, in

early spring in colder regions. Dig and store the corms in fall in cold-winter climates.

Tiger flower (*Tigridia pavonia*) Bulb, zones 8–11. Regular water; full sun, partial shade in hot-summer areas. Flashy summer blooms are up to 6 inches across. Plant grows 1½–2½ feet tall. The three outer segments of each triangular flower are red, pink, orange, yellow, or white. Individual flowers last only a day, but bloom lasts several weeks. Plant in spring after the weather warms. Set bulbs 2–4 inches deep and 4–8 inches apart. Dig and store in fall in cold climates.

Tulip (*Tulipa*) Bulb, zones 3–11. Regular water during growth and bloom; full sun to partial shade. Hybrid tulips come in a multitude of colors, including bright shades, pastels, and even nearly black. Eleven categories include early- to late-blooming kinds that grow from 6 inches to 3 feet tall. Flowers vary

widely in form, from the classic egg-shaped blossoms to those that look like lilies or peonies. Bloom season ranges from mid- to late spring, depending on variety. Most need an extended period of winter chill for best performance. In mild climates, refrigerate tulip bulbs for six weeks before planting (but never store near apples) and treat the plants as annuals. Otherwise, plant bulbs in fall, setting them three times as deep as they are wide, spaced 4–8 inches apart.

Common calla (*Zantedeschia aethiopica*) Rhizome, zones 8–11. Moderate to ample water; full sun, light shade in hottest regions. Large, cream-colored flowers, 2–4 feet tall, rise above shiny green arrow-shaped leaves, in spring and early summer. Excellent cut flower. Plant from fall through early spring. Set rhizomes 4 inches deep and 1 foot apart. Needs moist soil year-round. Can become weedy. Low-growing hybrids with cream, pink, orange, or lavender blooms are available.

ornamental grasses
STRIKING TEXTURES PLUS A REFINED, NATURAL LOOK

IF YOU'RE LOOKING FOR SPECIAL EFFECTS IN YOUR GARDEN, CONSIDER PLANTING ORNAMENTAL grasses. These versatile plants offer beauty and grace while demanding minimal care in return. Once used almost exclusively in prairie or native gardens, they are now finding their way into elegant and even formal landscapes.

Ornamental grasses line a pathway, and flowering grasses create an arch over the entry gate.

Ornamental grasses bring new dimensions of texture, color, height, and graceful motion to the border, highlighting and enlivening groups of more traditional perennials. Varying in size from low tufts to giants rising to 8 feet or taller, the many kinds of grasses can serve as edgings, mix with midsize perennials, and provide accents or focal points. Most are also excellent for containers. Many have variegated or colored leaves as well as interesting blooms, and the foliage and flowering stems often persist into autumn and winter.

Massed groups of clumping grasses can create the same color impact as landscape shrubs. The taller plants, such as zebra grass (*Miscanthus sinensis* 'Zebrinus'), can make effective hedges and privacy screens. In small gardens, use ornamental grasses as specimens or as accents in borders. In large gardens, fill wide borders with grasses that have airy textures and interesting colors. If you have a pond in your garden, try planting some moisture-loving grasses, such as purple moor grass (*Molinia caerulea*), close to the water's edge, where they will help establish a naturalistic setting.

Early spring is the best time for both planting and dividing ornamental grasses. It's also the time to tidy up the clumps before new growth begins, cutting back dead foliage.

Of course, grasses aren't perfect plants. While many are well behaved, others can be invasive. For example, maiden grass (*Miscanthus sinensis* 'Gracillimus'), is known to self-sow prolifically. Giant reed and ribbon grass (*Phalaris arundinacea*) spread quickly through the garden by underground rhizomes. Research these grasses before adding them to your landscape.

BELOW LEFT: Containers on pedestals filled with blue fescue and annual red fountain grass boost these shorter grasses to new heights.

BELOW RIGHT: The light of the setting sun catches upright seed stalks of feather reed grass. Arching stalks in right foreground are from blue oat grass.

BOTTOM RIGHT: Flowers of maiden grass drape over a path.

a sampler of ornamental grasses

Bulbous oat grass (*Arrhenatherum elatius bulbosum* 'Variegatum')

Feather reed grass (*Calamagrostis acutiflora* 'Karl Foerster')

Goldband Japanese sedge (*Carex morrowii* 'Goldband')

Yellow foxtail grass (*Alopecurus pratensis* 'Aureus') Zones 5–10 (5–11W). Regular water; full sun, partial shade in hottest areas. Translucent 12-inch-long blades range from green striped with gold to almost entirely yellow. In partial shade, it is chartreuse. To keep foliage attractive and prevent seedlings, shear flower heads when they form in midspring. Grows best in cool weather.

Bulbous oat grass (*Arrhenatherum elatius bulbosum* 'Variegatum') Zones 3–10, sun or partial shade. Blooms in summer; height under 2 feet. White-striped blades. Showy, erect, oatlike flower spike. Short-lived in hot inland areas. Dormant in summer. Effective as an accent in perennial borders and large rock gardens.

Rattlesnake grass (*Briza maxima*) Zones 3–9 (3–11W), sun or partial shade. Blooms in spring; height under 2 feet. Heart-shaped florets resemble

rattlesnake rattles and are good in arrangements. Green foliage.

Feather reed grass (*Calamagrostis acutiflora* 'Karl Foerster') Zones 4–9 (4–11W), full sun. Blooms late spring to fall; height under 5 feet. Bright green foliage. Erect flower spikes. Blooms vary depending on climate. Good in arrangements. Deciduous in colder areas. Makes a strong vertical accent. Plant in groups or at rear of a border.

Leather leaf sedge (*Carex buchananii*) Zones 6–9 (6–11W), sun or partial shade. Height under 2 feet. Coppery red-brown foliage with curled leaf tips. May be short-lived. Evergreen. Use as accent, in groups, or combined with blue, gray, or dark green foliage.

Goldband Japanese sedge (*Carex morrowii* 'Goldband') Zones 5–9 (5–11W), shade or partial shade. Height under 2 feet. Lustrous, white-

striped blades. May be short-lived. Evergreen. Use for accent, alone or in groups; in borders, or spilling over rocks or walls.

Sea oats (*Chasmanthium latifolium*) Zones 5–11, 2–3 feet. Water regularly; plant in full sun, partial shade in hottest areas. Broad bamboo-like leaves form a 2-foot-wide clump topped in midsummer by arching 2- to 5-foot flowering stems. The stems carry showers of silver-green spikelets that resemble flattened clusters of oats. Leaves turn brown in winter, when the plant should be cut back to the ground. May need staking. Potentially invasive in moist soils.

Job's tears (*Coix lacryma-jobi*) All zones as an annual, full sun. Grown for its ornamental beadlike seeds. Leaves are 1½ inches wide and 2 feet long. They grow in loose, sprawling clumps that become 1½ feet across. In fall, jointed 6-foot-long stems bear flower spikelets, and the outside

Blue oat grass (*Helictotrichon sempervirens*)

Japanese blood grass (*Imperata cylindrica* 'Rubra')

Giant feather grass (*Stipa gigantea*)

coverings of female flowers harden and resemble beads.

Common blue fescue (*Festuca glauca*)

Zones 3–11, full sun or partial shade. Blooms in spring; height under 2 feet. Evergreen. Foliage may be green, blue, or gray. *F. amethystina*, with blue-green weeping foliage and pink flowers, is the best bloomer. Use as ground cover or as a single accent. Makes good edging for borders.

Blue oat grass (*Helictotrichon sempervirens*)

Zones 4–9 (4–11W), full sun. Blooms in late summer to fall; height 2–4 feet. Evergreen. Blue-gray foliage with pointed tips. Showy flowers. Blooms best in cool areas. In hot areas with wet, heavy soil, root rot may occur. Makes a good accent alone or in groups, in borders as well as in rock gardens.

Japanese blood grass (*Imperata cylindrica* 'Rubra')

Zones 5–11, full sun but afternoon shade in the hottest regions. Height under 2 feet. Blades are bright green with blood red tips, which turn reddish brown in fall. Spreads slowly.

Blue lyme grass (*Leymus arenarius*)

Zones 4–11, 2–3 feet. Little to moderate water; full sun to light shade. Attractive, vigorous (spreads by underground runners) low clump of gray-blue leaves topped with flower heads 3–4 feet tall. Looks best in cool weather. Cut back just as flowers begin to form to maintain crisp blue color. Also sold as *Elymus glaucus*.

Eulalia grass (*Miscanthus sinensis*)

Zones 4–11, sun or shade. Blooms in late summer; height 2–4 feet. Narrow, green foliage. Showy beige flowers are good for cutting. Use as a specimen or plant at back of a border. Recommended varieties include 'Cabaret', with cream-and-green leaves, and 'Stricta', with green leaves with horizontal yellow stripes. Avoid invasive 'Gracillimus'.

Mexican feather grass (*Nassella tenuissima*)

Zones 7–11, sun or partial shade. Blooms in summer; height under 2 feet. Fine-textured, open, airy flowers and green foliage clumps. Flowers tall, fine textured, filmy, green turning tan in winter. Might be invasive in some regions.

Purple fountain grass (*Pennisetum setaceum* 'Rubrum')

Zones 8–11, full sun. Blooms summer to fall; height 2–4 feet. Evergreen or deciduous according to climate. Noninvasive. Purple foliage topped by red-purple plumes is good in arrangements. Cold-hardiness varies greatly. Effective as accent or in groups in perennial or shrub borders.

Giant feather grass (*Stipa gigantea*)

Zones 6–8, full sun. Blooms in summer; height 2–4 feet. Evergreen. Narrow, arching, evergreen leaves in 2- to 3-foot wide-open, airy clump. Use as a specimen or in groups, particularly in perennial borders.

wildflowers
NATURE'S CAREFREE COLOR

WITH THEIR EVOCATIVE NAMES AND BRILLIANT COLORS, WILDFLOWERS OFFER YOU A CHANCE TO bring Native American and pioneer history as well as ecologically suitable plants into the garden. For example, you can sow wildflowers native to your region in a 4- to 8-foot border to create a cheery transition between lawn and woods. You can also sprinkle wildflowers in gaps between ground covers, or you can simply designate a corner or circle of your property as a "wild" patch where children can explore and play.

Growing wildflowers is purely a regional affair, with different parts of the country planting locally adapted favorites. Specialty seed companies offer regional mixes that work well in most areas. Local native plant societies can provide additional information on growing wildflowers in your area.

The prairie native cone-flower meanders down a slope into a garden.

in the west, miner's lettuce, milk maids, sugar-scoops, baby blue eyes, California poppies, farewell-to-springs, lupines, myriad penstemons, and shooting stars are just a few of the many wildflowers that thrive. Although wildflowers are often naturalized in the garden, don't be afraid to include flowers such as the delicate western columbine (*Aquilegia formosa*) in formal borders. And feel free to intersperse native species with their modern hybrid offspring (such as Pacific Coast irises, hybrids of *Iris douglasiana*) and other garden flowers.

in the south, reseeding annuals, including calliopsis, Drummond phlox, Indian paint-brush, Indian blanket, and bluebonnets, can be grown in great sweeps in sunny naturalized areas, such as fields, roadsides, hillsides, and informal lawns. The drier and leaner the soil, the better these flowers seem to grow. Other wildflowers find a good home in traditional perennial borders. Orange coneflower, pur-ple coneflower, and goldenrod are tough, carefree, dependable performers that come back year after year.

Many native flowers prefer the moist, rich soil and dappled shade of a woodland garden. They bloom better beneath trees pruned to allow the maximum amount of light through, or at the edge of a stand of trees rather than in dense woods. Favorite wildflowers include Virginia bluebells and wild columbine.

in the midwest and northeast, doll's eyes, Quaker ladies, rattlesnake master,

FAR LEFT: 'Crown of Rays' goldenrod is laden with millions of golden flowers in fall.

LEFT: Instead of a lawn in this desert garden, golden California poppies cover the soil.

BELOW LEFT: Blue flax *(Linum perenne)* in West Virginia is punctuated by naturalized daisies.

BELOW CENTER: *Gaura lindheimeri* 'Pink Cloud' is a native of east Texas and Louisiana.

BELOW RIGHT: *Iris douglasiana* is a native of the West Coast. Many named varieties are available.

sneezeweed, and tickseed thrive. Good candidates are coneflowers (*Echinacea purpurea*) and threadleaf coreopsis (*Coreopsis verticillata*). With exotic garden flowers, you can include natives and their modern hybrid offspring—such as bee balm (*Monarda didyma*) and its varieties 'Cambridge Scarlet', 'Jacob Kline', and 'Marshall's Delight', or spike gayfeather (*Liatris spicata*) and its varieties 'Alba', 'Floristan Violett', and 'Kobold'.

growing wildflowers

Weeds are the primary cause of failure in wildflower gardens. So whether you're seeding a wildflower border or painstakingly planting an area with small starts of perennial grasses and flowers, prepare the planting bed as carefully as you would for any flower border. With luck, you'll get a good display the first year. Keep an eye out for weed

seedlings and remove them as they start to emerge and before they take over.

After the plants have finished blooming, your natural meadow may take on a ragged or even weedy appearance. Enjoy it. Let the plants set seeds, and then allow the seeds to dry and naturally spill onto the ground. They'll sprout new plants (and attract wild birds) the following year. You can also gather some seeds by hand and save them for later plantings or to fill out any bare spots.

In early winter or very early spring, mow or cut the dry stems down to 6 to 8 inches. At the same time, pull out any weeds, such as oxalis or dandelion. This once-a-year trim will give perennial wildflowers room and light to spread before the next crop of annuals has emerged from their seeds. In regions that typically have a lot of rain in winter, irrigate a wildflower patch only when rains are light.

american native plants
SELF-RELIANT, TOUGH, AND LOW MAINTENANCE

EVERY REGION OF THE UNITED STATES HAS ITS OWN DISTINCT CLIMATE AND RECOGNIZABLE PALETTE of native plants that create the area's unique natural landscape. Whether it's the cactus of the desert Southwest, the aromatic scrub of California's chaparral, or the delicate woodland plants of the Northwest, native plants are supremely adapted to areas in which they grow naturally, which makes them excellent landscape choices.

Native plants give your garden a sense of place, making it part of the overall landscape of the region where you live. They attract wildlife such as birds, butterflies, lizards, and insects to your garden. And because they are so naturally suited to the climate, they're generally self-sufficient, needing little care after they're established.

planting and caring for native plants

When setting out container plants, start with young ones that are not root-bound. They may not be much to look at when first planted, but they'll adapt more successfully than larger plants. Water immediately after planting, being sure to saturate the soil. Then water

carefully and steadily during dry weather in the first summer or two. Don't inundate your plants, but don't let them dry out either.

After you've taken care to establish your natives, they should do well with little or no supplemental watering. In general, natives don't require fertilizing; some are even weakened by it. Still, a light mulch is usually beneficial. But to avoid rot, keep mulch away from plant crowns.

in the northeast: natives of the woodland

As winter releases its grip, the snow cover melts, the ground begins to thaw, and spring ephemerals that have been dormant since the previous summer stir into growth. Overhead, the tree canopy is

ABOVE LEFT: In the Northeast, ferns and wildflowers carpet the forest floor in early spring.

ABOVE RIGHT: Feathery plumes of prairie smoke (*Geum triflorum*) produce a rose pink mist above common prairie grasses.

open to the sky, allowing the sun to reach the ground. Small bulbs and tubers, such as bloodroot (*Sanguinaria*) and dogtooth violets (*Erythronium*), as well as sweet violets, come into bloom. Later come the taller bulbs and perennials: mayapples, trilliums, white foamflower (*Tiarella*), Solomon's seal (*Polygonatum*), meadow rue (*Thalictrum*), and red-and-yellow columbines. And tender, green ferns are everywhere.

As the deciduous trees fill in with foliage, the middle story of the woodland comes into bloom. White-flowered dogwood and redbud join viburnums, native azaleas, spicebush (*Lindera*), mountain laurel (*Kalmia*), and clethra to fill the woods with color and fragrance. Spring rains give way to dry summer, and in clearings and on the woodland's edges, the stately blooms of native Canada and Turk's cap lilies join with cardinal flower and scarlet bee balm (*Monarda*). Asters, goldenrod, and sweet autumn clematis, with its cloud of white flowers, follow in fall.

But it is probably autumn's fireworks that most distinguish the northeastern woodland. Every plant is a player in the fall pageant, but probably none more than the deciduous trees and shrubs, flashing deep orange and gold, scarlet to burgundy, lemon yellow, and lush purple to the deepest mahogany.

in the midwest: jewels of the prairie

Prairie flowers that are tough enough to compete successfully with native grasses need no coddling in the garden. In early spring, the single lavender blooms of pasque flower (*Pulsatilla patens*), the state flower of South Dakota, open above their low, clumping leaves. Soon after it, the blue flower spikes of false indigo (*Baptisia minor*) appear.

In midsummer, giant red-violet blossom spires top Kansas gayfeather (*Liatris pycnostachya*). Drooping yellow petals surround the prominent brown centers of prairie coneflowers (*Ratibida pinnata*). Butterflies float and dart around vivid orange butterfly weed (*Asclepias tuberosa*).

Many prairie gems bloom for months. Deep blue blooms cover tiny prairie skullcap (*Scutellaria resinosa*) throughout summer. Wide-spreading Missouri primrose (*Oenothera macro-carpa* and *O. missouriensis*) blooms all summer, too, flaunting its many showy saucer-shaped yellow blooms.

In autumn, lavender-blue blossoms cover 3-foot-tall smooth asters (*Aster laevis*). And as the flowers bow out, prairie grasses dominate the landscape. The russet red of little bluestem (*Schizachyrium scoparium*), Willa Cather's beloved red grass, persists throughout winter.

in the west: stars of the chaparral

Chaparral plants are brilliant in spring. Smothered with yellow flowers, flannel bush (*Fremontodendron*)—native to the Sierra Nevada foothills and the inland slopes of Southern California's mountains—is almost its own parade float. And lavender *Salvia clevelandii* provides much of chaparral's pungent scent.

The qualities that make these plants survivors in the wild also make them some of the best choices for western gardens. Take your design cues from nature. You'll need the conditions that naturally embrace these plants: gritty, sun-baked soil; well-drained slopes; and full sun. Give them room to grow, as many, like woolly blue curls (*Trichostema lanatum*), hate to be crowded. Use them together or mix them with plants from other Mediterranean climates. Plant in fall, letting winter rains establish them.

Drought tolerant and hardy, a lawn of blue grama grass is a good choice for this New Mexico garden.

vegetables
BEAUTIFUL, NUTRITIOUS, AND FUN

TO MAKE YOUR VEGETABLE PATCH A SUCCESS, DO A LITTLE PLANNING BEFORE YOU PLANT. IF YOU'RE new to vegetable gardening, start small. An area of just 100 to 130 square feet can provide a substantial harvest. As you gain experience, you may want to expand the plot. List the vegetables your family really enjoys, and then consider how much room each kind requires. If space is limited, raise plants that give a good yield for the area they occupy. Beans, tomatoes, and summer squash, for example, can overwhelm you with their bounty from a small plot. At the other extreme are melons, corn, and some other kinds of squash, which all require a great deal of space relative to their yield.

vegetable seasons

Vegetables are designated as warm-season or cool-season, depending on the weather they need for best growth. Warm-season vegetables, such as peppers and tomatoes, are summer crops. They require both warm soil and high temperatures to grow and produce fruit. They are killed by frost. Plant them after the last frost in spring.

Cool-season vegetables grow best at average temperatures 10 to 15 degrees F below those needed by warm-season types. They can be planted in very early spring for early-summer harvest or in late summer for harvest in fall and, in mild regions, winter. Many will endure short spells of frost, but in hot weather they become bitter and often bolt to seed. In areas with short growing seasons (fewer than 100 days) or cool, foggy summers, cool-season vegetables can be grown in summer.

choosing a location

Vegetables grow best with at least 6 hours of full sun each day. To avoid both shade and root competition, locate the vegetable patch away from trees and large shrubs. It's also important to choose a spot protected from cold winds in spring and hot, dry winds in summer. Steer clear of frost pockets—low-lying areas that may experience frosts later in spring and earlier in fall than other parts of the garden. Watering and other routine tasks are easier on a level site. If only sloping land is available, try to find a south- or southeast-facing slope to take full advantage of the sun.

working with the growing season

After you've chosen a site and decided which vegetables it can accommodate, you'll need to consider your climate and the length of your growing season. Calculate the length of your growing season by counting the number of days between the average last-frost date in spring and the first-frost date in fall. Any Lowe's garden associate can help you with this.

Vegetables are natural companions to herbs and flowers. Here, sunflowers and white cosmos daisies back up squash, basil, and sage.

Last-frost dates let you know when it's safe to set out tender vegetable plants or sow seeds. First-frost dates tell you when you'll probably have to provide protection for tender kinds late in the season. Aim to select vegetables that can mature and bear a good crop in the interval between these two dates. For example, if the seed packet says a certain variety of winter squash requires 120 days from seed to harvest but your growing season lasts only 100 days, look instead for a variety adapted to short growing seasons or plan to use season-extending techniques, such as cold frames or row covers.

planting vegetables

Before actually digging your plot, draw a rough plan on paper. Be sure to place tall vegetables to the north so they won't shade short ones.

Start with careful soil preparation. You will be repaid with faster growth and a substantially larger harvest. Remove any weeds from the plot and spread the soil with a 3- to 4-inch layer of compost or well-rotted manure. If you're planting a wide bed, scatter a complete fertilizer over the area, following package directions for amounts. If you are planting in rows, apply fertilizer in furrows alongside the rows after planting. Work in amendments and fertilizer by hand or with a rotary tiller, then rake the area smooth. If your soil is poor or doesn't drain well, you may elect to grow vegetables in raised beds filled with a mixture of compost and good topsoil.

You can start vegetables by planting seeds outdoors in the garden or by setting out transplants you have started yourself or purchased from a nursery. Vegetables that require a long growing season—peppers and tomatoes, for example—need many weeks of warm weather before they produce fruit, so they are best set out as transplants. Many other vegetables, including broccoli, cabbage, and lettuce, can be seeded directly or transplanted. Some vegetables, especially beans, carrots, corn, and peas, grow better when started from seed sown directly in the garden. For more on starting and setting out transplants, see page 305.

caring for vegetables

For the best possible harvest, keep your vegetables growing steadily throughout the season. Thin those started from seed sown directly in the ground so that each plant will have enough space to develop properly. Thin plants when they are a few inches tall, spacing them as indicated in the descriptions beginning on page 382 or on the seed packet. Water and fertilize regularly, as any disruption in soil moisture or lack of nutrients will reduce the harvest. Apply a thick mulch of organic matter.

FAR LEFT: Plant tomatoes deep enough to bury the root-ball and a portion of the stem.

LEFT: A mulch of weed-free straw stops most weeds and dresses up the vegetable garden.

a sampler of annual vegetables

Beans, snap

Melons

Tomatoes

warm-season vegetables

Beans, snap Snap beans have tender, fleshy pods. Besides the familiar green, pods can also be yellow or purple. Choose self-supporting (bush) or climbing (pole) varieties. Plant seeds of bush types 2 inches apart in rows spaced 2–3 feet apart. Thin seedlings to 4 inches apart. Space pole types 4–6 inches apart and allow 3 feet between rows. Support the plants on a trellis or plant them around a tepee. Thin seedlings to 6 inches apart. Begin harvest 50 to 70 days after sowing seeds.

Corn Most kinds of corn do best in hot-summer areas, but early-maturing hybrid varieties will grow even where summers are cool or short. Sow seeds directly in the garden, spacing them 4–6 inches apart in rows 1½–3 feet apart. Thin seedlings to 1–2 feet apart. Harvest begins 60 to 100 days later, depending on the variety.

Cucumbers In spring, sow groups of four seeds in hills 4–6 feet apart. Thin

seedlings to two or three per hill. Or sow two or three seeds in groups spaced 1½ feet apart at the base of a trellis and then thin seedlings to one per group. Harvest begins 50 to 100 days after sowing. Harvest frequently in order to promote the growth of more fruits.

Melons Cantaloupes are the easiest melons to grow, because they ripen the fastest. Planting through black plastic speeds harvest. In spring, sow four or five seeds per hill, spacing hills 4–6 feet apart. Thin seedlings to two per hill. Harvest 70 to 115 days after sowing.

Peppers Sweet peppers come in a range of colors, shapes, and sizes— from bell types to long, slender frying peppers, in hues from green to bright yellow and purple. Hot peppers likewise offer a range of sizes, colors, and pungencies. Start seeds of sweet or hot peppers in flats indoors 6 to 8 weeks before planting time, or buy transplants. Set out plants in spring,

spacing them 1½–2 feet apart in rows 2½ feet apart. Harvest 60 to 95 days after setting out plants.

Squash Summer squash (zucchini, crookneck, pattypan) are eaten when the fruit is small and tender. Harvest 50 to 60 days after sowing. Winter squash form hard shells. They are harvested in fall (80 to 120 days after sowing) and can be stored for winter use. Sow seeds of both types in the spring, bush types 1 foot apart in rows 3–5 feet apart. Thin seedlings to 2 feet apart. Sow vining squash about 5 feet apart, placing four or five seeds in each hill. Thin to two per hill.

Tomatoes Start seeds in flats indoors six weeks before planting time. Or buy transplants without buds or flowers, and set them out in spring, spacing plants 2–4 feet apart in rows 3–4 feet apart. Cover the leafless stem with soil. Stake large, sprawling varieties. Weed regularly, and water to maintain soil moisture. Harvest when tomatoes begin to soften.

Cabbage

Chard

Peas

cool-season vegetables

Beets Besides basic red beets, look for seeds of golden yellow and white varieties. The tender young leaves are edible. Sow in early spring for an early summer crop, or in late summer for a fall crop. Plant seeds 1 inch apart in rows spaced 1½ feet apart, or broadcast them in wide beds. Thin seedlings to 2–3 inches apart. Harvest 45 to 65 days after sowing.

Broccoli and cabbage Start seeds indoors six weeks before planting time, or buy transplants. In early spring, or in mid- to late summer for a fall crop, set out plants 15–24 inches apart in rows spaced 2–3 feet apart. Cut the heads before the buds begin to open. After the central head is harvested, side shoots will produce additional, smaller heads. Harvest shoots or heads 50 to 100 days after transplanting.

Carrots Plant seeds in early spring or, for a fall crop, in late summer. Sow 1 inch apart in rows 1–2 feet apart,

or broadcast seeds in wide beds. Thin seedlings to 2–4 inches apart. Harvest baby carrots 30 to 40 days after sowing, but wait for 50 to 80 days after sowing before harvesting mature carrots.

Chard This is one of the most ornamental vegetables, with bright red, white, and green leaves. Plant seed in early spring, or in late summer for a fall crop, in rows spaced 2 feet apart. Thin seedlings to 1 foot apart. Harvest leaves about 60 days after sowing seeds, through summer and into winter in mild-winter climates. 'Bright Lights' is a particularly decorative variety with leaves ranging from green to burgundy and stalks in shades of orange, red, pink, purple, green, and white.

Lettuce Start seeds in flats indoors about four weeks before best planting time, or buy transplants. Plant transplants, or sow seed directly in the garden, in early spring. Make successive plantings or sowings until

daytime temperatures reach 75–80 degrees F. Harvest leaf lettuce 40 to 55 days after sowing. Plant again in late summer and early autumn.

Peas Some kinds of peas are for shelling, some have edible pods, and some can be used either way. Bush and vining types of all kinds are available; the latter reach 6 feet tall and bear heavier. In early spring, or in early fall for a fall crop, sow seeds 1 inch apart in rows spaced 2–3 feet apart. Later, thin seedlings to 2–4 inches apart. Set up a trellis for vining types at planting time. Begin harvesting 55 to 70 days after sowing.

Spinach Spinach is a cool-season annual that bolts quickly into flower if the weather gets too warm or the days get too long. For best results, sow seeds in early spring, or in early fall for a fall crop. Space seedlings 1 inch apart in rows 1–1½ feet apart, or broadcast seeds over wide beds. Thin seedlings to 3–4 inches apart. Harvest 40–50 days after sowing.

kitchen herbs

THEY'RE TOO GOOD AND TOO EASY TO IGNORE

FOR THOUSANDS OF YEARS, GARDENERS HAVE KNOWN THE CULINARY AND MEDICINAL VALUE OF herbs. Today, herbs are equally valuable as adornments—planted in a kitchen window box, mixed with other plants in a scented garden, or used as hedges along a garden path. Most herbs are easy to grow, adapting well to home gardens. Compared to their commercial dried counterparts, many fresh herbs have a more intense flavor and fragrance.

planting herbs

Perennial herbs are easier to start from purchased transplants than from seed. Nurseries offer many sorts in spring, typically in 2- or 4-inch pots. Rosemary and sage are also sold in gallon containers. Annual and biennial herbs, such as basil, cilantro, dill, and parsley, can be started from seed. All perennial herbs can be grown as annuals in areas where they aren't cold hardy.

Water herbs after planting to get them established. After they're growing steadily, though, most will need only occasional irrigation. Exceptions are basil, chives, and parsley, all of which prefer evenly moist soil.

drying herbs

Harvest herbs for drying just as the first flower buds begin to open. The oils in the leaves are most concentrated at this time, and the herbs will maintain their flavor when dried and preserved. Cut sprigs or branches in the morning after the dew has evaporated. Tie them together at the cut ends and hang them upside down in a warm, dry, well-ventilated place that is out of direct sunlight. When the leaves feel brittle and crisp to the touch, strip them from the stems and store them in airtight jars.

You can also dry herbs by removing the leaves from the stems and spreading them on screens placed in a warm, dry, airy place out of direct sunlight. Stir the leaves in the trays every few days. When they feel crisp and crumble easily, store them in airtight jars. With herbs grown for their seeds, harvest the seed heads or pods when they turn brown. Dry them in paper bags until you can shake the seeds loose. Again, store the seeds in jars that are airtight.

Bright yellow-green leaves of common sage 'Icterina' are flanked by lavender-flowered thyme, marjoram, and rosemary.

a sampler of herbs

BASIL DILL MINT OREGANO PARSLEY

Basil This fragrant annual needs warm weather to grow well. Plants typically reach 1½–2 feet tall. Besides varieties with large green leaves, you'll find purple basils and dwarf or small-leafed sorts.

Chives A hardy perennial in all zones, chives make a pretty addition to an ornamental garden. Each plant forms a clump of narrow onion-flavored leaves up to 2 feet high. Rosy purple flowers are also edible.

Dill The fresh or dried leaves and the seeds of this versatile annual herb are a popular seasoning for many foods—including, of course, dill pickles. The plants grow 3–4 feet high, sporting soft, feathery leaves and flat clusters of small yellow flowers.

Mint These perennial herbs spread by underground stems. Their hardiness varies by type. Spearmint is the preferred kind for cooking. It has shiny, bright green leaves and reaches 1–2 feet tall. Peppermint,

favored for flavoring tea, grows to 2 feet or taller. Unlike most other herbs, mint thrives not only in sun but also in partial to full shade.

Oregano A perennial herb that grows well in all zones, oregano is popular in Italian, Greek, and Spanish cooking. Use its leaves fresh or dried. Many kinds are available. Of these, Greek oregano is considered one of the most flavorful. Plants reach 2 feet tall and spread at a moderate rate by underground stems.

Parsley A biennial that's usually grown as an annual, curly-leaf parsley is an attractive edging for herb, vegetable, or flower gardens. In cooking, it's prized for garnishes. Flat-leaf parsley, also called Italian parsley, has a stronger flavor and is favored for seasoning many dishes. Both sorts grow 6–12 inches tall.

Rosemary A shrubby perennial with aromatic needlelike foliage, rosemary is available in numerous varieties, in

heights ranging from 1½ to 6 feet. Most are hardy in zones 8–11, but 'Arp' has survived temperatures as low as –10 degrees F. Rosemary is widely used as a ground cover or low hedge and needs little water. Set plants 2–3 feet apart.

Sage This perennial is adapted to zones 5–11 but isn't picky about where it grows. Strong-flavored sage comes not only in the traditional soft gray-green variety but also in decorative forms with leaves of yellow and green, purple, or tricolored in gray, white, and purplish pink. Plants form dense bushes up to 3 feet tall.

Sweet marjoram Sweet marjoram is a perennial in zones 9–11. Elsewhere grow it as a summer-season annual, or grow it in containers that are moved indoors for winter. Plants reach 1–2 feet tall. The tiny gray-green leaves have a sweet floral scent and a somewhat milder flavor than oregano, to which sweet marjoram is closely related.

care and maintenance

DESIGNING, BUILDING, AND PLANTING YOUR LANDSCAPE ARE

only the first, although usually the most intense, phases of

landscaping. What follows planting is the establishment

phase, which usually lasts at least two seasons. During

that time, new plants are more vulnerable than they will

ultimately be, and some will require special pruning or

attention just to help them get started right. This chapter

spells out that care.

These are the basic gardening

principles and procedures that

will make the difference for

your landscape over the long

haul. And that's why dealing

with watering, fertilizing,

pruning, and pests

in effective, sound,

and efficient ways

is so important.

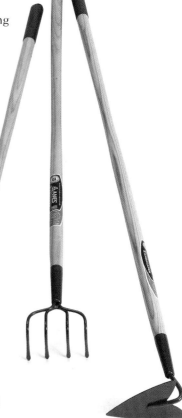

watering and composting
WHEN, HOW, AND HOW MUCH

HOW MUCH WATER DO PLANTS NEED? HOW OFTEN SHOULD YOU WATER, AND WHAT'S THE BEST WAY to do it? How can you conserve water? This section addresses these and other important, and often perplexing, questions.

watering guidelines

Plants, like animals, need water to live. A seed must absorb water before it can germinate. Roots can take up nutrients only when water is present in the soil, and water transports nutrients throughout plants. Water is also essential to photosynthesis.

But how much water your plants need and how frequently they need it depend on a number of interrelated factors, including soil texture, the plants themselves, their age, and the weather.

Your soil's ability to absorb and retain water is closely related to its composition. Clay soils absorb water slowly and also drain slowly, retaining water longer than other soils. Sandy soils, in contrast, absorb water quickly and drain just as quickly. Loam soils absorb water fairly rapidly and drain well but not too fast. You can work organic amendments into clay soils so they absorb water faster and drain better; amendments can also make sandy soils retain more moisture. For more about organic amendments and soil texture, see pages 300–301.

After their roots are established, different sorts of plants have widely differing water needs. Plants native to semiarid and arid climates, called *xerophytes*, have evolved features that allow them to survive with little water and low relative humidity. They may have deep root systems, for example, or leaves that are small, hairy, or waxy. The majority of familiar garden plants, however, are adapted to moist soil and high relative humidity. Called *mesophytes*, they usually have broad, thin leaves.

Keep in mind that all young plants, including xerophytes, require more frequent watering than mature plants until their root systems become well established in their new environment. And many annuals and vegetables require regular moisture throughout the growing season if they are to bloom well or produce a good crop.

Weather also affects water needs. When it's hot, dry, and windy, plants use water very rapidly, and young or shallow-rooted ones sometimes can't absorb water fast enough to keep foliage from wilting. Such plants will need frequent watering to keep leaves cool and to prevent wilting. During cool, damp weather, on the other hand, plants require much less water. Similarly, water needs are

Watering with a watering can or a handheld nozzle is just right for seed beds and seedlings but is usually inadequate for mature plants that need enough water to soak the entire rootball.

lower during winter, when the days are short and the sun is low on the horizon.

Because soil texture, weather, and plant type and age are all variable, following a fixed watering schedule year-round (or even all summer) isn't the most efficient way to meet your plants' needs. If there's any doubt, test the soil for moisture and look at the plants before you water. To check the soil around new transplants and in vegetable and flower beds, dig down a few inches with your fingers or a trowel. If the top 1 to 2 inches of soil is dry, you probably need to water. In a lawn or around established trees and shrubs, a soil-sampling tube (shown at right) is useful. It allows you to test moisture at deeper levels without digging a hole that could disturb roots. Leaves can also tell you when it's time to water—they look dull or roll in at the edges just before they wilt.

When you do water, aim to soak the plants' root zones. As a general guideline, the roots of lawn grasses grow about 1 foot deep, while roots of small shrubs and other plants reach 1 to 2 feet deep. While taproots of some trees and shrubs grow more deeply, most roots concentrate in the top 2 to 3 feet. Watering below the root zone only wastes water.

To check how far water penetrates into your soil, water for a set amount of time—say, 30 minutes. Wait 24 hours and then use a soil-sampling tube or dig a hole to check for moisture. You'll soon learn to judge how long to water each plant in order to soak its root zone thoroughly.

Water trees and shrubs by soaking soil up to and just beyond the drip line, the area below outermost branch tips. Feeder roots are normally concentrated here because rain usually collects here. As plants grow and roots extend beyond the canopy, irrigation must too.

watering methods

Ways to apply water to your landscape range from simple handheld sprayers and hose-end sprinklers to more complex drip systems and underground rigid-pipe systems. The combination of devices that's best for you depends on how often you need to water and your desire to maximize efficiency.

Traditionally used for watering lawns, underground pipe systems with risers for sprinkler heads remain the best system for watering medium-size to large lawns and low-growing ground covers. For more information on installing a rigid-pipe irrigation system, see pages 208–213.

To use water effectively, you need to know how fast it penetrates your soil and the delivery rate of your sprinklers. As the illustration below left shows, 1 inch of water from sprinkling or rainfall moistens about 12 inches deep in sandy soil, 7 inches in loam, and 4 to 5 inches in clay. Thus, if you want to water to a depth of 12 inches, you'll need to apply about 1 inch of water to sandy soil, 2½ to 3 inches to clay soil.

To determine delivery rate, place a number of equal size containers (straight-sided coffee cups, for example) at regular intervals outward from the sprinkler, as shown above. Then turn on the water and note how long it takes to fill a container with an inch of water. This test will also show you the delivery pattern, because the containers will typically fill at different rates. To ensure that every area ultimately receives the same amount of water, you'll need to move the sprinklers so that their coverage overlaps.

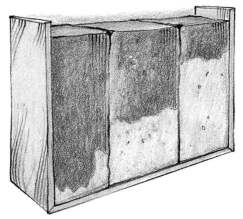

Applied to sandy soil (left), 1 inch of water penetrates about 12 inches deep. In loam soil (center), the same amount of water reaches a depth of 7 inches. One inch of water penetrates only 4 to 5 inches in clay soil (right).

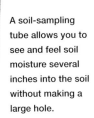

A soil-sampling tube allows you to see and feel soil moisture several inches into the soil without making a large hole.

Check a sprinkler's delivery rate and pattern by placing equal-size containers at regularly spaced distances from the sprinkler.

sprinkling Watering with a handheld nozzle or sprinkler may be enjoyable for you, but it takes far too long to truly soak the soil enough for established plants. Hand watering is more useful for new transplants, seedlings, and container plants, because you can apply the water gently and exactly where it's needed.

Sprinklers, whether hose-end or permanent, produce an artificial rainfall and are the simplest way to apply water over a large surface. Many plants, particularly those that like a cool, humid atmosphere, thrive under overhead sprinkling. Watering with sprinklers also rinses foliage of dust that encourages certain pests, especially spider mites.

But overhead water has some negative aspects. First, it can be wasteful. Wind often blows some water away before it even reaches the ground, and water that falls or runs off

A portable sprinkler with an adjustable watering pattern lets you select the size of the area covered and, to some degree, the shape.

onto pavement is lost. And in humid climates, sprinkling encourages foliage diseases, such as black spot and rust, although you can minimize that risk by sprinkling early in the morning so that leaves dry quickly. A final drawback is that plants with weak stems bend and can break under a heavy load of water.

ABOUT HOSES

A hose can make the task of watering your garden easy or difficult. If you buy an inexpensive hose that's prone to kinking, you'll spend more time cursing than watering. But if you purchase a durable, kink-free type, it will last much longer and work more efficiently.

Unreinforced vinyl hoses are inexpensive and lightweight, but are also less durable and most prone to kinking. Reinforced vinyl hoses are less likely to kink and are lightweight, which is important if you have to move the hose around a lot. Rubber hoses, which have dull surfaces, are the heaviest and toughest types. They kink in hot weather but work well in cold weather. Reinforced rubber-vinyl hoses are flexible, kink resistant, moderately heavy, and durable.

Hoses are sold by length and have various inside diameters ($5/8$-inch, $3/4$-inch, and 1-inch hoses are common). Although the difference in diameters may seem slight, the water volume each carries varies greatly. If you have low water pressure or if you must run your hose uphill, you will need all the pressure and flow you can get. Buy the largest-diameter, shortest hose that's practical for your situation.

Soaker hoses are either perforated plastic or porous rubber, like this one. Attach it to a hose, and water seeps out along its entire length.

Like drip systems, furrows are advised for plants prone to leaf diseases. Use a bubbler attachment on a hose to break the water's flow.

soaker hoses These forerunners of drip-irrigation systems are still quite useful for slow, steady water delivery to plants in rows. They're long tubes made of perforated or porous plastic or rubber, with hose fittings at one or both ends. When you attach a soaker to a regular hose and turn on the water supply, water seeps or sprinkles from the soaker along its entire length. You can also water wide beds by snaking soakers back and forth around the plants. Trees and shrubs can be watered with a soaker coiled in a circle around the plant. You'll probably need to leave soakers on longer than you would sprinklers. Check water penetration with a trowel or soil-sampling tube.

flood watering Flooding, or soaking, is an effective way to supply enough water to the extensive, deep root systems of large shrubs and trees. Make a level basin for the plant by forming a ridge of soil several inches high around its drip line. You'll usually need to fill the basin more than once to ensure that water penetrates throughout the entire root zone. If the soil in the basin hasn't absorbed all the water within a few hours, make a channel in the ridge around it so that the excess can drain away.

If you grow vegetables or flowers in rows, you can build adjoining basins for large plants, like squash or pumpkins, or make furrows between rows (as shown above). To minimize potential damage to roots caused by making the furrows, construct them when the plants are young, before their root systems have spread. Broad, shallow furrows are generally better than deep, narrow ones. The wider the furrow, the wider the root area you can soak, because water moves primarily downward rather than to either side. And a shallow furrow is safer for plants, as nearby roots are less likely to be disturbed when you scoop out the furrow. They're also less apt to be exposed if a strong flow of water comes through.

drip watering For the greatest water savings, use drip irrigation for trees, shrubs, perennials, and vegetables. The opposite of flood watering, drip watering means applying water slowly, drip by drip. Drip sprinklers, called emitters, operate at low pressure, and they deliver a low volume of water compared to standard sprinklers. Because the water is applied slowly on or near the ground, there is no waste from runoff and little loss to evaporation. Position emitters to deliver water just where the plants need it, and control infiltration by varying the time the system runs and/or varying the emitters' delivery capacity. You can regulate the volume of water delivered to each plant by varying the type and number of emitters.

Besides water conservation, the chief advantage of drip systems is flexibility. You can tailor them to water individual plants by providing each with its own emitter(s), or you can distribute water over larger areas with microsprays. A standard layout may include hookups to two or more valves. The limber plastic lines are easily concealed with mulch, so changing the system is simple. Just add or subtract tubes and emitters as needed.

Your drip system can be attached to a hose end or screwed into a hose bibb. If you prefer, you can connect it permanently to your main water source. For more on how to install a drip-irrigation system, see page 214.

mulch

Like many other seeds, most weed seeds require sunlight, warmth, and moisture to germinate and grow. Mulches prevent light from reaching weed seeds, thus preventing their germination and growth. Mulch also helps keep soil moist and helps reduce water evaporation. Many mulches also reduce soil temperature.

The two broad categories of mulch to choose between are organic or inorganic.

organic mulches, such as compost and straw, gradually decompose, adding humus to the soil and improving its structure. They also moderate soil temperature extremes. Before

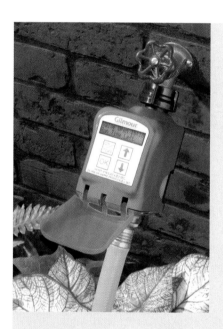

To prevent overwatering, control hose-end sprinklers with a battery-powered, programmable timer.

WAYS TO USE LESS WATER

Water is a limited resource everywhere. Although the eastern half of the United States typically receives enough precipitation to replenish reservoirs, droughts do occur, and some regions have suffered extended droughts in recent years. Similarly, most low-elevation areas of the western United States have low rainfall rates and a long dry season. Although the overall water supply remains virtually fixed, ever more people are putting demands on it. Thus, conserving water is, or should be, a concern everywhere. Here are a few tips for water-wise gardening.

USE WATER-CONSERVING PLANTS Some plants need a lot of water to survive, while others perform better with less. You can find water-thrifty trees, shrubs, flowering plants, ground covers, and even some grasses for your garden. Some provide seasonal color, others year-round green. The key is to choose plants that are well adapted to the natural conditions of your region.

GROUP PLANTS WISELY Place thirsty ones together and drought-resistant plants elsewhere.

Put plants that need regular watering on a separate irrigation system and schedule.

LIMIT TURF AREAS A lawn requires more irrigation than almost any other landscape feature. Limit its size to just what you need for your purposes, and choose a grass or grass mix adapted to your climate (see page 339). Consider replacing at least part of your lawn with hardscape materials or alternative plants.

IRRIGATE EFFICIENTLY Make sure your watering practices, schedules, and devices use water as efficiently as possible.

IMPROVE THE SOIL Routinely cultivate your soil and incorporate organic matter. Doing so will improve the soil's ability to resist evaporation and retain moisture.

MULCH Place a layer of organic or mineral mulch material over soil and around plants. Mulch will significantly reduce the amount of moisture lost by reducing evaporation. It also discourages weeds and slows erosion.

MAINTAIN YOUR GARDEN Repair faucets so they don't drip. Water plants only when needed, not by the clock or calendar. Avoid runoff, which wastes water.

CONTROL WEEDS These garden intruders consume water needed by more desirable plants.

Mulch of black plastic conserves moisture and prevents weed growth.

Use a drip emitter to deliver water at a precise rate and to a specific place.

Weed-free straw makes an excellent and attractive mulch.

applying an organic mulch, clear existing weeds from the soil, as those that are already established can likely grow right through the mulch. Use a 2- to 4-inch-thick layer on paths and around plants, but take care not to cover the plants' crowns. Too much moisture near the crown will rot many plants.

gravel, river rock, and other kinds of stones make permanent mulches that can suppress weeds effectively, as long as you install them over weed-free soil to begin with. Many gardeners place a weed-blocking landscape fabric (see below) under gravel.

black plastic is available in rolls and is used primarily in vegetable gardens. Besides preventing weed growth, it speeds the growth of heat-loving plants like melons, squash, and pumpkins. Prepare the soil for planting and place a soil-soaking hose or drip lines, or prepare furrows. Place the plastic over the soil and cut slits in it where you want to plant seeds or transplants. You'll need to remove and dispose of the plastic at the end of the growing season because by then it usually will have degraded too much to be used again.

landscape fabrics are made of woven polypropylene, spun-bonded polyethylene, or a combination of other synthetic materials. Unlike plastic sheeting, they are porous and allow air and water to reach the soil. Density

Spread landscape fabric or mulch over the planting area and secure corners and sides with wire staples or soil.

Use a knife to cut openings; tuck flaps back around plants.

and porosity vary, and denser fabrics are better for suppressing weeds.

Landscape fabrics are available in various widths and lengths. They're best used in permanent plantings around trees and shrubs. Install them around existing plants or cut slits in them to accommodate new plants.

Before you install a landscape fabric, eliminate existing weeds. Unroll the fabric and estimate where to cut it. Overlap seams by at least 3 inches to avoid gaps that weeds can penetrate. Secure the outer edges of the fabric with plastic pegs, large nails, or heavy wire staples.

After installation, cover the fabric with 2 to 3 inches of mulch, such as bark chips, or with a layer of pea gravel or stone mulch. The mulch will protect the fabric against degradation caused by ultraviolet light and improve its appearance.

composting

Composting is a natural process that converts raw organic materials into a valuable soil conditioner. Use it to improve a soil's texture, boost its nutrient content, and make it more water retentive. Besides benefiting the garden, composting lightens the load at the landfill, as you recycle garden debris at home rather than consign it to the dump.

A pile of leaves, branches, and other garden trimmings will eventually decompose with no intervention on your part. This type of composting is called slow or cold composting. With a little effort, however, you can speed up the process. If you create optimum conditions for the organisms responsible for decay by giving them the mixture of air, water, and carbon- and nitrogen-rich nutrients they need, the compost pile will heat up quickly and decompose in a few months. Hot composting also destroys many (though not all) weeds and disease pathogens.

You can make compost in a freestanding pile, as shown in the photo on the facing page, but using some sort of an enclosure is neater and more space efficient.

assemble materials You will need approximately equal amounts, by volume, of brown and green matter. Brown matter is high in carbon and includes dry leaves, hay, sawdust, straw, wood chips, and woody prunings. Green matter, which has more nitrogen, includes grass clippings, fruit and vegetable scraps, coffee grounds, tea bags, and manures. The compost will heat up faster if you collect all the ingredients in advance and assemble the pile all at once. Don't put in bones, cat or dog waste, dairy products, scraps of meat, badly diseased or insect-infested plants, or weeds that might survive composting.

chop materials Shredding or chopping branches and stems into smaller pieces allows decay-producing organisms to reach more surfaces and thus speeds up the composting process. Shredder-chippers and lawn mowers are useful for this purpose. Shred dry leaves by gathering them into low piles and running a lawn mower over them several times.

build the pile Building a compost pile is like making a layer cake. Start by spreading a 4- to 8-inch layer of brown material over an area at least 3 feet square. Then add a layer of green material about 2 to 8 inches deep. Make layers of grass clippings no more than 2 inches deep, but those of less dense green materials can be thicker. Add another layer of brown material and sprinkle the pile with

TEA TIME FOR PLANTS

One of the best liquid fertilizers is a simple brew that you can easily make yourself: compost tea. Not only does it provide balanced nutrition for plants, but evidence suggests that it can also help prevent plant diseases. All you need are a bucket, some cheesecloth, and compost. If you don't have access to a fresh supply, a high-quality bagged compost from a nursery will work.

To make the tea, fill the bucket about one-third of the way with compost. Add water to fill the bucket, then let the mixture steep for three to four days. Strain the mixture through cheesecloth. Return the remaining solids to your compost bin or add them to the potting mix in one of your containers.

Before using the brew, dilute it until it reaches the color of weak tea. Apply it as you would any liquid fertilizer. To use compost tea as a foliar feed (see page 398), add $1/8$ teaspoon vegetable oil or mild dishwashing liquid to each gallon of tea. This will help the solution adhere to plants' foliage. One caution: strong sunlight can damage the wet leaves, so do your spraying in the morning or on an overcast day.

When a variety of garden debris is available all at once, build a freestanding compost pile by alternating green and brown materials.

water. Continue adding layers, watering, and mixing. To heat up efficiently, the pile should be about 4 feet wide and 3 feet tall, giving it a volume of about 1 cubic yard.

turn the pile In a few days, the pile should have heated up dramatically. In time, it will decompose on its own, but you can hurry the process along by turning the contents to introduce more oxygen, which is needed by the decomposition organisms. Use a spading fork or pitchfork, restack the pile, redistributing it so that the materials originally on the outside are moved to the center, where they'll be exposed to higher heat. Add water if necessary to keep the pile moist, like a

wrung-out sponge. Turn the pile weekly, if possible, until it is no longer generating internal heat.

use the compost Finished compost is dark and crumbly, with a pleasant, earthy aroma. Mix it into your planting beds or use it as a mulch. If some of the material from the pile's exterior is still coarser than you prefer for either a soil amendment or mulch, compost it a second time. And to produce fine textured compost that you can use as potting soil for containers or for starting seeds, sift the finished material through a screen with a ½-inch mesh.

composting systems

In addition to making compost in a free-standing pile, you can use a homemade structure or purchase a manufactured composter.

wire cylinders Use welded wire or chicken wire, supporting it with stakes if necessary. The cylinder or hoop should be about 4 feet in diameter and 3 to 4 feet tall. To turn the pile, lift the cylinder, move it to one side, then fork the materials back into it.

manufactured composters These include tumblers, which make it easier to turn materials and produce finished compost quickly. Most are turned with a crank, but some roll on the ground.

Manufactured compost bins that you regularly add to and rarely turn are practical for many gardens. Remove finished compost through an opening at the base.

LOWE'S QUICK TIP

Three-bin compost systems are very flexible. One bin holds new green and brown material, the center one contains partly decomposed compost, and the third bin holds compost nearly ready to use. The bin for nearly finished compost will be empty for a few weeks at the start. For a picture of a three-bin compost system and construction details, see page 262.

Compost bins with tops that close and keep pests out are suitable for kitchen scraps. Add only yard waste to open bins.

WIRE CYLINDER

TUMBLER

STATIC BIN

a guide to fertilizers
WHEN, HOW, AND HOW MUCH

WHEN PLANTS ARE ACTIVELY GROWING, THEY NEED A STEADY SUPPLY OF NUTRIENTS. THOUGH MANY of these are present in soil, water, and air, gardeners need to supply others. Most likely to require supplemental feeding are fast-growing annuals such as vegetables and flowers, lawns, perennials, fruit trees, and immature plants of numerous kinds. Mature trees and shrubs, on the other hand, may need little or no fertilizing.

Knowing what to supply, in what quantities, and when begins with understanding the nutrients plants need, when, and why.

Plants' needs often change during the season. And at any given time, a plant may need more of one nutrient, such as phosphorus, than others. The trick is to give them just the right amount, in order to maintain a nutrient balance in the soil. Too much phosphorus, for example, causes something else (perhaps nitrogen) to be in short supply.

what's in fertilizer

Every fertilizer label states the percentage, by weight, of the three macronutrients in this order: nitrogen (N), phosphorus (P), and potassium (K). This is called the fertilizer's grade. A fertilizer labeled 10-8-6 contains 10 percent nitrogen, 8 percent phosphorus, and 6 percent potassium. The label also tells you the source of each nutrient.

nitrogen may be included in a fertilizer in nitrate form, which is water soluble and fast acting. But it also washes out of the soil readily and so can pollute surface and ground water if used to excess. Nitrogen in the form of ammonium may have organic, synthetic, or both origins. This form is released more slowly and lasts longer in the soil.

phosphorus is expressed on product labels as phosphate, P_2O_5, and listed as "available phosphoric acid."

potassium is noted on fertilizer labels as potassium oxide, or K_2O. Also called potash, it is described in various ways, including "available phosphate" and "water-soluble potash." Phosphorus and potassium do not move readily through the soil in solution and must be applied near plant roots to do the most good.

ORGANIC, INCOMPLETE

ORGANIC, COMPLETE

INORGANIC, COMPLETE

ORGANIC BASE, COMPLETE

In some coastal areas, runoff has caused serious pollution. Inland, the water quality of lakes and streams also suffers when garden runoff contains residue from chemical fertilizers and pesticides. Here are some things you can do to curb such runoff.

GARDEN SMART Don't apply any chemicals to your garden when rain is likely. You can easily miss your intended target, and instead the chemicals will wash off into storm drains. In addition, avoid overwatering plants before and after you apply chemicals. Never dispose of lawn or garden chemicals in the storm drain or trash, and bag or compost yard waste so it won't clog drains.

USE PERMEABLE PAVING Gravel and permeable concrete allow rainwater through into the soil, which acts as a filter. Impermeable surfaces simply move along rainwater or excess irrigation water to storm drains.

INSTALL AN INFILTRATION SYSTEM In some coastal communities, local ordinances require new building sites to include an infiltration pit or other subsurface runoff-retention system. These may be underground tanks or chambers that are connected to downspouts. They can be installed about 5 feet beneath a driveway or lawn. Before putting in new landscaping near the coast, check local ordinances, or consult a structural engineer or geologist about installing such a system.

kinds of fertilizers

simple versus complete Complete fertilizers contain all three macronutrients: nitrogen (N), phosphorus (P), and potassium (K). Some may also include secondary and/or micronutrients, which are also listed on the label. Simple fertilizers supply just one macronutrient. Most familiar are the types that contain only nitrogen, such as ammonium sulfate (21-0-0), and phosphorus-only superphosphate (0-20-0). Between complete and simple types are incomplete fertilizers. An example is 0-10-10, which provides only phosphorus and potassium.

general-purpose and special-purpose The various fertilizers labeled "general-purpose" or "all-purpose" usually contain equal or nearly equal amounts of the macronutrients N, P, and K, such as a 10-10-10 formulation. They are intended to meet most plants' requirements throughout the growing season. Other formulas are designed to meet specific needs. For instance, high-nitrogen blends (such as 29-3-4) help keep lawns green and growing quickly, while higher-phosphorus mixes (6-10-4, for instance) are intended to promote flowering and fruiting. Some packaged fertilizers are formulated for specific

INORGANIC, COMPLETE

types of plants. Those designed for acid lovers such as camellias, rhododendrons, and azaleas are especially useful, as are fertilizers for citrus and roses.

Use a hand-cranked spreader to scatter fertilizer granules, and a cultivator to work them into soil.

types of fertilizer

inorganic fertilizers are made from synthetic substances with concentrated amounts of specific nutrients, primarily nitrogen, phosphorus, and potassium. When you apply an inorganic fertilizer, you see almost instant results because the nutrients are immediately available to your plants.

organic fertilizers are made from the remains or by-products of living or once living organisms. Manure, fish emulsion, bone meal, and kelp meal are all examples of organic fertilizers that can be used alone or in various combinations. They release their nutrients more slowly than inorganic fertilizers. Many manufacturers combine several natural fertilizers to produce a complete fertilizer.

dry fertilizers may be powders, granules, or pellets that are designed to be spread on the ground or scratched or dug into the soil. Controlled-release types may be bead-like granules, spikes, or tablets. Dig granules into the soil at planting time or scratch them into the surface of the soil (they're especially useful for containers). Use a mallet to pound spikes into the ground, and place tablets at the bottom of planting holes.

liquid fertilizers are sold as water-soluble crystals or granules, or as liquid concentrates that you mix with water and apply with a hose, watering can, or spray bottle. The spray types, known as foliar feeds, are generally used to deliver instant supplies of specific nutrients. Liquid fertilizers must be reapplied frequently, as their nutrients leach through the root zone rapidly.

To avoid burning leaves, water plants thoroughly before spraying them, follow label directions, and don't apply fertilizer if outdoor temperatures rise above 85 degrees F.

LOWE'S QUICK TIPS

- Wait two to three weeks after planting to apply liquid fertilizers.
- Controlled-release fertilizers are more convenient and less polluting than others.
- Organic fertilizers improve soil structure as they release nutrients.

Apply dry fertilizers over the root area and use a cultivator or water it into soil. Be careful not to damage surface roots.

Use a spading fork to work a dry granular fertilizer deep into a new garden bed where nutrients will do the most good. Water afterward.

applying fertilizer

Use a spading fork to work a dry granular fertilizer into a new garden bed. This technique puts phosphorus and potassium at a level where they can interact with the soil and eventually be absorbed by plant roots, which are several inches below the soil surface. Water thoroughly after incorporating the fertilizer but avoid overwatering.

With a cultivator, scratch the soil beneath plants, as roots are close to the surface. Water thoroughly after application. Because roots may extend several feet beyond the drip line, you'll need to spread fertilizer out wide enough to reach all the roots.

The simplest way to apply liquid fertilizers is with a watering can. You can also use an injector device to run the fertilizer through your hose or watering system. The simplest kind connects between your faucet and hose, draws concentrated fertilizer from a bucket, and injects it into your hose.

fertilizer selection guide

This table describes several common natural and chemical fertilizers. The N-P-K ratios listed are typical, but they vary widely according to specific sources and manufacturers. In general, fertilizers formulated for lawns and other plants grown for their leaves have relatively higher nitrogen levels, while fertilizers that maximize flowering and fruiting have higher phosphorus.

When you shop, you'll also see specialty fertilizers formulated for specific plants, such as roses, fruits, vegetables, and lawns. While these fertilizers are not necessarily unique, the directions on the label are specific to the featured plants, so they're more useful for those plants than are the directions on a general-purpose fertilizer.

organic

FERTILIZER TYPE	Blood meal	Cotton seed meal	Fish emulsion	Fish pellets
N-P-K RATIO	13-0-0	6-2-1	5-1-1	8-5-1
BENEFITS, USES	Good source of nitrogen in both soluble and insoluble forms. Scratch it into the soil around plants. Store away from cats and dogs.	Acidifies soil as it fertilizes, so is useful where soils are commonly alkaline and for plants, such as azaleas.	Acts fairly quickly and gently. Excellent for container plants and leafy vegetables. Fishy odor can attract cats and raccoons.	Blend the pellets into the soil of vegetable beds at planting time. Fish odor can attract animals.

inorganic

FERTILIZER TYPE	Liquid (including water-soluble crystals)	Solid granules or pellets (above) or spikes (right)
N-P-K RATIO	Varies; 20-20-20 is common	10-10-10 (all purpose); 6-10-4 (flowers); 29-3-4 (lawns); 10-20-20 (vegetables)
BENEFITS, USES	Works well for most kinds of plants but requires frequent application.	Generally more nutrient per pound of fertilizer than organic fertilizers and often tailored to benefit specific types of plants.

pruning
KEEP PLANTS HEALTHY AND GOOD-LOOKING

IN A WELL-PLANNED, WELL-PRUNED GARDEN, YOU'RE RARELY AWARE OF PRUNING. TREES AND SHRUBS grow in perfect proportion to each other, complementing your house and other structures rather than overwhelming them. In fact, most people notice pruning only when it's done badly.

This section discusses how and when branches grow—information that is the basis of how and when to prune. For more about pruning trees, see page 309; for shrubs, see page 319; for vines, see page 329; for perennials, see page 347; and for roses, see page 355.

why prune?

If you choose the right plant for the right location and give it plenty of room to expand, you probably won't need to prune too often. You may have to cut back a few stems or branches now and then as the plant matures, but pruning won't be a major task.

Sometimes, however, circumstances make pruning necessary. A tree's branches may block your view as you back out of your driveway, creating a safety hazard. Or you may move into a house with a garden so woefully neglected that it has turned into a jungle. These and several other key reasons to prune are listed here.

for safety Remove low-growing branches if they impede passing vehicles or obscure oncoming traffic from view. You may also need to take out split or broken branches before they come crashing down on a person, car, or building. It's also wise to prune out low-hanging whiplike branches (especially those with thorns) that may strike passersby.

to rejuvenate growth Neglected, overgrown shrubs can sometimes be turned into small multitrunk trees if you remove their lower limbs. This may be a better approach than digging out the shrub and planting another in its place.

to redirect growth Pruning influences the direction in which a plant grows. Each time you make a cut, you stop growth in one direction and encourage it in another. This principle is important to keep in mind when you train young trees to develop a strong branching structure.

to remove undesirable growth Prune out unwanted growth periodically. Cut out wayward branches, as well as thin, twiggy growth that's too dense, and remove suckers (stems growing up from the roots) and water

Generally, trees, shrubs, and vines need pruning to look and flower their best. Make most pruning cuts just above a leaf bud, as shown here.

sprouts, those vigorous shoots that grow straight up from the trunk and main branches.

to promote plant health Maximize the health and vigor of trees and shrubs by removing branches that are diseased, dead, pest-ridden, or rubbing together.

to shape You can prune a line of closely planted trees or shrubs as a unit to create a hedge. If you're a hobbyist who practices topiary, you can prune trees and shrubs into fanciful shapes.

to promote flowers or fruits Flowering plants and some fruit trees are pruned to increase the yield of blossoms and fruit and to improve their quality. For example, you'll need to remove spent flowers from roses throughout their bloom time. For some fruit trees, you'll make many small, precise cuts each dormant season. Although this sort of pruning sometimes ranks as a tedious chore, remember that your efforts will pay off in lavish bloom and generous crops of fruit at harvest time.

when to prune

Learning when to prune a particular plant is as important as knowing how to do the actual job. The timing is easier to understand if you know a little about plant metabolism. Most plants produce new leaves and stem growth from spring through midsummer. Photosynthesis proceeds most intensively during this time, producing food for the plant in the form of sugars.

As full summer heat sets in, the sugars are gradually transferred to the plant's woody parts and its roots, where they're stored during the winter dormant period. When spring arrives, the stored sugars are used to start new growth. Pruning is timed to harmonize with this cycle. It is typically done either late in dormancy or during summer. For some plants, a combination of both late-dormancy and summer pruning often yields the best results.

Note that these guidelines are most pertinent in climates with four distinct seasons and definite winter chill. In warmer-winter

remove dead and damaged branches

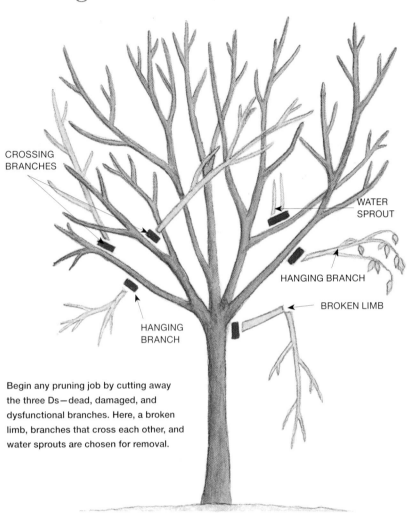

CROSSING BRANCHES

WATER SPROUT

HANGING BRANCH

BROKEN LIMB

HANGING BRANCH

Begin any pruning job by cutting away the three Ds—dead, damaged, and dysfunctional branches. Here, a broken limb, branches that cross each other, and water sprouts are chosen for removal.

areas, optimum timing will vary depending on the particular plant's native climate. If you have any reservations about the best time to prune a particular plant, ask a Lowe's sales associate or your cooperative extension office for advice.

pruning in late dormancy Many plants, especially deciduous trees and shrubs, are best pruned in late winter, or early spring just before they break dormancy. In early spring, heavy frosts have abated, so the plants are less likely to suffer cold damage at the point where you make your cuts. Sugars are stored in larger branches, trunks, and roots, so little of the plant's energy reserves will be lost to pruning. Deciduous plants are still bare, so

1 PRUNE CRAPE MYRTLES In the late dormant season. This one has too much twiggy growth.

2 THIN OUT twiggy growth, and leave one or two shoots at the end of each limb.

3 IN SUMMER, remove branches that are too weak to support heavy flower clusters.

you can easily spot broken and awkwardly growing branches and decide how to direct growth. And because growth will start soon, your pruning cuts will stimulate new growth in the direction you want.

For flowering trees and shrubs, determine whether flowers are produced on old or new growth. If early spring flowers come on last year's growth—as in the case of forsythia, flowering quince (*Chaenomeles*), and flowering trees such as peach and plum (*Prunus*)—wait until flowering has finished before pruning. Otherwise you'll lose many flowers. But plants like cinquefoil (*Potentilla*) that bear flowers on leafy new growth formed in spring can safely be pruned while dormant.

pruning in summer A second time to prune is in late summer, when sugars needed for the next year's growth are moving into large limbs, trunks, and roots and will not be seriously depleted by pruning. Some gardeners like to thin plants in summer because it's easier to see how much thinning is really needed when branches are still thickly foliaged. And because growth is slower at this time of year, pruning is less likely to stimulate new growth—an advantage when you're thinning. In cold-winter regions, don't do summer pruning later than one month before the first frost. If you do, an early frost may damage the plant at the point of the cuts.

pruning evergreens

Although evergreen trees and shrubs don't drop their leaves, they approach a near-dormant state during winter. The group includes broadleaf evergreens, such as boxwood and camellia, and conifers, among them spruce and pine.

ANVIL-CUT SHEARS

SCISSOR-CUT SHEARS

Broadleaf evergreens are usually best pruned in late dormancy or in summer, as outlined above. For flowering broadleaf evergreens, however, timing is a bit more precise, as you'll need to prune with an eye toward preserving flower buds. Prune broadleaf evergreens that bloom in early spring after spring flowers fade; prune those that flower in late spring or summer in late winter, before spring growth begins.

Most conifers are pruned only in their first two or three years in order to direct their basic shape. From then on, they're best left alone. Some of the most badly botched pruning you'll see is on conifers that have been pruned too severely, usually to keep them confined to a too-small location—although a few conifers, including arborvitae (*Platycladus* and *Thuja*), yew (*Taxus*), and hemlock (*Tsuga*), lend themselves to shearing into hedges. When you do need to prune a conifer, the timing will depend on whether the plant is a whorl-branching or random-branching type.

In whorl-branching conifers, the branches radiate out from the trunk in whorls. Mem-

bers of this group include fir (*Abies*), spruce (*Picea*), and pine (*Pinus*). These trees produce all their new growth in spring. Buds appear at the tips of new shoots as well as along their length and at their bases. On pines, the new shoots are called candles because that's what they look like before the needles open out.

Shorten new spring growth to control the size and shape of whorl-branching conifers, such as this pine.

Prune whorl-branching conifers in early spring. Pinch or cut anywhere along the new growth, being sure to do so while shoots are still new and soft, to induce branching. When the tree is still relatively small, you can nip back the pliant new growth of the leader (the central upward-growing stem) and

all side branches to make a denser, bushier plant. However, if you cut into an older stem, even at a point where it bears foliage, no new growth will sprout from below the cut.

Unlike whorl-branching sorts, random-branching conifers have branches that grow randomly along the trunk. These plants do not limit their new growth to spring but instead grow in spurts throughout the growing season. Trees of this type include cedar (*Cedrus*), cypress (*Cupressus*), dawn redwood (*Metasequoia*), redwood (*Sequoia*), giant sequoia (*Sequoiadendron*), bald cypress (*Taxodium*), and hemlock (*Tsuga*). Prune these as you would deciduous and broadleaf

REMOVING A BRANCH

It is essential to avoid ripping the bark on the main trunk of a tree when removing a heavy limb. The key is to shorten the branch to a stub before cutting it off close to the trunk. Use a sharp pruning saw and make three cuts as described below:

1. About a foot from the branch base, make a cut from the underside approximately a third of the way through.

2. About an inch farther out, cut through the top of the branch until it breaks off. The branch should separate cleanly between the two cuts.

3. Make the final cut by placing the saw beside the branch bark ridge and cutting downward just outside the branch collar. If the branch angle is very narrow, cut upward from the bottom to avoid cutting into the branch collar.

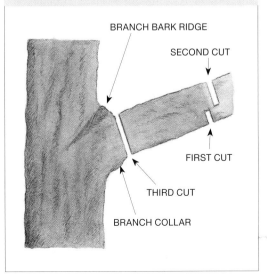

BRANCH BARK RIDGE

SECOND CUT

FIRST CUT

THIRD CUT

BRANCH COLLAR

growth buds on a branch

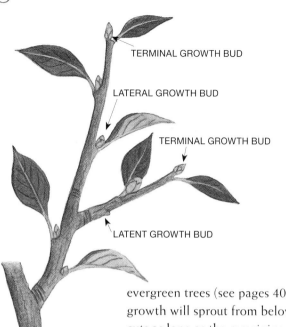

TERMINAL GROWTH BUD

LATERAL GROWTH BUD

TERMINAL GROWTH BUD

LATENT GROWTH BUD

cutting above the bud

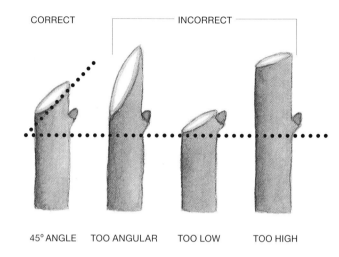

CORRECT

INCORRECT

45° ANGLE   TOO ANGULAR   TOO LOW   TOO HIGH

evergreen trees (see pages 402–403). New growth will sprout from below the pruning cuts as long as the remaining branch bears some foliage. In general, no new growth will develop from bare branches, though hemlock is an exception. It's best to prune random-branching conifers right before new growth begins in spring.

growth buds

Pruning makes sense when you understand the roles and locations of growth buds. Select the bud you want to keep, then cut just beyond it. The resulting growth will vary depending on the bud. If your pruning is to have the effect you want, you'll need to learn to recognize three different kinds of growth buds.

A terminal bud grows at the tip of a shoot and causes the shoot to grow longer. These buds produce hormones that move downward along the shoot, inhibiting the growth of other buds on that shoot.

Lateral buds grow along the sides of a shoot and give rise to the sideways growth that makes a plant bushy. These buds stay dormant until the shoot has grown long enough to diminish the influence of the hormones produced in the terminal bud, or until that terminal bud is removed, at which point they grow. When you remove lateral buds, growth is directed to the terminal bud. The shoot will lengthen and tend to grow upward.

Latent buds lie dormant beneath the bark. If a branch breaks or is cut off above a latent bud, the bud may develop a new shoot to replace the wood that has been removed. If you need to repair a damaged plant, look for a latent bud and cut above it.

BOW SAW

HEDGE SHEARS

LOPPERS

pruning cuts

There are four basic pruning cuts, each aimed at producing a different effect. For all cuts except shearing that involve cutting above a growth bud, make your cut as shown on the facing page. Angle it at about 45 degrees, with the lowest point of the cut opposite the bud but even with it, and the highest point about ¼ inch above the bud.

ELECTRIC HEDGE SHEARS

pinching is the most basic pruning cut, used primarily on annuals and perennials. Use your thumb and forefinger or a pair of shears to nip off the tips of new growth. Pinching side shoots causes stems to lengthen; removing terminal growth causes side shoots to grow.

thinning is the most common pruning cut. It opens up a plant and stimulates minimal regrowth. Remove an entire stem or branch, taking it back to its point of origin, which in most cases is its junction with another branch. In the case of plants that send up stems directly from the roots, cut it all the way to the ground. When removing one branch at a junction, be sure the remaining one is at least one-third the diameter of the branch being removed.

THINNING

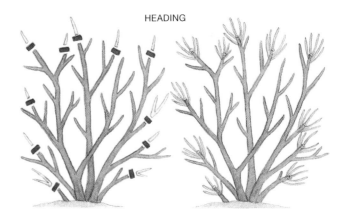

HEADING

heading removes a stem or branch back to a bud or to a twig or branch too small to take over the terminal role. Heading stimulates the growth of lateral buds just below the cut, producing clusters of shoots.

For maintenance pruning of most trees and shrubs, heading is less desirable than thinning. Though it may initially make a plant more compact, heading promotes vigorous growth from lateral buds, eventually ruining the natural shape of the plant. Use heading to force branching at a specific point, to fill a hole in the crown of a tree, or to increase blooms of a flowering shrub.

SHEARING

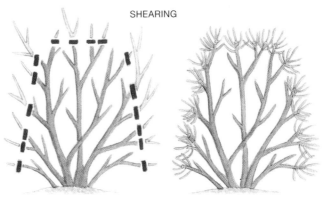

shearing is an indiscriminate form of heading that involves clipping a plant's outer foliage to create an even surface or specific shape. The plants best suited to shearing have main and lateral branches bearing closely spaced buds, so almost every cut ends up near a growing point.

lawn care

WATERING, MOWING, AND FERTILIZING

THE KEY TO GROWING A GREAT LAWN—ONE THAT IS DENSE, IS EVENLY GREEN, AND HAS FEW PESTS OR weeds—is not doing just one thing perfectly. It's doing several things pretty well. A great lawn results from proper watering, fertilizing, mowing, and aerating. And that's assuming you've planted a type of grass that's well adapted to your area (for more about choosing the right grass, see pages 338–345). Assuming you have a reasonably healthy lawn to start with, here's how to keep it beautiful.

watering

In general, warm-season grasses require less water than cool-season types; tall fescue needs the least among the cool-season kinds. On average, however, most grasses need 1 to 2 inches of water per week, whether from rainfall, irrigation, or both. To encourage roots to grow deep, water infrequently, providing the 1 to 2 inches all in one go. If you simply sprinkle on a little water each day, the roots will stay near the surface. If there is then a prolonged dry spell or if you forget to water, the root system will not be able to draw enough water from deeper in the soil to survive.

Watering too frequently can cause problems, just as can watering too much. Both waste nutrients by washing them from the soil, and the perpetually moist conditions can promote disease.

After watering, let the top inch or two of soil dry before watering again. To check, probe the soil with a thick piece of wire or a long screwdriver. The tool will move easily through moist soil and stop when it reaches dry soil. You can also use a soil-sampling tube (see page 389). An even faster way to determine whether a lawn needs watering is simply to walk across it. If the lawn has enough water, the grass under your footsteps will spring right back. But if your footprints remain clearly visible for several minutes, it's a sure sign that it's time to water.

Water in the morning, when there's less water lost to evaporation and when wind is less likely to blow water away. If you need to water later in the day, do so well before dusk so the grass will dry before nightfall. Grass that stays damp for long periods is typically more susceptible to disease.

watering efficiently

Most lawns use relatively more water than other plants, largely because they have shallow root systems that dry out quickly. For

A smaller lawn requires less water and fertilizer, and less of your time mowing. Savings compound if you choose a drought-tolerant, low-maintenance grass.

Portable sprinklers are convenient if you live where lawns need supplemental watering only occasionally.

Where rain does not reliably sustain lawn growth, an underground sprinkler system is essential. Maximum efficiency is achieved through proper operation and maintenance.

that reason, and because in many areas water resources are stretched thin, it's important to get all the benefit possible out of the water you use. Here are the key considerations.

eliminate runoff Adjust sprinkler spray patterns so water isn't wasted irrigating paved surfaces. If your sprinkler system showers water over a sidewalk, patio, or driveway, replace the heads with models that deliver water only where it is needed. If necessary, redesign the system. Sloping land and heavy clay soils both invite runoff, because of gravity in the first case and slow water penetration in the second. To avoid runoff in such situations, adjust the rate at which water is applied. If you use sprinklers, you can improve penetration by watering in successive short intervals, giving the water time to soak in between sprinklings. On slopes, use terraces and basins to help prevent runoff.

irrigate slowly Slow soaking limits runoff and encourages plants to develop deep root systems that are better able to tolerate drought. The heavier your soil, the more important slow soaking is in preventing runoff. Using an oscillating sprinkler to water large areas helps reduce runoff. But if you see puddling, turn the water off for an hour, then start again. To minimize evaporation, irrigate in the early morning or evening.

You can also upgrade an existing underground sprinkler system by simply replacing older sprinkler heads with new, low-volume kinds that apply water more slowly.

use timers With the simplest timers, you set the dial for how long you want the water to run, then turn on the water. The timer turns the faucet off for you. More sophisticated timers operate on batteries or household current. You set them to a schedule, and they turn the water on and off as programmed. Such timers ensure that your garden will be watered whether you're at home or away. What's more, you can select a schedule that will give your lawn the precise amount of water it needs to thrive.

A weakness of automatic controllers is that they follow the set schedule regardless of the weather. They'll turn on the water during a deluge or apply amounts appropriate for hot summer weather on a cool fall day. To solve this problem, reset the controller seasonally, taking rainfall and weather conditions into account. Or use electronic attachments that function as weather sensors. By linking a soil moisture sensor to the controller, for example, you can trigger the sprinklers to switch on only when the sensor indicates that soil moisture has dropped to the point where water is needed. Another useful attachment is a rain shutoff device. It accumulates rainwater in a collector pan, turns off the controller when the pan is filled to a prescribed depth, and triggers it to resume watering when the collected water has evaporated. But before

Little noise and no fumes are the key virtues of electric mowers.

installing either of these sensors, first check to ensure that they are compatible with your automatic controller.

mowing

A simple secret to maintaining a healthy lawn is to mow high and mow often.

Mowing high produces a stronger, healthier grass that has deeper roots and fewer pest problems. The ideal height of specific lawn grasses varies, but most lawns are best mowed to 1½ to 3½ inches high. Maintain this height by mowing off as little as is practical with each pass. The rule is to cut no

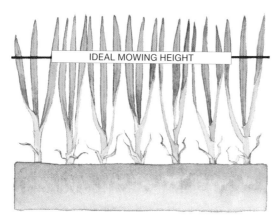

IDEAL MOWING HEIGHT

Aim to cut off no more than the top third of grass blades with each mowing, as removing more than that slows regrowth. Leave clippings on the lawn.

more than one-third the height. That means frequent mowing when the lawn is growing fastest. And when you mow, don't collect the clippings unless you must. Leaving them to melt back into the lawn returns useful nutrients, cutting the amount of fertilizer the lawn needs by about a third.

Warm-season grasses grow fastest in hot weather, cool-season grasses in spring. At the peak of the growing season, mowing may be needed more than once a week. At other times of the year, every two weeks or even once a month may be enough. Mow cool-season grasses highest during hot weather.

Here are the recommended mowing heights for common lawn grasses:

- Creeping bent grass: 1 inch
- Blue grama grass: 4 inches
- Buffalo grass: 4 inches
- Hybrid bermuda: 1 inch
- Centipede grass: 2 inches
- Tall fescue: 3 inches
- Fine fescue: 2½ inches
- Perennial ryegrass: 2 inches
- Bahia grass: 3 inches
- Seashore paspalum: 1 inch
- Kentucky bluegrass: 3 inches
- St. Augustine grass: 2 inches
- Zoysia: 2 inches

lawn mowers Push-type reel mowers were once the only type of mower sold. The original models were cumbersome, and their popularity declined with the advent of self-propelled gasoline and electric mowers, which are easier to use. You just walk along behind them, guiding their direction. Older gas mowers, like car engines, require regular maintenance, can be fussy about starting, and spew fumes into the air. Older electric mowers, though fume-free, can cause problems too. You need to have an outdoor electrical receptacle and, to mow a large lawn, a very long cord.

In recent years, all types of lawn mowers have been improved significantly. The new push-types, suitable for small to medium-size lawns, are more compact and lighter in weight than their predecessors, and many can easily be carried in one hand. Their blades cut cleaner and stay sharper longer than those of self-propelled mowers. Most models have either four or seven blades. A four-blade mower is a good choice for most home lawns, while a seven-blade model will cut a bent-grass lawn to putting-green perfection.

Electric mowers have also changed. They are still self-propelled and without the gas fumes or noise typical of other lawn mowers. Use of corded types is limited to 100 feet from an outlet. Battery-powered electric mowers carry sufficient charge to mow an average-size lawn on a single charge and are not restricted by a cord.

The most common lawn mowers have gasoline-powered engines. The newest kinds are cleaner, quieter, more efficient, and easier to operate than their predecessors. Most are self-propelled, some with a variable drive to accommodate your walking speed. There's a huge range of sizes available at your local Lowe's store, from walk-behind through riding, so finding one to match your lawn shouldn't be a problem.

Most gasoline and electric mowers include a mulching function that chops the cut grass blades into smaller pieces and deposits them back onto the lawn. While it's always a good idea to leave grass clippings on the lawn for their nutrients, mulching mowers produce a particularly neat look (because the clippings are so fine) and speed up the decomposition process.

Mower blades should be sharpened at least once a year, more frequently if the grass begins to look chewed rather than sharply cut. A sharp blade makes mowing easier, requires less power from the engine, and leaves the lawn looking more attractive.

GASOLINE-POWERED SELF-PROPELLED

PUSH-TYPE REEL MOWER

GASOLINE-POWERED WITH ELECTRIC START

STRING TRIMMER

edging a lawn can take as much time as mowing it. Concrete or brick mowing strips reduce the need for edging. For edging small areas, handheld shears are effective. For larger lawns, however, battery- or gas-powered trimmers are more efficient. But be careful using these for edging around large shrubs or trees. The nylon cord can easily cut into bark and damage it. They're also risky around annual and perennial beds. Angle the trimmer the wrong way for even a split second, and you will decapitate your plants.

fertilizing
To grow well, lawns need fertilizer. Without it, they'll grow poorly, if at

all, and primarily it will be the less desirable grasses and weeds that survive. Grass that is insufficiently nourished is also more susceptible to pests and diseases.

Fertilizing three to five times a year is sufficient for most lawns. If you're growing a cool-season grass, apply most fertilizer in fall. Make the final application at the same time as the final mowing of the year. Roots will be nourished, and the stored nutrients will give new growth a boost in spring. Depending on the lawn's overall health and growth, you may want to fertilize again in late spring or early summer. Fertilize warm-season grasses in spring after dormant lawns are revived and green, then again in July or August.

For any grass, use a fertilizer formulated specially for lawns, particularly one that releases nitrogen gradually. To make it easy, buy a product that includes application directions for the model spreader you have and apply the fertilizer at that setting.

To use a fertilizer for which there is no recommended spreader setting, apply about 5 pounds of 20-0-0 per 1,000 square feet at each application, or 10 pounds of 10-0-0, or 2½ pounds of 40-0-0. All of these amounts of fertilizer equal 1 pound of actual nitrogen per 1,000 square feet. If more than 50 percent of the fertilizer is slow-release, you can safely apply fertilizer at twice this rate.

A soil test is the best way to know if phosphorus and potassium are needed. Check with the local cooperative extension office about soil tests and these nutrients.

Some fertilizers are mixed with herbicides to kill existing weeds or to prevent weeds from growing in the lawn. Use these products with great care. They can certainly perform as advertised, but they can also damage the lawn and pollute local water systems if spilled or washed into the street.

To ensure even fertilizer distribution, use a spreader, as shown below. Uneven distribution often results in fertilizer burn or unevenly green grass.

solving lawn problems

The best way to solve many lawn problems is to prevent them in the first place, by watering, mowing, fertilizing, aerating, and dethatching (see page 412) regularly. Some of the most common problems are described in this section. If you're not sure what's causing the symptoms, ask for help at a Lowe's Garden Center, check with your cooperative extension office, or hire a professional to inspect your lawn and make an assessment. For more about products and remedies, see pages 414–425.

chemical spill or dog urine causes patches of dead grass. The remedy is to immediately drench the area with water; later rake away any dead grass. Fill in the bare patch with sod or by reseeding.

USING A DROP SPREADER

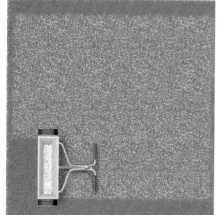

On each pass, overlap wheels to avoid gaps in coverage. To guarantee even coverage, cut the rate in half and cover the lawn twice, walking opposite directions.

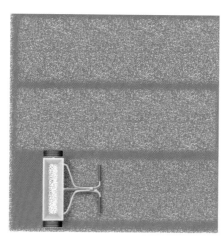

If you include wheels in swath width, unfertilized tracks will appear later as pale green stripes.

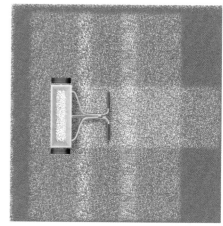

Avoid inadvertently covering the same area twice. Overdoses of fertilizer can cause uneven greening or dead grass.

CHEMICAL SPILL OR DOG URINE

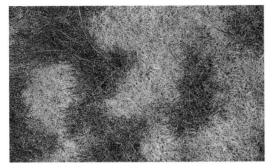
UNEVEN FERTILIZER APPLICATION

CHINCH BUGS

SOD WEBWORMS

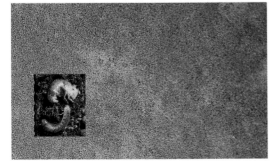
WHITE GRUBS

uneven fertilizer application can result in dead or yellow patches. Parts of the lawn that received the right amount of fertilizer turn dark green, areas that didn't get enough are pale green or yellow, and those that received too much fertilizer burn and turn brown. Remove the dead patches and water the area well. If the grass doesn't come back on its own, reseed or resod.

chinch bugs are ¼-inch-long gray-black insects that suck juices from grass blades. They cause brownish yellow patches in lawns, primarily in St. Augustine and zoysia grasses (and sometimes in bluegrass and creeping bent grass), especially in hot or drought-stressed conditions. To diagnose, sink an empty can (open at both ends) into the ground at the edge of a patch. Fill the can with water. If chinch bugs are present, they'll soon float to the surface. To minimize spread, keep the area well watered. Chemical controls include insecticidal soap, one of the pyrethroids, or trichlorfon.

sod webworms are small, hairless gray caterpillars—the larvae of tiny buff-colored moths that, if present, can be seen flying close to the lawn's surface in the evening. Sod webworms feed on grass blades. Symptoms are small dead patches of lawn that appear in spring and enlarge during summer. To diagnose, drench an area of lawn near the dead spots with a solution of 1 tablespoon liquid dishwashing detergent diluted in a gallon of water. The larvae will come to the surface. If you find more than 15 larvae in 1 square yard, treat the lawn.

If you don't want to use chemicals, you may be able to reduce the pest population by improving lawn care. Don't overwater or overfertilize, and do dethatch and aerate regularly (see page 412).

For chemical control, use *Bacillus thuringiensis*, insecticidal soap, a neem concentrate, a pyrethroid, or trichlorfon.

white grubs is a catchall name for the soil-dwelling larvae of various kinds of beetles, including June bugs, rose chafers, and Japanese beetles. The larvae of all these

lawn weeds

beetles feed on lawn roots. They're white with brown heads, and when exposed they curl up in a C shape. Signs of their presence include distinct, irregularly shaped brown patches in the lawn, usually in late summer. Because the roots have been eaten, the dead patches pull up easily. Remove a patch and dig into the soil. If you find more than one grub per square foot, treat the soil. Beneficial nematodes control many kinds of grubs. Chemical controls include trichlorfon and imidacloprid.

fairy rings are small to large circular patches of dark green grass surrounding areas of dead or light-colored grass. Mushrooms may or may not be present at the perimeter of the green area. The rings result from a fungal disease common in lawns growing in soil that's high in organic matter. To control the problem, aerate the soil, apply a nitrogen fertilizer formulated for lawn care, and keep the lawn wet for three to five days.

rust is a fungal disease. Among lawns, it affects primarily bluegrass and ryegrass. Grass blades turn yellowish to reddish brown throughout, small reddish pustules form in groups on older blades and stems, and the blades eventually die. The best solution for rust is to apply a nitrogen fertilizer formulated for lawn care, water regularly, and mow more frequently.

weeds

Weeds that infest the rest of your garden will also attempt to establish themselves in the lawn, and many are quite successful. A healthy, vigorous lawn isn't at high risk. It grows thick enough that it is difficult for weed seeds to reach soil, germinate, and take root. But if the lawn is in poor condition and patchy soil is exposed, weed infestation becomes more likely. Some warm-season grasses, particularly bermuda and zoysia, can

BERMUDA GRASS

DANDELION

QUACK GRASS

YELLOW OXALIS

themselves be weeds if accidentally introduced into a lawn of another type of grass. Other lawn weeds include common mallow, crabgrass, dandelion, oxalis, plantain, quack grass, and spotted spurge.

improving a poor lawn

Sufficient fertilizer and water plus weed control are the primary ways to improve a poor lawn. Aeration and thatch removal are two other techniques that are often useful. Thatch is the layer of dead grass, roots, and debris that accumulates between the soil surface and the green grass blades above. Once it forms a thick mat, water and air cannot reach the soil.

DETHATCHING RAKE

dethatching Almost every lawn needs dethatching approximately once a year or whenever the thatch reaches a thickness of ½ inch or more. Dethatch cool-season grasses in early fall, warm-season types in early spring.

If your lawn is small, use a dethatching rake (shown above). The sturdy, very sharp, crescent-shaped tines slice into the thatch, which you then rake up. For larger lawns, rent a dethatching machine. Similar in appearance to a large, heavy gas mower, it has knifelike blades that slice into the turf vertically. Make several crisscrossing passes to cut and loosen the thatch.

Dethatching machines have several settings. For most grasses, adjust the blades to a high setting and 3 inches apart. For tougher grasses, such as bermuda and zoysia, set the blades lower and about an inch apart.

aeration Punching holes into the lawn to allow water, air, and nutrients to more easily enter the soil is called *aeration*. Its primary function is to loosen compacted soil, and it's often needed for lawns growing in clay soils and those subjected to heavy foot traffic. Aeration also helps break up thatch. You can do the job more than once a year if necessary. If you aerate once annually, do it in fall for cool-season grasses and in spring for warm-season varieties.

lawn renovation

1 CHECK FOR THATCH. A thatch layer that's more than 1/2 inch thick is too much.

2 SLICE THROUGH and pull up thatch with a rake or machine to improve air circulation.

3 AERATE SOIL to create small holes that reduce soil compaction and make spaces favorable to new seeds.

4 RAKE UP and remove soil and debris brought to the surface by the dethatching and aerating processes.

5 SOW LAWN SEED over the aerated and dethatched lawn. Follow up with fertilizer, a light mulch, and water.

You can aerate soil with a hand tool. Press it into the soil with your foot, and then lift it out along with a 2-inch cylindrical plug of sod. Aerating by hand is certainly good exercise, but it is time consuming if you have a large lawn. For good-sized areas, a gas-powered aerator does the job faster. Rent one from a supply center that rents garden equipment.

After the lawn has been aerated, clear away the plugs and spread a layer of organic matter, such as compost or soil conditioner, over the lawn. Water the organic matter in, and it will seep into the holes left by the plugs, improving the soil's texture.

lawn renovation

If your lawn is in poor condition, improve basic care. Water, fertilize, and mow according to the guidelines provided in this chapter. Eliminate major weed infestations with a selective herbicide. If these steps prove inadequate, then consider renovating,

a process that involves dethatching, aerating, and reseeding.

Renovate your lawn at the optimum time of year for your type of grass. Renovate warm-season grasses in late spring and cool-season grasses in early fall. For more about different kinds of grasses and where they grow, see page 339 and also inquire at a Lowe's Garden Center.

Choose a grass seed that is well suited to your climate, and spread both seed and a starter fertilizer over the lawn. Cover seeds with a seed germination mat to protect them from drying, washing away, or being damaged by birds.

Water lightly until the new grass is about a third taller than its optimum height, or about 3 inches tall. Water often enough to maintain soil moisture. After the new grass is tall enough, mow it, removing only 1/2 inch or so. Gradually reduce watering frequency, and minimize use of the lawn for another 1 to 2 months.

coping with garden pests
WHEN TO TAKE ACTION, WHEN TO WAIT

THE NOTION OF PEST CONTROL—WHERE CONTROL IMPLIES ERADICATION—HAS BEEN SUPERSEDED by the concept of pest management. The management concept acknowledges that many perceived "problems" are natural components of gardens and that the presence of pests doesn't necessarily spell trouble. In a diversified garden, most insect pests are kept in check by natural forces, such as predators and weather. If pests reach damaging levels, however, temporary intervention may be needed to restore a balance.

Because of this natural system of checks and balances in a garden, it makes sense to determine which form of intervention will return the situation to a normal balance with the least risk of destroying helpful (as well as harmless) organisms that maintain the equilibrium. Action choices range from doing nothing (giving nature a chance to correct the imbalance), using restraints (washing plants, thereby repelling or physically destroying the damagers), implementing biological controls (improving the helpful side of nature's control system) or, as a last resort, using chemical controls.

Pest problems are minimal when gardens include a diversity of plants that are native or well adapted to the region.

an integrated approach
More and more gardeners are turning to physical restraints and biological controls as a first line of defense against garden pests because they want natural gardens that are safer for children, pets, and wildlife. Yet garden experts acknowledge the need for at least occasional treatment with chemical controls. This approach—the preferred use of natural and mechanical controls, plus chemicals as

Pick large pests like tomato hornworms by hand or with a tool.

Ladybugs earn their good name by consuming common pests.

Yellow cards attract and trap tiny whiteflies on the sticky surface.

a discretionary second choice—is called integrated pest management, or IPM. Increasingly, IPM is being used in parks, city landscapes, and greenhouses.

The following points explain how to implement IPM in your own garden. Most aspects are just good common sense, but it helps to see how basic gardening practices influence pest problems.

select well-adapted plants Choose plants that are adapted to your area and that are resistant to your region's pest and disease problems. Plants stressed by inhospitable climate or by lack of water or nutrients are more vulnerable to damaging organisms than are their healthy, well-cared-for counterparts.

adjust planting time If by planting early you can avoid a pest, do so. For instance, spider mites, a common pest of beans, are most troublesome when the weather turns hot. By planting beans early, as soon as soil warms, you can avoid mites. Keep records of planting dates and temperatures so you can make adjustments from season to season.

use physical controls Handpicking, traps, barriers, floating row covers, or strong water sprays can reduce or thwart many pests, especially in the early stages of a potential problem. Cleanup of plant debris can remove the environment in which certain pests and diseases breed or overwinter.

accept minor damage A totally pest-free garden is neither possible nor desirable. Allow natural control methods to play the major role in maintaining a healthy balance among pests, beneficial insects, and the many harmless insects and creatures that are normal in gardens. That means ignoring minor damage to plants, and not applying a pesticide to every potential threat.

use less toxic alternatives Release or encourage beneficial insects. Use soaps, horticultural oils, botanical insecticides (such as natural pyrethrins and neem), and one of several packaged forms of *Bacillus thuringiensis* (see pages 416–417). Realize that beneficial insects may take a while to reduce the pests they prey upon and that you may have to use nonchemical controls at more frequent intervals than you would chemical controls. And although many natural insecticides have a relatively low impact on the environment, they can be harmful to humans if used carelessly. Follow instructions exactly.

use chemicals carefully and rarely Before you buy a chemical control and apply it, be sure you have correctly identified the problem. Use a pesticide only if both the pest and the plant it is preying on are listed on the pesticide's label.

If you are at all uncertain, ask a Lowe's sales associate or your nearest cooperative extension office.

kinds of pesticides

SYNTHETIC PESTICIDES ARE MANUFACTURED COMPOUNDS THAT DO NOT NORMALLY OCCUR in nature. Natural pesticides, on the other hand, are products whose active ingredients originate in a plant, animal, or mineral, or whose action results from a biological process (as in the case of *Bacillus thuringiensis*). Be aware that "natural" does not mean "harmless." Some natural products can still harm people, pets, or plants if they are used incorrectly, and most of them will kill beneficial insects along with the pests.

When using any pesticide, read the label carefully and follow the manufacturer's directions exactly. The label will clearly state the plants and pests for which the control is registered.

Following are the common names of active ingredients. You'll have to read the label to see if these ingredients are included in a particular product. See pages 418–419 for specific control measures for common pests.

natural pesticides

azadirachtin is derived from the tropical neem tree. It repels many pests and, when ingested by those it doesn't, interferes with growth. Effective against aphids, beetles, caterpillars, grasshoppers, leaf miners, mealybugs, root weevils, and whiteflies. Products that contain only neem oil and not azadirachtin act like other horticultural oils (see facing page).

bacillus thuringiensis (Bt) is a naturally occurring bacterium. Several strains exist, and each targets different kinds of insects. The most common, *B. t. kurstaki*, controls leaf-feeding caterpillars. *B. t. tenebrionis* is effective against leaf beetles. All Bt products must be ingested by the target insect.

diatomaceous earth (DE) is a powdery substance made from the skeletons of microscopic marine organisms. It works by damaging the protective coats of pests such as ants, aphids, cutworms, slugs, snails, and cucumber beetles. Be sure to use the horticultural product, not the one intended for swimming pool filters. Wear a breathing mask during application to avoid inhaling the dust. Sometimes DE is combined with a pyrethrin insecticide.

food-grade oils and extracts are commercial versions of homemade repellents and pesticides that gardeners have relied on for centuries. Active ingredients include kitchen standbys such as citrus peels, sesame oil, garlic, hot pepper, mint, and rosemary. Effectiveness varies.

horticultural oils are mainly highly refined petroleum oils, but some are also derived from fish or seeds, such as cottonseed, neem, or soybean. The oil must be mixed with water and acts primarily by smothering the insect. Oils are widely effective against pests such as scale insects, mites, and whiteflies. Do not apply oils when plants are under drought stress and temperatures are high.

insecticidal soap is made not from dish detergent but from potassium salts of fatty acids found in plants and animals. Soaps kill on contact pests including aphids, mealybugs, mites, scales, thrips, and whiteflies. Hard water inactivates the soap, so mix the concentrated product with soft water, distilled water, or rainwater.

iron phosphate is very common in nature. It is applied to soil as part of a pellet that also contains bait to attract snails and slugs. When the pests eat the pellets, the iron phosphate causes the snails and slugs to stop eating your plants almost immediately. They die three to six days later.

pyrethrins are derived from compounds found in the dried flowers of the marigold *Tanacetum cinerariifolium*. They work as both a contact and a stomach poison and are lethal to many pests. They break down quickly in sunlight. To give them more time to act, apply after sundown. Some products combine pyrethrins with other pesticides. The dried flowers, known as pyrethrum, are also sold as an insecticide.

spinosad is a newer insecticide made from the extracts of a soil microbe, *Saccharopolysproa spinosa*. It is used primarily to control caterpillars and thrips, but it can also help control some beetles and sawflies. Although it is quite selective, some beneficial species can be killed if directly sprayed.

sulfur is dusted or sprayed over plants to control mites as well as some plant diseases. Do not use sulfur in conjunction with horticultural oils or when the air temperature is above 85 degrees F. Can irritate eyes.

synthetic pesticides

acephate is a systemic poison—one absorbed by the plant and incorporated into its tissues. It is a broad-spectrum product used against many pests; hazardous to many beneficials. Use on nonedibles only.

carbaryl is a broad-spectrum contact insecticide. It controls most chewing insects but is not effective against many sucking types. In fact, it often increases problems with the latter, namely spider mites, by destroying natural predators. Registered for use on edible crops.

imidacloprid is a systemic that controls a wide variety of pests. Registered for use on lawns for grubs, and on some tree crops primarily as a soil drench. Do not use it on edible plants. Very toxic to bees. Do not use it on or near flowering plants that bees are likely to visit.

pyrethroids are synthetic versions of plant-based pyrethrins, are being used increasingly in pesticides, and are effective against many garden and household pests. Active ingredients include bifenthrin, permethrin, cyfluthrin, and esfenvalerate.

trichlorfon is an organophosphate insecticide used to control cockroaches, crickets, fleas, flies, ticks, leafminers, and leafhoppers. Trichlorfon is toxic to target insects through direct contact and ingestion. It is somewhat selective, meaning that it kills primarily targeted insects and spares most others. It is relatively safe to use around bees but is highly toxic to birds.

LOWE'S SAFETY TIP

Pesticides are available in formulations that are ready to use or in concentrates that you dilute before applying. Keep a separate set of measuring spoons for pesticide concentrates, and prepare the minimum amount needed. Wear goggles and a hat to shield your head and eyes when applying any pesticide that includes a "warning" or "danger" label. Wash up with soap and water after using a pesticide.

common insect pests

The following insects are familiar garden troublemakers throughout most of North America.

aphids are tiny green, yellow, black, or pink insects that cluster on new growth. Heavy infestations stunt growth. In trees, their secretion, called honeydew, drips from branches.
controls Hose them off or spray them with insecticidal soap or oils.

beetles are hard-shelled insects that chew holes in leaves and flowers. Japanese beetles (left) are a common pest in eastern North America.
controls Handpick or use neem, spinosad, imidacloprid, acephate, or carbaryl.

borers are insects that cause limbs and branches to die. Signs include small holes in a tree or shrub branch accompanied by bits of sawdust. Entry holes of borers that tunnel beneath bark may not be visible. Young trees and plants stressed from drought are particularly vulnerable. Wrap trunks of newly planted trees with protective wrap to prevent borers. Reduce plant stress with consistent watering.
controls Beneficial nematodes. Drench soil with imidacloprid.

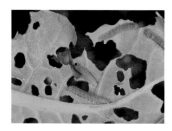

caterpillars and worms include many multileg, crawling larvae of moths and butterflies. They range from the relatively innocuous inchworm to the voracious, highly destructive gypsy moth caterpillar.
controls Handpick or spray with *Bacillus thuringiensis*, spinosad, or carbaryl.

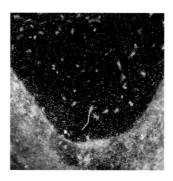

mites are tiny spiders found on leaf undersides (webbing is often present). The leaf surface is pale and stippled. Foliage eventually dries out and turns brown.
controls Wash mites from foliage with a strong blast of water. Use native predatory spider mites. Spray with insecticidal soap, horticultural oil, or sulfur spray or dust.

scale insects attach themselves to stems and leaves, covering their bodies with protective, waxy shells. They usually occur in large colonies.
controls Adult scale can be rubbed off by hand or sprayed with an oil. For the juvenile crawler stage, spray with horticultural oil, insecticidal soap, or imidacloprid.

snails and slugs are night-feeding pests. Snails have shells; slugs don't. They feast on leaves, stems, and flowers, leaving a silvery trail.
controls Handpick and destroy. Containers filled with beer and set at ground level attract the pests, which then fall in and drown. Use barriers. Surround plants or beds with rings of diatomaceous earth or enclose containers and raised beds with copper strips. Use baits containing iron phosphate.

whiteflies are tiny white pests that fly up in a cloud when disturbed, kind of like plant dandruff. They suck plant juices from leaf undersides. Damaged foliage is sometimes stippled and may eventually curl and turn brown, and die.
controls Hose off plants frequently with water jets; spray directly with insecticidal soap. Or use horticultural oil or imidacloprid.

common beneficial insects

Some of the creatures described here are naturally present in gardens. Others, as noted, can be introduced to reduce various pest populations. Spiders and centipedes are also important predators, as are toads, frogs, and birds.

beneficial nematodes are nearly microscopic round-worms that kill insects by introducing a bacterium into their body. Nematodes can help control pests that spend at least some part of their lives in the soil, such as grubs and sod webworms. Beneficial nematodes are available from many mail-order suppliers. They must be applied to moist soil to be effective.

ground beetles range from ½ to 1 inch long. Most are shiny black, though some are also marked with bright colors. The smaller species eat other insects, caterpillars, cutworms, and soil-dwelling grubs. Some larger species eat slugs and snails and their eggs.

lacewings in adulthood are inch-long flying insects with lacy, netted wings and long antennae. The immature or larval form looks something like a ½-inch-long alligator. It has visible legs and is equipped with pincers at the mouth end. Lacewing larvae devour aphids, mites, whiteflies, and many other small insect pests. Adults of most species feed only on nectar, pollen, and honeydew from garden plants. Lacewing larvae that you can release into your garden are commercially available.

ladybugs are familiar to gardeners, and more than 100 species are common in North America. Adults of most ladybugs are brightly colored and patterned, although some are solid black. The larvae are ¾ inch long and dark with some bright patterns, resembling miniature six-legged alligators. The larvae feed on aphids, mites, and scale as well as many other garden pests. Attract ladybugs by planting flowers that provide nectar and pollen for the adults, and by allowing some aphids to remain on a few plants or plant parts. Mail-order companies and garden centers sell ladybugs, but once released, the insects often fly away rather than stay in your garden. Freeing them at night or keeping them contained for the first few days may encourage them to remain.

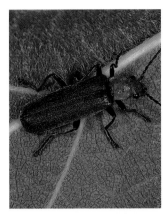

soldier beetles are narrow, ¾-inch-long, typically red or orange insects with leathery-looking black, gray, or brown wing covers. Adults eat aphids and other soft-bodied insects. The tiny soil-dwelling larvae attack smaller insects. Adults also feed on pollen and nectar.

syrphid flies, also known as flower or hover flies, are important beneficial insects that naturally occur in most gardens. Adults have bodies banded with yellow. They look like bees but have only one set of wings. Adults feed only on nectar and pollen, while the larvae (tapered green or gray maggots with small fangs) consume dozens of aphids each day.

tachinid flies are generally hairy flies that are easily mistaken for houseflies. However, their habits are very different because they develop as parasites of other insects. Adults lay their eggs on various caterpillars and beetles, which are then killed by the developing larvae. Many species, each attacking specific insects.

animal pests

A number of animals, including gophers, moles, squirrels, field mice, and deer, can damage gardens and plants. You can keep tunneling moles, gophers, and ground squirrels out of beds by surrounding the beds with underground fencing 3 to 4 feet deep. You can also use barriers for raised beds (see pages 260–261), or plant bulbs and land-scape plants in wire baskets. Use traps or poison baits as a last resort.

Continued ➤

The best way to keep aboveground animals out of your garden is to build a strong fence. Deer fencing should be at least 7 feet high. Fencing to keep out rabbits should be a few feet high but also extend 6 inches below the ground. To keep mice and other animals from feeding on bark, wrap trunks with protective materials. For more information on keeping animals out of your garden, consult a sales associate at the Lowe's Garden Center, or your local cooperative extension office.

Pets can do as much damage to gardens as wild animals, and they are often harder to control or exclude. Fences can keep out neighborhood dogs, but your own canine may need to be trained to avoid certain areas. If you can, give Rover a fenced-in area for playing. Cats are attracted to the soft earth of newly seeded beds, which they will use as litter boxes. Placing wire fencing directly on the soil, so that plants will grow through its holes, is effective.

plant diseases

A healthy plant, like a healthy human being, is better able to resist the microorganisms that cause disease. Focus on keeping your plants strong and vigorous, and you'll have already taken an important step toward preventing problems. Sometimes, however, diseases will appear despite your best efforts. But if you're familiar with their symptoms and the controls that can be used against them,

you'll have a better chance of stopping them before they can get established.

Fungi, bacteria, and viruses are the pathogens most often responsible for plant diseases. Unlike green plants, these organisms are incapable of manufacturing their own food and must instead take it from a host plant. Fungi can live in the soil, but the bacteria and viruses that cause plant problems can't survive outside their host.

Fungi multiply by tiny reproductive bodies called spores (their equivalent of seeds), which they produce in great quantity. Spores of some fungi enter plants through the roots, while others land on leaves, where they attach and complete their life cycle. In fact, a single fungus-infected leaf may release 100 million spores, which drift through the garden and onto new hosts with even the slightest breath of air.

Bacteria need water and warmth to multiply, so the diseases they cause tend to be more prevalent in warm, wet climates. These single-celled organisms are easily transmitted by rain and splashing irrigation water as well as by gardeners working among plants. They are able to enter plants through a wound or natural opening.

Viruses are even smaller than bacteria. They can reproduce only within the actual cells of the host organism. Some viruses are transmitted by insects, such as aphids, leafhoppers, and thrips. Others are carried by

BELOW LEFT: Deer are thriving throughout North America, and a pair like this can decimate a garden in one evening.

BELOW RIGHT: A high but attractive sloping deer fence encloses a garden that would otherwise serve as a deer's salad bar.

infected seeds and pollen. Viruses also enter plants through wounds and cuts.

disease prevention

You can't always prevent a disease from attacking a prized plant. The bacterial infection fire blight, for example, can enter blossoms easily if rain occurs at just the right time during bloom. Similarly, a bare-root rose infected with mosaic virus won't exhibit symptoms until it leafs out.

Good gardening practices will prevent most common diseases. Here's how to keep plant problems under control.

keep plants healthy by giving them the water, light, healthy soil, and fertilizer they need to flourish.

buy disease-resistant plants Search for them and you'll find tomatoes that are resistant to fusarium and verticillium wilts, and flowering pear trees that are less likely to succumb to fire blight, for example. Tomato and other vegetable seed packets are labeled to indicate the particular plant's disease resistance. Tags on fruit trees or ornamental trees and shrubs sometimes also include this information. Ask at a Lowe's Garden Center or at your cooperative extension office for more information on plants that are naturally resistant to the diseases most likely to cause problems in your area.

transplant with care to minimize root damage. When broken, roots are susceptible to certain soilborne diseases.

avoid injuring plants when you work in the garden. An open wound on a plant stem or tree trunk will readily admit disease-causing bacteria and fungi.

avoid wet-weather garden work or you may unwittingly spread waterborne pathogens as you move about from one spot to the next.

install a drip-irrigation system or use soaker hoses to minimize the splashing water that can spread waterborne diseases.

Raking is more than a fall ritual that keeps the garden neat. It also removes diseased leaves so they can't infect new growth next spring.

remove diseased plants If certain plants are constantly afflicted by disease, eliminate them from the garden and replace them with less trouble-prone choices. This solution is simpler than attempting to control the disease, and it removes sources of further infection.

dispose of infected plants and plant parts right away. Throw them out with the trash, and don't compost them. Some disease pathogens may be killed by the heat generated during decomposition, but it's better not to take the chance.

keep the garden clean with a thorough fall cleanup each year. Remove weeds, as pathogens may overwinter on them. In mild-winter areas, strip off any diseased leaves remaining on plants. Rake up and discard all diseased leaves on the ground. You may also want to rake up other garden debris. Although it can serve as a good mulch if undiseased, it also shelters ground-dwelling pests.

common diseases

anthracnose is a fungus that attacks new shoots and leaves in spring, causing them to turn brown and die. In older leaves it causes large, irregular brown patches and premature leaf drop. Spores are spread by rainfall and sprinkling, so the disease is severe in wet

springs but disappears in warm, dry weather. It overwinters in cankers on twigs it has killed, then reinfects the new growth in spring. To prevent this, cut out all dead twigs and branches.

controls Spray with lime sulfur during the dormant season. Use chlorothalonil in spring (check with your cooperative extension office for timing in your area).

black spot is a fungal disease that thrives in high-humidity areas with ample summer rain. It attacks roses exclusively. Black, irregular circles, sometimes surrounded with a yellow halo, appear on young leaves, which then drop from the plant. Heavy infestation

can defoliate a plant, thus preventing it from building up nutrient reserves. In cold-weather regions, badly infected plants can become so depleted that they may not survive winter.

controls Prevent the disease by planting resistant rose varieties. Remove and destroy all diseased foliage in fall. Some gardeners have had good luck controlling black spot with weekly applications of a baking soda and oil spray. To make the solution, mix 2 teaspoons baking soda and 2 teaspoons summer oil with a gallon of water. Some gardeners report success with soap sprays or sulfur. Chemical controls include chlorothalonil and triforine. Repeated applications will be needed as long as the weather conditions favor the development of the fungus.

powdery mildew shows up as a powdery white to gray coating on leaves, stems, and flower buds. It attacks a wide variety of plants, including beans, clematis, dahlia,

grape, hydrangea, rose, strawberry, tomato, and zinnia, as well as apple, maple, oak, peach, and sycamore trees. Heavy infestations debilitate and disfigure plants. Favored by moist air, poor air circulation, and shade but, requires leaves to be dry in order to become established.

controls Plant resistant varieties and routinely spray plants with jets of water to

SYNTHETIC FUNGICIDES

CHLOROTHALONIL Broad-spectrum liquid fungicide used to prevent powdery mildew, leaf spots, gray mold, scab, and a variety of lawn and other diseases. Toxic to fish.

TEBUCONAZOLE Liquid systemic fungicide used to treat and prevent black spot, leaf spot, petal blight, powdery mildew, rust, and scab on landscape plants.

TRIADIMEFON Wettable powder systemic used for the prevention or eradication of powdery mildew, rust, and some lawn diseases.

TRIFORINE Liquid systemic for prevention and eradication of powdery mildew, rust, black spot, and a variety of other diseases.

BAKING SODA (SODIUM BICARBONATE) Helps control powdery mildew on roses. You can make your own by mixing 2 teaspoons each of baking soda and fine-grade horticultural oil with a gallon of water. Also add a "sticker" ingredient to help keep the spray on the plant.

BIOFUNGICIDES These preventive products use naturally occurring fungi and bacteria to protect plants from harmful fungi without upsetting the soil's natural microbial balance. Used as a foliar spray, *Ampelomyces quisqualis* prevents powdery mildew on both edibles and ornamentals, and it will also parasitize newly established spores. A strain of *Bacillus subtilis* is a broad-spectrum product that controls numerous bacterial and fungal diseases. Other biofungicides, such as *Streptomyces griseo-viridis*, *Trichoderma harzianum*, and *Gliocladium virens*, used as soil drenches at planting time, prevent a number of seed, stem, and root rots.

COPPER COMPOUNDS General-purpose fungicides and bactericides used to prevent brown rot, fire blight, peach leaf curl, shot hole, and other foliar diseases.

COPPER SOAP FUNGICIDE Broad-spectrum fungicide used to control many plant diseases, including black spot, downy mildew, gray mold, powdery mildew, and rust.

GARLIC Controls many fungal diseases, including rust, black spot, mildew, and dollar spot and brown patch on lawns. You can buy commercial sprays and soil drenches. Or make your own using this formula: 3 ounces minced garlic with 1 ounce mineral oil. Let soak for at least 24 hours. Strain, stir in 1 tablespoon of liquid castile soap, and store the mixture in a sealed glass container. It will keep at room temperature for several months. To use, mix 2 tablespoons of the garlic oil with 1 pint of water.

LIME SULFUR Spray in winter when plants are dormant to prevent various leaf spots and peach leaf curl. Very caustic. Wear plastic gloves and goggles when applying.

NEEM OIL Useful for preventing and controlling black spot and powdery mildews. Also used as an insecticide and miticide. Toxic to fish.

POTASSIUM BICARBONATE Used to control powdery mildew.

SULFUR Controls powdery mildew, rust, and other diseases. Do not use in conjunction with horticultural oil sprays or when the outdoor temperature is above 85 degrees F.

wash off fungus spores. Increase sunlight to plants by avoiding overcrowding. In fall, discard infected flowers, fruits, and plants. Sulfur may help. On roses and other flowering plants, try a baking soda and summer oil spray (see black spot, facing page). Some gardeners report success with antitranspirant sprays, which are sold to protect tender plants from cold. These sprays keep the surface temperature of leaves somewhat higher than that of the surrounding air. Apparently they also prevent mildew spores from attaching to foliage. Chemical controls include triforine.

root rots are caused by fungi and are active mostly in warm, wet, or poorly drained soils. Young leaves usually turn yellow and wilt. Plants may be stunted or may wilt and die, even in moist soil. Trees and shrubs may die a branch at a time.

controls Plant resistant varieties. Keep soils moist but do not overwater. Improve drainage. No chemical management. Consult your local cooperative extension office for additional information.

rust is a fungus of many different types, and each type is specific to a certain plant. Yellow, orange, red, or brown pustules appear on leaf undersides. The powdery spores are spread

by wind and water.
controls Buy resistant plant varieties. Because rust spreads fastest in wet conditions (leaves must be wet for at least 4 to 5 hours for spores to germinate), you can minimize spread by curtailing overhead watering. Remove and discard most-affected leaves. Dispose of infected leaves that drop to the ground, and clean up all debris in fall. Sulfur and horticultural oil may help, but do not apply them simultaneously, as the combination is toxic to plants. Chemical controls include chlorothalonil, triadimefon, and triforine (especially on roses).

sooty mold is caused by a number of different fungi. This disease can afflict any plant. It shows up as a powdery dark brown or black

coating on leaves, hence the name. The responsible fungi live on a plant's natural secretions and on the honeydew excreted by aphids, mealybugs, and scale. While fairly harmless on its own, sooty mold may weaken a plant if combined with extensive insect damage.
controls Reduce the population of the honeydew-excreting insects. Rinse small ornamental plants by hand. Hose down larger infected areas such as trees or expanses of ground covers. There is no chemical control.

controlling weeds

Whether a plant is labeled a weed depends on several factors. Some plants, like bindweed and yellow oxalis, are regarded as weeds wherever they grow. Other ones may be considered weeds in some situations and garden plants in others. For example, common yarrow is an annoying weed when it invades a lawn, but it is a very useful ornamental ground cover in a hot, dry part of the garden. Certain plants spread so aggressively that they are often thought of as weeds. Examples include some asters, bamboo, mint, Mexican evening primrose, sweet woodruff, and Jerusalem artichoke. Similarly, some ornamentals have gone beyond invading the garden alone, jumping the fence to overwhelm native plants in wild lands.

Despite their undesirable qualities from the gardener's point of view, weedy plants do have their positive side. An assemblage of weeds can hold the soil on a steep bank, preventing erosion. Some weeds provide nectar and shelter for beneficial insects and butterflies. When they die and decompose, weeds add humus to the soil. And even the dreaded poison oak and poison ivy are important to the deer, birds, and rabbits that eat their berries.

identifying weeds Weeds are classified by the length of their life cycle. Annual weeds grow shoots and leaves, flower, set seed, and die within one season. Most of these are summer annuals, germinating in spring or summer and dying by fall. Winter annual weeds begin growth in fall or early winter, then set seed in early spring while the weather is still cool. Biennial weeds produce a cluster or rosette of leaves in their first year of growth, and in the following year they flower, set seed, and die. Annuals and biennials reproduce by seed.

Perennial weeds, which live for several years, also reproduce by seed. Once mature, however, perennial weeds also produce spreading roots, stolons, rhizomes, bulbs, or tubers, making control more difficult.

Weeds are also classed as either broadleaf or grassy. The most common grassy weed is crabgrass. Other common grassy weeds are Bermuda grass, Dallis grass, and quack grass. All nongrassy plants that invade your yard are considered broadleaf weeds. Bindweed, dandelion, and chickweed are common examples.

Herbicides are classified according to what stage of weed growth they affect, as well as by how they kill weeds.

preemergence herbicides work by inhibiting the growth of germinating weed seeds and very young seedlings. They do not affect established plants or weeds already growing. To be effective, they must be applied before the seeds sprout. Before applying these chemicals in ornamental gardens, remove any existing weeds. Some preemergence products must be watered into the soil, while others are best cultivated into it. Some may also harm seeds you sow later in the season. Check the label to learn how long a product remains active in the soil.

postemergence herbicides act on growing weeds. Ones that kill roots must be absorbed by the plant through its leaves or stems. They then kill it by interfering with its metabolism. Contact herbicides kill only the plant parts on which they are sprayed. Regrowth can still occur from roots or unsprayed buds of perennial weeds.

Two common weeds often require repeated treatments to eliminate. They are yellow nutsedge (above) and wild morning glory (below).

SYNTHETIC HERBICIDES

GLUFOSINATE-AMMONIUM (postemergence) Contact herbicide that damages or kills many kinds of weeds. Take care not to apply to desirable plants.

GLYPHOSATE (postemergence) Translocated herbicide that kills or damages any plant it contacts. Effective on a broad range of troublesome weeds but must be used with care to avoid contacting desirable plants.

ORYZALIN (preemergence) Used to control annual grasses and many broadleaf weeds in warm-season turf grasses and in gardens.

PENDIMETHALIN (preemergence) Used to control many grasses and broadleaf weeds in turf and in ornamental plantings. Toxic to fish.

SETHOXYDIM (postemergence) Translocated herbicide that controls many grasses growing in ornamental plantings. Check the label.

TRICLOPYR (postemergence) Translocated herbicide. Depending on formulation, used on cool-season turf to control broadleaf weeds and bermuda grass. Also used to control hard-to-kill woody plants. Use with care to avoid damaging desirable plants.

TRIFLURALIN (preemergence) Controls many grasses and broadleaf weeds in turf and ornamental plantings. Toxic to fish.

NATURAL HERBICIDES

CORN GLUTEN MEAL (preemergence) Prevents sprouting seeds from developing normal roots, thereby making them susceptible to dehydration in dry soil. The roots of established plants are not affected. It is most often used to control weeds, especially crabgrass, in lawns, but it is also effective in garden beds. This product is also a fertilizer, serving to thicken lawns and thus suppress weed growth in that way as well. It poses no health risk to animals—in fact, it's a common ingredient in food for dogs, cats, fish, poultry, and cows. But some people have allergic reactions to corn and corn by-products.

HERBICIDAL SOAPS (postemergence) Contact herbicides that degrade quickly. Made from fatty acids (as are insecticidal soaps), they kill top growth of young, actively growing weeds. Most effective on annual weeds.

VINEGAR (postemergence) A number of organic-gardening catalogs sell vinegar-based herbicides, usually with soap and/or lemon juice added for extra sticking and to increase their penetrating power.

index

index

index

credits

Each image is identified by its position on the page. Use the following key to decode the position of the image: B (bottom); F (far); I (inset); L (left); LL (lower left); M (middle); R (right); T (top); U (upper); and 2 (second from top, bottom, left, or right). Many photos require a combination of letters; for example, "UMR," for upper middle right. A page number with no directionals indicates the photographer or designer is responsible for all the photos or designs on that page.

Photography

Ian Adams: 103. Larry Albee/Longwood Gardens: 202B. Jean Allsopp: 17TL; 31T; 33B; 53TR; 123TR; 139M; 191R; 330M. Ralph Anderson: 19BL; 33T. Scott Atkinson: 246–247 (main); 303; 347BL; 347BM; 347BR; 385FL; 385ML; 385M; 385MR; 385FR. Max E. Badgley: 411BI. Tom Barnett of SA Creative for Gilmour: 390MR; 392; 407L; 425T. Laurie Black: 79B. Paul Bousquet: 9TL; 30; 63T; 113R. Marion Brenner: 1; 2; 16; 101L; 109R; 142–143 (main); 187TL; 199TL; 199TR; 315L; 320M; 338; 363R; 377MR; 394; 413BL; Kathleen Brenzel: 295BL. Rob D. Brodman: 9TR; 24; 39BR; 68; 79TR; 99TR; 104; 105L; 293TR; 393BM; 393BR. Tod Bryant: 413R; 413BM. Gay Bumgarner: 126. Karen Bussolini: 111TR; 129TL; 351R. Karen Bussolini/Jackson Scofield: 173. Cal Spas: 282TL. Rob Cardillo: 39BL. David Cavagnaro: 55BR; 193B; 282B; 351L; 353M; 374R; 375R; 383R. Walter Chandoha: 85TR; 125BR; 131L; 132TL; 291BR. Van Chaplin: 15TR; 23TL; 25BL; 35BR; 37B; 41BR; 45TR; 55TL; 71BR; 73BR; 99TL; 117TM; 122; 125TR; 129MR; 135BR; 204; 220T; 216–217 (main); 310M; 314R; 323M; 337L; 341; 356M; 386–387 (main). Carolyn Chatterton: 420L. Gary Clark: 293TL. Connie Coleman: 62. Glenn Cormier: 381R. Richard S. Cowles: 411B. Crandall & Crandall: 279TR; 279BR; 289TR; 407R; 411T2; 411B2; 411B2I; 415L. Claire Curran: 34; 35TR; 123TL; 312R; 320R; 324M; 361R; 365M. Robin Bachtler Cushman: 55TR. Janet Davis: 86; 140. R. Todd Davis: 324R; 348L; 351M. Joseph De Sciose: 5TR; 63BR; 402TL; 402TM; 402TR. Deckorators: 97R. Alan & Linda Detrick: 352R; 375M. William Dickey: 292L. Laurie Dickson: 15BL. Andrew Drake: 38; 111B; 166TR; 166BR; 167; 263TL; 263TR. Beth Dreiling: 292R. Ken Druse: 49TL; 184L; 368L. Laura Dunkin-Hubby: 201MR; 201BL; 201BR; 214TL; 297BR; 377M. Thomas E. Eltzroth: 422BL; 424T. Derek Fell: 193TL; 313M; 313R; 315R; 320L; 322M; 331L; 369L. Cheryl Fenton: 77BR; 94BL; 232. Scott Fitzgerrell: 94TL; 94TR; 95TR; 95BR; 171BR. Roger Foley: 69TL; 108; 115TL; 120–121 (main); 135BL; 144–145 (main); 146–147; 147TR; 154L; 154R; 155T; 187TR; 189TR; 281T. Brian Francis: 279BL. Frank Gaglione: 198; 217BR; 223BL; 223BM; 223BR; 226TR; 226BL; 226BR; 227TL; 227TR; 227BL; 227BR; 229TL; 229TR; 229ML; 229MR; 229BL; 229BR. Scott Gibson: 254. Fiona Gilsenan: 400. David Goldberg: 397TR; 412T; 413TL; 425MR; 412B2. Jay Graham: 138; 83R. John Granen: 47TR; 12–13 (main). Art Gray: 87R; 101R; 113TL; 277BL. Geoffrey Gross: 255. Steven Gunther: 14; 20; 25TL; 26; 27TL; 32; 43L; 50; 51TR; 53BR; 54; 59BL; 65TL; 69BR; 73TR; 100; 105R; 107TR; 112; 115BL; 139R; 149TR; 149BL; 149BR; 161TL; 161TR; 161B; 162TL; 162TR; 162–163B; 163TR; 271TL; 316L; 345R; 406. Jamie Hadley: 29BR; 57TR; 97L; 258; 259TL; 259TR; 259BL; 259BR. Eric Hanson: 252–253. Marcus Harpur: 130. Lynne Harrison: 51BR; 271TR; 273BR; 294; 349L; 353L. Philip Harvey: 47L; 57MR; 69BL; 76–77 (main); 79TL; 84; 132TM; 179; 199BL; 199BR; 202T; 234T; 247BR; 282TR; 302L. Marijke Heuff/GPL: 134. David Hewitt/Anne Garrison: 57ML. Saxon Holt: 31B; 45BL; 52; 55BL; 71TR; 102; 113BL; 114; 119TR; 125BL; 184R; 189TL; 189B; 205BL; 266–267 (main); 310R; 318; 319TL; 319TM; 319TR; 321L; 326M; 327M; 349R; 357L; 358; 367TL; 367TR; 368R; 393TR; 398BR; 403L. D.A. Horchner/Design Workshop: 49B. Jean-Claude Hurni: 98; 118; 135TR. ©iStockphoto.com/Jason Lugo: 411T. Arthur Lee Jacobson/Photo Garden: 315M. Andrea Jones: 111TM. Lynn Karlin: 107BR; 298R. Dennis Kennedy: 273T; 283BL; 283BM; 285T; 285M; 287L2; 387BR; 398T; 402BR; 404B; 405T; 409BR. Ben Klaffke: 75BL. Bert Klassen: 188. Ernst Kucklich: 22. Chuck Kuhn: 203. A.M. Leonard: 409TR. Janet Loughrey: 23B; 107TL; 164–165B; 164TR; 165TR; 313L; 336R; 364L. Lowe's: 3; 119TL; 267BR; 268; 269MR; 269ML; 269BL; 269BR; 270B; 271BL; 271BR; 274TR; 275TR; 275MR; 276BR; 277TR; 277BR; 279TL; 281BL; 281BR; 283BR; 284T; 284B; 285BR; 286B; 287BL; 287BR; 287R2; 289BR; 291BL; 291BM; 396L; 396ML; 396MR; 396R; 397BL; 397BM; 397BR; 402BL; 408T; 409TL; 409ML. Renee Lynn: 333BR. Michael MacCaskey: 7BR; 23TR; 60; 61TL; 61BR; 65TR; 172; 295TM; 295 R; 369M; 418T2L. Maggie MacLaren: 136L. Allan Mandell: 25BR; 27TR; 27BR; 39TL; 39TR; 58; 59TL; 67TL; 248; 280; 325R; 350R; 357R; 373TR. Charles Mann: 41BL; 61TR; 61BL; 72; 73BL; 83L; 107BL; 296–297 (main); 298L; 322R; 325L; 331R; 332T; 353L; 374L; 374M; 375L; 376; 377TR; 383M; 414. Tom Mannion: 144TL; 168L. Sylvia Martin: 116; 168–169 (main); 170–171 (main); 317M. Ells Marugg: 356R. Maslowski Photo: 295TL. S. Maslowski/Visuals Unlimited: 295BM. Jim McCausland: 67BR; 78; 372. David McDonald/Photo Garden: 18; 87L; 336L; 321R; 373BR. E. Andrew McKinney: 121BR; 125TL; 236L; 236M; 236R; 240; 283T; 293B. N. et P. Mioulane/MAP: 366. Terrence Moore: 71BL; 272; 290. Netherlands Flowers: 371M. C. Nichols/MAP: 273ML. Russell J. Nirella/Thermal Industries: 95MR. Don Normark: 312L. Lauren S. Ogden: 335M. John O'Hagan: 37TR. Carole Ottesen: 129ML; 193TR. Jerry Pavia: 59TR; 63BL; 110; 129M; 133TL; 133TR; 136R; 141R; 192; 219TL; 273MR; 302R; 317L; 323L; 325M; 326L; 330L; 335L; 348R; 349M; 356L; 363M; 364R; 365R; 367BL; 371R; 393TL. Joanne Pavia: 360L; 383L. Pamela K. Peirce: 412B; 425BR. Leonard Phillips: 378L. Chuck Place: 74. Norm Plate: 15BR; 17BR; 19TL; 21TR; 25TR; 36; 37TL; 42; 46; 47BR; 53TL; 57TL; 67TR; 73TL; 85L; 85BR; 106; 109L; 117TR; 131BR; 132BR; 151B; 174; 260; 261TL; 261TR; 261BL; 261BM; 261BR; 289L; 304; 379. Norman A. Plate: 21B; 27BL; 51BL; 53BL; 70; 71TL; 124; 131TR; 136M; 141L; 208; 218; 242M; 243TL; 243TM; 243TR; 243ML; 243M; 243MR; 249TR; 249BL; 249BM; 249BR; 250; 251TL; 251TR; 251BL; 251BR; 256; 257TL; 257TR; 257BL; 257BR; 291TR; 306L; 306ML; 306MR; 306R; 308; 322L; 332B; 340T; 340B; 342TL; 342TM; 342TR; 342BM; 342BR; 343TL; 343TR; 343BL; 343BM; 343BR; 344L; 344M; 344R; 345L; 345M; 350M; 352M; 353R; 360R; 365L; 367FL; 367ML; 367M; 367MR; 367FR; 370L; 380; 381L; 382R; 384; 389BR; 390BL; 398BL; 399TL; 399TML; 399TMR; 399TR; 399BL; 399BM; 399BR; 416. Matthew Plut: 244M; 132TR. Jay Pscheidt: 422TL. Rain Bird Corp.: 211MR. Rapid Cool: 275TL. Kenneth Rice: 82. John Rizzo: 288. Allen Rokach: 51TL; 66; 178. Lisa Romerein: 17BL; 274B. Nancy Rotenberg: 44; 67BL. Susan A. Roth: 64; 137; 311M; 312M; 324L; 328; 331M; 334R; 335R; 336M; 337R; 348M; 354; 355T; 361L; 362R; 364M; 369R; 377TL; 422R. Mark Rutherford: 206T; 206B; 210; 211B; 214BL; 214BR; 233TL; 233TR; 233B. Greg Ryan & Sally Beyer: 186T; 187B; 373L. Scotts Co.: 411M; 411MI. Richard Shiell: 330R; 334L; 337M. Steve Sibbett: 412T2; 423. Richard Hamilton Smith: 378R. Southern Progress: 28–29 (main); 41T; 48; 65BR; 117TL; 129TR; 132BL; 139L; 191BL; 300; 311L; 415R; 200–201 (main). Lynn Steiner: 346. Thomas J. Story: 5TL; 6–7 (main); 8; 11TL; 11TR; 11BL; 15TL; 17TR; 19TR; 19BR; 21TL; 35TL; 43TR; 43BR; 45TL; 45BR; 69TR; 96; 97M; 111TL; 115BR; 150B; 152TL; 152TR; 152BR; 153; 157T; 157B; 158; 159TL; 159B; 219TR; 228; 269TL; 269TR; 276TL; 277BM; 278; 420R. Joseph G. Strauch, Jr.: 314M. Tim Street-Porter: 49TR. Dan Stultz: 223TL; 223TM; 223TR. Shaun Sullivan: 291TM. Michael S. Thompson: 75R; 311R; 314L; 317R; 321M; 323R; 326R; 334M; 350L; 357M; 360M; 362L; 362M; 363L; 368M; 370M; 371L; 382L; 382M; 388; 393TM; 395T; 421. Connie Toops: 377ML. E. Spencer Toy: 11BR. Andreas Trauttmannsdorff: 224. Mark Turner: 135TL. Union Tools, Inc.: 412TM; 413TM. Jessie Walker: 191TL. Deidra Walpole Photography: 56; 115TR; 270T; 277TL. Washington State University: 418B2L. Darrow M. Watt: 264M; 370R; 391TL. www.philipwegener.com: 230B. Ron West/Nature Photography: 418TL; 418BL; 418TR; 418T2R; 418B2R; 418BR; 419L; 419TR; 419MR; 419BR; 424B. Rick Wetherbee: 190. judywhite/GardenPhotos.com: 273BL. Peter O. Whiteley: 59BR; 286T; 286TI. Bob Wigand: 35BL; 65BL. Tom Wilhite: 143BR. David Winger: 327L; 40. Tom Woodward: 13BR. Cynthia Woodyard: 327R; 361M. Tom Wyatt: 219BR. Ed Young: 415M. Linda Quartman Younker: 128; 310L. David Zaitz: 75TL.

Design

Alida Aldrich, the Aldrich Company (plant design): 271TL. Arentz Landscape Architects: 108; 281T. Allison Banks (stylist): 279BL. Ralph Barnes: 293TR. Rick Bayless: 282B. David C. Becker: 260, 261. Tom Berger, the Berger Partnership: 85BR. Phoebe and Charles Blackston: 23TL. Greg Bobich, Designs by Sundown: 30. Pat Brodie Landscape Design: 65TL. Pat Brodie: 69BR. Jon Buerk, J. Buerk Landscape Maintenance: 24; 79TR; 104. Barbara Butler Artist-Builder (playhouse): 165TR. Susan Calhoun, Plantswoman Design: 12–13 (main); 106. Scott Calhoun, Zona-Gardens: 272. Carlotta from Paradise: 73TL. Aldon Caron, Outdoor Lighting Perspectives: 286T; 286TI. Julie Chai: 228. Yunghi Choi: 187TR. Dan Cleveland: 15TR. Shelly Coglizer and Ron Lutsko: 1. Cindy Combs: 190. Michelle Comeau Landscape Design: 53BR. Erick Cortina/Roger's Gardens: 293B. Conni Cross: 64. Karen Donnelly: 68. Pamela Dreyfuss Interior Design and Exteriors Landscape Architecture: 278. Puck Erickson, Arcadia Studio: 132BR. Wood and Patti Farless: 17TL; 139M. Julie Fehlauer/Sweet Oregon Grill: 23B. Kathleen Ferguson Landscapes: 37TL; 54. David, Celestina, and Sharon Finkle with Teri Ravel Kane (landscape architect): 159TL; 159B. Jamie Fogle, Design Workshop: 49B. Forest Pryde Landscape Design: 109L. Michael Glassman & Associates: 150B. Will Green: 47BR; 117TR. Green Scene Landscape Design: 277TL. Griffith and Cletta: 51TR. Tony Gwilliam: 19BR. Paul Harris, Imagine Sonoma: 21TL. Julie Hart and Associates, Griffith & Cletta (landscape design):17BL. Cynthia Hayes, Mozaic Landscape Design Group: 57TL. Paul Hendershot Design: 269TR. HLD Group Landscape Architecture: 43BR. Cathy Hoekman/Concept Landscapes: 280. T. M. Holtschlag: 111B. Thomas Bateman Hood, Architect: 276TL. Linda Hostetler: 37TR. Scott Huston, Columbine Design: 113R. Virginia Israelit (garden), and Marcia Donahue (sculpture), Portland: 58. Jordan Jackson: 67BR; 135TL. Chris Jacobson GardenArt Group: 45BR. Laurie Jekel, the Last Detail: 63T. Margaret Joplin, Design Collaborations: 131BR. Raymond Jungles: 69TL. Judy Kameon with Michael Kirchmann Jr. and Ivette Soler, Elysian Landscapes: 14; 20; 105R; 112. Michelle Kaufmann Designs: 97M. Vi Kono, Creative Designs: 78. Amy Korn and Matt Randolph, KornRandolph: 277BM. Olivier Le Clerc/Les Jardins du Magnolia: 118. Le Jardin Home, Garden and Ranch Design: 372. Terry LeBlanc: 25TR. Deirdre Lee, Urban Jungle Art & Design: 59BL. Jill Lewis and Lane Williams, Coop 15: 79B. Mark Licht, Clemens & Associates (design), Santa Fe Awning (installation): 274B. Jeff Lightbody: 174. George Little and David Lewis: 18. Eileen & Pat Mangan: 376. Tom Mannion: 144TL; 144–145 (main); 146–147 (main); 147TR; 154L; 154R; 155T; 168–169 (main). Mark Marcinik, Greenmeadow Architects: 99TR. Gary Marsh Design: 97L. Shelly Marsterson: 273BL. Sarah McCarty Garden Design: 289L. Mia McCarville, Cedros Gardens: 32. Carolyn and Doug McCord: 21TR; 46. Melissa McDonald, Santa Fe Permaculture: 61BL. Christy and Bob McLaughlin: 5TR. Steve Morgan, Steve Morgan Landscape Architecture–Eco-Logical Design: 115BR. Vanessa Nagel, Milieux Design Studio: 59TL. Ben Page & Associates: 328. Pamela Palmer, Artecho: 25TL. Patkau Architects: 420R. David Pfeiffer, Garden Architecture Inc.: 166TR; 166BR; 167. Grace Phillips Garden Design: 107TR. Ahna Pietras-Dominski: 19TR. Putnam Construction & Landscaping: 100. Safdie Rabines Architects: 96. Jim Robinson, Daichi Landscape: 42. Chris Rosmini Garden Design: 26. KenCairn Sager Landscape Architects: 55TR. Rebecca Sams and Buell Steelman, Moasic Gardens: 47TR. Greg Sanchez, GDS Designs: 87R; 101R. JoAnna and Gary Sasnett with Carlotte Rose (designer): 191R. Herb Schaal, EDAW: 40. Hendrikus Schraven: 67TR. Elaine Schreve: 248. Jeffrey Gordon Smith Landscape Architecture: 162–163B; 269TL. Rob Steiner, Landscape Architect: 50; 149TR; 149BL; 149BR. Chuck Stopherd, Hidden Garden: 43L; 113TL. Stout garden: 39BL. Katsy Swan: 35TL. Freeland Tanner, Proscape Landscape Design: 16. Sasha Tarnopolsky, Dry Design: 161TL; 161TR; 161B. Ten Eyck Landscape Architects: 15BR. Stefan Thuilot with Joseph Huettl, Huettl Thuilot Associates: 15TL; 45TL. Huettl Thuilot Associates: 157T; 157B. Bernard Trainor Design: 338. Bernard Trainor + Associates: 5TL. Truxell & Valentino Landscape Development, Inc.: 36. Nicholas Walker, Jardin du Jour; Crain Prunty and Mario Navarro, All Oregon Landscaping: 164–165B; 164TR. Birte Walter (prop styling): 152TR; 152BR; 153. John and Charlotte Waters: 33T. Shirley Alexandra Watts, landscape designer: 151B. Kim Weinheimer: 292L. Wendy White: 63BR. Peter O. Whiteley: 219TR. Mark Wienke: 277BL. Richard Wilder, Wilder Landscaping: 379. Tom Wilhite: 142–143. Nick Williams & Associates: 115BL. Windsmith Design: 105L. Richard William Wogisch: 71TR; 113BL. Mary Zahl: 31T. Raul Zumba, Zumba Gardens: 102.